THE

TRIUMPH

OF

GOD'S LOVE

*The Story of the Vindication of the Character
of God and the Salvation of Mankind*

by E. G. WHITE

Author of *Prophets and Kings*
The Desire of Ages
The Acts of the Apostles
Patriarchs and Prophets

Volume 1

Published jointly by
REVIEW AND HERALD® PUBLISHING ASSOCIATION
Hagerstown, MD 21740

PACIFIC PRESS PUBLISHING ASSOCIATION
Boise, ID 83707
Oshawa, Ontario, Canada

Foreword

THIS book is published to strengthen the most deeply cherished of all our hopes—the final and right solution of human affairs. It is not published to tell us that there is sin and woe and misery in the world. It is not published to tell us that there is a mighty struggle between darkness and light, sin and righteousness, death and life. In our heart of hearts we know it, and know that we are participants in the conflict. But many are fearful and perplexed. They are not so sure that love will triumph at last over the forces of wrong.

In every human heart there is a longing to know more about the conflict between good and evil, the issues involved and the characters, seen and unseen, who lead out in the struggle. How did this conflict between right and wrong begin? How am I related to it? I find myself in this world by no choice of my own. Does that mean evil or good for me? What are the great principles involved? How long will this struggle continue? Will this world of ours sink, as some scientists tell us, into the depths of a sunless and eternal night? Or is there a bright future before us, radiant with the light of life? In short, will God's great love for lost humanity and His plan for our redemption finally triumph?

The questions come closer home: How may the struggle between good and evil in my own heart be settled in the triumph of the right? What has God to teach us upon this question, eternally important to every man? What does the Bible say? Surely that God who created in us a hungering for righteousness and the desire for truth will not withhold from us that knowledge which is essential to our happiness here and hereafter.

The purpose of this book is to help you as an honest seeker for truth to a solution of these perplexing questions. It is written by one who knew God from deep personal experience, and who learned, in communion with Him and in the study of His Holy Word, that the secret of the Lord is with them that fear Him, and that He will show them His covenant.

That we may better understand the principles of the agelong controversy, the author has set before us events and developments of Christian times that serve as object lessons in the struggle between truth and error. The book opens with the stirring, climactic scenes of Jerusalem's destruction by Titus in A.D. 70. The city of God's chosen, after her rejection of the Man of Calvary, is left in ruins. Thence onward along the great highway of the nations it reviews the persecutions of Christians during the first centuries; the great departure from the faith which followed; the world awakening of Christianity in the latter part of the Middle Ages; the awful lesson of the rejection of God's Word during the revolution in France; the revival of the study of the Holy Scriptures and their lifesaving influence; the religious awakening of modern times; and the unsealing of the prophecies of God's Word with regard to the future. Simply and lucidly this book sets forth the present and impending problems that the religious world is facing, and the great fundamental principles involved, concerning which none can be neutral.

Last of all, this work portrays the eternal and glorious triumph of good over evil, right over wrong, light over darkness, joy over sorrow, hope over despair, glory over shame, life over death, and everlasting, long-suffering love over vindictive hate.

This volume was formerly published under the title *The Great Controversy Between Christ and Satan.* In this edition the title of the book has been changed, as well as the titles of some of the chapters. But in no instance has the textual matter of the book itself been altered in any way. The small numbers in brackets at the foot of each page at the inside margin indicate the location of the corresponding page in the reference edition.

Beginning with its first edition (1888), followed by an author's revision (1911), this outstanding work has achieved worldwide circulation through many editions and translations. The reader will find that the author writes frankly and vigorously, pointing out errors and suggesting solutions based on the infallible Word of God. And even though the last few decades have witnessed shifts and adjustments in the socioreligious world, the main scheme and the future projections presented in this book maintain today full timeliness and absorbing interest.

The attention of the reader is called to a number of study helps at the close of the volume, all of which will prove to be helpful. These include Appendix Notes, Scripture Index referring to all Bible texts quoted, and the General Index.

Former printings of this book have brought many inquiring readers to the true Shepherd; it is the prayer of the publishers that this edition may be even more fruitful of present and eternal good.

THE PUBLISHERS.

Page numbers in brackets in this book indicate the pages in the standard edition used for compiling the *Comprehensive Index to the Writings of E. G. White.*

Introduction

BEFORE the entrance of sin, Adam enjoyed open communion with his Maker; but since man separated himself from God by transgression, the human race has been cut off from this high privilege. By the plan of redemption, however, a way has been opened whereby the inhabitants of the earth may still have connection with heaven. God has communicated with men by His Spirit, and divine light has been imparted to the world by revelations to His chosen servants. "Holy men of God spake as they were moved by the Holy Ghost." 2 Peter 1:21.

During the first twenty-five hundred years of human history, there was no written revelation. Those who had been taught of God, communicated their knowledge to others, and it was handed down from father to son, through successive generations. The preparation of the written word began in the time of Moses. Inspired revelations were then embodied in an inspired book. This work continued during the long period of sixteen hundred years—from Moses, the historian of creation and the law, to John, the recorder of the most sublime truths of the gospel.

The Bible points to God as its author; yet it was written by human hands; and in the varied style of its different books it presents the characterstics of the several writers. The truths revealed are all "given by inspiration of God" (2 Timothy 3:16); yet they are expressed in the words of men. The Infinite One by His Holy Spirit has shed light into the minds and hearts of His servants. He has given dreams and visions, symbols and figures; and those to whom the truth was thus revealed have themselves embodied the thought in human language.

The Ten Commandments were spoken by God Himself, and were written by His own hand. They are of divine, and not of human composition. But the Bible, with its God-given truths expressed in the language of men, presents a union of the divine and the human. Such a union existed in the nature of Christ, who was the Son of God and the Son of man. Thus it is true of the Bible, as it was of Christ, that "the Word was made flesh, and dwelt among us." John 1:14.

Written in different ages, by men who differed widely in rank and occupation, and in mental and spiritual endowments, the books of the Bible present a wide contrast in style, as well as a diversity in the nature of the subjects unfolded. Different forms of expression are employed by different writers; often the same truth is more strikingly presented by one than by another. And as several writers present a subject under varied aspects and relations, there may appear, to the superficial, care- less, or prejudiced reader, to be discrepancy or contradiction, where the thoughtful, reverent student, with clearer insight, discerns the under- lying harmony.

As presented through different individuals, the truth is brought out in its varied aspects. One writer is more strongly impressed with one phase of the subject; he grasps those points that harmonize with his ex- perience or with his power of perception and appreciation; another seizes upon a different phase; and each, under the guidance of the Holy Spirit, presents what is most forcibly impressed upon his own mind—a different aspect of the truth in each, but a perfect harmony through all. And the truths thus revealed unite to form a perfect whole, adapted to meet the wants of men in all the circumstances and experiences of life.

God has been pleased to communicate His truth to the world by human agencies, and He Himself, by His Holy Spirit, qualified men and enabled them to do this work. He guided the mind in the selection of what to speak and what to write. The treasure was entrusted to earthen vessels, yet it is, nonetheless, from Heaven. The testimony is conveyed through the imperfect expression of human language, yet it is the testi- mony of God; and the obedient, believing child of God beholds in it the glory of a divine power, full of grace and truth.

In His word, God has committed to men the knowledge necessary for salvation. The Holy Scriptures are to be accepted as an authoritative, infallible revelation of His will. They are the standard of character, the revealer of doctrines, and the test of experience. "Every scripture inspired of God is also profitable for teaching, for reproof, for correction, for in- struction which is in righteousness; that the man of God may be com- plete, furnished completely unto every good work." 2 Timothy 3:16, 17, R.V.

Yet the fact that God has revealed His will to men through His word, has not rendered needless the continued presence and guiding of the Holy Spirit. On the contrary, the Spirit was promised by our Saviour, to open the word to His servants, to illuminate and apply its teachings. And since it was the Spirit of God that inspired the Bible, it is impossible that the teaching of the Spirit should ever be contrary to that of the word.

The Spirit was not given—nor can it ever be bestowed—to supersede the Bible; for the Scriptures explicitly state that the word of God is the standard by which all teaching and experience must be tested. Says the apostle John, "Believe not every spirit, but try the spirits whether they are of God: because many false prophets are gone out into the world." 1 John 4:1. And Isaiah declares, "To the law and to the testimony: if they speak not according to this word, it is because there is no light in them." Isaiah 8:20.

Great reproach has been cast upon the work of the Holy Spirit by the errors of a class that, claiming its enlightenment, profess to have no further need of guidance from the word of God. They are governed by impressions which they regard as the voice of God in the soul. But the spirit that controls them is not the Spirit of God. This following of impressions, to the neglect of the Scriptures, can lead only to confusion, to deception and ruin. It serves only to further the designs of the evil one. Since the ministry of the Holy Spirit is of vital importance to the church of Christ, it is one of the devices of Satan, through the errors of extremists and fanatics, to cast contempt upon the work of the Spirit and cause the people of God to neglect this source of strength which our Lord Himself has provided.

In harmony with the word of God, His Spirit was to continue its work throughout the period of the gospel dispensation. During the ages while the Scriptures of both the Old and the New Testament were being given, the Holy Spirit did not cease to communicate light to individual minds, apart from the revelations to be embodied in the Sacred Canon. The Bible itself relates how, through the Holy Spirit, men received warning, reproof, counsel, and instruction, in matters in no way relating to the giving of the Scriptures. And mention is made of prophets in different ages, of whose utterances nothing is recorded. In like manner, after the close of the canon of the Scripture, the Holy Spirit was still to continue its work, to enlighten, warn, and comfort the children of God.

Jesus promised His disciples, "The Comforter which is the Holy Ghost, whom the Father will send in My name, He shall teach you all things, and bring all things to your remembrance, whatsoever I have said unto you." "When He, the Spirit of truth, is come, He will guide you into all truth: . . . and He will show you things to come." John 14:26; 16:13. Scripture plainly teaches that these promises, so far from being limited to apostolic days, extend to the church of Christ in all ages. The Saviour assures His followers, "I am with you alway, even unto the end of the world." Matthew 28:20. And Paul declares that the gifts and manifestations of the Spirit were set in the church "for the perfecting of the saints, for the work of the ministry, for the edifying of the body of Christ: till we all come in the unity of the faith, and of the knowledge of the Son of God, unto a perfect man, unto the measure of the stature of the fullness of Christ." Ephesians 4:12, 13.

For the believers at Ephesus the apostle prayed, "That the God of our Lord Jesus Christ, the Father of glory, may give unto you the *Spirit of wisdom and revelation* in the knowledge of Him: *the eyes of your understanding being enlightened;* that ye may know what is the hope of His calling, and . . . what is the *exceeding greatness* of His power to usward who believe." Ephesians 1:17-19. The ministry of the divine Spirit in enlightening the understanding and opening to the mind the deep things of God's holy word, was the blessing which Paul thus besought for the Ephesian church.

After the wonderful manifestation of the Holy Spirit on the Day of Pentecost, Peter exhorted the people to repentance and baptism in the name of Christ, for the remission of their sins; and he said: "Ye shall receive the gift of the Holy Ghost. For the promise is unto you, and to your children, and to all that are afar off, even as many as the Lord our God shall call." Acts 2:38, 39.

In immediate connection with the scenes of the great day of God, the Lord by the prophet Joel has promised a special manifestation of His Spirit. Joel 2:28. This prophecy received a partial fulfillment in the outpouring of the Spirit on the Day of Pentecost; but it will reach its full accomplishment in the manifestation of divine grace which will attend the closing work of the gospel.

The great controversy between good and evil will increase in intensity to the very close of time. In all ages the wrath of Satan has been manifested against the church of Christ; and God has bestowed His grace and Spirit upon His people to strengthen them to stand against the power of the evil one. When the apostles of Christ were to bear His gospel to the world and to record it for all future ages, they were especially endowed with the enlightenment of the Spirit. But as the church approaches her final deliverance, Satan is to work with greater power. He comes down "having great wrath, because he knoweth that he hath but a short time." Revelation 12:12. He will work "with all power and signs and lying wonders." 2 Thessalonians 2:9. For six thousand years that mastermind that once was highest among the angels of God has been wholly bent to the work of deception and ruin. And all the depths of satanic skill and subtlety acquired, all the cruelty developed, during these struggles of the ages, will be brought to bear against God's people in the final conflict. And in this time of peril the followers of Christ are to bear to the world the warning of the Lord's second advent; and a people are to be prepared to stand before Him at His coming, "without spot, and blameless." 2 Peter 3:14. At this time the special endowment of divine grace and power is not less needful to the church than in apostolic days.

Through the illumination of the Holy Spirit, the scenes of the long-continued conflict between good and evil have been opened to the writer of these pages. From time to time I have been permitted to behold the working, in different ages, of the great controversy between Christ, the Prince of life, the Author of our salvation, and Satan, the prince of evil, the author of sin, the first transgressor of God's holy law. Satan's enmity against Christ has been manifested against His followers. The same hatred of the principles of God's law, the same policy of deception, by which error is made to appear as truth, by which human laws are substituted for the law of God, and men are led to worship the creature rather than the Creator, may be traced in all the history of the past. Satan's efforts to misrepresent the character of God, to cause men to cherish a false conception of the Creator, and thus to regard Him with fear and hate rather than with love; his endeavors to set aside the divine law, leading the people to think themselves free from its requirements; and his persecution of those who dare to resist his deceptions, have been steadfastly pursued in all ages. They may be traced in the history of patriarchs, prophets, and apostles, of martyrs and reformers.

In the great final conflict, Satan will employ the same policy, manifest the same spirit, and work for the same end as in all preceding ages. That which has been, will be, except that the coming struggle will be marked with a terrible intensity such as the world has never witnessed. Satan's deceptions will be more subtle, his assaults more determined. If it were possible, he would lead astray the elect. Mark 13:22, R.V.

As the Spirit of God has opened to my mind the great truths of His word, and the scenes of the past and the future, I have been bidden to make known to others that which has thus been revealed—to trace the history of the controversy in past ages, and especially so to present it as to shed a light on the fast-approaching struggle of the future. In pursuance of this purpose, I have endeavored to select and group together events in the history of the church in such a manner as to trace the unfolding of the great testing truths that at different periods have been given to the world, that have excited the wrath of Satan, and the enmity of a world-loving church, and that have been maintained by the witness of those who "loved not their lives unto the death."

In these records we may see a foreshadowing of the conflict before us. Regarding them in the light of God's word, and by the illumination of His Spirit, we may see unveiled the devices of the wicked one, and the dangers which they must shun who would be found "without fault" before the Lord at His coming.

The great events which have marked the progress of reform in past ages are matters of history, well known and universally acknowledged by the Protestant world; they are facts which none can gainsay. This history I have presented briefly, in accordance with the scope of the book, and the brevity which must necessarily be observed, the facts having been condensed into as little space as seemed consistent with a proper understanding of their application. In some cases where a historian has so grouped together events as to afford, in brief, a comprehensive view of the subject, or has summarized details in a convenient manner, his words have been quoted; but in some instances no specific credit has been given, since the quotations are not given for the purpose of citing that writer as authority, but because his statement affords a ready and forcible presentation of the subject. In narrating the experience and views of those carrying forward the work of reform in our own time, similar use has been made of their published works.

It is not so much the object of this book to present new truths concerning the struggles of former times, as to bring out facts and principles which have a bearing on coming events. Yet viewed as a part of the controversy between the forces of light and darkness, all these records of the past are seen to have a new significance; and through them a light is cast upon the future, illumining the pathway of those who, like the reformers of past ages, will be called, even at the peril of all earthly good, to witness "for the word of God, and for the testimony of Jesus Christ."

To unfold the scenes of the great controversy between truth and error; to reveal the wiles of Satan, and the means by which he may be successfully resisted; to present a satisfactory solution of the great problem of evil, shedding such a light upon the origin and the final disposition of sin as to make fully manifest the justice and benevolence of God in all His dealings with His creatures; and to show the holy, unchanging nature of His law, is the object of this book. That through its influence souls may be delivered from the power of darkness, and become "partakers of the inheritance of the saints in light," to the praise of Him who loved us, and gave Himself for us, is the earnest prayer of the writer.

E. G. W.

Contents

chapter 1

The Love and Long-Suffering of Christ

"IF THOU hadst known, even thou, at least in this thy day, the things which belong unto thy peace! but now they are hid from thine eyes. For the days shall come upon thee, that thine enemies shall cast a trench about thee, and compass thee round, and keep thee in on every side, and shall lay thee even with the ground, and thy children within thee; and they shall not leave in thee one stone upon another; because thou knewest not the time of thy visitation." Luke 19:42-44.

From the crest of Olivet, Jesus looked upon Jerusalem. Fair and peaceful was the scene spread out before Him. It was the season of the Passover, and from all lands the children of Jacob had gathered there to celebrate the great national festival. In the midst of gardens and vineyards, and green slopes studded with pilgrims' tents, rose the terraced hills, the stately palaces, and massive bulwarks of Israel's capital. The daughter of Zion seemed in her pride to say, I sit a queen and shall see no sorrow; as lovely then, and deeming herself as secure in Heaven's favor, as when, ages before, the royal minstrel sang: "Beautiful for situation, the joy of the whole earth, is Mount Zion, . . . the city of the great King." Psalm 48:2. In full view were the magnificent buildings of the temple. The rays of the setting sun lighted up the snowy whiteness of its marble walls and gleamed from golden gate and tower and pinnacle. "The perfection of beauty" it stood, the pride of the Jewish nation. What child of Israel could gaze upon the scene without a thrill of joy and admiration! But far other thoughts occupied the mind of Jesus.

Because God's chosen people rejected and crucified Jesus, God had to allow them to suffer the results of transgression.

THE TRIUMPH OF GOD'S LOVE

"When He was come near, He beheld the city, and wept over it." Luke 19:41. Amid the universal rejoicing of the triumphal entry, while palm branches waved, while glad hosannas awoke the echoes of the hills, and thousands of voices declared Him king, the world's Redeemer was overwhelmed with a sudden and mysterious sorrow. He, the Son of God, the Promised One of Israel, whose power had conquered death and called its captives from the grave, was in tears, not of ordinary grief, but of intense, irrepressible agony.

His tears were not for Himself, though He well knew whither His feet were tending. Before Him lay Gethsemane, the scene of His approaching agony. The sheepgate also was in sight, through which for centuries the victims for sacrifice had been led, and which was to open for Him when He should be "brought as a lamb to the slaughter." Isaiah 53:7. Not far distant was Calvary, the place of crucifixion. Upon the path which Christ was soon to tread must fall the horror of great darkness as He should make His soul an offering for sin. Yet it was not the contemplation of these scenes that cast the shadow upon Him in this hour of gladness. No foreboding of His own superhuman anguish clouded that unselfish spirit. He wept for the doomed thousands of Jerusalem—because of the blindness and impenitence of those whom He came to bless and to save.

The history of more than a thousand years of God's special favor and guardian care, manifested to the chosen people, was open to the eye of Jesus. There was Mount Moriah, where the son of promise, an unresisting victim, had been bound to the altar—emblem of the offering of the Son of God. There the covenant of blessing, the glorious Messianic promise, had been confirmed to the father of the faithful. Genesis 22:9, 16-18. There the flames of the sacrifice ascending to heaven from the threshing floor of Ornan had turned aside the sword of the destroying angel (1 Chronicles 21)—fitting symbol of the Saviour's sacrifice and mediation for guilty men. Jerusalem had been honored of God above all the earth. The Lord had "chosen Zion," He had "desired it for His habitation." Psalm 132:13. There, for ages, holy prophets had uttered their messages of warning. There priests had waved their censers, and the cloud of incense, with the prayers of the worshipers, had ascended before God. There daily the blood of slain lambs had been offered, pointing forward to the Lamb of God. There Jehovah had revealed His presence in the cloud of glory above the mercy seat. There rested the base of that mystic ladder connecting earth with heaven (Genesis 28:12; John 1:51)—that ladder upon which angels of God descended and ascended, and which opened to the world the way into the holiest of all. Had Israel as a nation preserved her allegiance to Heaven, Jerusalem would have stood forever, the elect of God. Jeremiah 17:21-25. But the history of that favored people was a record of backsliding and rebellion. They had resisted Heaven's grace, abused their privileges, and slighted their opportunities.

Although Israel had "mocked the messengers of God, and despised His words, and misused His prophets" (2 Chronicles 36:16), He had still manifested Himself to them, as "the Lord God, merciful and gracious, long-suffering, and abundant in goodness and truth" (Exodus 34:6); notwithstanding repeated rejections, His mercy had continued its pleadings. With more than a father's pitying love for the son of his care, God had "sent to them by His messengers, rising up betimes, and sending; because He had compassion on His people, and on His dwelling place." 2 Chronicles 36:15. When remonstrance, entreaty, and rebuke had failed, He sent to them the best gift of heaven; nay, He poured out all heaven in that one Gift.

The Son of God Himself was sent to plead with the impenitent city. It was Christ that had brought Israel as a goodly vine out of Egypt. Psalm 80:8. His own hand had cast out the heathen before it. He had planted it "in a very fruitful hill." His guardian care had hedged it about. His servants had been sent to nurture it. "What could have been done more to My vineyard," He exclaims, "that I have not done in it?" Isaiah 5:1-4. Though when He looked that it should bring forth grapes, it brought forth wild grapes, yet with a still yearning hope of fruitfulness He came in person to His vineyard, if haply it might be saved from destruction. He digged about His vine; He pruned and cherished it. He was unwearied in His efforts to save this vine of His own planting.

For three years the Lord of light and glory had gone in and out among His people. He "went about doing good, and healing all that were oppressed of the devil," binding up the brokenhearted, setting at liberty them that were bound, restoring sight to the blind, causing the lame to walk and the deaf to hear, cleansing the lepers, raising the dead, and preaching the gospel to the poor. Acts 10:38; Luke 4:18; Matthew 11:5. To all classes alike was addressed the gracious call: "Come unto Me, all ye that labor and are heavy-laden, and I will give you rest." Matthew 11:28.

Though rewarded with evil for good, and hatred for His love (Psalm 109:5), He had steadfastly pursued His mission of mercy. Never were those repelled that sought His grace. A homeless wanderer, reproach and penury His daily lot, He lived to minister to the needs and lighten the woes of men, to plead with them to accept the gift of life. The waves of mercy, beaten back by those stubborn hearts, returned in a stronger tide of pitying, inexpressible love. But Israel had turned from her best Friend and only Helper. The pleadings of His love had been despised, His counsels spurned, His warnings ridiculed.

The hour of hope and pardon was fast passing; the cup of God's long-deferred wrath was almost full. The cloud that had been gathering through ages of apostasy and rebellion, now black with woe, was about to burst upon a guilty people; and He who alone could save them from their impending fate had been slighted, abused, rejected, and was soon to be crucified. When Christ should hang upon the cross of Calvary, Israel's day as a nation favored and blessed of God would be ended. The loss of even one soul is a calamity infinitely outweighing the gains and treasures of a world; but as Christ looked upon Jerusalem, the doom of a whole city, a whole nation, was before Him—that city, that nation, which had once been the chosen of God, His peculiar treasure.

Prophets had wept over the apostasy of Israel and the terrible desolations by which their sins were visited. Jeremiah wished that his eyes were a fountain of tears, that he might weep day and night for the slain of the daughter of his people, for the Lord's flock that was carried away captive. Jeremiah 9:1; 13:17. What, then, was the grief of Him whose prophetic glance took in, not years, but ages! He beheld the destroying angel with sword uplifted against the city which had so long been Jehovah's dwelling place. From the ridge of Olivet, the very spot afterward occupied by Titus and his army, He looked across the valley upon the sacred courts and porticoes, and with tear-dimmed eyes He saw, in awful perspective, the walls surrounded by alien hosts. He heard the tread of armies marshaling for war. He heard the voice of mothers and children crying for bread in the besieged city. He saw her holy and beautiful house, her palaces and towers, given to the flames, and where once they stood, only a heap of smoldering ruins.

Looking down the ages, He saw the covenant people scattered in every land, "like wrecks on a desert shore." In the temporal retribution about to fall upon her children, He saw but the first draft from that cup of wrath which at the final judgment she must drain to its dregs. Divine pity, yearning love, found utterance in the mournful words: "O Jerusalem, Jerusalem, thou that killest the prophets, and stonest them which are sent unto thee, how often would I have gathered thy children together, even as a hen gathereth her chickens under her wings, and ye would not!" O that thou, a nation favored above every other, hadst known the time of thy visitation, and the things that belong unto thy peace! I have stayed the angel of justice, I have called thee to repentance, but in vain. It is not merely servants, delegates, and prophets, whom thou hast refused and rejected, but the Holy One of Israel, thy Redeemer. If thou art destroyed, thou alone art responsible. "Ye will not come to Me, that ye might have life." Matthew 23:37; John 5:40.

Christ saw in Jerusalem a symbol of the world hardened in unbelief and rebellion, and hastening on to meet the retributive judgments of God. The woes of a fallen race, pressing upon His soul, forced from His lips that exceeding bitter cry. He saw the record of sin traced in human misery, tears, and blood; His heart was moved with infinite pity for the afflicted and suffering ones of earth; He yearned to relieve them all. But even His hand might not turn back the tide of human woe; few would seek their only Source of help. He was willing to pour out His soul unto death, to bring salvation within their reach; but few would come to Him that they might have life.

The Majesty of heaven in tears! the Son of the infinite God troubled in spirit, bowed down with anguish! The scene filled all heaven with wonder. That scene reveals to us the exceeding sinfulness of sin; it shows how hard a task it is, even for Infinite Power, to save the guilty from the consequences of transgressing the law of God. Jesus, looking down to the last generation, saw the world involved in a deception similar to that which caused the destruction of Jerusalem. The great sin of the Jews was their rejection of Christ; the great sin of the Christian world would be their rejection of the law of God, the foundation of His government in heaven and earth. The precepts of Jehovah would be despised and set at nought. Millions in bondage to sin, slaves of Satan, doomed to suffer the second death, would refuse to listen to the words of truth in their day of visitation. Terrible blindness! strange infatuation!

Two days before the Passover, when Christ had for the last time departed from the temple, after denouncing the hypocrisy of the Jewish rulers, He again went out with His disciples to the Mount of Olives and seated Himself with them upon the grassy slope overlooking the city. Once more He gazed upon its walls, its towers, and its palaces. Once more He beheld the temple in its dazzling splendor, a diadem of beauty crowning the sacred mount.

A thousand years before, the psalmist had magnified God's favor to Israel in making her holy house His dwelling place: "In Salem also is His tabernacle, and His dwelling place in Zion." He "chose the tribe of Judah, the Mount Zion which He loved. And He built His sanctuary like high palaces." Psalms 76:2; 78:68, 69. The first temple had been erected during the most prosperous period of Israel's history. Vast stores of treasure for this purpose had been collected by King David, and the plans for its construction were made by divine inspiration. 1 Chronicles 28:12, 19. Solomon, the wisest of Israel's monarchs, had completed the work. This temple was the most magnificent building which the world ever saw. Yet the Lord had declared by the prophet Haggai, concerning the second temple: "The glory of this latter house shall be greater than of the former." "I will shake all nations, and the Desire of all nations shall come: and I will fill this house with glory, saith the Lord of hosts." Haggai 2:9, 7.

After the destruction of the temple by Nebuchadnezzar it was rebuilt about five hundred years before the birth of Christ by a people who from a lifelong captivity had returned to a wasted and almost deserted country. There were then among them aged men who had seen the glory of Solomon's temple, and who wept at the foundation of the new building, that it must be so inferior to the former. The feeling that prevailed is forcibly described by the prophet: "Who is left among you that saw this house in her first glory? and how do ye see it now? is it not in your eyes in comparison of it as nothing?" Haggai 2:3; Ezra 3:12. Then was given the promise that the glory of this latter house should be greater than that of the former.

But the second temple had not equaled the first in magnificence; nor was it hallowed by those visible tokens of the divine presence which pertained to the first temple. There was no manifestation of supernatural power to mark its dedication. No cloud of glory was seen to fill the newly erected sanctuary. No fire from heaven descended to consume the sacrifice upon its altar. The Shekinah no longer abode between the cherubim in the most holy place; the ark, the mercy seat, and the tables of the testimony were not to be found therein. No voice sounded from heaven to make known to the inquiring priest the will of Jehovah.

For centuries the Jews had vainly endeavored to show wherein the promise of God given by Haggai had been fulfilled; yet pride and unbelief blinded their minds to the true meaning of the prophet's words. The second temple was not honored with the cloud of Jehovah's glory, but with the living presence of One in whom dwelt the fullness of the Godhead bodily—who was God Himself manifest in the flesh. The "Desire of all nations" had indeed come to His temple when the Man of Nazareth taught and healed in the sacred courts. In the presence of Christ, and in this only, did the second temple exceed the first in glory. But Israel had put from her the proffered Gift of heaven. With the humble Teacher who had that day passed out from its golden gate, the glory had forever departed from the temple. Already were the Saviour's words fulfilled: "Your house is left unto you desolate." Matthew 23:38.

The disciples had been filled with awe and wonder at Christ's prediction of the overthrow of the temple, and they desired to understand more fully the meaning of His words. Wealth, labor, and architectural skill had for more than forty years been freely expended to enhance its splendors. Herod the Great had lavished upon it both Roman wealth and Jewish treasure, and even the emperor of the world had enriched it with his gifts. Massive blocks of white marble, of almost fabulous size, forwarded from Rome for this purpose, formed a part of its structure; and to these the disciples had called the attention of their Master, saying: "See what manner of stones and what buildings are here!" Mark 13:1.

To these words, Jesus made the solemn and startling reply: "Verily I say unto you, There shall not be left here one stone upon another, that shall not be thrown down." Matthew 24:2.

With the overthrow of Jerusalem the disciples associated the events of Christ's personal coming in temporal glory to take the throne of universal empire, to punish the impenitent Jews, and to break from off the nation the Roman yoke. The Lord had told them that He would come the second time. Hence at the mention of judgments upon Jerusalem, their minds reverted to that coming; and as they were gathered about the Saviour upon the Mount of Olives, they asked: "When shall these things be? and what shall be the sign of Thy coming, and of the end of the world?" Verse 3.

The future was mercifully veiled from the disciples. Had they at that time fully comprehended the two awful facts—the Redeemer's sufferings and death, and the destruction of their city and temple—they would have been overwhelmed with horror. Christ presented before them an outline of the prominent events to take place before the close of time. His words were not then fully understood; but their meaning was to be unfolded as His people should need the instruction therein given. The prophecy which He uttered was twofold in its meaning; while foreshadowing the destruction of Jerusalem, it prefigured also the terrors of the last great day.

Jesus declared to the listening disciples the judgments that were to fall upon apostate Israel, and especially the retributive vengeance that would come upon them for their rejection and crucifixion of the Messiah. Unmistakable signs would precede the awful climax. The dreaded hour would come suddenly and swiftly. And the Saviour warned His followers: "When ye therefore shall see the abomination of desolation, spoken of by Daniel the prophet, stand in the holy place, (whoso readeth, let him understand:) then let them which be in Judea flee into the mountains." Matthew 24:15, 16; Luke 21:20, 21. When the idolatrous standards of the Romans should be set up in the holy ground, which extended some furlongs outside the city walls, then the followers of Christ were to find safety in flight. When the warning sign should be seen, those who would escape must make no delay. Throughout the land of Judea, as well as in Jerusalem itself, the signal for flight must be immediately obeyed. He who chanced to be upon the housetop must not go down into his house, even to save his most valued treasures. Those who were working in the fields or vineyards must not take time to return for the outer garment laid aside while they should be toiling in the heat of the day. They must not hesitate a moment, lest they be involved in the general destruction.

In the reign of Herod, Jerusalem had not only been greatly beautified, but by the erection of towers, walls, and fortresses, adding to the natural strength of its situation, it had been rendered apparently impregnable. He who would at this time have foretold publicly its destruction, would, like Noah in his day, have been called a crazed alarmist. But Christ had said: "Heaven and earth shall pass away, but My words shall not pass away."

Matthew 24:35. Because of her sins, wrath had been denounced against Jerusalem, and her stubborn unbelief rendered her doom certain.

The Lord had declared by the prophet Micah: "Hear this, I pray you, ye heads of the house of Jacob, and princes of the house of Israel, that abhor judgment, and pervert all equity. They build up Zion with blood, and Jerusalem with iniquity. The heads thereof judge for reward, and the priests thereof teach for hire, and the prophets thereof divine for money: yet will they lean upon the Lord, and say, Is not the Lord among us? none evil can come upon us." Micah 3:9-11.

These words faithfully described the corrupt and self-righteous inhabitants of Jerusalem. While claiming to observe rigidly the precepts of God's law, they were transgressing all its principles. They hated Christ because His purity and holiness revealed their inquity; and they accused Him of being the cause of all the troubles which had come upon them in consequence of their sins. Though they knew Him to be sinless, they had declared that His death was necessary to their safety as a nation. "If we let Him thus alone," said the Jewish leaders, "all men will believe on Him: and the Romans shall come and take away both our place and nation." John 11:48. If Christ were sacrificed, they might once more become a strong, united people. Thus they reasoned, and they concurred in the decision of their high priest, that it would be better for one man to die than for the whole nation to perish.

Thus the Jewish leaders had built up "Zion with blood, and Jerusalem with iniquity." Micah 3:10. And yet, while they slew their Saviour because He reproved their sins, such was their self-righteousness that they regarded themselves as God's favored people and expected the Lord to deliver them from their enemies. "Therefore," continued the prophet, "shall Zion for your sake be plowed as a field, and Jerusalem shall become heaps, and the mountain of the house as the high places of the forest." Verse 12.

For nearly forty years after the doom of Jerusalem had been pronounced by Christ Himself, the Lord delayed His judgments upon the city and the nation. Wonderful was the long-suffering of God toward the rejectors of His gospel and the murderers of His Son. The parable of the unfruitful tree represented God's dealings with the Jewish nation. The command had gone forth, "Cut it down; why cumbereth it the ground?" (Luke 13:7) but divine mercy had spared it yet a little longer. There were still many among the Jews who were ignorant of the character and the work of Christ. And the children had not enjoyed the opportunities or received the light which their parents had spurned. Through the preaching of the apostles and their associates, God would cause light to shine upon them; they would be permitted to see how prophecy had been fulfilled, not only in the birth and life of Christ, but in His death and resurrection. The children were not condemned for the sins of the parents; but when, with a knowledge of all the light given to their parents, the children rejected the additional light granted to themselves, they became partakers of the parents' sins, and filled up the measure of their iniquity.

The long-suffering of God toward Jerusalem only confirmed the Jews in their stubborn impenitence. In their hatred and cruelty toward the disciples of Jesus they rejected the last offer of mercy. Then God withdrew His protection from them and removed His restraining power from Satan and his angels, and the nation was left to the control of the leader she had chosen. Her children had spurned the grace of Christ, which would have enabled them to subdue their evil impulses, and now these became the conquerors. Satan aroused the fiercest and most debased passions of the soul. Men did not reason; they were beyond reason—controlled by impulse and blind rage. They became satanic in their cruelty. In the family and in the nation, among the highest and the lowest classes alike, there was suspicion, envy, hatred, strife, rebellion, murder. There was no safety anywhere. Friends and kindred betrayed one another. Parents slew their children, and children their parents. The rulers of the people had no power to rule themselves. Uncontrolled passions made them tyrants. The Jews had accepted false testimony to condemn the innocent Son of God. Now false accusations made their own lives uncertain. By their actions they had long been saying: "Cause the Holy One of Israel to cease from before us." Isaiah 30:11. Now their desire was granted. The fear of God no longer disturbed them. Satan was at the head of the nation, and the highest civil and religious authorities were under his sway.

The leaders of the opposing factions at times united to plunder and torture their wretched victims, and again they fell upon each other's forces and slaughtered without mercy. Even the sanctity of the temple could not restrain their horrible ferocity. The worshipers were stricken down before the altar, and the sanctuary was polluted with the bodies of the slain. Yet in their blind and blasphemous presumption the instigators of this hellish work publicly declared that they had no fear that Jerusalem would be destroyed, for it was God's own city. To establish their power more firmly, they bribed false prophets to proclaim, even while Roman legions were besieging the temple, that the people were to wait for deliverance from God. To the last, multitudes held fast to the belief that the Most High would interpose for the defeat of their adversaries. But Israel had spurned the divine protection, and now she had no defense. Unhappy Jerusalem! rent by internal dissensions, the blood of her children slain by one another's hands crimsoning her streets, while alien armies beat down her fortifications and slew her men of war!

All the predictions given by Christ concerning the destruction of Jerusalem were fulfilled to the letter. The Jews experienced the truth of His words of warning: "With what measure ye mete, it shall be measured to you again." Matthew 7:2.

Signs and wonders appeared, foreboding disaster and doom. In the midst of the night an unnatural light shone over the temple and the altar. Upon the clouds at sunset were pictured chariots and men of war gathering for battle. The priests ministering by night in the sanctuary were terrified by mysterious sounds; the earth trembled, and a multitude of voices were heard crying: "Let us depart hence." The great eastern gate, which was so heavy that it could hardly be shut by a score of men, and which was secured by immense bars of iron fastened deep in the pavement of solid stone, opened at midnight, without visible agency. —Milman, *The History of the Jews,* book 13.

For seven years a man continued to go up and down the streets of Jerusalem, declaring the woes that were to come upon the city. By day and by night he chanted the wild dirge: "A voice from the east! a voice from the west! a voice from the four winds! a voice against Jerusalem and against the temple! a voice against the bridegrooms and the brides! a voice against the whole people!"—*Ibid.* This strange being was imprisoned and scourged, but no complaint escaped his lips. To insult and abuse he answered only: "Woe, woe to Jerusalem!" "woe, woe to the inhabitants thereof!" His warning cry ceased not until he was slain in the siege he had foretold.

Not one Christian perished in the destruction of Jerusalem. Christ had given His disciples warning, and all who believed His words watched for the promised sign. "When ye shall see Jerusalem compassed with armies," said Jesus, "then know that the desolation thereof is nigh. Then let them which are in Judea flee to the mountains; and let them which are in the midst of it depart out." Luke 21:20, 21. After the Romans under Cestius had surrounded the city, they unexpectedly abandoned the siege when everything seemed favorable for an immediate attack. The besieged, despairing of successful resistance, were on the point of surrender, when the Roman general withdrew his forces without the least apparent reason. But God's merciful providence was directing events for the good of His own people. The promised sign had been given to the waiting Christians, and now an opportunity was offered for all who would, to obey the Saviour's warning. Events were so overruled that neither Jews nor Romans should hinder the flight of the Christians. Upon the retreat of Cestius, the Jews, sallying from Jerusalem, pursued after his retiring army; and while both forces were thus fully engaged, the Christians had an opportunity to leave the city. At this time the country also had been cleared of enemies who might have endeavored to intercept them. At the time of the siege, the Jews were assembled at Jerusalem to keep the Feast of Tabernacles, and thus the Christians throughout the land were able to make their escape unmolested. Without delay they fled to a place of safety—the city of Pella, in the land of Perea, beyond Jordan.

The Jewish forces, pursuing after Cestius and his army, fell upon their rear with such fierceness as to threaten them with total destruction. It was with great difficulty that the Romans succeeded in making their retreat. The Jews escaped almost without loss, and with their spoils returned in triumph to Jerusalem. Yet this apparent success brought them only evil. It inspired them with that spirit of stubborn resistance to the Romans which speedily brought unutterable woe upon the doomed city.

Terrible were the calamities that fell upon Jerusalem when the siege was resumed by Titus. The city was invested at the time of the Passover, when millions of Jews were assembled within its walls. Their stores of provision, which if carefully preserved would have supplied the inhabitants for years, had previously been destroyed through the jealousy and revenge of the contending factions, and now all the horrors of starvation were experienced. A measure of wheat was sold for a talent. So fierce were the pangs of hunger that men would gnaw the leather of their belts and sandals and the covering of their shields. Great numbers of the people would steal out at night to gather wild plants growing outside the city walls, though many were seized and put to death with cruel torture, and often those who returned in safety were robbed of what they had gleaned at so great peril. The most inhuman tortures were inflicted by those in power, to force from the want-stricken people the last scanty supplies which they might have concealed. And these cruelties were not infrequently practiced by men who were themselves well fed, and who were merely desirous of laying up a store of provision for the future.

Thousands perished from famine and pestilence. Natural affection seemed to have been destroyed. Husbands robbed their wives, and wives their husbands. Children would be seen snatching the food from the mouths of their aged parents. The question of the prophet, "Can a woman forget her sucking child?" received the answer within the walls of that doomed city: "The hands of the pitiful women have sodden their own children: they were their meat in the destruction of the daughter of my people." Isaiah 49:15; Lamentations 4:10. Again was fulfilled the warning prophecy given fourteen centuries before: "The tender and delicate woman among you, which would not adventure to set the sole of her foot upon the ground for delicateness and tenderness, her eye shall be evil toward the husband of her bosom, and toward her son, and toward her daughter, . . . and toward her children which she shall bear: for she shall eat them for want of all things secretly in the siege and straitness, wherewith thine enemy shall distress thee in thy gates." Deuteronomy 28:56, 57.

The Roman leaders endeavored to strike terror to the Jews and thus cause them to surrender. Those prisoners who resisted when taken, were scourged, tortured, and crucified before the wall of the city. Hundreds were daily put to death in this manner, and the dreadful work continued until, along the Valley of Jehoshaphat and at Calvary, crosses were erected in so great numbers that there was scarcely room to move among them. So terribly was visited that awful imprecation uttered before the

THE TRIUMPH OF GOD'S LOVE

judgment seat of Pilate: "His blood be on us, and on our children." Matthew 27:25.

Titus would willingly have put an end to the fearful scene, and thus have spared Jerusalem the full measure of her doom. He was filled with horror as he saw the bodies of the dead lying in heaps in the valleys. Like one entranced, he looked from the crest of Olivet upon the magnificent temple and gave command that not one stone of it be touched. Before attempting to gain possession of this stronghold, he made an earnest appeal to the Jewish leaders not to force him to defile the sacred place with blood. If they would come forth and fight in any other place, no Roman should violate the sanctity of the temple. Josephus himself, in a most eloquent appeal, entreated them to surrender, to save themselves, their city, and their place of worship. But his words were answered with bitter curses. Darts were hurled at him, their last human mediator, as he stood pleading with them. The Jews had rejected the entreaties of the Son of God, and now expostulation and entreaty only made them more determined to resist to the last. In vain were the efforts of Titus to save the temple; One greater than he had declared that not one stone was to be left upon another.

The blind obstinacy of the Jewish leaders, and the detestable crimes perpetrated within the besieged city, excited the horror and indignation of the Romans, and Titus at last decided to take the temple by storm. He determined, however, that if possible it should be saved from destruction. But his commands were disregarded. After he had retired to his tent at night, the Jews, sallying from the temple, attacked the soldiers without. In the struggle, a firebrand was flung by a soldier through an opening in the porch, and immediately the cedar-lined chambers about the holy house were in a blaze. Titus rushed to the place, followed by his generals and legionaries, and commanded the soldiers to quench the flames. His words were unheeded. In their fury the soldiers hurled blazing brands into the chambers adjoining the temple, and then with their swords they slaughtered in great numbers those who had found shelter there. Blood flowed down the temple steps like water. Thousands upon thousands of Jews perished. Above the sound of battle, voices were heard shouting: "Ichabod!"—the glory is departed.

"Titus found it impossible to check the rage of the soldiery; he entered with his officers, and surveyed the interior of the sacred edifice. The splendor filled them with wonder; and as the flames had not yet penetrated to the holy place, he made a last effort to save it, and springing

14 [*32-33*]

Roman soldiers, incensed by the blind obstinancy of the Jews, destroyed the magnificent temple at Jerusalem.

Roman soldiers, incensed by the blind obstinancy of the Jews, destroyed the magnificent temple at Jerusalem.

forth, again exhorted the soldiers to stay the progress of the conflagration. The centurion Liberalis endeavored to force obedience with his staff of office; but even respect for the emperor gave way to the furious animosity against the Jews, to the fierce excitement of battle, and to the insatiable hope of plunder. The soldiers saw everything around them radiant with gold, which shone dazzlingly in the wild light of the flames; they supposed that incalculable treasures were laid up in the sanctuary. A soldier, unperceived, thrust a lighted torch between the hinges of the door: the whole building was in flames in an instant. The blinding smoke and fire forced the officers to retreat, and the noble edifice was left to its fate.

"It was an appalling spectacle to the Roman—what was it to the Jew? The whole summit of the hill which commanded the city, blazed like a volcano. One after another the buildings fell in, with a tremendous crash, and were swallowed up in the fiery abyss. The roofs of cedar were like sheets of flame; the gilded pinnacles shone like spikes of red light; the gate towers sent up tall columns of flame and smoke. The neighboring hills were lighted up; and dark groups of people were seen watching in horrible anxiety the progress of the destruction: the walls and heights of the upper city were crowded with faces, some pale with the agony of despair, others scowling unavailing vengeance. The shouts of the Roman soldiery as they ran to and fro, and the howlings of the insurgents who were perishing in the flames, mingled with the roaring of the conflagration and the thundering sound of falling timbers. The echoes of the mountains replied or brought back the shrieks of the people on the heights; all along the walls resounded screams and wailings; men who were expiring with famine rallied their remaining strength to utter a cry of anguish and desolation.

"The slaughter within was even more dreadful than the spectacle from without. Men and women, old and young, insurgents and priests, those who fought and those who entreated mercy, were hewn down in indiscriminate carnage. The number of the slain exceeded that of the slayers. The legionaries had to clamber over heaps of dead to carry on the work of extermination."—Milman, *The History of the Jews*, book 16.

After the destruction of the temple, the whole city soon fell into the hands of the Romans. The leaders of the Jews forsook their impregnable towers, and Titus found them solitary. He gazed upon them with amazement, and declared that God had given them into his hands; for no engines, however powerful, could have prevailed against those stupendous battlements. Both the city and the temple were razed to their foundations, and the ground upon which the holy house had stood was "plowed like a field." Jeremiah 26:18. In the siege and the slaughter that followed, more than a million of the people perished; the survivors were carried away as captives, sold as slaves, dragged to Rome to grace the conqueror's triumph, thrown to wild beasts in the amphitheaters, or scattered as homeless wanderers throughout the earth.

The Jews had forged their own fetters; they had filled for themselves the cup of vengeance. In the utter destruction that befell them as a nation, and in all the woes that followed them in their dispersion, they were but reaping the harvest which their own hands had sown. Says the prophet: "O Israel, thou hast destroyed thyself;" "for thou hast fallen by thine iniquity." Hosea 13:9; 14:1. Their sufferings are often represented as a punishment visited upon them by the direct decree of God. It is thus that the great deceiver seeks to conceal his own work. By stubborn rejection of divine love and mercy, the Jews had caused the protection of God to be withdrawn from them, and Satan was permitted to rule them according to his will. The horrible cruelties enacted in the destruction of Jerusalem are a demonstration of Satan's vindictive power over those who yield to his control.

We cannot know how much we owe to Christ for the peace and protection which we enjoy. It is the restraining power of God that prevents mankind from passing fully under the control of Satan. The disobedient and unthankful have great reason for gratitude for God's mercy and long-suffering in holding in check the cruel, malignant power of the evil one. But when men pass the limits of divine forbearance, that restraint is removed. God does not stand toward the sinner as an executioner of the sentence against transgression; but He leaves the rejectors of His mercy to themselves, to reap that which they have sown. Every ray of light rejected, every warning despised or unheeded, every passion indulged, every transgression of the law of God, is a seed sown which yields its unfailing harvest. The Spirit of God, persistently resisted, is at last withdrawn from the sinner, and then there is left no power to control the evil passions of the soul, and no protection from the malice and enmity of Satan. The destruction of Jerusalem is a fearful and solemn warning to all who are trifling with the offers of divine grace and resisting the pleadings of divine mercy. Never was there given a more decisive testimony to God's hatred of sin and to the certain punishment that will fall upon the guilty.

THE TRIUMPH OF GOD'S LOVE

The Saviour's prophecy concerning the visitation of judgments upon Jerusalem is to have another fulfillment, of which that terrible desolation was but a faint shadow. In the fate of the chosen city we may behold the doom of a world that has rejected God's mercy and trampled upon His law. Dark are the records of human misery that earth has witnessed during its long centuries of crime. The heart sickens, and the mind grows faint in contemplation. Terrible have been the results of rejecting the authority of Heaven. But a scene yet darker is presented in the revelations of the future. The records of the past—the long procession of tumults, conflicts, and revolutions, the "battle of the warrior . . . with confused noise, and garments rolled in blood" (Isaiah 9:5)—what are these, in contrast with the terrors of that day when the restraining Spirit of God shall be wholly withdrawn from the wicked, no longer to hold in check the outburst of human passion and satanic wrath! The world will then behold, as never before, the results of Satan's rule.

But in that day, as in the time of Jerusalem's destruction, God's people will be delivered, everyone that shall be found written among the living. Isaiah 4:3. Christ has declared that He will come the second time to gather His faithful ones to Himself: "Then shall all the tribes of the earth mourn, and they shall see the Son of man coming in the clouds of heaven with power and great glory. And He shall send His angels with a great sound of a trumpet, and they shall gather together His elect from the four winds, from one end of heaven to the other. Matthew 24:30, 31. Then shall they that obey not the gospel be consumed with the spirit of His mouth and be destroyed with the brightness of His coming. 2 Thessalonians 2:8. Like Israel of old the wicked destroy themselves; they fall by their iniquity. By a life of sin, they have placed themselves so out of harmony with God, their natures have become so debased with evil, that the manifestation of His glory is to them a consuming fire.

Let men beware lest they neglect the lesson conveyed to them in the words of Christ. As He warned His disciples of Jerusalem's destruction, giving them a sign of the approaching ruin, that they might make their escape; so He has warned the world of the day of final destruction and has given them tokens of its approach, that all who will may flee from the wrath to come. Jesus declares: "There shall be signs in the sun, and in the moon, and in the stars; and upon the earth distress of nations." Luke 21:25; Matthew 24:29; Mark 13:24-26; Revelation 6:12-17. Those who behold these harbingers of His coming are to "know that it is near, even at the doors." Matthew 24:33. "Watch ye therefore," are His words of admonition. Mark 13:35. They that heed the warning shall not be left in darkness, that that day should overtake them unawares. But to them that will not watch, "the day of the Lord so cometh as a thief in the night." 1 Thessalonians 5:2-5.

The world is no more ready to credit the message for this time than were the Jews to receive the Saviour's warning concerning Jerusalem. Come when it may, the day of God will come unawares to the ungodly. When life is going on in its unvarying round; when men are absorbed in pleasure, in business, in traffic, in money-making; when religious leaders are magnifying the world's progress and enlightenment, and the people are lulled in a false security—then, as the midnight thief steals within the unguarded dwelling, so shall sudden destruction come upon the careless and ungodly, "and they shall not escape." Verse 3.

chapter 2

The First Christians--
Loyal and True

WHEN Jesus revealed to His disciples the fate of Jerusalem and the scenes of the second advent, He foretold also the experience of His people from the time when He should be taken from them, to His return in power and glory for their deliverance. From Olivet the Saviour beheld the storms about to fall upon the apostolic church; and penetrating deeper into the future, His eye discerned the fierce, wasting tempests that were to beat upon His followers in the coming ages of darkness and persecution. In a few brief utterances of awful significance He foretold the portion which the rulers of this world would mete out to the church of God. Matthew 24:9, 21, 22. The followers of Christ must tread the same path of humiliation, reproach, and suffering which their Master trod. The enmity that burst forth against the world's Redeemer would be manifested against all who should believe on His name.

The history of the early church testified to the fulfillment of the Saviour's words. The powers of earth and hell arrayed themselves against Christ in the person of His followers. Paganism foresaw that should the gospel triumph, her temples and altars would be swept away; therefore she summoned her forces to destroy Christianity. The fires of persecution were kindled. Christians were stripped of their possessions and driven from their homes. They "endured a great fight of afflictions." Hebrews 10:32. They "had trial of cruel mockings and scourgings, yea, moreover of bonds and imprisonment." Hebrews 11:36. Great numbers sealed their testimony with their blood. Noble and slave,

Enticements to compromise their faith in Christ in order to save themselves from torture and death were steadfastly resisted by Christians of the pagan Roman Empire.

rich and poor, learned and ignorant, were alike slain without mercy.

These persecutions, beginning under Nero about the time of the martyrdom of Paul, continued with greater or less fury for centuries. Christians were falsely accused of the most dreadful crimes and declared to be the cause of great calamities—famine, pestilence, and earthquake. As they became the objects of popular hatred and suspicion, informers stood ready, for the sake of gain, to betray the innocent. They were condemned as rebels against the empire, as foes of religion, and pests to society. Great numbers were thrown to wild beasts or burned alive in the amphitheaters. Some were crucified; others were covered with the skins of wild animals and thrust into the arena to be torn by dogs. Their punishment was often made the chief entertainment at public fetes. Vast multitudes assembled to enjoy the sight and greeted their dying agonies with laughter and applause.

Wherever they sought refuge, the followers of Christ were hunted like beasts of prey. They were forced to seek concealment in desolate and solitary places. "Destitute, afflicted, tormented; (of whom the world was not worthy:) they wandered in deserts, and in mountains, and in dens and caves of the earth." Verses 37, 38. The catacombs afforded shelter for thousands. Beneath the hills outside the city of Rome, long galleries had been tunneled through earth and rock; the dark and intricate network of passages extended for miles beyond the city walls. In these underground retreats the followers of Christ buried their dead; and here also, when suspected and proscribed, they found a home. When the Life-giver shall awaken those who have fought the good fight, many a martyr for Christ's sake will come forth from those gloomy caverns.

Under the fiercest persecution these witnesses for Jesus kept their faith unsullied. Though deprived of every comfort, shut away from the light of the sun, making their home in the dark but friendly bosom of the earth, they uttered no complaint. With words of faith, patience, and hope they encouraged one another to endure privation and distress. The loss of every earthly blessing could not force them to renounce their belief in Christ. Trials and persecution were but steps bringing them nearer their rest and their reward.

Like God's servants of old, many were "tortured, not accepting deliverance; that they might obtain a better resurrection." Verse 35. These called to mind the words of their Master, that when persecuted for Christ's sake, they were to be exceeding glad, for great would be their reward in heaven; for so the prophets had been persecuted before them.

They rejoiced that they were accounted worthy to suffer for the truth, and songs of triumph ascended from the midst of crackling flames. Looking upward by faith, they saw Christ and angels leaning over the battlements of heaven, gazing upon them with the deepest interest and regarding their steadfastness with approval. A voice came down to them from the throne of God: "Be thou faithful unto death, and I will give thee a crown of life." Revelation 2:10.

In vain were Satan's efforts to destroy the church of Christ by violence. The great controversy in which the disciples of Jesus yielded up their lives did not cease when these faithful standard-bearers fell at their post. By defeat they conquered. God's workmen were slain, but His work went steadily forward. The gospel continued to spread and the number of its adherents to increase. It penetrated into regions that were inaccessible even to the eagles of Rome. Said a Christian, expostulating with the heathen rulers who were urging forward the persecution: You may "kill us, torture us, condemn us. . . . Your injustice is the proof that we are innocent. . . . Nor does your cruelty . . . avail you." It was but a stronger invitation to bring others to their persuasion. "The oftener we are mown down by you, the more in number we grow; the blood of Christians is seed."—Tertullian, *Apology,* paragraph 50.

Thousands were imprisoned and slain, but others sprang up to fill their places. And those who were martyred for their faith were secured to Christ and accounted of Him as conquerors. They had fought the good fight, and they were to receive the crown of glory when Christ should come. The sufferings which they endured brought Christians nearer to one another and to their Redeemer. Their living example and dying testimony were a constant witness for the truth; and where least expected, the subjects of Satan were leaving his service and enlisting under the banner of Christ.

Satan therefore laid his plans to war more successfully against the government of God by planting his banner in the Christian church. If the followers of Christ could be deceived and led to displease God, then their strength, fortitude, and firmness would fail, and they would fall an easy prey.

The great adversary now endeavored to gain by artifice what he had failed to secure by force. Persecution ceased, and in its stead were substituted the dangerous allurements of temporal prosperity and worldly honor. Idolaters were led to receive a part of the Christian faith, while they rejected other essential truths. They professed to accept Jesus as the Son of God and to believe in His death and resurrection, but they had no conviction of sin and felt no need of repentance or of a change of heart. With some concessions on their part they proposed that Christians should make concessions, that all might unite on the platform of belief in Christ.

Now the church was in fearful peril. Prison, torture, fire, and sword were blessings in comparison with this. Some of the Christians stood firm, declaring that they could make no compromise. Others were in favor of yielding or modifying some features of their faith and uniting with those who had accepted a part of Christianity, urging that this might be the means of their full conversion. That was a time of deep anguish to the faithful followers of Christ. Under a cloak of pretended Christianity, Satan was insinuating himself into the church, to corrupt their faith and turn their minds from the word of truth.

Most of the Christians at last consented to lower their standard, and a union was formed between Christianity and paganism. Although the worshipers of idols professed to be converted, and united with the church, they still clung to their idolatry, only changing the objects of their worship to images of Jesus, and even of Mary and the saints. The foul leaven of idolatry, thus brought into the church, continued its baleful work. Unsound doctrines, superstitious rites, and idolatrous ceremonies were incorporated into her faith and worship. As the followers of Christ united with idolaters, the Christian religion became corrupted, and the church lost her purity and power. There were some, however, who were not misled by these delusions. They still maintained their fidelity to the Author of truth and worshiped God alone.

There have ever been two classes among those who profess to be followers of Christ. While one class study the Saviour's life and earnestly seek to correct their defects and conform to the Pattern, the other class shun the plain, practical truths which expose their errors. Even in her best estate the church was not composed wholly of the true, pure, and sincere. Our Saviour taught that those who willfully indulge in sin are not to be received into the church; yet He connected with Himself men who were faulty in character, and granted them the benefits of His teachings and example, that they might have an opportunity to see their errors and correct them. Among the twelve apostles was a traitor. Judas was accepted, not because of his defects of character, but notwithstanding them. He was connected with the disciples, that, through the instruction and example of Christ, he might learn what constitutes Christian character, and thus be led to see his errors, to repent, and, by the aid of divine grace, to purify his soul "in obeying the truth." But Judas did not walk in the light so graciously permitted to shine upon him. By indulgence in sin he invited the temptations of Satan. His evil traits of character became predominant. He yielded his mind to the control of the powers of darkness, he became angry when his faults were reproved, and thus he was led to commit the fearful crime of betraying his Master. So do all who cherish evil under a profession of godliness hate those who disturb their peace by condemning their course of sin. When a favorable opportunity is presented, they will, like Judas, betray those who for their good have sought to reprove them.

The apostles encountered those in the church who professed godliness while they were secretly cherishing iniquity. Ananias and Sapphira acted the part of deceivers, pretending to make an entire sacrifice for God, when they were covetously withholding a portion for themselves. The Spirit of truth revealed to the apostles the real character of these pretenders, and the judgments of God rid the church of this foul blot upon its purity. This signal evidence of the discerning Spirit of Christ in the church was a terror to hypocrites and evildoers. They could not long remain in connection with those who were, in habit and disposition, constant representatives of Christ; and as trials and persecution came upon His followers, those only who were willing to forsake all for the truth's sake desired to become His disciples. Thus, as long as persecution continued, the church remained comparatively pure. But as it ceased, converts were added who were less sincere and devoted, and the way was open for Satan to obtain a foothold.

But there is no union between the Prince of light and the prince of darkness, and there can be no union between their followers. When Christians consented to unite with those who were but half converted from paganism, they entered upon a path which led further and further from the truth. Satan exulted that he had succeeded in deceiving so large a number of the followers of Christ. He then brought his power to bear more fully upon these, and inspired them to persecute those who remained true to God. None understood so well how to oppose the true Christian faith as did those who had once been its defenders; and these apostate Christians, uniting with their half-pagan companions, directed their warfare against the most essential features of the doctrines of Christ.

It required a desperate struggle for those who would be faithful to stand firm against the deceptions and abominations which were disguised in sacerdotal garments and introduced into the church. The Bible was not accepted as the standard of faith. The doctrine of religious freedom was termed heresy, and its upholders were hated and proscribed.

After a long and severe conflict, the faithful few decided to dissolve all union with the apostate church if she still refused to free herself from falsehood and idolatry. They saw that separation was an absolute necessity if they would obey the word of God. They dared not tolerate errors fatal to their own souls, and set an example which would imperil the faith of their children and children's children. To secure peace and unity they were ready to make any concession consistent with fidelity to God; but they felt that even peace would be too dearly purchased at the sacrifice of principle. If unity could be secured only by the compromise of truth and righteousness, then let there be difference, and even war.

Well would it be for the church and the world if the principles that actuated those steadfast souls were revived in the hearts of God's professed people. There is an alarming indifference in regard to the doctrines which are the pillars of the Christian faith. The opinion is gaining ground, that, after all, these are not of vital importance. This degeneracy is strengthening the hands of the agents of Satan, so that false theories and fatal delusions which the faithful in ages past imperiled their lives to resist and expose, are now regarded with favor by thousands who claim to be followers of Christ.

The early Christians were indeed a peculiar people. Their blameless deportment and unswerving faith were a continual reproof that disturbed the sinner's peace. Though few in numbers, without wealth, position, or honorary titles, they were a terror to evildoers wherever their character and doctrines were known. Therefore they were hated by the wicked, even as Abel was hated by the ungodly Cain. For the same reason that Cain slew Abel, did those who sought to throw off the restraint of the Holy Spirit, put to death God's people. It was for the same reason that the Jews rejected and crucified the Saviour—because the purity and holiness of His character was a constant rebuke to their selfishness and corruption. From the days of Christ until now His faithful disciples have excited the hatred and opposition of those who love and follow the ways of sin.

How, then, can the gospel be called a message of peace? When Isaiah foretold the birth of the Messiah, he ascribed to Him the title, "Prince of Peace." When angels announced to the shepherds that Christ was born, they sang above the plains of Bethlehem: "Glory to God in the highest, and on earth peace, good will toward men." Luke 2:14. There is a seeming contradiction between these prophetic declarations and the words of Christ: "I came not to send peace, but a sword." Matthew 10:34. But, rightly understood, the two are in perfect harmony. The gospel is a message of peace. Christianity is a system which, received and obeyed, would spread peace, harmony, and happiness throughout the earth. The religion of Christ will unite in close brotherhood all who accept its teachings. It was the mission of Jesus to reconcile men to God, and thus to one another. But the world at large are under the control of Satan, Christ's bitterest foe. The gospel presents to them principles of life which are wholly at variance with their habits and desires, and they rise in rebellion against it. They hate the purity which reveals and condemns their sins, and they persecute and destroy those who would urge upon them its just and holy claims. It is in this sense—because the exalted truths it brings occasion hatred and strife—that the gospel is called a sword.

The mysterious providence which permits the righteous to suffer persecution at the hand of the wicked has been a cause of great perplexity to many who are weak in faith. Some are even ready to cast away their confidence in God because He suffers the basest of men to prosper, while the best and purest are afflicted and tormented by their cruel power. How, it is asked, can One who is just and merciful, and who is also infinite in power, tolerate such injustice and oppression? This is a question with which we have nothing to do. God has given us sufficient evidence of His love, and we are not to doubt His goodness because we cannot understand the workings of His providence. Said the Saviour to His disciples, foreseeing the doubts that would press upon their souls in days of trial and darkness: "Remember the word that I said unto you, The servant is not greater than his lord. If they have persecuted Me, they will also persecute you." John 15:20. Jesus suffered for us more than any of His followers can be made to suffer through the cruelty of wicked men. Those who are called to endure torture and martyrdom are but following in the steps of God's dear Son.

"The Lord is not slack concerning His promise." 2 Peter 3:9. He does not forget or neglect His children; but He permits the wicked to reveal their true character, that none who desire to do His will may be deceived concerning them. Again, the righteous are placed in the furnace of affliction, that they themselves may be purified; that their example may convince others of the reality of faith and godliness; and also that their consistent course may condemn the ungodly and unbelieving.

God permits the wicked to prosper and to reveal their enmity against Him, that when they shall have filled up the measure of their iniquity all may see His justice and mercy in their utter destruction. The day of His vengeance hastens, when all who have transgressed His law and oppressed His people will meet the just recompense of their deeds; when every act of cruelty or injustice toward God's faithful ones will be punished as though done to Christ Himself.

There is another and more important question that should engage the attention of the churches of today. The apostle Paul declares that "all that will live godly in Christ Jesus shall suffer persecution." 2 Timothy 3:12. Why is it, then, that persecution seems in a great degree to slumber? The only reason is that the church has conformed to the world's standard and therefore awakens no opposition. The religion which is current in our day is not of the pure and holy character that marked the Christian faith in the days of Christ and His apostles. It is only because of the spirit of compromise with sin, because the great truths of the word of God are so indifferently regarded, because there is so little vital godliness in the church, that Christianity is apparently so popular with the world. Let there be a revival of the faith and power of the early church, and the spirit of persecution will be revived, and the fires of persecution will be rekindled.

chapter 3

Rejecting God's Word

THE apostle Paul, in his second letter to the Thessalonians, foretold the great apostasy which would result in the establishment of the papal power. He declared that the day of Christ should not come, "except there come a falling away first, and that man of sin be revealed, the son of perdition; who opposeth and exalteth himself above all that is called God, or that is worshiped; so that he as God sitteth in the temple of God, showing himself that he is God." And furthermore, the apostle warns his brethren that "the mystery of iniquity doth already work." 2 Thessalonians 2:3, 4, 7. Even at that early date he saw, creeping into the church, errors that would prepare the way for the development of the papacy.

Little by little, at first in stealth and silence, and then more openly as it increased in strength and gained control of the minds of men, "the mystery of iniquity" carried forward its deceptive and blasphemous work. Almost imperceptibly the customs of heathenism found their way into the Christian church. The spirit of compromise and conformity was restrained for a time by the fierce persecutions which the church endured under paganism. But as persecution ceased, and Christianity entered the courts and palaces of kings, she laid aside the humble simplicity of Christ and His apostles for the pomp and pride of pagan priests and rulers; and in place of the requirements of God, she substituted human theories and traditions. The nominal conversion of Constantine, in the early part of the fourth century, caused great rejoicing; and the world, cloaked with a form of righteousness, walked into the church. Now the work of corruption rapidly progressed. Paganism, while appearing to be vanquished, became the conqueror. Her spirit controlled the church. Her doctrines, ceremonies, and superstitions were incorporated into the faith and worship of the professed followers of Christ.

This compromise between paganism and Christianity resulted in the development of "the man of sin" foretold in prophecy as opposing and exalting himself above God. That gigantic system of false religion is a masterpiece of Satan's power—a monument of his efforts to seat himself upon the throne to rule the earth according to his will.

Satan once endeavored to form a compromise with Christ. He came to the Son of God in the wilderness of temptation, and showing Him all the kingdoms of the world and the glory of them, offered to give all into His hands if He would but acknowledge the supremacy of the prince of darkness. Christ rebuked the presumptuous tempter and forced him to depart. But Satan meets with greater success in presenting the same temptations to man. To secure worldly gains and honors, the church was led to seek the favor and support of the great men of earth; and having thus rejected Christ, she was induced to yield allegiance to the representative of Satan—the bishop of Rome.

It is one of the leading doctrines of Romanism that the pope is the visible head of the universal church of Christ, invested with supreme authority over bishops and pastors in all parts of the world. More than this, the pope has been given the very titles of Deity. He has been styled "Lord God the Pope" (see Appendix), and has been declared infallible. He demands the homage of all men. The same claim urged by Satan in the wilderness of temptation is still urged by him through the Church of Rome, and vast numbers are ready to yield him homage.

But those who fear and reverence God meet this heaven-daring assumption as Christ met the solicitations of the wily foe: "Thou shalt worship the Lord thy God, and Him only shalt thou serve." Luke 4:8. God has never given a hint in His word that He has appointed any man to be the head of the church. The doctrine of papal supremacy is directly opposed to the teachings of the Scriptures. The pope can have no power over Christ's church except by usurpation.

Romanists have persisted in bringing against Protestants the charge of heresy and willful separation from the true church. But these accusations apply rather to themselves. They are the ones who laid down the banner of Christ and departed from "the faith which was once delivered unto the saints." Jude 3.

Satan well knew that the Holy Scriptures would enable men to discern his deceptions and withstand his power. It was by the word that even the Saviour of the world had resisted his attacks. At every assault, Christ presented the shield of eternal truth, saying, "It is written." To every suggestion of the adversary, He opposed the wisdom and power of the word. In order for Satan to maintain his sway over men, and establish the authority of the papal usurper, he must keep them in ignorance of the Scriptures. The Bible would exalt God and place finite men in their true position; therefore its sacred truths must be concealed and suppressed. This logic was adopted by the Roman Church. For hundreds of years the circulation of the Bible was prohibited. The people were forbidden to read it or to have it in their houses, and unprincipled priests and prelates interpreted its teachings to sustain their pretensions. Thus the pope came to be almost universally acknowledged as the vicegerent of God on earth, endowed with authority over church and state.

The detector of error having been removed, Satan worked according to his will. Prophecy had declared that the papacy was to "think to change times and laws." Daniel 7:25. This work it was not slow to attempt. To afford converts from heathenism a substitute for the worship of idols, and thus to promote their nominal acceptance of Christianity, the adoration of images and relics was gradually introduced into the Christian worship. The decree of a general council (see Appendix) finally established this system of idolatry. To complete the sacrilegious work, Rome presumed to expunge from the law of God the second commandment, forbidding image worship, and to divide the tenth commandment, in order to preserve the number.

The spirit of concession to paganism opened the way for a still further disregard of Heaven's authority. Satan, working through unconsecrated leaders of the church, tampered with the fourth commandment also, and essayed to set aside the ancient Sabbath, the day which God had blessed and sanctified (Genesis 2:2, 3), and in its stead to exalt the festival observed by the heathen as "the venerable day of the sun." This change was not at first attempted openly. In the first centuries the true Sabbath had been kept by all Christians. They were jealous for the honor of God, and, believing that His law is immutable, they zealously guarded the sacredness of its precepts. But with great subtlety Satan worked through his agents to bring about his object. That the attention of the people might be called to the Sunday, it was made a festival in honor of the resurrection of Christ. Religious services were held upon it; yet it was regarded as a day of recreation, the Sabbath being still sacredly observed.

To prepare the way for the work which he designed to accomplish, Satan had led the Jews, before the advent of Christ, to load down the Sabbath with the most rigorous exactions, making its observance a burden. Now, taking advantage of the false light in which he had thus caused it to be regarded, he cast contempt upon it as a Jewish institution. While Christians generally continued to observe the Sunday as a joyous festival, he led them, in order to show their hatred of Judaism, to make the Sabbath a fast, a day of sadness and gloom.

In the early part of the fourth century the emperor Constantine issued a decree making Sunday a public festival throughout the Roman Empire. (See Appendix.) The day of the sun was reverenced by his pagan subjects and was honored by Christians; it was the emperor's policy to unite the conflicting interests of heathenism and Christianity. He was urged to do this by the bishops of the church, who, inspired by ambition and thirst for power, perceived that if the same day was observed by both Christians and heathen, it would promote the nominal acceptance of Christianity by pagans and thus advance the power and glory of the church. But while many God-fearing Christians were gradually led to regard Sunday as possessing a degree of sacredness, they still held the true Sabbath as the holy of the Lord and observed it in obedience to the fourth commandment.

The archdeceiver had not completed his work. He was resolved to gather the Christian world under his banner and to exercise his power through his vicegerent, the proud pontiff who claimed to be the representative of Christ. Through half-converted pagans, ambitious prelates, and world-loving churchmen he accomplished his purpose. Vast councils were held from time to time, in which the dignitaries of the church were convened from all the world. In nearly every council the Sabbath which God had instituted was pressed down a little lower, while the Sunday was correspondingly exalted. Thus the pagan festival came finally to be honored as a divine institution, while the Bible Sabbath was pronounced a relic of Judaism, and its observers were declared to be accursed.

The great apostate had succeeded in exalting himself "above all that is called God, or that is worshiped." 2 Thessalonians 2:4. He had dared to change the only precept of the divine law that unmistakably points all mankind to the true and living God. In the fourth commandment, God is revealed as the Creator of the heavens and the earth, and is thereby distinguished from all false gods. It was as a memorial of the work of creation that the seventh day was sanctified as a rest day for man. It was designed to keep the living God ever before the minds of men as the source of being and the object of reverence and worship. Satan strives to turn men from their allegiance to God, and from rendering obedience to His law; therefore he directs his efforts especially against that commandment which points to God as the Creator.

Protestants now urge that the resurrection of Christ on Sunday made it the Christian Sabbath. But Scripture evidence is lacking. No such honor was given to the day by Christ or His apostles. The observance of Sunday as a Christian institution had its origin in that "mystery of lawlessness" (2 Thessalonians 2:7, R.V.) which, even in Paul's day, had begun its work. Where and when did the Lord adopt this child of the papacy? What valid reason can be given for a change which the Scriptures do not sanction?

In the sixth century the papacy had become firmly established. Its seat of power was fixed in the imperial city, and the bishop of Rome was declared to be the head over the entire church. Paganism had given place to the papacy. The dragon had given to the beast "his power, and his seat, and great authority." Revelation 13:2. And now began the 1260 years of papal oppression foretold in the prophecies of Daniel and the Revelation. Daniel 7:25; Revelation 13:5-7. (See Appendix.) Christians were forced to choose either to yield their integrity and accept the papal ceremonies and worship, or to wear away their lives in dungeons or suffer death by the rack, the fagot, or the headsman's ax. Now were fulfilled the words of Jesus: "Ye shall be betrayed both by parents, and brethren, and kinsfolks, and friends; and some of you shall they cause to be put to death. And ye shall be hated of all men for My name's sake." Luke 21:16, 17. Persecution opened upon the faithful with greater fury than ever before, and the world became a vast battlefield. For hundreds of years the church of Christ found refuge in seclusion and obscurity. Thus says the prophet: "The woman fled into the wilderness, where she hath a place prepared of God, that they should feed her there a thousand two hundred and threescore days." Revelation 12:6.

The accession of the Roman Church to power marked the beginning of the Dark Ages. As her power increased, the darkness deepened. Faith was transferred from Christ, the true foundation, to the pope of Rome. Instead of trusting in the Son of God for forgiveness of sins and for eternal salvation, the people looked to the pope, and to the priests and prelates to whom he delegated authority. They were taught that the pope was their earthly mediator and that none could approach God except through him; and, further, that he stood in the place of God to them and was therefore to be implicitly obeyed. A deviation from his requirements was sufficient cause for the severest punishment to be visited upon the bodies and souls of the offenders. Thus the minds of the people were turned away from God to fallible, erring, and cruel men, nay, more, to the prince of darkness himself, who exercised his power through them. Sin was disguised in a garb of sanctity. When the Scriptures are suppressed, and man comes to regard himself as supreme, we need look only for fraud, deception, and debasing iniquity. With the elevation of human laws and traditions was manifest the corruption that ever results from setting aside the law of God.

Those were days of peril for the church of Christ. The faithful standard-bearers were few indeed. Though the truth was not left without witnesses, yet at times it seemed that error and superstition would wholly prevail, and true religion would be banished from the earth. The gospel was lost sight of, but the forms of religion were multiplied, and the people were burdened with rigorous exactions.

They were taught not only to look to the pope as their mediator, but to trust to works of their own to atone for sin. Long pilgrimages, acts of penance, the worship of relics, the erection of churches, shrines, and altars, the payment of large sums to the church—these and many similar acts were enjoined to appease the wrath of God or to secure His favor;

as if God were like men, to be angered at trifles, or pacified by gifts or acts of penance!

Notwithstanding that vice prevailed, even among the leaders of the Roman Church, her influence seemed steadily to increase. About the close of the eighth century, papists put forth the claim that in the first ages of the church the bishops of Rome had possessed the same spiritual power which they now assumed. To establish this claim, some means must be employed to give it a show of authority; and this was readily suggested by the father of lies. Ancient writings were forged by monks. Decrees of councils before unheard of were discovered, establishing the universal supremacy of the pope from the earliest times. And a church that had rejected the truth greedily accepted these deceptions. (See Appendix.)

The few faithful builders upon the true foundation (1 Corinthians 3:10, 11) were perplexed and hindered as the rubbish of false doctrine obstructed the work. Like the builders upon the wall of Jerusalem in Nehemiah's day, some were ready to say: "The strength of the bearers of burdens is decayed, and there is much rubbish; so that we are not able to build." Nehemiah 4:10. Wearied with the constant struggle against persecution, fraud, iniquity, and every other obstacle that Satan could devise to hinder their progress, some who had been faithful builders became disheartened; and for the sake of peace and security for their property and their lives, they turned away from the true foundation. Others, undaunted by the opposition of their enemies, fearlessly declared: "Be not ye afraid of them: remember the Lord, which is great and terrible" (verse 14); and they proceeded with the work, everyone with his sword girded by his side. Ephesians 6:17.

The same spirit of hatred and opposition to the truth has inspired the enemies of God in every age, and the same vigilance and fidelity have been required in His servants. The words of Christ to the first disciples are applicable to His followers to the close of time: "What I say unto you I say unto all, Watch." Mark 13:37.

The darkness seemed to grow more dense. Image worship became more general. Candles were burned before images, and prayers were offered to them. The most absurd and superstitious customs prevailed. The minds of men were so completely controlled by superstition that reason itself seemed to have lost its sway. While priests and bishops were themselves pleasure-loving, sensual, and corrupt, it could only be expected that the people who looked to them for guidance would be sunken in ignorance and vice.

Another step in papal assumption was taken, when, in the eleventh century, Pope Gregory VII proclaimed the perfection of the Roman Church. Among the propositions which he put forth was one declaring that the church had never erred, nor would it ever err, according to the Scriptures. But the Scripture proofs did not accompany the assertion. The proud pontiff also claimed the power to depose emperors, and declared that no sentence which he pronounced could be reversed by anyone, but that it was his prerogative to reverse the decisions of all others. (See Appendix.)

A striking illustration of the tyrannical character of this advocate of infallibility was given in his treatment of the German emperor, Henry IV. For presuming to disregard the pope's authority, this monarch was declared to be excommunicated and dethroned. Terrified by the desertion and threats of his own princes, who were encouraged in rebellion against him by the papal mandate, Henry felt the necessity of making his peace with Rome. In company with his wife and a faithful servant he crossed the Alps in midwinter, that he might humble himself before the pope. Upon reaching the castle whither Gregory had withdrawn, he was conducted, without his guards, into an outer court, and there, in the severe cold of winter, with uncovered head and naked feet, and in a miserable dress, he awaited the pope's permission to come into his presence. Not until he had continued three days fasting and making confession, did the pontiff condescend to grant him pardon. Even then it was only upon condition that the emperor should await the sanction of the pope before resuming the insignia or exercising the power of royalty. And Gregory, elated with his triumph, boasted that it was his duty to pull down the pride of kings.

How striking the contrast between the overbearing pride of this haughty pontiff and the meekness and gentleness of Christ, who represents Himself as pleading at the door of the heart for admittance, that He may come in to bring pardon and peace, and who taught His disciples: "Whosoever will be chief among you, let him be your servant." Matthew 20:27.

The advancing centuries witnessed a constant increase of error in the doctrines put forth from Rome. Even before the establishment of the papacy the teachings of heathen philosophers had received attention and exerted an influence in the church. Many who professed conversion still clung to the tenets of their pagan philosophy, and not only continued its study themselves, but urged it upon others as a means of extending their influence among the heathen. Serious errors were thus introduced into the Christian faith. Prominent among these was the belief in man's natural immortality and his consciousness in death. This doctrine laid the foundation upon which Rome established the invocation of saints and the adoration of the Virgin Mary. From this sprang also the heresy of eternal torment for the finally impenitent, which was early incorporated into the papal faith.

Then the way was prepared for the introduction of still another invention of paganism, which Rome named purgatory, and employed to terrify the credulous and superstitious multitudes. By this heresy is affirmed the existence of a place of torment, in which the souls of such as have not merited eternal damnation are to suffer punishment for their sins, and from which, when freed from impurity, they are admitted to heaven. (See Appendix.)

Still another fabrication was needed to enable Rome to profit by the fears and the vices of her adherents. This was supplied by the doctrine of indulgences. Full remission of sins, past, present, and future, and release from all the pains and penalties incurred, were promised to all who would enlist in the pontiff's wars to extend his temporal dominion, to punish his enemies, or to exterminate those who dared deny his spiritual supremacy. The people were also taught that by the payment of money to the church they might free themselves from sin, and also release the souls of their deceased friends who were confined in the tormenting flames. By such means did Rome fill her coffers and sustain the magnificence, luxury, and vice of the pretended representatives of Him who had not where to lay His head. (See Appendix.)

The Scriptural ordinance of the Lord's Supper had been supplanted by the idolatrous sacrifice of the mass. Papal priests pretended, by their senseless mummery, to convert the simple bread and wine into the actual "body and blood of Christ."—Cardinal Wiseman, *The Real Presence of the Body and Blood of Our Lord Jesus Christ in the Blessed Eucharist, Proved From Scripture*, lecture 8, sec. 3, par. 26. With blasphemous presumption, they openly claimed the power of creating God, the Creator of all things. Christians were required, on pain of death, to avow their faith in this horrible, Heaven-insulting heresy. Multitudes who refused were given to the flames. (See Appendix.)

In the thirteenth century was established that most terrible of all the engines of the papacy—the Inquisition. The prince of darkness wrought with the leaders of the papal hierarchy. In their secret councils Satan and his angels controlled the minds of evil men, while unseen in the midst stood an angel of God, taking the fearful record of their iniquitous decrees and writing the history of deeds too horrible to appear to human eyes. "Babylon the great" was "drunken with the blood of the saints." The mangled forms of millions of martyrs cried to God for vengeance upon that apostate power.

Popery had become the world's despot. Kings and emperors bowed to the decrees of the Roman pontiff. The destinies of men, both for time and for eternity, seemed under his control. For hundreds of years the doctrines of Rome had been extensively and implicitly received, its rites reverently performed, its festivals generally observed. Its clergy were honored and liberally sustained. Never since has the Roman Church attained to greater dignity, magnificence, or power.

But "the noon of the papacy was the midnight of the world."—J. A. Wylie, *The History of Protestantism*, b. I, ch. 4. The Holy Scriptures were almost unknown, not only to the people, but to the priests. Like the Pharisees of old, the papal leaders hated the light which would reveal their sins. God's law, the standard of righteousness, having been removed, they exercised power without limit, and practiced vice without restraint. Fraud, avarice, and profligacy prevailed. Men shrank from no crime by which they could gain wealth or position. The palaces of popes and prelates were scenes of the vilest debauchery. Some of the reigning pontiffs were guilty of crimes so revolting that secular rulers endeavored to depose these dignitaries of the church as monsters too vile to be tolerated. For centuries Europe had made no progress in learning, arts, or civilization. A moral and intellectual paralysis had fallen upon Christendom.

The condition of the world under the Romish power presented a fearful and striking fulfillment of the words of the prophet Hosea: "My people are destroyed for lack of knowledge: because thou hast rejected knowledge, I will also reject thee: . . . seeing thou hast forgotten the law of thy God, I will also forget thy children." "There is no truth, nor mercy, nor knowledge of God in the land. By swearing, and lying, and killing, and stealing, and committing adultery, they break out, and blood toucheth blood." Hosea 4:6, 1, 2. Such were the results of banishing the word of God.

chapter 4

Defending the Faith in the Mountains

AMID the gloom that settled upon the earth during the long period of papal supremacy, the light of truth could not be wholly extinguished. In every age there were witnesses for God—men who cherished faith in Christ as the only mediator between God and man, who held the Bible as the only rule of life, and who hallowed the true Sabbath. How much the world owes to these men, posterity will never know. They were branded as heretics, their motives impugned, their characters maligned, their writings suppressed, misrepresented, or mutilated. Yet they stood firm, and from age to age maintained their faith in its purity, as a sacred heritage for the generations to come.

The history of God's people during the ages of darkness that followed upon Rome's supremacy is written in heaven, but they have little place in human records. Few traces of their existence can be found, except in the accusations of their persecutors. It was the policy of Rome to obliterate every trace of dissent from her doctrines or decrees. Everything heretical, whether persons or writings, she sought to destroy. Expressions of doubt, or questions as to the authority of papal dogmas, were enough to forfeit the life of rich or poor, high or low. Rome endeavored also to destroy every record of her cruelty toward dissenters. Papal councils decreed that books and writings containing such records should be committed to the flames. Before the invention of printing, books were few in number, and in a form not favorable for preservation; therefore there was little to prevent the Romanists from carrying out their purpose.

Waldensian Christians, steadfast in their faith in the Bible, often worshiped under trying circumstances.

[61-62] 41

THE TRIUMPH OF GOD'S LOVE

No church within the limits of Romish jurisdiction was long left undisturbed in the enjoyment of freedom of conscience. No sooner had the papacy obtained power than she stretched out her arms to crush all that refused to acknowledge her sway, and one after another the churches submitted to her dominion.

In Great Britain primitive Christianity had very early taken root. The gospel received by the Britons in the first centuries was then uncorrupted by Romish apostasy. Persecution from pagan emperors, which extended even to these far-off shores, was the only gift that the first churches of Britain received from Rome. Many of the Christians, fleeing from persecution in England, found refuge in Scotland; thence the truth was carried to Ireland, and in all these countries it was received with gladness.

When the Saxons invaded Britain, heathenism gained control. The conquerors disdained to be instructed by their slaves, and the Christians were forced to retreat to the mountains and the wild moors. Yet the light, hidden for a time, continued to burn. In Scotland, a century later, it shone out with a brightness that extended to far-distant lands. From Ireland came the pious Columba and his colaborers, who, gathering about them the scattered believers on the lonely island of Iona, made this the center of their missionary labors. Among these evangelists was an observer of the Bible Sabbath, and thus this truth was introduced among the people. A school was established at Iona, from which missionaries went out, not only to Scotland and England, but to Germany, Switzerland, and even Italy.

But Rome had fixed her eyes on Britain, and resolved to bring it under her supremacy. In the sixth century her missionaries undertook the conversion of the heathen Saxons. They were received with favor by the proud barbarians, and they induced many thousands to profess the Romish faith. As the work progressed, the papal leaders and their converts encountered the primitive Christians. A striking contrast was presented. The latter were simple, humble, and Scriptural in character, doctrine, and manners, while the former manifested the superstition, pomp, and arrogance of popery. The emissary of Rome demanded that these Christian churches acknowledge the supremacy of the sovereign pontiff. The Britons meekly replied that they desired to love all men, but that the pope was not entitled to supremacy in the church, and they could render to him only that submission which was due to every follower of Christ. Repeated attempts were made to secure their allegiance to Rome; but these humble Christians, amazed at the pride displayed by her emissaries, steadfastly replied that they knew no other master than Christ. Now the true spirit of the papacy was revealed. Said the Romish leader: "If you will not receive brethren who bring you peace, you shall receive enemies who will bring you war. If you will not unite with us in showing the Saxons the way of life, you shall receive from them the stroke of death." —J. H. Merle D'Aubigné, *History of the Reformation of the Sixteenth Century*, b. 17, ch. 2. These were no idle threats. War, intrigue, and deception were employed against these witnesses for a Bible faith, until the churches of Britain were destroyed, or forced to submit to the authority of the pope.

In lands beyond the jurisdiction of Rome there existed for many centuries bodies of Christians who remained almost wholly free from papal corruption. They were surrounded by heathenism and in the lapse of ages were affected by its errors; but they continued to regard the Bible as the only rule of faith and adhered to many of its truths. These Christians believed in the perpetuity of the law of God and observed the Sabbath of the fourth commandment. Churches that held to this faith and practice existed in Central Africa and among the Armenians of Asia.

But of those who resisted the encroachments of the papal power, the Waldenses stood foremost. In the very land where popery had fixed its seat, there its falsehood and corruption were most steadfastly resisted. For centuries the churches of Piedmont maintained their independence; but the time came at last when Rome insisted upon their submission. After ineffectual struggles against her tyranny, the leaders of these churches reluctantly acknowledged the supremacy of the power to which the whole world seemed to pay homage. There were some, however, who refused to yield to the authority of pope or prelate. They were determined to maintain their allegiance to God and to preserve the purity and simplicity of their faith. A separation took place. Those who adhered to the ancient faith now withdrew; some, forsaking their native Alps, raised the banner of truth in foreign lands; others retreated to the secluded glens and rocky fastnesses of the mountains, and there preserved their freedom to worship God.

The faith which for centuries was held and taught by the Waldensian Christians was in marked contrast to the false doctrines put forth from Rome. Their religious belief was founded upon the written word of God, the true system of Christianity. But those humble peasants, in their obscure retreats, shut away from the world, and bound to daily toil among their flocks and their vineyards, had not by themselves arrived at the truth in opposition to the dogmas and heresies of the apostate church. Theirs was not a faith newly received. Their religious belief was their inheritance from their fathers. They contended for the faith of the apostolic church—"the faith which was once delivered unto the saints." Jude 3. "The church in the wilderness," and not the proud hierarchy enthroned in the world's great capital, was the true church of Christ, the guardian of the treasures of truth which God has committed to His people to be given to the world.

Among the leading causes that had led to the separation of the true church from Rome was the hatred of the latter toward the Bible Sabbath. As foretold by prophecy, the papal power cast down the truth to the ground. The law of God was trampled in the dust, while the traditions and customs of men were exalted. The churches that were under the rule of the papacy were early compelled to honor the Sunday as a holy day. Amid the prevailing error and superstition, many, even of the true people of God, became so bewildered that while they observed the Sabbath, they refrained from labor also on the Sunday. But this did not satisfy the papal leaders. They demanded not only that Sunday be hallowed, but that the Sabbath be profaned; and they denounced in the strongest language those who dared to show it honor. It was only by fleeing from the power of Rome that any could obey God's law in peace. (See Appendix.)

The Waldenses were among the first of the peoples of Europe to obtain a translation of the Holy Scriptures. (See Appendix.) Hundreds of years before the Reformation they possessed the Bible in manuscript in their native tongue. They had the truth unadulterated, and this rendered them the special objects of hatred and persecution. They declared the Church of Rome to be the apostate Babylon of the Apocalypse, and at the peril of their lives they stood up to resist her corruptions. While, under the pressure of long-continued persecution, some compromised their faith, little by little yielding its distinctive principles, others held fast the truth. Through ages of darkness and apostasy there were Waldenses who denied the supremacy of Rome, who rejected image worship as idolatry, and who kept the true Sabbath. Under the fiercest tempests of opposition they maintained their faith. Though gashed by the Savoyard spear, and scorched by the Romish fagot, they stood unflinchingly for God's word and His honor.

Behind the lofty bulwarks of the mountains—in all ages the refuge of the persecuted and oppressed—the Waldenses found a hiding place. Here the light of truth was kept burning amid the darkness of the Middle

Ages. Here, for a thousand years, witnesses for the truth maintained the ancient faith.

God had provided for His people a sanctuary of awful grandeur, befitting the mighty truths committed to their trust. To those faithful exiles the mountains were an emblem of the immutable righteousness of Jehovah. They pointed their children to the heights towering above them in unchanging majesty, and spoke to them of Him with whom there is no variableness nor shadow of turning, whose word is as enduring as the everlasting hills. God had set fast the mountains and girded them with strength; no arm but that of Infinite Power could move them out of their place. In like manner He had established His law, the foundation of His government in heaven and upon earth. The arm of man might reach his fellowmen and destroy their lives; but that arm could as readily uproot the mountains from their foundations, and hurl them into the sea, as it could change one precept of the law of Jehovah, or blot out one of His promises to those who do His will. In their fidelity to His law, God's servants should be as firm as the unchanging hills.

The mountains that girded their lowly valleys were a constant witness to God's creative power, and a never-failing assurance of His protecting care. Those pilgrims learned to love the silent symbols of Jehovah's presence. They indulged no repining because of the hardships of their lot; they were never lonely amid the mountain solitudes. They thanked God that He had provided for them an asylum from the wrath and cruelty of men. They rejoiced in their freedom to worship before Him. Often when pursued by their enemies, the strength of the hills proved a sure defense. From many a lofty cliff they chanted the praise of God, and the armies of Rome could not silence their songs of thanksgiving.

Pure, simple, and fervent was the piety of these followers of Christ. The principles of truth they valued above houses and lands, friends, kindred, even life itself. These principles they earnestly sought to impress upon the hearts of the young. From earliest childhood the youth were instructed in the Scriptures and taught to regard sacredly the claims of the law of God. Copies of the Bible were rare; therefore its precious words were committed to memory. Many were able to repeat large portions of both the Old and the New Testament. Thoughts of God were associated alike with the sublime scenery of nature and with the humble blessings of daily life. Little children learned to look with gratitude to God as the giver of every favor and every comfort.

Parents, tender and affectionate as they were, loved their children too wisely to accustom them to self-indulgence. Before them was a life of trial and hardship, perhaps a martyr's death. They were educated from childhood to endure hardness, to submit to control, and yet to think and act for themselves. Very early they were taught to bear responsibilities, to be guarded in speech, and to understand the wisdom of silence. One indiscreet word let fall in the hearing of their enemies might imperil not only the life of the speaker, but the lives of hundreds of his brethren; for as wolves hunting their prey did the enemies of truth pursue those who dared to claim freedom of religious faith.

The Waldenses had sacrificed their worldly prosperity for the truth's sake, and with persevering patience they toiled for their bread. Every spot of tillable land among the mountains was carefully improved; the valleys and the less fertile hillsides were made to yield their increase. Economy and severe self-denial formed a part of the education which the children received as their only legacy. They were taught that God designs life to be a discipline, and that their wants could be supplied only by personal labor, by forethought, care, and faith. The process was laborious and wearisome, but it was wholesome, just what man needs in his fallen state, the school which God has provided for his training and development. While the youth were inured to toil and hardship, the culture of the intellect was not neglected. They were taught that all their powers belonged to God, and that all were to be improved and developed for His service.

The Vaudois churches, in their purity and simplicity, resembled the church of apostolic times. Rejecting the supremacy of the pope and prelate, they held the Bible as the only supreme, infallible authority. Their pastors, unlike the lordly priests of Rome, followed the example of their Master, who "came not to be ministered unto, but to minister." They fed the flock of God, leading them to the green pastures and living fountains of His holy word. Far from the monuments of human pomp and pride the people assembled, not in magnificent churches or grand cathedrals, but beneath the shadow of the mountains, in the Alpine valleys, or, in time of danger, in some rocky stronghold, to listen to the words of truth from the servants of Christ. The pastors not only preached the gospel, but they visited the sick, catechized the children, admonished the erring, and labored to settle disputes and promote harmony and brotherly love. In times of peace they were sustained by the freewill offerings of the people; but, like Paul the tentmaker, each learned some trade or profession by which, if necessary, to provide for his own support.

From their pastors the youth received instruction. While attention was given to branches of general learning, the Bible was made the chief study. The Gospels of Matthew and John were committed to memory, with many of the Epistles. They were employed also in copying the Scriptures. Some manuscripts contained the whole Bible, others only brief selections, to which some simple explanations of the text were added by those who were able to expound the Scriptures. Thus were brought forth the treasures of truth so long concealed by those who sought to exalt themselves above God.

By patient, untiring labor, sometimes in the deep, dark caverns of the earth, by the light of torches, the Sacred Scriptures were written out, verse by verse, chapter by chapter. Thus the work went on, the revealed will of God shining out like pure gold; how much brighter, clearer, and more powerful because of the trials undergone for its sake only those could realize who were engaged in the work. Angels from heaven surrounded these faithful workers.

Satan had urged on the papal priests and prelates to bury the word of truth beneath the rubbish of error, heresy, and superstition; but in a most wonderful manner it was preserved uncorrupted through all the ages of darkness. It bore not the stamp of man, but the impress of God. Men have been unwearied in their efforts to obscure the plain, simple meaning of the Scriptures, and to make them contradict their own testimony; but like the ark upon the billowy deep, the word of God outrides the storms that threaten it with destruction. As the mine has rich veins of gold and silver hidden beneath the surface, so that all must dig who would discover its precious stores, so the Holy Scriptures have treasures of truth that are revealed only to the earnest, humble, prayerful seeker. God designed the Bible to be a lessonbook to all mankind, in childhood, youth, and manhood, and to be studied through all time. He gave His word to men as a revelation of Himself. Every new truth discerned is a fresh disclosure of the character of its Author. The study of the Scriptures is the means divinely ordained to bring men into closer connection with their Creator and to give them a clearer knowledge of His will. It is the medium of communication between God and man.

While the Waldenses regarded the fear of the Lord as the beginning of wisdom, they were not blind to the importance of a contact with the world, a knowledge of men and of active life, in expanding the mind and quickening the perceptions. From their schools in the mountains some of the youth were sent to institutions of learning in the cities of France or Italy, where was a more extended field for study, thought, and observation than in their native Alps. The youth thus sent forth were exposed to temptation, they witnessed vice, they encountered Satan's wily agents, who urged upon them the most subtle heresies and the most dangerous deceptions. But their education from childhood had been of a character to prepare them for all this.

In the schools whither they went, they were not to make confidants of any. Their garments were so prepared as to conceal their greatest treasure—the precious manuscripts of the Scriptures. These, the fruit of months and years of toil, they carried with them, and whenever they could do so without exciting suspicion, they cautiously placed some portion in the way of those whose hearts seemed open to receive the truth. From their mother's knee the Waldensian youth had been trained with this purpose in view; they understood their work and faithfully performed it. Converts to the true faith were won in these institutions of learning, and frequently its principles were found to be permeating the entire school; yet the papal leaders could not, by the closest inquiry, trace the so-called corrupting heresy to its source.

The spirit of Christ is a missionary spirit. The very first impulse of the renewed heart is to bring others also to the Saviour. Such was the spirit of the Vaudois Christians. They felt that God required more of them than merely to preserve the truth in its purity in their own churches; that a solemn responsibility rested upon them to let their light shine forth to those who were in darkness; by the mighty power of God's word they sought to break the bondage which Rome had imposed. The Vaudois ministers were trained as missionaries, everyone who expected to enter the ministry being required first to gain an experience as an evangelist. Each was to serve three years in some mission field before taking charge of a church at home. This service, requiring at the outset self-denial and sacrifice, was a fitting introduction to the pastor's life in those times that tried men's souls. The youth who received ordination to the sacred office saw before them, not the prospect of earthly wealth and glory, but a life of toil and danger, and possibly a martyr's fate. The missionaries went out two and two, as Jesus sent forth His disciples. With each young man was usually associated a man of age and experience, the youth being under the guidance of his companion, who was held responsible for his training, and whose instruction he was required to heed. These colaborers were not always together, but often met for prayer and counsel, thus strengthening each other in the faith.

To have made known the object of their mission would have ensured its defeat; therefore they carefully concealed their real character. Every minister possessed a knowledge of some trade or profession, and the missionaries prosecuted their work under cover of a secular calling. Usually they chose that of merchant or peddler. "They carried silks, jewelry, and other articles, at that time not easily purchasable save at distant marts; and they were welcomed as merchants where they would have been spurned as missionaries."—Wylie, b. 1, ch. 7. All the while their hearts were uplifted to God for wisdom to present a treasure more precious than gold or gems. They secretly carried about with them copies of the Bible, in whole or in part; and whenever an opportunity was presented, they called the attention of their customers to these manuscripts. Often an interest to read God's word was thus awakened, and some portion was gladly left with those who desired to receive it.

The work of these missionaries began in the plains and valleys at the foot of their own mountains, but it extended far beyond these limits. With naked feet and in garments coarse and travel-stained as were those of their Master, they passed through great cities and penetrated to distant lands. Everywhere they scattered the precious seed. Churches sprang up in their path, and the blood of martyrs witnessed for the truth. The day of God will reveal a rich harvest of souls garnered by the labors of these faithful men. Veiled and silent, the word of God was making its way

through Christendom and meeting a glad reception in the homes and hearts of men.

To the Waldenses the Scriptures were not merely a record of God's dealings with men in the past, and a revelation of the responsibilities and duties of the present, but an unfolding of the perils and glories of the future. They believed that the end of all things was not far distant, and as they studied the Bible with prayer and tears they were the more deeply impressed with its precious utterances and with their duty to make known to others its saving truths. They saw the plan of salvation clearly revealed in the sacred pages, and they found comfort, hope, and peace in believing in Jesus. As the light illuminated their understanding and made glad their hearts, they longed to shed its beams upon those who were in the darkness of papal error.

They saw that under the guidance of pope and priest, multitudes were vainly endeavoring to obtain pardon by afflicting their bodies for the sin of their souls. Taught to trust to their good works to save them, they were ever looking to themselves, their minds dwelling upon their sinful condition, seeing themselves exposed to the wrath of God, afflicting soul and body, yet finding no relief. Thus conscientious souls were bound by the doctrines of Rome. Thousands abandoned friends and kindred, and spent their lives in convent cells. By oft-repeated fasts and cruel scourgings, by midnight vigils, by prostration for weary hours upon the cold, damp stones of their dreary abode, by long pilgrimages, by humiliating penance and fearful torture, thousands vainly sought to obtain peace of conscience. Oppressed with a sense of sin, and haunted with the fear of God's avenging wrath, many suffered on, until exhausted nature gave way, and without one ray of light or hope they sank into the tomb.

The Waldenses longed to break to these starving souls the bread of life, to open to them the messages of peace in the promises of God, and to point them to Christ as their only hope of salvation. The doctrine that good works can atone for the transgression of God's law they held to be based upon falsehood. Reliance upon human merit intercepts the view of Christ's infinite love. Jesus died as a sacrifice for man because the fallen race can do nothing to recommend themselves to God. The merits of a crucified and risen Saviour are the foundation of the Christian's faith. The dependence of the soul upon Christ is as real, and its connection with Him must be as close, as that of a limb to the body, or of a branch to the vine.

The teachings of popes and priests had led men to look upon the char-

The Waldenses, eager to share their faith, went everywhere as missionaries, often disguised as itinerant merchants.

acter of God, and even of Christ, as stern, gloomy, and forbidding. The Saviour was represented as so far devoid of sympathy with man in his fallen state that the mediation of priests and saints must be invoked. Those whose minds had been enlightened by the word of God longed to point these souls to Jesus as their compassionate, loving Saviour, standing with outstretched arms, inviting all to come to Him with their burden of sin, their care and weariness. They longed to clear away the obstructions which Satan had piled up that men might not see the promises, and come directly to God, confessing their sins, and obtaining pardon and peace.

Eagerly did the Vaudois missionary unfold to the inquiring mind the precious truths of the gospel. Cautiously he produced the carefully written portions of the Holy Scriptures. It was his greatest joy to give hope to the conscientious, sin-stricken soul, who could see only a God of vengeance, waiting to execute justice. With quivering lip and tearful eye did he, often on bended knees, open to his brethren the precious promises that reveal the sinner's only hope. Thus the light of truth penetrated many a darkened mind, rolling back the cloud of gloom, until the Sun of Righteousness shone into the heart with healing in His beams. It was often the case that some portion of Scripture was read again and again, the hearer desiring it to be repeated, as if he would assure himself that he had heard aright. Especially was the repetition of these words eagerly desired: "The blood of Jesus Christ His Son cleanseth us from all sin." 1 John 1:7. "As Moses lifted up the serpent in the wilderness, even so must the Son of man be lifted up: that whosoever believeth in Him should not perish, but have eternal life." John 3:14, 15.

Many were undeceived in regard to the claims of Rome. They saw how vain is the mediation of men or angels in behalf of the sinner. As the true light dawned upon their minds they exclaimed with rejoicing: "Christ is my priest; His blood is my sacrifice; His altar is my confessional." They cast themselves wholly upon the merits of Jesus, repeating the words, "Without faith it is impossible to please Him." Hebrews 11:6. "There is none other name under heaven given among men, whereby we must be saved." Acts 4:12.

The assurance of a Saviour's love seemed too much for some of these poor tempest-tossed souls to realize. So great was the relief which it brought, such a flood of light was shed upon them, that they seemed transported to heaven. Their hands were laid confidingly in the hand of Christ; their feet were planted upon the Rock of Ages. All fear of death was banished. They could now covet the prison and the fagot if they might thereby honor the name of their Redeemer.

In secret places the word of God was thus brought forth and read, sometimes to a single soul, sometimes to a little company who were longing for light and truth. Often the entire night was spent in this manner. So great would be the wonder and admiration of the listeners that the messenger of mercy was not infrequently compelled to cease his reading until the understanding could grasp the tidings of salvation. Often would words like these be uttered: "Will God indeed accept *my* offering? Will He smile upon *me?* Will He pardon *me?*" The answer was read: "Come unto Me, all ye that labor and are heavy-laden, and I will give you rest." Matthew 11:28.

Faith grasped the promise, and the glad response was heard: "No more long pilgrimages to make; no more painful journeys to holy shrines. I may come to Jesus just as I am, sinful and unholy, and He will not spurn the penitential prayer. 'Thy sins be forgiven thee.' Mine, even mine, may be forgiven!"

A tide of sacred joy would fill the heart, and the name of Jesus would be magnified by praise and thanksgiving. Those happy souls returned to their homes to diffuse light, to repeat to others, as well as they could, their new experience; that they had found the true and living Way. There was a strange and solemn power in the words of Scripture that spoke directly to the hearts of those who were longing for the truth. It was the voice of God, and it carried conviction to those who heard.

The messenger of truth went on his way; but his appearance of humility, his sincerity, his earnestness and deep fervor, were subjects of frequent remark. In many instances his hearers had not asked him whence he came or whither he went. They had been so overwhelmed, at first with surprise, and afterward with gratitude and joy, that they had not thought to question him. When they had urged him to accompany them to their homes, he had replied that he must visit the lost sheep of the flock. Could he have been an angel from heaven? they queried.

In many cases the messenger of truth was seen no more. He had made his way to other lands, or he was wearing out his life in some unknown dungeon, or perhaps his bones were whitening on the spot where he had witnessed for the truth. But the words he had left behind could not be destroyed. They were doing their work in the hearts of men; the blessed results will be fully known only in the judgment.

The Waldensian missionaries were invading the kingdom of Satan, and the powers of darkness aroused to greater vigilance. Every effort to advance the truth was watched by the prince of evil, and he excited the fears of his agents. The papal leaders saw a portent of danger to their cause from the labors of these humble itinerants. If the light of truth were allowed to shine unobstructed, it would sweep away the heavy clouds of error that enveloped the people. It would direct the minds of men to God alone and would eventually destroy the supremacy of Rome.

The very existence of this people, holding the faith of the ancient church, was a constant testimony to Rome's apostasy, and therefore excited the most bitter hatred and persecution. Their refusal to surrender the Scriptures was also an offense that Rome could not tolerate. She determined to blot them from the earth. Now began the most terrible crusades against God's people in their mountain homes. Inquisitors were put upon their track, and the scene of innocent Abel falling before the murderous Cain was often repeated.

Again and again were their fertile lands laid waste, their dwellings and chapels swept away, so that where once were flourishing fields and the homes of an innocent, industrious people, there remained only a desert. As the ravenous beast is rendered more furious by the taste of blood, so the rage of the papists was kindled to greater intensity by the sufferings of their victims. Many of these witnesses for a pure faith were pursued across the mountains and hunted down in the valleys where they were hidden, shut in by mighty forests and pinnacles of rock.

No charge could be brought against the moral character of this proscribed class. Even their enemies declared them to be a peaceable, quiet, pious people. Their grand offense was that they would not worship God according to the will of the pope. For this crime every humiliation, insult, and torture that men or devils could invent was heaped upon them.

When Rome at one time determined to exterminate the hated sect, a bull was issued by the pope, condemning them as heretics, and delivering them to slaughter. (See Appendix.) They were not accused as idlers, or dishonest, or disorderly; but it was declared that they had an appearance of piety and sanctity that seduced "the sheep of the true fold." Therefore the pope ordered "that malicious and abominable sect of malignants," if they "refuse to abjure, to be crushed like venomous snakes."—Wylie, b. 16, ch. 1. Did this haughty potentate expect to meet those words again? Did he know that they were registered in the books of heaven, to confront him at the judgment? "Inasmuch as ye have done it unto one of the least of these My brethren," said Jesus, "ye have done it unto Me." Matthew 25:40.

This bull called upon all members of the church to join the crusade against the heretics. As an incentive to engage in this cruel work, it "absolved from all ecclesiastical pains and penalties, general and particular; it released all who joined the crusade from any oaths they might have taken; it legitimatized their title to any property they might have illegally acquired; and promised remission of all their sins to such as should kill any heretic. It annulled all contracts made in favor of Vaudois, ordered their domestics to abandon them, forbade all persons to give them any aid whatever, and empowered all persons to take possession of their property."—Wylie, b. 16, ch. 1. This document clearly reveals the master spirit behind the scenes. It is the roar of the dragon, and not the voice of Christ, that is heard therein.

The papal leaders would not conform their characters to the great standard of God's law, but erected a standard to suit themselves, and determined to compel all to conform to this because Rome willed it. The most horrible tragedies were enacted. Corrupt and blasphemous priests and popes were doing the work which Satan appointed them. Mercy had no place in their natures. The same spirit that crucified Christ and slew the apostles, the same that moved the bloodthirsty Nero against the faithful in his day, was at work to rid the earth of those who were beloved of God.

The persecutions visited for many centuries upon this God-fearing people were endured by them with a patience and constancy that honored their Redeemer. Notwithstanding the crusades against them, and the inhuman butchery to which they were subjected, they continued to send out their missionaries to scatter the precious truth. They were hunted to death; yet their blood watered the seed sown, and it failed not of yielding fruit. Thus the Waldenses witnessed for God centuries before the birth of Luther. Scattered over many lands, they planted the seeds of the Reformation that began in the time of Wycliffe, grew broad and deep in the days of Luther, and is to be carried forward to the close of time by those who also are willing to suffer all things for "the word of God, and for the testimony of Jesus Christ." Revelation 1:9.

chapter 5

The Light Breaks in England

BEFORE the Reformation there were at times but very few copies of the Bible in existence, but God had not suffered His word to be wholly destroyed. Its truths were not to be forever hidden. He could as easily unchain the words of life as He could open prison doors and unbolt iron gates to set His servants free. In the different countries of Europe men were moved by the Spirit of God to search for the truth as for hid treasures. Providentially guided to the Holy Scriptures, they studied the sacred pages with intense interest. They were willing to accept the light at any cost to themselves. Though they did not see all things clearly, they were enabled to perceive many long-buried truths. As Heaven-sent messengers they went forth, rending asunder the chains of error and superstition, and calling upon those who had been so long enslaved, to arise and assert their liberty.

Except among the Waldenses, the word of God had for ages been locked up in languages known only to the learned; but the time had come for the Scriptures to be translated and given to the people of different lands in their native tongue. The world had passed its midnight. The hours of darkness were wearing away, and in many lands appeared tokens of the coming dawn.

In the fourteenth century arose in England the "morning star of the Reformation." John Wycliffe was the herald of reform, not for England alone, but for all Christendom. The great protest against Rome which it was permitted him to utter was never to be silenced. That protest opened the struggle which was to result in the emancipation of individuals, of churches, and of nations.

Wycliffe received a liberal education, and with him the fear of the Lord was the beginning of wisdom. He was noted at college for his fervent piety as well as for his remarkable talents and sound scholarship. In his thirst for knowledge he sought to become acquainted with every branch of learning. He was educated in the scholastic philosophy, in the canons of the church, and in the civil law, especially that of his own country. In his after labors the value of this early training was apparent. A thorough acquaintance with the speculative philosophy of his time enabled him to expose its errors; and by his study of national and ecclesiastical law he was prepared to engage in the great struggle for civil and religious liberty. While he could wield the weapons drawn from the word of God, he had acquired the intellectual discipline of the schools, and he understood the tactics of the schoolmen. The power of his genius and the extent and thoroughness of his knowledge commanded the respect of both friends and foes. His adherents saw with satisfaction that their champion stood foremost among the leading minds of the nation; and his enemies were prevented from casting contempt upon the cause of reform by exposing the ignorance or weakness of its supporter.

While Wycliffe was still at college, he entered upon the study of the Scriptures. In those early times, when the Bible existed only in the ancient languages, scholars were enabled to find their way to the fountain of truth, which was closed to the uneducated classes. Thus already the way had been prepared for Wycliffe's future work as a Reformer. Men of learning had studied the word of God and had found the great truth of His free grace there revealed. In their teachings they had spread a knowledge of this truth, and had led others to turn to the living oracles.

When Wycliffe's attention was directed to the Scriptures, he entered upon their investigation with the same thoroughness which had enabled him to master the learning of the schools. Heretofore he had felt a great want, which neither his scholastic studies nor the teaching of the church could satisfy. In the word of God he found that which he had before sought in vain. Here he saw the plan of salvation revealed and Christ set forth as the only advocate for man. He gave himself to the service of Christ and determined to proclaim the truths he had discovered.

Like after Reformers, Wycliffe did not, at the opening of his work, foresee whither it would lead him. He did not set himself deliberately in opposition to Rome. But devotion to truth could not but bring him in conflict with falsehood. The more clearly he discerned the errors of the papacy, the more earnestly he presented the teaching of the Bible. He saw that Rome had forsaken the word of God for human tradition; he fearlessly accused the priesthood of having banished the Scriptures, and demanded that the Bible be restored to the people and that its authority be again established in the church. He was an able and earnest teacher and an eloquent preacher, and his daily life was a demonstration of the truths he preached. His knowledge of the Scriptures, the force of his reasoning, the purity of his life, and his unbending courage and integrity won for him general esteem and confidence. Many of the people had become dissatisfied with their former faith as they saw the iniquity that prevailed in the Roman Church, and they hailed with unconcealed joy the truths brought to view by Wycliffe; but the papal leaders were filled with rage when they perceived that this Reformer was gaining an influence greater than their own.

Wycliffe was a keen detector of error, and he struck fearlessly against many of the abuses sanctioned by the authority of Rome. While acting as chaplain for the king, he took a bold stand against the payment of tribute claimed by the pope from the English monarch and showed that the papal assumption of authority over secular rulers was contrary to both reason and revelation. The demands of the pope had excited great indignation, and Wycliffe's teachings exerted an influence upon the leading minds of the nation. The king and the nobles united in denying the pontiff's claim to temporal authority and in refusing the payment of the tribute. Thus an effectual blow was struck against the papal supremacy in England.

Another evil against which the Reformer waged long and resolute battle was the institution of the orders of mendicant friars. These friars swarmed in England, casting a blight upon the greatness and prosperity of the nation. Industry, education, morals, all felt the withering influence. The monk's life of idleness and beggary was not only a heavy drain upon the resources of the people, but it brought useful labor into contempt. The youth were demoralized and corrupted. By the influence of the friars many were induced to enter a cloister and devote themselves to a monastic life, and this not only without the consent of their parents, but even without their knowledge and contrary to their commands. One of the early Fathers of the Roman Church, urging the claims of monasticism above the obligations of filial love and duty, had declared: "Though thy father should lie before thy door weeping and lamenting, and thy mother should show the body that bore thee and the breasts that nursed thee, see that thou trample them underfoot, and go onward straightway to Christ." By this "monstrous inhumanity," as Luther afterward styled it, "savoring more of the wolf and the tyrant than of the Christian and the man," were the hearts of children steeled against their parents.— Barnas Sears, *The Life of Luther*, pages 70, 69. Thus did the papal leaders, like the Pharisees of old, make the commandment of God of none effect by their tradition. Thus homes were made desolate and parents were deprived of the society of their sons and daughters.

Even the students in the universities were deceived by the false representations of the monks and induced to join their orders. Many afterward repented this step, seeing that they had blighted their own lives and had brought sorrow upon their parents; but once fast in the snare it was impossible for them to obtain their freedom. Many parents, fearing the influence of the monks, refused to send their sons to the universities. There was a marked falling off in the number of students in attendance at the great centers of learning. The schools languished, and ignorance prevailed.

The pope had bestowed on these monks the power to hear confessions and to grant pardon. This became a source of great evil. Bent on enhancing their gains, the friars were so ready to grant absolution that criminals of all descriptions resorted to them, and, as a result, the worst vices rapidly increased. The sick and the poor were left to suffer, while the gifts that should have relieved their wants went to the monks, who with threats demanded the alms of the people, denouncing the impiety of those who should withhold gifts from their orders. Notwithstanding their profession of poverty, the wealth of the friars was constantly increasing, and their magnificent edifices and luxurious tables made more apparent the growing poverty of the nation. And while spending their time in luxury and pleasure, they sent out in their stead ignorant men, who could only recount marvelous tales, legends, and jests to amuse the people and make them still more completely the dupes of the monks. Yet the friars continued to maintain their hold on the superstitious multitudes and led them to believe that all religious duty was comprised in acknowledging the supremacy of the pope, adoring the saints, and making gifts to the monks, and that this was sufficient to secure them a place in heaven.

Men of learning and piety had labored in vain to bring about a reform in these monastic orders; but Wycliffe, with clearer insight, struck at the root of the evil, declaring that the system itself was false and that it should be abolished. Discussion and inquiry were awakening. As the monks traversed the country, vending the pope's pardons, many were led to doubt the possibility of purchasing forgiveness with money, and they questioned whether they should not seek pardon from God rather than from the pontiff of Rome. (See Appendix note for page 38.) Not a few were alarmed at the rapacity of the friars, whose greed seemed never to be satisfied. "The monks and priests of Rome," said they, "are eating us away like a cancer. God must deliver us, or the people will perish."—D'Aubigné, b. 17, ch. 7. To cover their avarice, these begging monks claimed that they were following the Saviour's example, declaring that Jesus and His disciples had been supported by the charities of the people. This claim resulted in injury to their cause, for it led many to the Bible to learn the truth for themselves—a result which of all others was least desired by Rome. The minds of men were directed to the Source of truth, which it was her object to conceal.

Wycliffe began to write and publish tracts against the friars, not, however, seeking so much to enter into dispute with them as to call the minds of the people to the teachings of the Bible and its Author. He declared that the power of pardon or of excommunication is possessed by the pope in no greater degree than by common priests, and that no man can be truly excommunicated unless he has first brought upon himself the condemnation of God. In no more effectual way could he have undertaken the overthrow of that mammoth fabric of spiritual and temporal dominion which the pope had erected and in which the souls and bodies of millions were held captive.

Again Wycliffe was called to defend the rights of the English crown against the encroachments of Rome; and being appointed a royal ambassador, he spent two years in the Netherlands, in conference with the commissioners of the pope. Here he was brought into communication with ecclesiastics from France, Italy, and Spain, and he had an opportunity to look behind the scenes and gain a knowledge of many things which would have remained hidden from him in England. He learned much that was to give point to his after labors. In these representatives from the papal court he read the true character and aims of the hierarchy. He returned to England to repeat his former teachings more openly and with greater zeal, declaring that covetousness, pride, and deception were the gods of Rome.

In one of his tracts he said, speaking of the pope and his collectors: "They draw out of our land poor men's livelihood, and many thousand marks, by the year, of the king's money, for sacraments and spiritual things, that is cursed heresy of simony, and maketh all Christendom assent and maintain this heresy. And certes though our realm had a huge hill of gold, and never other man took thereof but only this proud worldly priest's collector, by process of time this hill must be spended; for he taketh ever money out of our land, and sendeth nought again but God's curse for his simony."—John Lewis, *History of the Life and Sufferings of J. Wiclif*, page 37.

Soon after his return to England, Wycliffe received from the king the appointment to the rectory of Lutterworth. This was an assurance that the monarch at least had not been displeased by his plain speaking. Wycliffe's influence was felt in shaping the action of the court, as well as in molding the belief of the nation.

The papal thunders were soon hurled against him. Three bulls were dispatched to England—to the university, to the king, and to the prelates—all commanding immediate and decisive measures to silence the teacher of heresy. (Augustus Neander, *General History of the Christian Religion and Church*, period 6, sec. 2, pt. 1, par. 8. See also Appendix.) Before the arrival of the bulls, however, the bishops, in their zeal, had summoned Wycliffe before them for trial. But two of the most powerful princes in the kingdom accompanied him to the tribunal; and the people, surrounding the building and rushing in, so intimidated the judges that the proceedings were for the time suspended, and he was allowed to go his way in peace. A little later, Edward III, whom in his old age the prelates were seeking to influence against the Reformer, died, and Wycliffe's former protector became regent of the kingdom.

But the arrival of the papal bulls laid upon all England a peremptory command for the arrest and imprisonment of the heretic. These measures pointed directly to the stake. It appeared certain that Wycliffe must soon fall a prey to the vengeance of Rome. But He who declared to one of old, "Fear not: . . . I am thy shield" (Genesis 15:1), again stretched out His hand to protect His servant. Death came, not to the Reformer, but to the pontiff who had decreed his destruction. Gregory XI died, and the ecclesiastics who had assembled for Wycliffe's trial, dispersed.

God's providence still further overruled events to give opportunity for the growth of the Reformation. The death of Gregory was followed by the election of two rival popes. Two conflicting powers, each professedly infallible, now claimed obedience. (See Appendix notes for pages 30 and 63.) Each called upon the faithful to assist him in making war upon the other, enforcing his demands by terrible anathemas against his adversaries, and promises of rewards in heaven to his supporters. This occurrence greatly weakened the power of the papacy. The rival factions had all they could do to attack each other, and Wycliffe for a time had rest. Anathemas and recriminations were flying from pope to pope, and torrents of blood were poured out to support their conflicting claims. Crimes and scandals flooded the church. Meanwhile the Reformer, in the quiet retirement of his parish of Lutterworth, was laboring diligently to point men from the contending popes to Jesus, the Prince of Peace.

The schism, with all the strife and corruption which it caused, prepared the way for the Reformation by enabling the people to see what the papacy really was. In a tract which he published, *On the Schism of the Popes,* Wycliffe called upon the people to consider whether these two priests were not speaking the truth in condemning each other as the antichrist. "God," said he, "would no longer suffer the fiend to reign in only one such priest, but . . . made division among two, so that men, in Christ's name, may the more easily overcome them both."—R. Vaughan, *Life and Opinions of John de Wycliffe,* vol. 2, p. 6.

Wycliffe, like his Master, preached the gospel to the poor. Not content with spreading the light in their humble homes in his own parish of Lutterworth, he determined that it should be carried to every part of England. To accomplish this he organized a body of preachers, simple, devout men, who loved the truth and desired nothing so much as to extend it. These men went everywhere, teaching in the market places, in the streets of the great cities, and in the country lanes. They sought out the aged, the sick, and the poor, and opened to them the glad tidings of the grace of God.

As a professor of theology at Oxford, Wycliffe preached the word of God in the halls of the university. So faithfully did he present the truth to the students under his instruction, that he received the title of "the gospel doctor." But the greatest work of his life was to be the translation of the Scriptures into the English language. In a work, *On the Truth and Meaning of Scripture,* he expressed his intention to translate the Bible, so that every man in England might read, in the language in which he was born, the wonderful works of God.

But suddenly his labors were stopped. Though not yet sixty years of age, unceasing toil, study, and the assaults of his enemies had told upon his strength and made him prematurely old. He was attacked by a dangerous illness. The tidings brought great joy to the friars. Now they thought he would bitterly repent the evil he had done the church, and they hurried to his chamber to listen to his confession. Representatives from the four religious orders, with four civil officers, gathered about the supposed dying man. "You have death on your lips," they said; "be touched by your faults, and retract in our presence all that you have said to our injury." The Reformer listened in silence; then he bade his attendant raise him in his bed, and, gazing steadily upon them as they stood waiting for his recantation, he said, in the firm, strong voice which had so often caused them to tremble: "I shall not die, but live; and again declare the evil deeds of the friars."—D'Aubigné, b. 17, ch. 7. Astonished and abashed, the monks hurried from the room.

Wycliffe's words were fulfilled. He lived to place in the hands of his countrymen the most powerful of all weapons against Rome—to give them the Bible, the Heaven-appointed agent to liberate, enlighten, and evangelize the people. There were many and great obstacles to surmount in the accomplishment of this work. Wycliffe was weighed down with infirmities; he knew that only a few years for labor remained for him; he saw the opposition which he must meet; but, encouraged by the promises of God's word, he went forward nothing daunted. In the full vigor of his intellectual powers, rich in experience, he had been preserved and prepared by God's special providence for this, the greatest of his labors. While all Christendom was filled with tumult, the Reformer in his rectory at Lutterworth, unheeding the storm that raged without, applied himself to his chosen task.

At last the work was completed—the first English translation of the Bible ever made. The word of God was opened to England. The Reformer feared not now the prison or the stake. He had placed in the hands of the English people a light which should never be extinguished. In giving the Bible to his countrymen, he had done more to break the fetters of ignorance and vice, more to liberate and elevate his country, than was ever achieved by the most brilliant victories on fields of battle.

The art of printing being still unknown, it was only by slow and wearisome labor that copies of the Bible could be multiplied. So great was the interest to obtain the book, that many willingly engaged in the work of transcribing it, but it was with difficulty that the copyists could supply the demand. Some of the more wealthy purchasers desired the whole Bible. Others bought only a portion. In many cases, several families united to purchase a copy. Thus Wycliffe's Bible soon found its way to the homes of the people.

The appeal to men's reason aroused them from their passive submission to papal dogmas. Wycliffe now taught the distinctive doctrines of Protestantism—salvation through faith in Christ, and the sole infallibility of the Scriptures. The preachers whom he had sent out circulated the Bible, together with the Reformer's writings, and with such success that the new faith was accepted by nearly one half of the people of England.

The appearance of the Scriptures brought dismay to the authorities of the church. They had now to meet an agency more powerful than Wycliffe—an agency against which their weapons would avail little. There was at this time no law in England prohibiting the Bible, for it had never before been published in the language of the people. Such laws were afterward enacted and rigorously enforced. Meanwhile, notwithstanding the efforts of the priests, there was for a season opportunity for the circulation of the word of God.

Again the papal leaders plotted to silence the Reformer's voice. Before three tribunals he was successively summoned for trial, but without avail. First a synod of bishops declared his writings heretical, and, winning the young king, Richard II, to their side, they obtained a royal decree consigning to prison all who should hold the condemned doctrines.

Wycliffe appealed from the synod to Parliament; he fearlessly arraigned the hierarchy before the national council and demanded a reform of the enormous abuses sanctioned by the church. With convincing power he portrayed the usurpation and corruptions of the papal see. His enemies were brought to confusion. The friends and supporters of Wycliffe had been forced to yield, and it had been confidently expected that the Reformer himself, in his old age, alone and friendless, would bow to the combined authority of the crown and the miter. But instead of this the papists saw themselves defeated. Parliament, roused by the stirring appeals of Wycliffe, repealed the persecuting edict, and the Reformer was again at liberty.

A third time he was brought to trial, and now before the highest ecclesiastical tribunal in the kingdom. Here no favor would be shown to heresy. Here at last Rome would triumph, and the Reformer's work would be stopped. So thought the papists. If they could but accomplish their purpose, Wycliffe would be forced to abjure his doctrines, or would leave the court only for the flames.

But Wycliffe did not retract; he would not dissemble. He fearlessly maintained his teachings and repelled the accusations of his persecutors. Losing sight of himself, of his position, of the occasion, he summoned his hearers before the divine tribunal, and weighed their sophistries and deceptions in the balances of eternal truth. The power of the Holy Spirit was felt in the council room. A spell from God was upon the hearers. They seemed to have no power to leave the place. As arrows from the Lord's quiver, the Reformer's words pierced their hearts. The charge of heresy, which they had brought against him, he with convincing power threw back upon themselves. Why, he demanded, did they dare to spread their errors? For the sake of gain, to make merchandise of the grace of God?

"With whom, think you," he finally said, "are ye contending? With an old man on the brink of the grave? No! with Truth—Truth which is stronger than you, and will overcome you."—Wylie, b. 2, ch. 13. So saying, he withdrew from the assembly, and not one of his adversaries attempted to prevent him.

Wycliffe's work was almost done; the banner of truth which he had so long borne was soon to fall from his hand; but once more he was to bear witness for the gospel. The truth was to be proclaimed from the very stronghold of the kingdom of error. Wycliffe was summoned for trial before the papal tribunal at Rome, which had so often shed the blood of the saints. He was not blind to the danger that threatened him, yet he would have obeyed the summons had not a shock of palsy made it impossible for him to perform the journey. But though his voice was not to be heard at Rome, he could speak by letter, and this he determined to do.

For centuries men and women were willing to risk imprisonment and even death for possession of the Scriptures.

From his rectory the Reformer wrote to the pope a letter, which, while respectful in tone and Christian in spirit, was a keen rebuke to the pomp and pride of the papal see.

"Verily I do rejoice," he said, "to open and declare unto every man the faith which I do hold, and especially unto the bishop of Rome: which, forasmuch as I do suppose to be sound and true, he will most willingly confirm my said faith, or if it be erroneous, amend the same.

"First, I suppose that the gospel of Christ is the whole body of God's law. . . . I do give and hold the bishop of Rome, forasmuch as he is the vicar of Christ here on earth, to be most bound, of all other men, unto that law of the gospel. For the greatness among Christ's disciples did not consist in worldly dignity or honors, but in the near and exact following of Christ in His life and manners. . . . Christ, for the time of His pilgrimage here, was a most poor man, abjecting and casting off all worldly rule and honor. . . .

"No faithful man ought to follow either the pope himself or any of the holy men, but in such points as he hath followed the Lord Jesus Christ; for Peter and the sons of Zebedee, by desiring worldly honor, contrary to the following of Christ's steps, did offend, and therefore in those errors they are not to be followed. . . .

"The pope ought to leave unto the secular power all temporal dominion and rule, and thereunto effectually to move and exhort his whole clergy; for so did Christ, and especially by His apostles. Wherefore, if I have erred in any of these points, I will most humbly submit myself unto correction, even by death, if necessity so require; and if I could labor according to my will or desire in mine own person, I would surely present myself before the bishop of Rome; but the Lord hath otherwise visited me to the contrary, and hath taught me rather to obey God than men."

In closing he said: "Let us pray unto our God, that He will so stir up our Pope Urban VI, as he began, that he with his clergy may follow the Lord Jesus Christ in life and manners; and that they may teach the people effectually, and that they, likewise, may faithfully follow them in the same."—John Foxe, *Acts and Monuments,* vol. 3, pp. 49, 50.

Thus Wycliffe presented to the pope and his cardinals the meekness and humility of Christ, exhibiting not only to themselves but to all Christendom the contrast between them and the Master whose representatives they professed to be.

Wycliffe fully expected that his life would be the price of his fidelity. The king, the pope, and the bishops were united to accomplish his ruin, and it seemed certain that a few months at most would bring him to the stake. But his courage was unshaken. "Why do you talk of seeking the crown of martyrdom afar?" he said. "Preach the gospel of Christ to haughty prelates, and martyrdom will not fail you. What! I should live and be silent? . . . Never! Let the blow fall, I await its coming."—D'Aubigné, b. 17, ch. 8.

But God's providence still shielded His servant. The man who for a whole lifetime had stood boldly in defense of the truth, in daily peril of his life, was not to fall a victim of the hatred of its foes. Wycliffe had never sought to shield himself, but the Lord had been his protector; and now, when his enemies felt sure of their prey, God's hand removed him beyond their reach. In his church at Lutterworth, as he was about to dispense the communion, he fell, stricken with palsy, and in a short time yielded up his life.

God had appointed to Wycliffe his work. He had put the word of truth in his mouth, and He set a guard about him that this word might come to the people. His life was protected, and his labors were prolonged, until a foundation was laid for the great work of the Reformation.

Wycliffe came from the obscurity of the Dark Ages. There were none who went before him from whose work he could shape his system of reform. Raised up like John the Baptist to accomplish a special mission, he was the herald of a new era. Yet in the system of truth which he presented there was a unity and completeness which Reformers who followed him did not exceed, and which some did not reach, even a hundred years later. So broad and deep was laid the foundation, so firm and true was the framework, that it needed not to be reconstructed by those who came after him.

The great movement that Wycliffe inaugurated, which was to liberate the conscience and the intellect, and set free the nations so long bound to the triumphal car of Rome, had its spring in the Bible. Here was the source of that stream of blessing, which, like the water of life, has flowed down the ages since the fourteenth century. Wycliffe accepted the Holy Scriptures with implicit faith as the inspired revelation of God's will, a sufficient rule of faith and practice. He had been educated to regard the Church of Rome as the divine, infallible authority, and to accept with unquestioning reverence the established teachings and customs of a thousand years; but he turned away from all these to listen to God's holy word. This was the authority which he urged the people to acknowledge. Instead of the church speaking through the pope, he declared the only true authority to be the voice of God speaking through His word. And he taught not only that the Bible is a perfect revelation of God's will, but that the Holy Spirit is its only interpreter, and that every man is, by the study of its teachings, to learn his duty for himself. Thus he turned the minds of men from the pope and the Church of Rome to the word of God.

Wycliffe was one of the greatest of the Reformers. In breadth of intellect, in clearness of thought, in firmness to maintain the truth, and in boldness to defend it, he was equaled by few who came after him. Purity of life, unwearying diligence in study and in labor, incorruptible integrity, and Christlike love and faithfulness in his ministry, characterized the first of the Reformers. And this notwithstanding the intellectual darkness and moral corruption of the age from which he emerged.

The character of Wycliffe is a testimony to the educating, transforming power of the Holy Scriptures. It was the Bible that made him what he was. The effort to grasp the great truths of revelation imparts freshness and vigor to all the faculties. It expands the mind, sharpens the perceptions, and ripens the judgment. The study of the Bible will ennoble every thought, feeling, and aspiration as no other study can. It gives stability of purpose, patience, courage, and fortitude; it refines the character and sanctifies the soul. An earnest, reverent study of the Scriptures, bringing the mind of the student in direct contact with the infinite mind, would give to the world men of stronger and more active intellect, as well as of nobler principle, than has ever resulted from the ablest training that human philosophy affords. "The entrance of Thy words," says the psalmist, "giveth light; it giveth understanding." Psalm 119:130.

The doctrines which had been taught by Wycliffe continued for a time to spread; his followers, known as Wycliffites and Lollards, not only traversed England, but scattered to other lands, carrying the knowledge of the gospel. Now that their leader was removed, the preachers labored with even greater zeal than before, and multitudes flocked to listen to their teachings. Some of the nobility, and even the wife of the king, were among the converts. In many places there was a marked reform in the manners of the people, and the idolatrous symbols of Romanism were removed from the churches. But soon the pitiless storm of persecution burst upon those who had dared to accept the Bible as their guide. The English monarchs, eager to strengthen their power by securing the support of Rome, did not hesitate to sacrifice the Reformers. For the first time in the history of England the stake was decreed against the disciples of the gospel. Martyrdom succeeded martyrdom. The advocates of truth, proscribed and tortured, could only pour their cries into the ear of the Lord of Sabaoth. Hunted as foes of the church and traitors to the realm, they continued to preach in secret places, finding shelter as best they could in the humble homes of the poor, and often hiding away even in dens and caves.

Notwithstanding the rage of persecution, a calm, devout, earnest, patient protest against the prevailing corruption of religious faith continued for centuries to be uttered. The Christians of that early time had only a partial knowledge of the truth, but they had learned to love and obey God's word, and they patiently suffered for its sake. Like the disciples in apostolic days, many sacrificed their worldly possessions for the cause of Christ. Those who were permitted to dwell in their homes gladly sheltered their banished brethren, and when they too were driven forth they cheerfully accepted the lot of the outcast. Thousands, it is true, terrified by the fury of their persecutors, purchased their freedom at the sacrifice of their faith, and went out of their prisons, clothed in penitents' robes, to publish their recantation. But the number was not small—and among them were men of noble birth as well as the humble and lowly —who bore fearless testimony to the truth in dungeon cells, in "Lollard towers," and in the midst of torture and flame, rejoicing that they were counted worthy to know "the fellowship of His sufferings."

The papists had failed to work their will with Wycliffe during his life, and their hatred could not be satisfied while his body rested quietly in the grave. By the decree of the Council of Constance, more than forty years after his death his bones were exhumed and publicly burned, and the ashes were thrown into a neighboring brook. "This brook," says an old writer, "hath conveyed his ashes into Avon, Avon into Severn, Severn into the narrow seas, they into the main ocean. And thus the ashes of Wycliffe are the emblem of his doctrine, which now is dispersed all the world over."—T. Fuller, *Church History of Britain,* b. 4, sec. 2, par. 54. Little did his enemies realize the significance of their malicious act.

It was through the writings of Wycliffe that John Huss, of Bohemia, was led to renounce many of the errors of Romanism and to enter upon the work of reform. Thus in these two countries, so widely separated, the seed of truth was sown. From Bohemia the work extended to other lands. The minds of men were directed to the long-forgotten word of God. A divine hand was preparing the way for the Great Reformation.

chapter 6

Two Heroes Face Death

THE gospel had been planted in Bohemia as early as the ninth century. The Bible was translated, and public worship was conducted, in the language of the people. But as the power of the pope increased, so the word of God was obscured. Gregory VII, who had taken it upon himself to humble the pride of kings, was no less intent upon enslaving the people, and accordingly a bull was issued forbidding public worship to be conducted in the Bohemian tongue. The pope declared that "it was pleasing to the Omnipotent that His worship should be celebrated in an unknown language, and that many evils and heresies had arisen from not observing this rule."—Wylie, b. 3, ch. 1. Thus Rome decreed that the light of God's word should be extinguished and the people should be shut up in darkness. But Heaven had provided other agencies for the preservation of the church. Many of the Waldenses and Albigenses, driven by persecution from their homes in France and Italy, came to Bohemia. Though they dared not teach openly, they labored zealously in secret. Thus the true faith was preserved from century to century.

Before the days of Huss there were men in Bohemia who rose up to condemn openly the corruption in the church and the profligacy of the people. Their labors excited widespread interest. The fears of the hierarchy were roused, and persecution was opened against the disciples of the gospel. Driven to worship in the forests and the mountains, they were hunted by soldiers, and many were put to death. After a time it was decreed that all who departed from the Romish worship should be

72 [*97-98*]

burned. But while the Christians yielded up their lives, they looked forward to the triumph of their cause. One of those who "taught that salvation was only to be found by faith in the crucified Saviour," declared when dying: "The rage of the enemies of the truth now prevails against us, but it will not be forever; there shall arise one from among the common people, without sword or authority, and against him they shall not be able to prevail."—*Ibid.*, b. 3, ch. 1. Luther's time was yet far distant; but already one was rising, whose testimony against Rome would stir the nations.

John Huss was of humble birth, and was early left an orphan by the death of his father. His pious mother, regarding education and the fear of God as the most valuable of possessions, sought to secure this heritage for her son. Huss studied at the provincial school, and then repaired to the university at Prague, receiving admission as a charity scholar. He was accompanied on the journey to Prague by his mother; widowed and poor, she had no gifts of worldly wealth to bestow upon her son, but as they drew near to the great city, she kneeled down beside the fatherless youth and invoked for him the blessing of their Father in heaven. Little did that mother realize how her prayer was to be answered.

At the university, Huss soon distinguished himself by his untiring application and rapid progress, while his blameless life and gentle, winning deportment gained him universal esteem. He was a sincere adherent of the Roman Church and an earnest seeker for the spiritual blessings which it professes to bestow. On the occasion of a jubilee he went to confession, paid the last few coins in his scanty store, and joined in the processions, that he might share in the absolution promised. After completing his college course, he entered the priesthood, and rapidly attaining to eminence, he soon became attached to the court of the king. He was also made professor and afterward rector of the university where he had received his education. In a few years the humble charity scholar had become the pride of his country, and his name was renowned throughout Europe

But it was in another field that Huss began the work of reform. Several years after taking priest's orders he was appointed preacher of the chapel of Bethlehem. The founder of this chapel had advocated, as a matter of great importance, the preaching of the Scriptures in the language of the people. Notwithstanding Rome's opposition to this practice, it had not been wholly discontinued in Bohemia. But there was great ignorance of the Bible, and the worst vices prevailed among the people of all ranks.

These evils Huss unsparingly denounced, appealing to the word of God to enforce the principles of truth and purity which he inculcated.

A citizen of Prague, Jerome, who afterward became so closely associated with Huss, had, on returning from England, brought with him the writings of Wycliffe. The queen of England, who had been a convert to Wycliffe's teachings, was a Bohemian princess, and through her influence also the Reformer's works were widely circulated in her native country. These works Huss read with interest; he believed their author to be a sincere Christian and was inclined to regard with favor the reforms which he advocated. Already, though he knew it not, Huss had entered upon a path which was to lead him far away from Rome.

About this time there arrived in Prague two strangers from England, men of learning, who had received the light and had come to spread it in this distant land. Beginning with an open attack on the pope's supremacy, they were soon silenced by the authorities; but being unwilling to relinquish their purpose, they had recourse to other measures. Being artists as well as preachers, they proceeded to exercise their skill. In a place open to the public they drew two pictures. One represented the entrance of Christ into Jerusalem, "meek, and sitting upon an ass" (Matthew 21:5), and followed by His disciples in travel-worn garments and with naked feet. The other picture portrayed a pontifical procession—the pope arrayed in his rich robes and triple crown, mounted upon a horse magnificently adorned, preceded by trumpeters and followed by cardinals and prelates in dazzling array.

Here was a sermon which arrested the attention of all classes. Crowds came to gaze upon the drawings. None could fail to read the moral, and many were deeply impressed by the contrast between the meekness and humility of Christ the Master and the pride and arrogance of the pope, His professed servant. There was great commotion in Prague, and the strangers after a time found it necessary, for their own safety, to depart. But the lesson they had taught was not forgotten. The pictures made a deep impression on the mind of Huss and led him to a closer study of the Bible and of Wycliffe's writings. Though he was not prepared, even yet, to accept all the reforms advocated by Wycliffe, he saw more clearly the true character of the papacy, and with greater zeal denounced the pride, the ambition, and the corruption of the hierarchy.

From Bohemia the light extended to Germany, for disturbances in the University of Prague caused the withdrawal of hundreds of German students. Many of them had received from Huss their first knowledge of the

Disciples of Wycliffe witnessed to
their faith in Prague by painting
pictures in places open to the public.

© P.P.P.A. JOHN STEEL, ARTIST

Bible, and on their return they spread the gospel in their fatherland.

Tidings of the work at Prague were carried to Rome, and Huss was soon summoned to appear before the pope. To obey would be to expose himself to certain death. The king and queen of Bohemia, the university, members of the nobility, and officers of the government united in an appeal to the pontiff that Huss be permitted to remain at Prague and to answer at Rome by deputy. Instead of granting this request, the pope proceeded to the trial and condemnation of Huss, and then declared the city of Prague to be under interdict.

In that age this sentence, whenever pronounced, created widespread alarm. The ceremonies by which it was accompanied were well adapted to strike terror to a people who looked upon the pope as the representative of God Himself, holding the keys of heaven and hell, and possessing power to invoke temporal as well as spiritual judgments. It was believed that the gates of heaven were closed against the region smitten with interdict; that until it should please the pope to remove the ban, the dead were shut out from the abodes of bliss. In token of this terrible calamity, all the services of religion were suspended. The churches were closed. Marriages were solemnized in the churchyard. The dead, denied burial in consecrated ground, were interred, without the rites of sepulture, in the ditches or the fields. Thus by measures which appealed to the imagination, Rome essayed to control the consciences of men.

The city of Prague was filled with tumult. A large class denounced Huss as the cause of all their calamities and demanded that he be given up to the vengeance of Rome. To quiet the storm, the Reformer withdrew for a time to his native village. Writing to the friends whom he had left at Prague, he said: "If I have withdrawn from the midst of you, it is to follow the precept and example of Jesus Christ, in order not to give room to the ill-minded to draw on themselves eternal condemnation, and in order not to be to the pious a cause of affliction and persecution. I have retired also through an apprehension that impious priests might continue for a longer time to prohibit the preaching of the word of God amongst you; but I have not quitted you to deny the divine truth, for which, with God's assistance, I am willing to die."—Bonnechose, *The Reformers Before the Reformation*, vol. 1, p. 87. Huss did not cease his labors, but traveled through the surrounding country, preaching to eager crowds. Thus the measures to which the pope resorted to suppress the gospel were causing it to be the more widely extended. "We can do nothing against the truth, but for the truth." 2 Corinthians 13:8.

"The mind of Huss, at this stage of his career, would seem to have been the scene of a painful conflict. Although the church was seeking to overwhelm him by her thunderbolts, he had not renounced her authority. The Roman Church was still to him the spouse of Christ, and the pope was the representative and vicar of God. What Huss was warring against was the abuse of authority, not the principle itself. This brought on a terrible conflict between the convictions of his understanding and the claims of his conscience. If the authority was just and infallible, as he believed it to be, how came it that he felt compelled to disobey it? To obey, he saw, was to sin; but why should obedience to an infallible church lead to such an issue? This was the problem he could not solve; this was the doubt that tortured him hour by hour. The nearest approximation to a solution which he was able to make was that it had happened again, as once before in the days of the Saviour, that the priests of the church had become wicked persons and were using their lawful authority for unlawful ends. This led him to adopt for his own guidance, and to preach to others for theirs, the maxim that the precepts of Scripture, conveyed through the understanding, are to rule the conscience; in other words, that God speaking in the Bible, and not the church speaking through the priesthood, is the one infallible guide."—Wylie, b. 3, ch. 2.

When after a time the excitement in Prague subsided, Huss returned to his chapel of Bethlehem, to continue with greater zeal and courage the preaching of the word of God. His enemies were active and powerful, but the queen and many of the nobles were his friends, and the people in great numbers sided with him. Comparing his pure and elevating teachings and holy life with the degrading dogmas which the Romanists preached, and the avarice and debauchery which they practiced, many regarded it an honor to be on his side.

Hitherto Huss had stood alone in his labors; but now Jerome, who while in England had accepted the teachings of Wycliffe, joined in the work of reform. The two were hereafter united in their lives, and in death they were not to be divided. Brilliancy of genius, eloquence and learning —gifts that win popular favor—were possessed in a preeminent degree by Jerome; but in those qualities which constitute real strength of character, Huss was the greater. His calm judgment served as a restraint upon the impulsive spirit of Jerome, who, with true humility, perceived his worth, and yielded to his counsels. Under their united labors the reform was more rapidly extended.

God permitted great light to shine upon the minds of these chosen men, revealing to them many of the errors of Rome; but they did not receive all the light that was to be given to the world. Through these, His servants, God was leading the people out of the darkness of Romanism; but there were many and great obstacles for them to meet, and He led them on, step by step, as they could bear it. They were not prepared to receive all the light at once. Like the full glory of the noontide sun to those who have long dwelt in darkness, it would, if presented, have caused them to turn away. Therefore He revealed it to the leaders little by little, as it could be received by the people. From century to century, other faithful workers were to follow, to lead the people on still further in the path of reform.

The schism in the church still continued. Three popes were now contending for the supremacy, and their strife filled Christendom with crime and tumult. Not content with hurling anathemas, they resorted to temporal weapons. Each cast about him to purchase arms and to obtain soldiers. Of course money must be had; and to procure this, the gifts, offices, and blessings of the church were offered for sale. (See Appendix note for page 38.) The priests also, imitating their superiors, resorted to simony and war to humble their rivals and strengthen their own power. With daily increasing boldness Huss thundered against the abominations which were tolerated in the name of religion; and the people openly accused the Romish leaders as the cause of the miseries that overwhelmed Christendom.

Again the city of Prague seemed on the verge of a bloody conflict. As in former ages, God's servant was accused as "he that troubleth Israel." 1 Kings 18:17. The city was again placed under interdict, and Huss withdrew to his native village. The testimony so faithfully borne from his loved chapel of Bethlehem was ended. He was to speak from a wider stage, to all Christendom, before laying down his life as a witness for the truth.

To cure the evils that were distracting Europe, a general council was summoned to meet at Constance. The council was called at the desire of the emperor Sigismund, by one of the three rival popes, John XXIII. The demand for a council had been far from welcome to Pope John, whose character and policy could ill bear investigation, even by prelates as lax in morals as were the churchmen of those times. He dared not, however, oppose the will of Sigismund. (See Appendix.)

The chief objects to be accomplished by the council were to heal the schism in the church and to root out heresy. Hence the two antipopes were summoned to appear before it, as well as the leading propagator of the new opinions, John Huss. The former, having regard to their own safety, did not attend in person, but were represented by their delegates. Pope John, while ostensibly the convoker of the council, came to it with many misgivings, suspecting the emperor's secret purpose to depose him, and fearing to be brought to account for the vices which had disgraced the tiara, as well as for the crimes which had secured it. Yet he made his entry into the city of Constance with great pomp, attended by ecclesiastics of the highest rank and followed by a train of courtiers. All the clergy and dignitaries of the city, with an immense crowd of citizens, went out to welcome him. Above his head was a golden canopy, borne by four of the chief magistrates. The host was carried before him, and the rich dresses of the cardinals and nobles made an imposing display.

Meanwhile another traveler was approaching Constance. Huss was conscious of the dangers which threatened him. He parted from his friends as if he were never to meet them again, and went on his journey feeling that it was leading him to the stake. Notwithstanding he had obtained a safe-conduct from the king of Bohemia, and received one also from the emperor Sigismund while on his journey, he made all his arrangements in view of the probability of his death.

In a letter addressed to his friends at Prague he said: "My brethren, . . . I am departing with a safe-conduct from the king to meet my numerous and mortal enemies. . . . I confide altogether in the all-powerful God, in my Saviour; I trust that He will listen to your ardent prayers, that He will infuse His prudence and His wisdom into my mouth, in order that I may resist them; and that He will accord me His Holy Spirit to fortify me in His truth, so that I may face with courage, temptations, prison, and, if necessary, a cruel death. Jesus Christ suffered for His well-beloved; and therefore ought we to be astonished that He has left us His example, in order that we may ourselves endure with patience all things for our own salvation? He is God, and we are His creatures; He is the Lord, and we are His servants; He is Master of the world, and we are contemptible mortals—yet He suffered! Why, then, should we not suffer also, particularly when suffering is for us a purification? Therefore, beloved, if my death ought to contribute to His glory, pray that it may come quickly, and that He may enable me to support all my calamities with constancy. But if it be better that I return amongst you, let us pray to God that I may return without stain—that is, that I may not suppress one tittle of the truth of the gospel, in order to leave my brethren an excellent example to follow. Probably, therefore, you will nevermore behold my face at Prague; but should the will of the all-powerful God deign to restore me to you, let us then advance with a firmer heart in the knowledge and the love of His law."—Bonnechose, vol. 1, pp. 147, 148.

In another letter, to a priest who had become a disciple of the gospel, Huss spoke with deep humility of his own errors, accusing himself "of having felt pleasure in wearing rich apparel and of having wasted hours in frivolous occupations." He then added these touching admonitions: "May the glory of God and the salvation of souls occupy thy mind, and not the possession of benefices and estates. Beware of adorning thy house more than thy soul; and, above all, give thy care to the spiritual edifice. Be pious and humble with the poor, and consume not thy substance in feasting. Shouldst thou not amend thy life and refrain from superfluities, I fear that thou wilt be severely chastened, as I am myself. . . . Thou knowest my doctrine, for thou hast received my instructions from thy childhood; it is therefore useless for me to write to thee any further. But I conjure thee, by the mercy of our Lord, not to imitate me in any of the vanities into which thou hast seen me fall." On the cover of the letter he added: "I conjure thee, my friend, not to break this seal until thou shalt have acquired the certitude that I am dead."—*Ibid.*, vol. 1, pp. 148, 149.

On his journey, Huss everywhere beheld indications of the spread of his doctrines and the favor with which his cause was regarded. The people thronged to meet him, and in some towns the magistrates attended him through their streets.

Upon arriving at Constance, Huss was granted full liberty. To the emperor's safe-conduct was added a personal assurance of protection by the pope. But, in violation of these solemn and repeated declarations, the Reformer was in a short time arrested, by order of the pope and cardinals, and thrust into a loathsome dungeon. Later he was transferred to a strong castle across the Rhine and there kept a prisoner. The pope, profiting little by his perfidy, was soon after committed to the same prison. *Ibid.*, vol. 1, p. 247. He had been proved before the council to be guilty of the basest crimes, besides murder, simony, and adultery, "sins not fit to be named." So the council itself declared, and he was finally deprived of the tiara and thrown into prison. The antipopes also were deposed, and a new pontiff was chosen.

Though the pope himself had been guilty of greater crimes than Huss had ever charged upon the priests, and for which he had demanded a reformation, yet the same council which degraded the pontiff proceeded to crush the Reformer. The imprisonment of Huss excited great indignation in Bohemia. Powerful noblemen addressed to the council earnest protests against this outrage. The emperor, who was loath to permit the violation of a safe-conduct, opposed the proceedings against him. But the enemies of the Reformer were malignant and determined. They appealed to the emperor's prejudices, to his fears, to his zeal for the church. They brought forward arguments of great length to prove that "faith ought not to be kept with heretics, nor persons suspected of heresy, though they are furnished with safe-conducts from the emperor and kings."—Jacques Lenfant, *History of the Council of Constance*, vol. 1, p. 516. Thus they prevailed.

Enfeebled by illness and imprisonment—for the damp, foul air of his dungeon had brought on a fever which nearly ended his life—Huss was at last brought before the council. Loaded with chains he stood in the presence of the emperor, whose honor and good faith had been pledged to protect him. During his long trial he firmly maintained the truth, and in the presence of the assembled dignitaries of church and state he uttered a solemn and faithful protest against the corruptions of the hierarchy. When required to choose whether he would recant his doctrines or suffer death, he accepted the martyr's fate.

THE TRIUMPH OF GOD'S LOVE

The grace of God sustained him. During the weeks of suffering that passed before his final sentence, heaven's peace filled his soul. "I write this letter," he said to a friend, "in my prison, and with my fettered hand, expecting my sentence of death tomorrow. . . . When, with the assistance of Jesus Christ, we shall again meet in the delicious peace of the future life, you will learn how merciful God has shown Himself toward me, how effectually He has supported me in the midst of my temptations and trials."—Bonnechose, vol. 2, p. 67.

In the gloom of his dungeon he foresaw the triumph of the true faith. Returning in his dreams to the chapel at Prague where he had preached the gospel, he saw the pope and his bishops effacing the pictures of Christ which he had painted on its walls. "This vision distressed him: but on the next day he saw many painters occupied in restoring these figures in greater number and in brighter colors. As soon as their task was ended, the painters, who were surrounded by an immense crowd, exclaimed, 'Now let the popes and bishops come; they shall never efface them more!'" Said the Reformer, as he related his dream: "I maintain this for certain, that the image of Christ will never be effaced. They have wished to destroy it, but it shall be painted afresh in all hearts by much better preachers than myself."—D'Aubigné, b. 1, ch. 6.

For the last time, Huss was brought before the council. It was a vast and brilliant assembly—the emperor, the princes of the empire, the royal deputies, the cardinals, bishops, and priests, and an immense crowd who had come as spectators of the events of the day. From all parts of Christendom had been gathered the witnesses of this first great sacrifice in the long struggle by which liberty of conscience was to be secured.

Being called upon for his final decision, Huss declared his refusal to abjure, and, fixing his penetrating glance upon the monarch whose plighted word had been so shamelessly violated, he declared: "I determined, of my own free will, to appear before this council, under the public protection and faith of the emperor here present."—Bonnechose, vol. 2, p. 84. A deep flush crimsoned the face of Sigismund as the eyes of all in the assembly turned upon him.

Sentence having been pronounced, the ceremony of degradation began. The bishops clothed their prisoner in the sacerdotal habit, and as he took the priestly robe, he said: "Our Lord Jesus Christ was covered with a white robe, by way of insult, when Herod had Him conducted before Pilate."—*Ibid.*, vol. 2, p. 86. Being again exhorted to retract, he replied, turning toward the people: "With what face, then, should I behold the heavens? How should I look on those multitudes of men to whom I have preached the pure gospel? No; I esteem their salvation more than this poor body, now appointed unto death." The vestments were removed one by one, each bishop pronouncing a curse as he performed his part of the ceremony. Finally "they put on his head a cap or pyramidal-shaped miter of paper, on which were painted frightful figures of demons, with the word 'Archheretic' conspicuous in front. 'Most joyfully,' said Huss, 'will I wear this crown of shame for Thy sake, O Jesus, who for me didst wear a crown of thorns.' "

When he was thus arrayed, "the prelates said, 'Now we devote thy soul to the devil.' 'And I,' said John Huss, lifting up his eyes toward heaven, 'do commit my spirit into Thy hands, O Lord Jesus, for Thou hast redeemed me.' "—Wylie, b. 3, ch. 7.

He was now delivered up to the secular authorities and led away to the place of execution. An immense procession followed, hundreds of men at arms, priests and bishops in their costly robes, and the inhabitants of Constance. When he had been fastened to the stake, and all was ready for the fire to be lighted, the martyr was once more exhorted to save himself by renouncing his errors. "What errors," said Huss, "shall I renounce? I know myself guilty of none. I call God to witness that all that I have written and preached has been with the view of rescuing souls from sin and perdition; and, therefore, most joyfully will I confirm with my blood that truth which I have written and preached."—*Ibid.*, b. 3, ch. 7. When the flames kindled about him, he began to sing, "Jesus, Thou Son of David, have mercy on me," and so continued till his voice was silenced forever.

Even his enemies were struck with his heroic bearing. A zealous papist, describing the martyrdom of Huss, and of Jerome, who died soon after, said: "Both bore themselves with constant mind when their last hour approached. They prepared for the fire as if they were going to a marriage feast. They uttered no cry of pain. When the flames rose, they began to sing hymns; and scarce could the vehemency of the fire stop their singing."—*Ibid.*, b. 3, ch. 7.

When the body of Huss had been wholly consumed, his ashes, with the soil upon which they rested, were gathered up and cast into the Rhine, and thus borne onward to the ocean. His persecutors vainly imagined that they had rooted out the truths he preached. Little did they dream that the ashes that day borne away to the sea were to be as seed scattered in all the countries of the earth; that in lands yet unknown it would yield abundant fruit in witnesses for the truth. The voice which had spoken in the council hall of Constance had wakened echoes that would be heard through all coming ages. Huss was no more, but the truths for which he died co ld never perish. His example of faith and constancy would encourage multitudes to stand firm for the truth, in the face of torture and death. His execution had exhibited to the whole world the perfidious cruelty of Rome. The enemies of truth, though they knew it not, had been furthering the cause which they vainly sought to destroy.

Yet another stake was to be set up at Constance. The blood of another witness must testify for the truth. Jerome, upon bidding farewell to Huss on his departure for the council, had exhorted him to courage and firmness, declaring that if he should fall into any peril, he himself would fly to his assistance. Upon hearing of the Reformer's imprisonment, the faithful disciple immediately prepared to fulfill his promise. Without a safe-conduct he set out, with a single companion, for Constance. On arriving there he was convinced that he had only exposed himself to peril, without the possibility of doing anything for the deliverance of Huss. He fled from the city, but was arrested on the homeward journey and brought back loaded with fetters and under the custody of a band of soldiers. At his first appearance before the council his attempts to reply to the accusations brought against him were met with shouts, "To the flames with him! to the flames!"—Bonnechose, vol. 1, p. 234. He was thrown into a dungeon, chained in a position which caused him great suffering, and fed on bread and water. After some months the cruelties of his imprisonment brought upon Jerome an illness that threatened his life, and his enemies, fearing that he might escape them, treated him with less severity, though he remained in prison for one year.

The death of Huss had not resulted as the papists had hoped. The violation of his safe-conduct had roused a storm of indignation, and as the safer course, the council determined, instead of burning Jerome, to force him, if possible, to retract. He was brought before the assembly, and offered the alternative to recant, or to die at the stake. Death at the beginning of his imprisonment would have been a mercy in comparison with the terrible sufferings which he had undergone; but now, weakened by illness, by the rigors of his prison house, and the torture of anxiety and suspense, separated from his friends, and disheartened by the death of Huss, Jerome's fortitude gave way, and he consented to submit to the council. He pledged himself to adhere to the Catholic faith, and accepted the action of the council in condemning the doctrines of Wycliffe and Huss, excepting, however, the "holy truths" which they had taught.—*Ibid.*, vol. 2, p. 141.

By this expedient Jerome endeavored to silence the voice of conscience and escape his doom. But in the solitude of his dungeon he saw more clearly what he had done. He thought of the courage and fidelity of Huss, and in contrast pondered upon his own denial of the truth. He thought of the divine Master whom he had pledged himself to serve, and who for his sake endured the death of the cross. Before his retraction he had found comfort, amid all his sufferings, in the assurance of God's favor; but now remorse and doubts tortured his soul. He knew that still other retractions must be made before he could be at peace with Rome. The path upon which he was entering could end only in complete apostasy. His resolution was taken: To escape a brief period of suffering he would not deny his Lord.

Soon he was again brought before the council. His submission had not satisfied his judges. Their thirst for blood, whetted by the death of Huss, clamored for fresh victims. Only by an unreserved surrender of the truth could Jerome preserve his life. But he had determined to avow his faith and follow his brother martyr to the flames.

He renounced his former recantation and, as a dying man, solemnly required an opportunity to make his defense. Fearing the effect of his words, the prelates insisted that he should merely affirm or deny the truth of the charges brought against him. Jerome protested against such cruelty and injustice. "You have held me shut up three hundred and forty days in a frightful prison," he said, "in the midst of filth, noisomeness, stench, and the utmost want of everything; you then bring me out before you, and lending an ear to my mortal enemies, you refuse to hear me. . . . If you be really wise men, and the lights of the world, take care not to sin against justice. As to me, I am only a feeble mortal; my life is but of little importance; and when I exhort you not to deliver an unjust sentence, I speak less for myself than for you."—*Ibid.*, vol. 2, pp. 146, 147.

His request was finally granted. In the presence of his judges, Jerome kneeled down and prayed that the divine Spirit might control his thoughts and words, that he might speak nothing contrary to the truth or unworthy of his Master. To him that day was fulfilled the promise of God to the first disciples: "Ye shall be brought before governors and kings for My sake. . . . But when they deliver you up, take no thought how or what ye shall speak: for it shall be given you in that same hour what ye shall speak. For it is not ye that speak, but the Spirit of your Father which speaketh in you." Matthew 10:18-20.

The words of Jerome excited astonishment and admiration, even in his enemies. For a whole year he had been immured in a dungeon, unable to read or even to see, in great physical suffering and mental anxiety. Yet his arguments were presented with as much clearness and power as if he had had undisturbed opportunity for study. He pointed his hearers to the long line of holy men who had been condemned by unjust judges. In almost every generation have been those who, while seeking to elevate the people of their time, have been reproached and cast out, but who in later times have been shown to be deserving of honor. Christ Himself was condemned as a malefactor at an unrighteous tribunal.

At his retraction, Jerome had assented to the justice of the sentence condemning Huss; he now declared his repentance and bore witness to the innocence and holiness of the martyr. "I knew him from his childhood," he said. "He was a most excellent man, just and holy; he was condemned, notwithstanding his innocence. . . . I also—I am ready to die: I will not recoil before the torments that are prepared for me by my enemies and false witnesses, who will one day have to render an account of their impostures before the great God, whom nothing can deceive."—Bonnechose, vol. 2, p. 151.

In self-reproach for his own denial of the truth, Jerome continued: "Of all the sins that I have committed since my youth, none weigh so heavily on my mind, and cause me such poignant remorse, as that which I committed in this fatal place, when I approved of the iniquitous sentence rendered against Wycliffe, and against the holy martyr, John Huss, my master and my friend. Yes! I confess it from my heart, and declare with horror that I disgracefully quailed when, through a dread of death, I condemned their doctrines. I therefore supplicate . . . Almighty God to deign to pardon me my sins, and this one in particular, the most heinous of all." Pointing to his judges, he said firmly: "You condemned Wycliffe and John Huss, not for having shaken the doctrine of the church, but simply because they branded with reprobation the scandals proceeding from the clergy—their pomp, their pride, and all the vices of the prelates and priests. The things which they have affirmed, and which are irrefutable, I also think and declare, like them."

His words were interrupted. The prelates, trembling with rage, cried out: "What need is there of further proof? We behold with our own eyes the most obstinate of heretics!"

Unmoved by the tempest, Jerome exclaimed: "What! do you suppose that I fear to die? You have held me for a whole year in a frightful dungeon, more horrible than death itself. You have treated me more cruelly than a Turk, Jew, or pagan, and my flesh has literally rotted off my bones alive; and yet I make no complaint, for lamentation ill becomes a man of heart and spirit; but I cannot but express my astonishment at such great barbarity toward a Christian."—*Ibid.*, vol. 2, pp. 151-153.

Again the storm of rage burst out, and Jerome was hurried away to prison. Yet there were some in the assembly upon whom his words had made a deep impression and who desired to save his life. He was visited by dignitaries of the church and urged to submit himself to the council. The most brilliant prospects were presented before him as the reward of renouncing his opposition to Rome. But like his Master when offered the glory of the world, Jerome remained steadfast.

"Prove to me from the Holy Writings that I am in error," he said, "and I will abjure it."

"The Holy Writings!" exclaimed one of his tempters, "is everything then to be judged by them? Who can understand them till the church has interpreted them?"

"Are the traditions of men more worthy of faith than the gospel of our Saviour?" replied Jerome. "Paul did not exhort those to whom he wrote to listen to the traditions of men, but said, 'Search the Scriptures.'"

"Heretic!" was the response, "I repent having pleaded so long with you. I see that you are urged on by the devil."—*Wylie*, b. 3, ch. 10.

Erelong sentence of condemnation was passed upon him. He was led out to the same spot upon which Huss had yielded up his life. He went singing on his way, his countenance lighted up with joy and peace. His gaze was fixed upon Christ, and to him death had lost its terrors. When the executioner, about to kindle the pile, stepped behind him, the martyr exclaimed: "Come forward boldly; apply the fire before my face. Had I been afraid, I should not be here."

His last words, uttered as the flames rose about him, were a prayer. "Lord, Almighty Father," he cried, "have pity on me, and pardon me my sins; for Thou knowest that I have always loved Thy truth."—Bonnechose, vol. 2, p. 168. His voice ceased, but his lips continued to move in prayer. When the fire had done its work, the ashes of the martyr, with the earth upon which they rested, were gathered up, and like those of Huss, were thrown into the Rhine.

So perished God's faithful light bearers. But the light of the truths which they proclaimed—the light of their heroic example—could not be extinguished. As well might men attempt to turn back the sun in its course as to prevent the dawning of that day which was even then breaking upon the world.

The execution of Huss had kindled a flame of indignation and horror in Bohemia. It was felt by the whole nation that he had fallen a prey to the malice of the priests and the treachery of the emperor. He was declared to have been a faithful teacher of the truth, and the council that decreed his death was charged with the guilt of murder. His doctrines now attracted greater attention than ever before. By the papal edicts the writings of Wycliffe had been condemned to the flames. But those that had escaped destruction were now brought out from their hiding places and studied in connection with the Bible, or such parts of it as the people could obtain, and many were thus led to accept the reformed faith.

The murderers of Huss did not stand quietly by and witness the triumph of his cause. The pope and the emperor united to crush out the movement, and the armies of Sigismund were hurled upon Bohemia.

But a deliverer was raised up. Ziska, who soon after the opening of the war became totally blind, yet who was one of the ablest generals of his age, was the leader of the Bohemians. Trusting in the help of God and the righteousness of their cause, that people withstood the mightiest armies that could be brought against them. Again and again the emperor, raising fresh armies, invaded Bohemia, only to be ignominiously repulsed. The Hussites were raised above the fear of death, and nothing could stand against them. A few years after the opening of the war, the brave Ziska died; but his place was filled by Procopius, who was an equally brave and skillful general, and in some respects a more able leader.

The enemies of the Bohemians, knowing that the blind warrior was dead, deemed the opportunity favorable for recovering all that they had lost. The pope now proclaimed a crusade against the Hussites, and again an immense force was precipitated upon Bohemia, but only to suffer terrible defeat. Another crusade was proclaimed. In all the papal countries of Europe, men, money, and munitions of war were raised. Multitudes flocked to the papal standard, assured that at last an end would be made of the Hussite heretics. Confident of victory, the vast force entered Bohemia. The people rallied to repel them. The two armies approached each other until only a river lay between them. "The crusaders were in greatly superior force, but instead of dashing across the stream, and closing in battle with the Hussites whom they had come so far to meet, they stood gazing in silence at those warriors."—Wylie, b. 3, ch. 17. Then suddenly a mysterious terror fell upon the host. Without striking a blow, that mighty force broke and scattered as if dispelled by an unseen power. Great numbers were slaughtered by the Hussite army, which pursued the fugitives, and an immense booty fell into the hands of the victors, so that the war, instead of impoverishing, enriched the Bohemians.

A few years later, under a new pope, still another crusade was set on foot. As before, men and means were drawn from all the papal countries of Europe. Great were the inducements held out to those who should engage in this perilous enterprise. Full forgiveness of the most heinous crimes was ensured to every crusader. All who died in the war were promised a rich reward in heaven, and those who survived were to reap honor and riches on the field of battle. Again a vast army was collected, and, crossing the frontier they entered Bohemia. The Hussite forces fell back before them, thus drawing the invaders farther and farther into the country, and leading them to count the victory already won. At last the army of Procopius made a stand, and turning upon the foe, advanced to give them battle. The crusaders, now discovering their mistake, lay in their encampment awaiting the onset. As the sound of the approaching force was heard, even before the Hussites were in sight, a panic again fell upon the crusaders. Princes, generals, and common soldiers, casting away their armor, fled in all directions. In vain the papal legate, who was the leader of the invasion, endeavored to rally his terrified and disorganized forces. Despite his utmost endeavors, he himself was swept along in the tide of fugitives. The rout was complete, and again an immense booty fell into the hands of the victors.

Thus the second time a vast army, sent forth by the most powerful nations of Europe, a host of brave, warlike men, trained and equipped for battle, fled without a blow before the defenders of a small and hitherto feeble nation. Here was a manifestation of divine power. The invaders were smitten with a supernatural terror. He who overthrew the hosts of Pharaoh in the Red Sea, who put to flight the armies of Midian before Gideon and his three hundred, who in one night laid low the forces of the proud Assyrian, had again stretched out His hand to wither the power of the oppressor. "There were they in great fear, where no fear was: for God hath scattered the bones of him that encampeth against thee: thou hast put them to shame, because God hath despised them." Psalm 53:5.

The papal leaders, despairing of conquering by force, at last resorted to diplomacy. A compromise was entered into, that while professing to grant to the Bohemians freedom of conscience, really betrayed them into the power of Rome. The Bohemians had specified four points as the condition of peace with Rome: the free preaching of the Bible; the right of the whole church to both the bread and the wine in the communion, and the use of the mother tongue in divine worship; the exclusion of the clergy from all secular offices and authority; and, in cases of crime, the jurisdiction of the civil courts over clergy and laity alike. The papal authorities at last "agreed that the four articles of the Hussites should be accepted, but that the right of explaining them, that is, of determining their precise import, should belong to the council—in other words, to the pope and the emperor."—Wylie, b. 3, ch. 18. On this basis a treaty was entered into, and Rome gained by dissimulation and fraud what she had failed to gain by conflict; for, placing her own interpretation upon the Hussite articles, as upon the Bible, she could pervert their meaning to suit her own purposes.

A large class in Bohemia, seeing that it betrayed their liberties, could not consent to the compact. Dissensions and divisions arose, leading to strife and bloodshed among themselves. In this strife the noble Procopius fell, and the liberties of Bohemia perished.

Sigismund, the betrayer of Huss and Jerome, now became king of Bohemia, and regardless of his oath to support the rights of the Bohemians, he proceeded to establish popery. But he had gained little by his subservience to Rome. For twenty years his life had been filled with labors and perils. His armies had been wasted and his treasuries drained by a long and fruitless struggle; and now, after reigning one year, he died, leaving his kingdom on the brink of civil war, and bequeathing to posterity a name branded with infamy.

Tumults, strife, and bloodshed were protracted. Again foreign armies invaded Bohemia, and internal dissension continued to distract the nation. Those who remained faithful to the gospel were subjected to a bloody persecution.

As their former brethren, entering into compact with Rome, imbibed her errors, those who adhered to the ancient faith had formed themselves into a distinct church, taking the name of "United Brethren." This act drew upon them maledictions from all classes. Yet their firmness was unshaken. Forced to find refuge in the woods and caves, they still assembled to read God's word and unite in His worship.

Through messengers secretly sent out into different countries, they learned that here and there were "isolated confessors of the truth, a few in this city and a few in that, the object, like themselves, of persecution; and that amid the mountains of the Alps was an ancient church, resting on the foundations of Scripture, and protesting against the idolatrous corruptions of Rome."—Wylie, b. 3, ch. 19. This intelligence was received with great joy, and a correspondence was opened with the Waldensian Christians.

Steadfast to the gospel, the Bohemians waited through the night of their persecution, in the darkest hour still turning their eyes toward the horizon like men who watch for the morning. "Their lot was cast in evil days, but . . . they remembered the words first uttered by Huss, and repeated by Jerome, that a century must revolve before the day should break. These were to the Taborites [Hussites] what the words of Joseph were to the tribes in the house of bondage: 'I die, and God will surely visit you, and bring you out.' "—*Ibid.*, b. 3, ch. 19. "The closing period of the fifteenth century witnessed the slow but sure increase of the churches of the Brethren. Although far from being unmolested, they yet enjoyed comparative rest. At the commencement of the sixteenth century their churches numbered two hundred in Bohemia and Moravia."—Ezra Hall Gillett, *Life and Times of John Huss*, vol. 2, p. 570. "So goodly was the remnant which, escaping the destructive fury of fire and sword, was permitted to see the dawning of that day which Huss had foretold."— Wylie, b. 3, ch. 19.

chapter 7

A Man for His Time

FOREMOST among those who were called to lead
the church from the darkness of popery into the
light of a purer faith, stood Martin Luther. Zealous, ardent, and devoted,
knowing no fear but the fear of God, and acknowledging no foundation
for religious faith but the Holy Scriptures, Luther was the man for his
time; through him God accomplished a great work for the reformation
of the church and the enlightenment of the world.

Like the first heralds of the gospel, Luther sprang from the ranks of
poverty. His early years were spent in the humble home of a German
peasant. By daily toil as a miner his father earned the means for his education. He intended him for a lawyer; but God purposed to make him a
builder in the great temple that was rising so slowly through the centuries. Hardship, privation, and severe discipline were the school in which
Infinite Wisdom prepared Luther for the important mission of his life.

Luther's father was a man of strong and active mind and great force
of character, honest, resolute, and straightforward. He was true to his
convictions of duty, let the consequences be what they might. His sterling
good sense led him to regard the monastic system with distrust. He was
highly displeased when Luther, without his consent, entered a monastery;
and it was two years before the father was reconciled to his son, and even
then his opinions remained the same.

Luther's parents bestowed great care upon the education and training
of their children. They endeavored to instruct them in the knowledge of
God and the practice of Christian virtues. The father's prayer often

With Luther's background of piety
and austerity, he was appalled at the
pomp and feasting he saw at Rome.

ascended in the hearing of his son that the child might remember the name of the Lord and one day aid in the advancement of His truth. Every advantage for moral or intellectual culture which their life of toil permitted them to enjoy was eagerly improved by these parents. Their efforts were earnest and persevering to prepare their children for a life of piety and usefulness. With their firmness and strength of character they sometimes exercised too great severity; but the Reformer himself, though conscious that in some respects they had erred, found in their discipline more to approve than to condemn.

At school, where he was sent at an early age, Luther was treated with harshness and even violence. So great was the poverty of his parents that upon going from home to school in another town he was for a time obliged to obtain his food by singing from door to door, and he often suffered from hunger. The gloomy, superstitious ideas of religion then prevailing filled him with fear. He would lie down at night with a sorrowful heart, looking forward with trembling to the dark future and in constant terror at the thought of God as a stern, unrelenting judge, a cruel tyrant, rather than a kind heavenly Father.

Yet under so many and so great discouragements Luther pressed resolutely forward toward the high standard of moral and intellectual excellence which attracted his soul. He thirsted for knowledge, and the earnest and practical character of his mind led him to desire the solid and useful rather than the showy and superficial.

When, at the age of eighteen, he entered the University of Erfurt, his situation was more favorable and his prospects were brighter than in his earlier years. His parents having by thrift and industry acquired a competence, they were able to render him all needed assistance. And the influence of judicious friends had somewhat lessened the gloomy effects of his former training. He applied himself to the study of the best authors, diligently treasuring their most weighty thoughts and making the wisdom of the wise his own. Even under the harsh discipline of his former instructors he had early given promise of distinction, and with favorable influences his mind rapidly developed. A retentive memory, a lively imagination, strong reasoning powers, and untiring application soon placed him in the foremost rank among his associates. Intellectual discipline ripened his understanding and aroused an activity of mind and a keenness of perception that were preparing him for the conflicts of his life.

The fear of the Lord dwelt in the heart of Luther, enabling him to maintain his steadfastness of purpose and leading him to deep humility before God. He had an abiding sense of his dependence upon divine aid, and he did not fail to begin each day with prayer, while his heart was continually breathing a petition for guidance and support. "To pray well," he often said, "is the better half of study."—D'Aubigné, b. 2, ch. 2.

While one day examining the books in the library of the university, Luther discovered a Latin Bible. Such a book he had never before seen. He was ignorant even of its existence. He had heard portions of the Gospels and Epistles, which were read to the people at public worship, and he supposed that these were the entire Bible. Now, for the first time, he looked upon the whole of God's word. With mingled awe and wonder he turned the sacred pages; with quickened pulse and throbbing heart he read for himself the words of life, pausing now and then to exclaim: "O that God would give me such a book for myself!"—*Ibid.*, b. 2, ch. 2. Angels of heaven were by his side, and rays of light from the throne of God revealed the treasures of truth to his understanding. He had ever feared to offend God, but now the deep conviction of his condition as a sinner took hold upon him as never before.

An earnest desire to be free from sin and to find peace with God led him at last to enter a cloister and devote himself to a monastic life. Here he was required to perform the lowest drudgery and to beg from house to house. He was at an age when respect and appreciation are most eagerly craved, and these menial offices were deeply mortifying to his natural feelings; but he patiently endured this humiliation, believing that it was necessary because of his sins.

Every moment that could be spared from his daily duties he employed in study, robbing himself of sleep and grudging even the time spent at his scanty meals. Above everything else he delighted in the study of God's word. He had found a Bible chained to the convent wall, and to this he often repaired. As his convictions of sin deepened, he sought by his own works to obtain pardon and peace. He led a most rigorous life, endeavoring by fasting, vigils, and scourgings to subdue the evils of his nature, from which the monastic life had brought no release. He shrank from no sacrifice by which he might attain to that purity of heart which would enable him to stand approved before God. "I was indeed a pious monk," he afterward said, "and followed the rules of my order more strictly than I can express. If ever monk could obtain heaven by his monkish works, I should certainly have been entitled to it. . . . If it had continued much longer, I should have carried my mortifications even to death."—*Ibid.*, b. 2, ch. 3. As the result of this painful discipline he lost strength and suffered from fainting spasms, from the effects of which he never fully recovered. But with all his efforts his burdened soul found no relief. He was at last driven to the verge of despair.

When it appeared to Luther that all was lost, God raised up a friend and helper for him. The pious Staupitz opened the word of God to Luther's mind and bade him look away from himself, cease the contemplation of infinite punishment for the violation of God's law, and look to Jesus, his sin-pardoning Saviour. "Instead of torturing yourself on account of your sins, throw yourself into the Redeemer's arms. Trust in Him, in the righteousness of His life, in the atonement of His death. . . . Listen to the Son of God. He became man to give you the assurance of divine favor." "Love Him who first loved you."—*Ibid.*, b. 2, ch. 4. Thus spoke this messenger of mercy. His words made a deep impression upon Luther's mind. After many a struggle with long-cherished errors, he was enabled to grasp the truth, and peace came to his troubled soul.

Luther was ordained a priest and was called from the cloister to a professorship in the University of Wittenberg. Here he applied himself to the study of the Scriptures in the original tongues. He began to lecture upon the Bible; and the book of Psalms, the Gospels, and the Epistles were opened to the understanding of crowds of delighted listeners. Staupitz, his friend and superior, urged him to ascend the pulpit and preach the word of God. Luther hesitated, feeling himself unworthy to speak to the people in Christ's stead. It was only after a long struggle that he yielded to the solicitations of his friends. Already he was mighty in the Scriptures, and the grace of God rested upon him. His eloquence captivated his hearers, the clearness and power with which he presented the truth convinced their understanding, and his fervor touched their hearts.

Luther was still a true son of the papal church and had no thought that he would ever be anything else. In the providence of God he was led to visit Rome. He pursued his journey on foot, lodging at the monasteries on the way. At a convent in Italy he was filled with wonder at the wealth, magnificence, and luxury that he witnessed. Endowed with a princely revenue, the monks dwelt in splendid apartments, attired themselves in the richest and most costly robes, and feasted at a sumptuous table. With painful misgivings Luther contrasted this scene with the self-denial and hardship of his own life. His mind was becoming perplexed.

At last he beheld in the distance the seven-hilled city. With deep emotion he prostrated himself upon the earth, exclaiming: "Holy Rome, I salute thee!"—*Ibid.*, b. 2, ch. 6. He entered the city, visited the churches, listened to the marvelous tales repeated by priests and monks, and performed all the ceremonies required. Everywhere he looked upon scenes that filled him with astonishment and horror. He saw that iniquity existed among all classes of the clergy. He heard indecent jokes from prelates, and was filled with horror at their awful profanity, even during mass. As he mingled with the monks and citizens he met dissipation, debauchery. Turn where he would, in the place of sanctity he found profanation. "No one can imagine," he wrote, "what sins and infamous actions are committed in Rome; they must be seen and heard to be believed. Thus they are in the habit of saying, 'If there is a hell, Rome is built over it: it is an abyss whence issues every kind of sin.'"—*Ibid.*, b. 2, ch. 6.

By a recent decretal an indulgence had been promised by the pope to all who should ascend upon their knees "Pilate's staircase," said to have been descended by our Saviour on leaving the Roman judgment hall and to have been miraculously conveyed from Jerusalem to Rome. Luther was one day devoutly climbing these steps, when suddenly a voice like thunder seemed to say to him: "The just shall live by faith." Romans 1:17. He sprang to his feet and hastened from the place in shame and horror. That text never lost its power upon his soul. From that time he saw more clearly than ever before the fallacy of trusting to human works for salvation, and the necessity of constant faith in the merits of Christ. His eyes had been opened, and were never again to be closed, to the delusions of the papacy. When he turned his face from Rome he had turned away also in heart, and from that time the separation grew wider, until he severed all connection with the papal church.

After his return from Rome, Luther received at the University of Wittenberg the degree of doctor of divinity. Now he was at liberty to devote himself, as never before, to the Scriptures that he loved. He had taken a solemn vow to study carefully and to preach with fidelity the word of God, not the sayings and doctrines of the popes, all the days of his life. He was no longer the mere monk or professor, but the authorized herald of the Bible. He had been called as a shepherd to feed the flock of God, that were hungering and thirsting for the truth. He firmly declared that Christians should receive no other doctrines than those which rest on the authority of the Sacred Scriptures. These words struck at the very foundation of papal supremacy. They contained the vital principle of the Reformation.

Luther saw the danger of exalting human theories above the word of God. He fearlessly attacked the speculative infidelity of the schoolmen and opposed the philosophy and theology which had so long held a controlling influence upon the people. He denounced such studies as not only worthless but pernicious, and sought to turn the minds of his hearers from the sophistries of philosophers and theologians to the eternal truths set forth by prophets and apostles.

Precious was the message which he bore to the eager crowds that hung upon his words. Never before had such teachings fallen upon their ears. The glad tidings of a Saviour's love, the assurance of pardon and peace through His atoning blood, rejoiced their hearts and inspired within them an immortal hope. At Wittenberg a light was kindled whose rays should extend to the uttermost parts of the earth, and which was to increase in brightness to the close of time.

But light and darkness cannot harmonize. Between truth and error there is an irrepressible conflict. To uphold and defend the one is to attack and overthrow the other. Our Saviour Himself declared: "I came not to send peace, but a sword." Matthew 10:34. Said Luther, a few years after the opening of the Reformation: "God does not guide me, He pushes me forward. He carries me away. I am not master of myself. I desire to live in repose; but I am thrown into the midst of tumults and revolutions." —D'Aubigné, b. 5, ch. 2. He was now about to be urged into the contest.

The Roman Church had made merchandise of the grace of God. The tables of the money-changers (Matthew 21:12) were set up beside her altars, and the air resounded with the shouts of buyers and sellers. Under the plea of raising funds for the erection of St. Peter's Church at Rome, indulgences for sin were publicly offered for sale by the authority of the pope. By the price of crime a temple was to be built up for God's worship —the cornerstone laid with the wages of iniquity! But the very means adopted for Rome's aggrandizement provoked the deadliest blow to her power and greatness. It was this that aroused the most determined and successful of the enemies of popery, and led to the battle which shook the papal throne and jostled the triple crown upon the pontiff's head.

The official appointed to conduct the sale of indulgences in Germany —Tetzel by name—had been convicted of the basest offenses against society and against the law of God; but having escaped the punishment due for his crimes, he was employed to further the mercenary and unscrupulous projects of the pope. With great effrontery he repeated the most glaring falsehoods and related marvelous tales to deceive an ignorant, credulous, and superstitious people. Had they possessed the word of God they would not have been thus deceived. It was to keep them under the control of the papacy, in order to swell the power and wealth of her ambitious leaders, that the Bible had been withheld from them. (See John C. L. Gieseler, *A Compendium of Ecclesiastical History,* per. 4, sec. 1, par. 5.)

As Tetzel entered a town, a messenger went before him, announcing: "The grace of God and of the holy father is at your gates."—D'Aubigné, b. 3, ch. 1. And the people welcomed the blasphemous pretender as if he were God Himself come down from heaven to them. The infamous traffic was set up in the church, and Tetzel, ascending the pulpit, extolled the indulgences as the most precious gift of God. He declared that by virtue of his certificates of pardon all the sins which the purchaser should afterward desire to commit would be forgiven him, and that "not even repentance is necessary."—*Ibid.,* b. 3, ch. 1. More than this, he assured his hearers that the indulgences had power to save not only the living but the dead; that the very moment the money should clink against the bottom of his chest, the soul in whose behalf it had been paid would escape from purgatory and make its way to heaven. (See K. R. Hagenbach, *History of the Reformation,* vol. 1, p. 96.)

When Simon Magus offered to purchase of the apostles the power to work miracles, Peter answered him: "Thy money perish with thee, because thou hast thought that the gift of God may be purchased with money." Acts 8:20. But Tetzel's offer was grasped by eager thousands. Gold and silver flowed into his treasury. A salvation that could be bought with money was more easily obtained than that which requires repentance, faith, and diligent effort to resist and overcome sin. (See Appendix note for page 38.)

The doctrine of indulgences had been opposed by men of learning and piety in the Roman Church, and there were many who had no faith in pretensions so contrary to both reason and revelation. No prelate dared lift his voice against this iniquitous traffic; but the minds of men were becoming disturbed and uneasy, and many eagerly inquired if God would not work through some instrumentality for the purification of His church.

Luther, though still a papist of the straitest sort, was filled with horror at the blasphemous assumptions of the indulgence mongers. Many of his own congregation had purchased certificates of pardon, and they soon began to come to their pastor, confessing their various sins, and expecting absolution, not because they were penitent and wished to reform, but on the ground of the indulgence. Luther refused them absolution, and warned them that unless they should repent and reform their lives, they must perish in their sins. In great perplexity they repaired to Tetzel with the complaint that their confessor had refused his certificates; and some boldly demanded that their money be returned to them. The friar was filled with rage. He uttered the most terrible curses, caused fires to be lighted in the public squares, and declared that he "had received an order from the pope to burn all heretics who presumed to oppose his most holy indulgences."—D'Aubigné, b. 3, ch. 4.

Luther now entered boldly upon his work as a champion of the truth. His voice was heard from the pulpit in earnest, solemn warning. He set before the people the offensive character of sin, and taught them that it is impossible for man, by his own works, to lessen its guilt or evade its punishment. Nothing but repentance toward God and faith in Christ can save the sinner. The grace of Christ cannot be purchased; it is a free gift. He counseled the people not to buy indulgences, but to look in faith to a crucified Redeemer. He related his own painful experience in vainly seeking by humiliation and penance to secure salvation, and assured his hearers that it was by looking away from himself and believing in Christ that he found peace and joy.

As Tetzel continued his traffic and his impious pretensions, Luther determined upon a more effectual protest against these crying abuses. An occasion soon offered. The castle church of Wittenberg possessed many relics, which on certain holy days were exhibited to the people, and full remission of sins was granted to all who then visited the church and made confession. Accordingly on these days the people in great numbers resorted thither. One of the most important of these occasions, the festival of All Saints, was approaching. On the preceding day, Luther, joining the crowds that were already making their way to the church, posted on its door a paper containing ninety-five propositions against the doctrine of indulgences. He declared his willingness to defend these theses next day at the university, against all who should see fit to attack them.

His propositions attracted universal attention. They were read and reread, and repeated in every direction. Great excitement was created in the university and in the whole city. By these theses it was shown that the power to grant the pardon of sin, and to remit its penalty, had never been committed to the pope or to any other man. The whole scheme was a farce—an artifice to extort money by playing upon the superstitions of the people—a device of Satan to destroy the souls of all who should trust to its lying pretensions. It was also clearly shown that the gospel of Christ is the most valuable treasure of the church, and that the grace of God, therein revealed, is freely bestowed upon all who seek it by repentance and faith.

Luther's theses challenged discussion; but no one dared accept the challenge. The questions which he proposed had in a few days spread through all Germany, and in a few weeks they had sounded throughout Christendom. Many devoted Romanists, who had seen and lamented the terrible iniquity prevailing in the church, but had not known how to arrest its progress, read the propositions with great joy, recognizing in them the voice of God. They felt that the Lord had graciously set His hand to arrest the rapidly swelling tide of corruption that was issuing from the see of Rome. Princes and magistrates secretly rejoiced that a check was to be put upon the arrogant power which denied the right of appeal from its decisions.

But the sin-loving and supersitious multitudes were terrified as the sophistries that had soothed their fears were swept away. Crafty ecclesiastics, interrupted in their work of sanctioning crime, and seeing their gains endangered, were enraged, and rallied to uphold their pretensions. The Reformer had bitter accusers to meet. Some charged him with acting hastily and from impulse. Others accused him of presumption, declaring

that he was not directed of God, but was acting from pride and forward-ness. "Who does not know," he responded, "that a man rarely puts forth any new idea without having some appearance of pride, and without being accused of exciting quarrels? . . . Why were Christ and all the martyrs put to death? Because they seemed to be proud contemners of the wisdom of the time, and because they advanced novelties without having first humbly taken counsel of the oracles of the ancient opinions."

Again he declared: "Whatever I do will be done, not by the prudence of men, but by the counsel of God. If the work be of God, who shall stop it? if it be not, who can forward it? Not my will, nor theirs, nor ours; but Thy will, O holy Father, which art in heaven."—*Ibid.*, b. 3, ch. 6.

Though Luther had been moved by the Spirit of God to begin his work, he was not to carry it forward without severe conflicts. The re-proaches of his enemies, their misrepresentation of his purposes, and their unjust and malicious reflections upon his character and motives, came in upon him like an overwhelming flood; and they were not without effect. He had felt confident that the leaders of the people, both in the church and in the schools, would gladly unite with him in efforts for reform. Words of encouragement from those in high position had in-spired him with joy and hope. Already in anticipation he had seen a brighter day dawning for the church. But encouragement had changed to reproach and condemnation. Many dignitaries, of both church and state, were convicted of the truthfulness of his theses; but they soon saw that the acceptance of these truths would involve great changes. To enlighten and reform the people would be virtually to undermine the authority of Rome, to stop thousands of streams now flowing into her treasury, and thus greatly to curtail the extravagance and luxury of the papal leaders. Furthermore, to teach the people to think and act as responsible beings, looking to Christ alone for salvation, would over-throw the pontiff's throne and eventually destroy their own authority. For this reason they refused the knowledge tendered them of God and arrayed themselves against Christ and the truth by their opposition to the man whom He had sent to enlighten them.

Luther trembled as he looked upon himself—one man opposed to the mightiest powers of earth. He sometimes doubted whether he had indeed been led of God to set himself against the authority of the church. "Who was I," he writes, "to oppose the majesty of the pope, before whom . . . the kings of the earth and the whole world trembled? . . . No one can know what my heart suffered during these first two years, and into what

Nailing his ninety-five theses on the church door at Wittenberg, Luther challenged religious error of his day.

despondency, I may say into what despair, I was sunk."—*Ibid.*, b. 3, ch. 6. But he was not left to become utterly disheartened. When human support failed, he looked to God alone and learned that he could lean in perfect safety upon that all-powerful arm.

To a friend of the Reformation Luther wrote: "We cannot attain to the understanding of Scripture either by study or by the intellect. Your first duty is to begin by prayer. Entreat the Lord to grant you, of His great mercy, the true understanding of His word. There is no other interpreter of the word of God than the Author of this word, as He Himself has said, 'They shall be all taught of God.' Hope for nothing from your own labors, from your own understanding: trust solely in God, and in the influence of His Spirit. Believe this on the word of a man who has had experience."—*Ibid.*, b. 3, ch. 7. Here is a lesson of vital importance to those who feel that God has called them to present to others the solemn truths for this time. These truths will stir the enmity of Satan and of men who love the fables that he has devised. In the conflict with the powers of evil there is need of something more than strength of intellect and human wisdom.

When enemies appealed to custom and tradition, or to the assertions and authority of the pope, Luther met them with the Bible and the Bible only. Here were arguments which they could not answer; therefore the slaves of formalism and superstition clamored for his blood, as the Jews had clamored for the blood of Christ. "He is a heretic," cried the Roman zealots. "It is high treason against the church to allow so horrible a heretic to live one hour longer. Let the scaffold be instantly erected for him!" —*Ibid.*, b. 3, ch. 9. But Luther did not fall a prey to their fury. God had a work for him to do, and angels of heaven were sent to protect him. Many, however, who had received from Luther the precious light were made the objects of Satan's wrath and for the truth's sake fearlessly suffered torture and death.

Luther's teachings attracted the attention of thoughtful minds throughout all Germany. From his sermons and writings issued beams of light which awakened and illuminated thousands. A living faith was taking the place of the dead formalism in which the church had so long been held. The people were daily losing confidence in the superstitions of Romanism. The barriers of prejudice were giving way. The word of God, by which Luther tested every doctrine and every claim, was like a two-edged sword, cutting its way to the hearts of the people. Everywhere there was awakening a desire for spiritual progress. Everywhere was such a hungering and thirsting after righteousness as had not been known for ages. The eyes of the people, so long directed to human rites and earthly mediators, were now turning in penitence and faith to Christ and Him crucified.

This widespread interest aroused still further the fears of the papal authorities. Luther received a summons to appear at Rome to answer to the charge of heresy. The command filled his friends with terror. They knew full well the danger that threatened him in that corrupt city, already drunk with the blood of the martyrs of Jesus. They protested against his going to Rome and requested that he receive his examination in Germany.

This arrangement was finally effected, and the pope's legate was appointed to hear the case. In the instructions communicated by the pontiff to this official, it was stated that Luther had already been declared a heretic. The legate was therefore charged "to prosecute and constrain without any delay." If he should remain steadfast, and the legate should fail to gain possession of his person, he was empowered "to proscribe him in every part of Germany; to banish, curse, and excommunicate all those who are attached to him."—*Ibid.*, b. 4, ch. 2. And, further, the pope directed his legate, in order entirely to root out the pestilent heresy, to excommunicate all, of whatever dignity in church or state, except the emperor, who should neglect to seize Luther and his adherents, and deliver them up to the vengeance of Rome.

Here is displayed the true spirit of popery. Not a trace of Christian principle, or even of common justice, is to be seen in the whole document. Luther was at a great distance from Rome; he had had no opportunity to explain or defend his position; yet before his case had been investigated, he was summarily pronounced a heretic, and in the same day, exhorted, accused, judged, and condemned; and all this by the self-styled holy father, the only supreme, infallible authority in church or state!

At this time, when Luther so much needed the sympathy and counsel of a true friend, God's providence sent Melanchthon to Wittenberg. Young in years, modest and diffident in his manners, Melanchthon's sound judgment, extensive knowledge, and winning eloquence, combined with the purity and uprightness of his character, won universal admiration and esteem. The brilliancy of his talents was not more marked than his gentleness of disposition. He soon became an earnest disciple of the gospel, and Luther's most trusted friend and valued supporter; his gentleness, caution, and exactness serving as a complement to Luther's courage and energy. Their union in the work added strength to the Reformation and was a source of great encouragement to Luther.

Augsburg had been fixed upon as the place of trial, and the Reformer set out on foot to perform the journey thither. Serious fears were entertained in his behalf. Threats had been made openly that he would be seized and murdered on the way, and his friends begged him not to venture. They even entreated him to leave Wittenberg for a time and find safety with those who would gladly protect him. But he would not leave the position where God had placed him. He must continue faithfully to maintain the truth, notwithstanding the storms that were beating upon him. His language was: "I am like Jeremiah, a man of strife and contention; but the more their threats increase, the more my joy is multiplied. . . . They have already destroyed my honor and my reputation. One single thing remains; it is my wretched body: let them take it; they will thus shorten my life by a few hours. But as for my soul, they cannot take that. He who desires to proclaim the word of Christ to the world, must expect death at every moment."—*Ibid.*, b. 4, ch. 4.

The tidings of Luther's arrival at Augsburg gave great satisfaction to the papal legate. The troublesome heretic who was exciting the attention of the whole world seemed now in the power of Rome, and the legate determined that he should not escape. The Reformer had failed to provide himself with a safe-conduct. His friends urged him not to appear before the legate without one, and they themselves undertook to procure it from the emperor. The legate intended to force Luther, if possible, to retract, or, failing in this, to cause him to be conveyed to Rome, to share the fate of Huss and Jerome. Therefore through his agents he endeavored to induce Luther to appear without a safe-conduct, trusting himself to his mercy. This the Reformer firmly declined to do. Not until he had received the document pledging him the emperor's protection, did he appear in the presence of the papal ambassador.

As a matter of policy, the Romanists had decided to attempt to win Luther by an appearance of gentleness. The legate, in his interviews with him, professed great friendliness; but he demanded that Luther submit implicitly to the authority of the church, and yield every point without argument or question. He had not rightly estimated the character of the man with whom he had to deal. Luther, in reply, expressed his regard for the church, his desire for the truth, his readiness to answer all objections to what he had taught, and to submit his doctrines to the decision of certain leading universities. But at the same time he protested against the cardinal's course in requiring him to retract without having proved him in error.

The only response was: "Retract, retract!" The Reformer showed that his position was sustained by the Scriptures and firmly declared that he could not renounce the truth. The legate, unable to reply to Luther's arguments, overwhelmed him with a storm of reproaches, gibes, and flattery, interspersed with quotations from tradition and the sayings of the Fathers, granting the Reformer no opportunity to speak. Seeing that the conference, thus continued, would be utterly futile, Luther finally obtained a reluctant permission to present his answer in writing.

"In so doing," said he, writing to a friend, "the oppressed find double gain; first, what is written may be submitted to the judgment of others; and second, one has a better chance of working on the fears, if not on the conscience, of an arrogant and babbling despot, who would otherwise overpower by his imperious language."—Martyn, *The Life and Times of Luther*, pages 271, 272.

At the next interview, Luther presented a clear, concise, and forcible exposition of his views, fully supported by many quotations from Scripture. This paper, after reading aloud, he handed to the cardinal, who, however, cast it contemptuously aside, declaring it to be a mass of idle words and irrelevant quotations. Luther, fully aroused, now met the haughty prelate on his own ground—the traditions and teachings of the church—and utterly overthrew his assumptions.

When the prelate saw that Luther's reasoning was unanswerable, he lost all self-control, and in a rage cried out: "Retract! or I will send you to Rome, there to appear before the judges commissioned to take cognizance of your cause. I will excommunicate you and all your partisans, and all who shall at any time countenance you, and will cast them out of the church." And he finally declared, in a haughty and angry tone: "Retract, or return no more."—D'Aubigné, London ed., b. 4, ch. 8.

The Reformer promptly withdrew with his friends, thus declaring plainly that no retraction was to be expected from him. This was not what the cardinal had purposed. He had flattered himself that by violence he could awe Luther to submission. Now, left alone with his supporters, he looked from one to another in utter chagrin at the unexpected failure of his schemes.

Luther's efforts on this occasion were not without good results. The large assembly present had opportunity to compare the two men, and to judge for themselves of the spirit manifested by them, as well as of the strength and truthfulness of their positions. How marked the contrast! The Reformer, simple, humble, firm, stood up in the strength of God, having truth on his side; the pope's representative, self-important, overbearing, haughty, and unreasonable, was without a single argument from the Scriptures, yet vehemently crying: "Retract, or be sent to Rome for punishment."

Notwithstanding Luther had secured a safe-conduct, the Romanists were plotting to seize and imprison him. His friends urged that as it was useless for him to prolong his stay, he should return to Wittenberg without delay, and that the utmost caution should be observed in order to conceal his intentions. He accordingly left Augsburg before daybreak, on horseback, accompanied only by a guide furnished him by the magistrate. With many forebodings he secretly made his way through the dark and silent streets of the city. Enemies, vigilant and cruel, were plotting his destruction. Would he escape the snares prepared for him? Those were moments of anxiety and earnest prayer. He reached a small gate in the wall of the city. It was opened for him, and with his guide he passed through without hindrance. Once safely outside, the fugitives hastened their flight, and before the legate learned of Luther's departure, he was beyond the reach of his persecutors. Satan and his emissaries were defeated. The man whom they had thought in their power was gone, escaped as a bird from the snare of the fowler.

At the news of Luther's escape the legate was overwhelmed with surprise and anger. He had expected to receive great honor for his wisdom and firmness in dealing with this disturber of the church; but his hope was disappointed. He gave expression to his wrath in a letter to Frederick, the elector of Saxony, bitterly denouncing Luther and demanding that Frederick send the Reformer to Rome or banish him from Saxony.

In defense, Luther urged that the legate or the pope show him his errors from the Scriptures, and pledged himself in the most solemn manner to renounce his doctrines if they could be shown to contradict the word of God. And he expressed his gratitude to God that he had been counted worthy to suffer in so holy a cause.

The elector had, as yet, little knowledge of the reformed doctrines, but he was deeply impressed by the candor, force, and clearness of Luther's words; and until the Reformer should be proved to be in error, Frederick resolved to stand as his protector. In reply to the legate's demand he wrote: " 'Since Dr. Martin has appeared before you at Augsburg, you should be satisfied. We did not expect that you would endeavor to make him retract without having convinced him of his errors. None of the learned men in our principality have informed me that Martin's doctrine is impious, antichristian, or heretical.' The prince refused, moreover, to send Luther to Rome, or to expel him from his states."—D'Aubigné, b. 4, ch. 10.

The elector saw that there was a general breaking down of the moral restraints of society. A great work of reform was needed. The complicated and expensive arrangements to restrain and punish crime would be unnecessary if men but acknowledged and obeyed the requirements of God and the dictates of an enlightened conscience. He saw that Luther was laboring to secure this object, and he secretly rejoiced that a better influence was making itself felt in the church.

He saw also that as a professor in the university Luther was eminently successful. Only a year had passed since the Reformer posted his theses on the castle church, yet there was already a great falling off in the number of pilgrims that visited the church at the festival of All Saints. Rome had been deprived of worshipers and offerings, but their place was filled by another class, who now came to Wittenberg, not pilgrims to adore her relics, but students to fill her halls of learning. The writings of Luther had kindled everywhere a new interest in the Holy Scriptures, and not only from all parts of Germany, but from other lands, students flocked to the university. Young men, coming in sight of Wittenberg for the first time, "raised their hands to heaven, and praised God for having caused the light of truth to shine forth from this city, as from Zion in times of old, and whence it spread even to the most distant countries."—*Ibid.*, b. 4, ch. 10.

Luther was as yet but partially converted from the errors of Romanism. But as he compared the Holy Oracles with the papal decrees and constitutions, he was filled with wonder. "I am reading," he wrote, "the decrees of the pontiffs, and . . . I do not know whether the pope is antichrist himself, or his apostle, so greatly is Christ misrepresented and crucified in them."—*Ibid.*, b. 5, ch. 1. Yet at this time Luther was still a supporter of the Roman Church, and had no thought that he would ever separate from her communion.

The Reformer's writings and his doctrine were extending to every nation in Christendom. The work spread to Switzerland and Holland. Copies of his writings found their way to France and Spain. In England his teachings were received as the word of life. To Belgium and Italy also the truth had extended. Thousands were awakening from their deathlike stupor to the joy and hope of a life of faith.

Rome became more and more exasperated by the attacks of Luther, and it was declared by some of his fanatical opponents, even by doctors in Catholic universities, that he who should kill the rebellious monk would be without sin. One day a stranger, with a pistol hidden under his cloak, approached the Reformer and inquired why he went thus alone. "I am in God's hands," answered Luther. "He is my strength and my shield. What can man do unto me?"—*Ibid.*, b. 6, ch. 2. Upon hearing these words, the stranger turned pale and fled away as from the presence of the angels of heaven.

Rome was bent upon the destruction of Luther; but God was his defense. His doctrines were heard everywhere—"in cottages and convents, . . . in the castles of the nobles, in the universities, and in the palaces of kings;" and noble men were rising on every hand to sustain his efforts. —*Ibid.*, b. 6, ch. 2.

It was about this time that Luther, reading the works of Huss, found that the great truth of justification by faith, which he himself was seeking to uphold and teach, had been held by the Bohemian Reformer. "We have all," said Luther, "Paul, Augustine, and myself, been Hussites without knowing it!" "God will surely visit it upon the world," he continued, "that the truth was preached to it a century ago, and burned!"— Wylie, b. 6, ch. 1.

In an appeal to the emperor and nobility of Germany in behalf of the reformation of Christianity, Luther wrote concerning the pope: "It is a horrible thing to behold the man who styles himself Christ's vicegerent, displaying a magnificence that no emperor can equal. Is this being like the poor Jesus, or the humble Peter? He is, say they, the lord of the world! But Christ, whose vicar he boasts of being, has said, 'My kingdom is not of this world.' Can the dominions of a vicar extend beyond those of his superior?"—D'Aubigné, b. 6, ch. 3.

He wrote thus of the universities: "I am much afraid that the universities will prove to be the great gates of hell, unless they diligently labor in explaining the Holy Scriptures, and engraving them in the hearts of youth. I advise no one to place his child where the Scriptures do not reign paramount. Every institution in which men are not unceasingly occupied with the word of God must become corrupt."—*Ibid.*, b. 6, ch. 3.

This appeal was rapidly circulated throughout Germany and exerted a powerful influence upon the people. The whole nation was stirred, and multitudes were roused to rally around the standard of reform. Luther's opponents, burning with a desire for revenge, urged the pope to take decisive measures against him. It was decreed that his doctrines should be immediately condemned. Sixty days were granted the Reformer and his adherents, after which, if they did not recant, they were all to be excommunicated.

That was a terrible crisis for the Reformation. For centuries Rome's sentence of excommunication had struck terror to powerful monarchs; it had filled mighty empires with woe and desolation. Those upon whom its condemnation fell were universally regarded with dread and horror; they were cut off from intercourse with their fellows and treated as outlaws, to be hunted to extermination. Luther was not blind to the tempest about to burst upon him; but he stood firm, trusting in Christ to be his support and shield. With a martyr's faith and courage he wrote: "What is about to happen I know not, nor do I care to know. . . . Let the blow light where it may, I am without fear. Not so much as a leaf falls, without the will of our Father. How much rather will He care for us! It is a light thing to die for the Word, since the Word which was made flesh hath Himself died. If we die with Him, we shall live with Him; and passing through that which He has passed through before us, we shall be where He is and dwell with Him forever."—*Ibid.*, 3d London ed., Walther, 1840, b. 6, ch. 9.

When the papal bull reached Luther, he said: "I despise and attack it, as impious, false. . . . It is *Christ* Himself who is condemned therein. . . . I rejoice in having to bear such ills for the best of causes. Already I feel greater liberty in my heart; for at last I know that the pope is antichrist, and that his throne is that of Satan himself."—D'Aubigné, b. 6, ch. 9.

Yet the mandate of Rome was not without effect. Prison, torture, and sword were weapons potent to enforce obedience. The weak and superstitious trembled before the decree of the pope; and while there was general sympathy for Luther, many felt that life was too dear to be risked in the cause of reform. Everything seemed to indicate that the Reformer's work was about to close.

But Luther was fearless still. Rome had hurled her anathemas against him, and the world looked on, nothing doubting that he would perish or be forced to yield. But with terrible power he flung back upon herself the sentence of condemnation and publicly declared his determination to abandon her forever. In the presence of a crowd of students, doctors, and citizens of all ranks Luther burned the pope's bull, with the canon laws, the decretals, and certain writings sustaining the papal power. "My enemies have been able, by burning my books," he said, "to injure the cause of truth in the minds of the common people, and destroy their souls; for this reason I consumed their books in return. A serious struggle has just begun. Hitherto I have been only playing with the pope. I began this work in God's name; it will be ended without me, and by His might." —*Ibid.*, b. 6, ch. 10.

To the reproaches of his enemies who taunted him with the weakness of his cause, Luther answered: "Who knows if God has not chosen and called me, and if they ought not to fear that, by despising me, they despise God Himself? Moses was alone at the departure from Egypt; Elijah was alone in the reign of King Ahab; Isaiah alone in Jerusalem; Ezekiel alone in Babylon. . . . God never selected as a prophet either the high priest or any other great personage; but ordinarily He chose low and despised men, once even the shepherd Amos. In every age, the saints have had to reprove the great, kings, princes, priests, and wise men, at the peril of their lives. . . . I do not say that I am a prophet; but I say that they ought to fear precisely because I am alone and that they are many. I am sure of this, that the word of God is with me, and that it is not with them."—*Ibid.*, b. 6, ch. 10.

Yet it was not without a terrible struggle with himself that Luther decided upon a final separation from the church. It was about this time that he wrote: "I feel more and more every day how difficult it is to lay aside the scruples which one has imbibed in childhood. Oh, how much pain it has caused me, though I had the Scriptures on my side, to justify it to myself that I should dare to make a stand alone against the pope, and hold him forth as antichrist! What have the tribulations of my heart not been! How many times have I not asked myself with bitterness that question which was so frequent on the lips of the papists: 'Art thou alone wise? Can everyone else be mistaken? How will it be, if, after all, it is thyself who art wrong, and who art involving in thy error so many souls, who will then be eternally damned?' 'Twas so I fought with myself and with Satan, till Christ, by His own infallible word, fortified my heart against these doubts."—Martyn, pages 372, 373.

The pope had threatened Luther with excommunication if he did not recant, and the threat was now fulfilled. A new bull appeared, declaring the Reformer's final separation from the Roman Church, denouncing him as accursed of Heaven, and including in the same condemnation all who should receive his doctrines. The great contest had been fully entered upon.

Opposition is the lot of all whom God employs to present truths specially applicable to their time. There was a present truth in the days of Luther—a truth at that time of special importance; there is a present truth for the church today. He who does all things according to the counsel of His will has been pleased to place men under various circumstances and to enjoin upon them duties peculiar to the times in which they live and the conditions under which they are placed. If they would prize the light given them, broader views of truth would be opened before them. But truth is no more desired by the majority today than it was by the papists who opposed Luther. There is the same disposition to accept the theories and traditions of men instead of the word of God

[*142-144*] 113

as in former ages. Those who present the truth for this time should not expect to be received with greater favor than were earlier reformers. The great controversy between truth and error, between Christ and Satan, is to increase in intensity to the close of this world's history.

Said Jesus to His disciples: "If ye were of the world, the world would love his own: but because ye are not of the world, but I have chosen you out of the world, therefore the world hateth you. Remember the word that I said unto you, The servant is not greater than his Lord. If they have persecuted Me, they will also persecute you; if they have kept My saying, they will keep yours also." John 15:19, 20. And on the other hand our Lord declared plainly: "Woe unto you, when all men shall speak well of you! for so did their fathers to the false prophets." Luke 6:26. The spirit of the world is no more in harmony with the spirit of Christ today than in earlier times, and those who preach the word of God in its purity will be received with no greater favor now than then. The forms of opposition to the truth may change, the enmity may be less open because it is more subtle; but the same antagonism still exists and will be manifested to the end of time.

chapter 8

A Champion of Truth

A NEW emperor, Charles V, had ascended the throne of Germany, and the emissaries of Rome hastened to present their congratulations and induce the monarch to employ his power against the Reformation. On the other hand, the elector of Saxony, to whom Charles was in great degree indebted for his crown, entreated him to take no step against Luther until he should have granted him a hearing. The emperor was thus placed in a position of great perplexity and embarrassment. The papists would be satisfied with nothing short of an imperial edict sentencing Luther to death. The elector had declared firmly that "neither his imperial majesty nor any other person had shown that Luther's writings had been refuted;" therefore he requested "that Dr. Luther should be furnished with a safe-conduct, so that he might appear before a tribunal of learned, pious, and impartial judges."—D'Aubigné, b. 6, ch. 11.

The attention of all parties was now directed to the assembly of the German states which convened at Worms soon after the accession of Charles to the empire. There were important political questions and interests to be considered by this national council; for the first time the princes of Germany were to meet their youthful monarch in deliberative assembly. From all parts of the fatherland had come the dignitaries of church and state. Secular lords, highborn, powerful, and jealous of their hereditary rights; princely ecclesiastics, flushed with their conscious superiority in rank and power; courtly knights and their armed retainers; and ambassadors from foreign and distant lands—all gathered at Worms.

Yet in that vast assembly the subject that excited the deepest interest was the cause of the Saxony Reformer.

Charles had previously directed the elector to bring Luther with him to the Diet, assuring him of protection, and promising a free discussion, with competent persons, of the questions in dispute. Luther was anxious to appear before the emperor. His health was at this time much impaired; yet he wrote to the elector: "If I cannot go to Worms in good health, I will be carried there, sick as I am. For if the emperor calls me, I cannot doubt that it is the call of God Himself. If they desire to use violence against me, and that is very probable (for it is not for their instruction that they order me to appear), I place the matter in the Lord's hands. He still lives and reigns who preserved the three young men in the burning fiery furnace. If He will not save me, my life is of little consequence. Let us only prevent the gospel from being exposed to the scorn of the wicked, and let us shed our blood for it, for fear they should triumph. It is not for me to decide whether my life or my death will contribute most to the salvation of all. . . . You may expect everything from me . . . except flight and recantation. Fly I cannot, and still less retract."—*Ibid.*, b. 7, ch. 1.

As the news was circulated at Worms that Luther was to appear before the Diet, a general excitement was created. Aleander, the papal legate to whom the case had been specially entrusted, was alarmed and enraged. He saw that the result would be disastrous to the papal cause. To institute inquiry into a case in which the pope had already pronounced sentence of condemnation would be to cast contempt upon the authority of the sovereign pontiff. Furthermore, he was apprehensive that the eloquent and powerful arguments of this man might turn away many of the princes from the cause of the pope. He therefore, in the most urgent manner, remonstrated with Charles against Luther's appearance at Worms. About this time the bull declaring Luther's excommunication was published; and this, coupled with the representations of the legate, induced the emperor to yield. He wrote to the elector that if Luther would not retract, he must remain at Wittenberg.

Not content with this victory, Aleander labored with all the power and cunning at his command to secure Luther's condemnation. With a persistence worthy of a better cause, he urged the matter upon the attention of princes, prelates, and other members of the assembly, accusing the Reformer of "sedition, rebellion, impiety, and blasphemy." But the vehemence and passion manifested by the legate revealed too plainly

Luther before the Diet at Worms
bravely defended the truths of the
Bible, saying, "I can do no other."

the spirit by which he was actuated. "He is moved by hatred and vengeance," was the general remark, "much more than by zeal and piety." —*Ibid.*, b. 7, ch. 1. The majority of the Diet were more than ever inclined to regard Luther's cause with favor.

With redoubled zeal Aleander urged upon the emperor the duty of executing the papal edicts. But under the laws of Germany this could not be done without the concurrence of the princes; and, overcome at last by the legate's importunity, Charles bade him present his case to the Diet. "It was a proud day for the nuncio. The assembly was a great one: the cause was even greater. Aleander was to plead for Rome, . . . the mother and mistress of all churches." He was to vindicate the princedom of Peter before the assembled principalities of Christendom. "He had the gift of eloquence, and he rose to the greatness of the occasion. Providence ordered it that Rome should appear and plead by the ablest of her orators in the presence of the most august of tribunals, before she was condemned."—Wylie, b. 6, ch. 4. With some misgivings those who favored the Reformer looked forward to the effect of Aleander's speech. The elector of Saxony was not present, but by his direction some of his councilors attended to take notes of the nuncio's address.

With all the power of learning and eloquence, Aleander set himself to overthrow the truth. Charge after charge he hurled against Luther as an enemy of the church and the state, the living and the dead, clergy and laity, councils and private Christians. "In Luther's errors there is enough," he declared, to warrant the burning of "a hundred thousand heretics."

In conclusion he endeavored to cast contempt upon the adherents of the reformed faith: "What are all these Lutherans? A crew of insolent pedagogues, corrupt priests, dissolute monks, ignorant lawyers, and degraded nobles, with the common people whom they have misled and perverted. How far superior to them is the Catholic party in number, ability, and power! A unanimous decree from this illustrious assembly will enlighten the simple, warn the imprudent, decide the waverers, and give strength to the weak."—D'Aubigné, b. 7, ch. 3.

With such weapons the advocates of truth in every age have been attacked. The same arguments are still urged against all who dare to present, in opposition to established errors, the plain and direct teachings of God's word. "Who are these preachers of new doctrines?" exclaim those who desire a popular religion. "They are unlearned, few in numbers, and of the poorer class. Yet they claim to have the truth, and to be the chosen people of God. They are ignorant and deceived. How greatly superior in numbers and influence is our church! How many great and learned men are among us! How much more power is on our side!" These are the arguments that have a telling influence upon the world; but they are no more conclusive now than in the days of the Reformer.

The Reformation did not, as many suppose, end with Luther. It is to be continued to the close of this world's history. Luther had a great work to do in reflecting to others the light which God had permitted to shine upon him; yet he did not receive all the light which was to be given to the world. From that time to this, new light has been continually shining upon the Scriptures, and new truths have been constantly unfolding.

The legate's address made a deep impression upon the Diet. There was no Luther present, with the clear and convincing truths of God's word, to vanquish the papal champion. No attempt was made to defend the Reformer. There was manifest a general disposition not only to condemn him and the doctrines which he taught, but if possible to uproot the heresy. Rome had enjoyed the most favorable opportunity to defend her cause. All that she could say in her own vindication had been said. But the apparent victory was the signal of defeat. Henceforth the contrast between truth and error would be more clearly seen, as they should take the field in open warfare. Never from that day would Rome stand as secure as she had stood.

While most of the members of the Diet would not have hesitated to yield up Luther to the vengeance of Rome, many of them saw and deplored the existing depravity in the church, and desired a suppression of the abuses suffered by the German people in consequence of the corruption and greed of the hierarchy. The legate had presented the papal rule in the most favorable light. Now the Lord moved upon a member of the Diet to give a true delineation of the effects of papal tyranny. With noble firmness, Duke George of Saxony stood up in that princely assembly and specified with terrible exactness the deceptions and abominations of popery, and their dire results. In closing he said:

"These are some of the abuses that cry out against Rome. All shame has been put aside, and their only object is . . . money, money, money, . . . so that the preachers who should teach the truth, utter nothing but falsehoods, and are not only tolerated, but rewarded, because the greater their lies, the greater their gain. It is from this foul spring that such tainted waters flow. Debauchery stretches out the hand to avarice. . . .

Alas, it is the scandal caused by the clergy that hurls so many poor souls into eternal condemnation. A general reform must be effected."—*Ibid.*, b. 7, ch. 4.

A more able and forcible denunciation of the papal abuses could not have been presented by Luther himself; and the fact that the speaker was a determined enemy of the Reformer's gave greater influence to his words.

Had the eyes of the assembly been opened, they would have beheld angels of God in the midst of them, shedding beams of light athwart the darkness of error and opening minds and hearts to the reception of truth. It was the power of the God of truth and wisdom that controlled even the adversaries of the Reformation, and thus prepared the way for the great work about to be accomplished. Martin Luther was not present; but the voice of One greater than Luther had been heard in that assembly.

A committee was at once appointed by the Diet to prepare an enumeration of the papal oppressions that weighed so heavily on the German people. This list, containing a hundred and one specifications, was presented to the emperor, with a request that he would take immediate measures for the correction of these abuses. "What a loss of Christian souls," said the petitioners, "what depredations, what extortions, on account of the scandals by which the spiritual head of Christendom is surrounded! It is our duty to prevent the ruin and dishonor of our people. For this reason we most humbly but most urgently entreat you to order a general reformation, and to undertake its accomplishment."—*Ibid.*, b.7, ch 4.

The council now demanded the Reformer's appearance before them. Notwithstanding the entreaties, protests, and threats of Aleander, the emperor at last consented, and Luther was summoned to appear before the Diet. With the summons was issued a safe-conduct, ensuring his return to a place of security. These were borne to Wittenberg by a herald, who was commissioned to conduct him to Worms.

The friends of Luther were terrified and distressed. Knowing the prejudice and enmity against him, they feared that even his safe-conduct would not be respected, and they entreated him not to imperil his life. He replied: "The papists do not desire my coming to Worms, but my condemnation and my death. It matters not. Pray not for me, but for the word of God. . . . Christ will give me His Spirit to overcome these ministers of error. I despise them during my life; I shall triumph over them by my death. They are busy at Worms about compelling me to retract;

and this shall be my retraction: I said formerly that the pope was Christ's vicar; now I assert that he is our Lord's adversary, and the devil's apostle."—*Ibid.*, b. 7, ch. 6.

Luther was not to make his perilous journey alone. Besides the imperial messenger, three of his firmest friends determined to accompany him. Melanchthon earnestly desired to join them. His heart was knit to Luther's, and he yearned to follow him, if need be, to prison or to death. But his entreaties were denied. Should Luther perish, the hopes of the Reformation must center upon his youthful colaborer. Said the Reformer as he parted from Melanchthon: "If I do not return, and my enemies put me to death, continue to teach, and stand fast in the truth. Labor in my stead. . . . If you survive, my death will be of little consequence."—*Ibid.*, b. 7, ch. 7. Students and citizens who had gathered to witness Luther's departure were deeply moved. A multitude whose hearts had been touched by the gospel, bade him farewell with weeping. Thus the Reformer and his companions set out from Wittenberg.

On the journey they saw that the minds of the people were oppressed by gloomy forebodings. At some towns no honors were proffered them. As they stopped for the night, a friendly priest expressed his fears by holding up before Luther the portrait of an Italian reformer who had suffered martyrdom. The next day they learned that Luther's writings had been condemned at Worms. Imperial messengers were proclaiming the emperor's decree and calling upon the people to bring the proscribed works to the magistrates. The herald, fearing for Luther's safety at the council, and thinking that already his resolution might be shaken, asked if he still wished to go forward. He answered: "Although interdicted in every city, I shall go on."—*Ibid.*, b. 7, ch. 7.

At Erfurt, Luther was received with honor. Surrounded by admiring crowds, he passed through the streets that he had often traversed with his beggar's wallet. He visited his convent cell, and thought upon the struggles through which the light now flooding Germany had been shed upon his soul. He was urged to preach. This he had been forbidden to do, but the herald granted him permission, and the friar who had once been made the drudge of the convent, now entered the pulpit.

To a crowded assembly he spoke from the words of Christ, "Peace be unto you." "Philosophers, doctors, and writers," he said, "have endeavored to teach men the way to obtain everlasting life, and they have not succeeded. I will now tell it to you: . . . God has raised one Man from the dead, the Lord Jesus Christ, that He might destroy death, extirpate sin, and shut the gates of hell. This is the work of salvation. . . . Christ has vanquished! this is the joyful news; and we are saved by His work, and not by our own. . . . Our Lord Jesus Christ said, 'Peace be unto you; behold My hands;' that is to say, Behold, O man! it is I, I alone, who have taken away thy sin, and ransomed thee; and now thou hast peace, saith the Lord.'

He continued, showing that true faith will be manifested by a holy life. "Since God has saved us, let us so order our works that they may be acceptable to Him. Art thou rich? let thy goods administer to the necessities of the poor. Art thou poor? let thy services be acceptable to the rich. If thy labor is useful to thyself alone, the service that thou pretendest to render unto God is a lie."—*Ibid.*, b. 7, ch. 7.

The people listened as if spellbound. The bread of life was broken to those starving souls. Christ was lifted up before them as above popes, legates, emperors, and kings. Luther made no reference to his own perilous position. He did not seek to make himself the object of thought or sympathy. In the contemplation of Christ he had lost sight of self. He hid behind the Man of Calvary, seeking only to present Jesus as the sinner's Redeemer.

As the Reformer proceeded on his journey, he was everywhere regarded with great interest. An eager multitude thronged about him, and friendly voices warned him of the purpose of the Romanists. "They will burn you," said some, "and reduce your body to ashes, as they did with John Huss." Luther answered, "Though they should kindle a fire all the way from Worms to Wittenberg, the flames of which reached to heaven,

I would walk through it in the name of the Lord; I would appear before them; I would enter the jaws of this behemoth, and break his teeth, confessing the Lord Jesus Christ."—*Ibid.*, b. 7, ch. 7.

The news of his approach to Worms created great commotion. His friends trembled for his safety; his enemies feared for the success of their cause. Strenuous efforts were made to dissuade him from entering the city. At the instigation of the papists he was urged to repair to the castle of a friendly knight, where, it was declared, all difficulties could be amicably adjusted. Friends endeavored to excite his fears by describing the dangers that threatened him. All their efforts failed. Luther, still unshaken, declared: "Even should there be as many devils in Worms as tiles on the housetops, still I would enter it."—*Ibid.*, b. 7, ch. 7.

Upon his arrival at Worms, a vast crowd flocked to the gates to welcome him. So great a concourse had not assembled to greet the emperor himself. The excitement was intense, and from the midst of the throng a shrill and plaintive voice chanted a funeral dirge as a warning to Luther of the fate that awaited him. "God will be my defense," said he, as he alighted from his carriage.

The papists had not believed that Luther would really venture to appear at Worms, and his arrival filled them with consternation. The emperor immediately summoned his councilors to consider what course should be pursued. One of the bishops, a rigid papist, declared: "We have long consulted on this matter. Let your imperial majesty get rid of this man at once. Did not Sigismund cause John Huss to be burnt? We are not bound either to give or to observe the safe-conduct of a heretic." "No," said the emperor, "we must keep our promise."—*Ibid.*, b. 7, ch. 8. It was therefore decided that the Reformer should be heard.

All the city were eager to see this remarkable man, and a throng of visitors soon filled his lodgings. Luther had scarcely recovered from his recent illness; he was wearied from the journey, which had occupied two full weeks; he must prepare to meet the momentous events of the morrow, and he needed quiet and repose. But so great was the desire to see him that he had enjoyed only a few hours' rest when noblemen, knights, priests, and citizens gathered eagerly about him. Among these were many of the nobles who had so boldly demanded of the emperor a reform of ecclesiastical abuses and who, says Luther, "had all been freed by my gospel."—Martyn, page 393. Enemies, as well as friends, came to look upon the dauntless monk; but he received them with unshaken calmness, replying to all with dignity and wisdom. His bearing was firm and courageous. His pale, thin face, marked with the traces of toil and illness, wore a kindly and even joyous expression. The solemnity and deep earnestness of his words gave him a power that even his enemies could not wholly withstand. Both friends and foes were filled with wonder. Some were convinced that a divine influence attended him; others declared, as had the Pharisees concerning Christ: "He hath a devil."

On the following day Luther was summoned to attend the Diet. An imperial officer was appointed to conduct him to the hall of audience; yet it was with difficulty that he reached the place. Every avenue was crowded with spectators eager to look upon the monk who had dared resist the authority of the pope.

As he was about to enter the presence of his judges, an old general, the hero of many battles, said to him kindly: "Poor monk, poor monk, thou art now going to make a nobler stand than I or any other captains have ever made in the bloodiest of our battles. But if thy cause is just, and thou art sure of it, go forward in God's name, and fear nothing. God will not forsake thee."—D'Aubigné, b. 7, ch. 8.

At length Luther stood before the council. The emperor occupied the throne. He was surrounded by the most illustrious personages in the empire. Never had any man appeared in the presence of a more imposing assembly than that before which Martin Luther was to answer for his faith. "This appearance was of itself a signal victory over the papacy. The pope had condemned the man, and he was now standing before a tribunal which, by this very act, set itself above the pope. The pope had laid him under an interdict, and cut him off from all human society; and yet he was summoned in respectful language, and received before the most august assembly in the world. The pope had condemned him to perpetual silence, and he was now about to speak before thousands of attentive hearers drawn together from the farthest parts of Christendom. An immense revolution had thus been effected by Luther's instrumentality. Rome was already descending from her throne, and it was the voice of a monk that caused this humiliation."—Ibid., b. 7, ch. 8.

In the presence of that powerful and titled assembly the lowly born Reformer seemed awed and embarrassed. Several of the princes, observing his emotion, approached him, and one of them whispered: "Fear not them which kill the body, but are not able to kill the soul." Another said: "When ye shall be brought before governors and kings for My sake, it shall be given you, by the Spirit of your Father, what ye shall say." Thus the words of Christ were brought by the world's great men to strengthen His servant in the hour of trial.

Luther was conducted to a position directly in front of the emperor's throne. A deep silence fell upon the crowded assembly. Then an imperial officer arose and, pointing to a collection of Luther's writings, demanded that the Reformer answer two questions—whether he acknowledged them as his, and whether he proposed to retract the opinions which he had therein advanced. The titles of the books having been read, Luther replied that as to the first question, he acknowledged the books to be his. "As to the second," he said, "seeing that it is a question which concerns faith and the salvation of souls, and in which the word of God, the greatest and most precious treasure either in heaven or earth, is involved, I should act imprudently were I to reply without reflection. I might affirm less than the circumstance demands, or more than truth requires, and so sin against this saying of Christ: 'Whosoever shall deny Me before men, him will I also deny before My Father which is in heaven.' [Matthew 10:33.] For this reason I entreat your imperial majesty, with all humility, to allow me time, that I may answer without offending against the word of God."—D'Aubigné, b. 7, ch. 8.

In making this request, Luther moved wisely. His course convinced the assembly that he did not act from passion or impulse. Such calmness and self-command, unexpected in one who had shown himself bold and uncompromising, added to his power, and enabled him afterward to answer with a prudence, decision, wisdom, and dignity that surprised and disappointed his adversaries, and rebuked their insolence and pride.

The next day he was to appear to render his final answer. For a time his heart sank within him as he contemplated the forces that were combined against the truth. His faith faltered; fearfulness and trembling came upon him, and horror overwhelmed him. Dangers multiplied before him; his enemies seemed about to triumph, and the powers of darkness to prevail. Clouds gathered about him and seemed to separate him from God. He longed for the assurance that the Lord of hosts would be with him. In anguish of spirit he threw himself with his face upon the earth and poured out those broken, heart-rending cries, which none but God can fully understand.

"O almighty and everlasting God," he pleaded, "how terrible is this world! Behold, it openeth its mouth to swallow me up, and I have so little trust in Thee. . . . If it is only in the strength of this world that I must put my trust, all is over. . . . My last hour is come, my condemnation has been pronounced. . . . O God, do Thou help me against all the wisdom of the world. Do this, . . . Thou alone; . . . for this is not my work, but Thine. I have nothing to do here, nothing to contend for with these great ones of the world. . . . But the cause is Thine, . . . and it is a righteous and eternal cause. O Lord, help me! Faithful and unchangeable God, in no man do I place my trust. . . . All that is of man is uncertain; all that cometh of man fails. . . . Thou hast chosen me for this work. . . . Stand at my side, for the sake of Thy well-beloved Jesus Christ, who is my defense, my shield, and my strong tower."—*Ibid.*, b. 7, ch. 8.

An all-wise Providence had permitted Luther to realize his peril, that he might not trust to his own strength and rush presumptuously into danger. Yet it was not the fear of personal suffering, a dread of torture or death, which seemed immediately impending, that overwhelmed him with its terror. He had come to the crisis, and he felt his insufficiency to meet it. Through his weakness the cause of truth might suffer loss. Not for his own safety, but for the triumph of the gospel did he wrestle with God. Like Israel's, in that night struggle beside the lonely stream, was the anguish and conflict of his soul. Like Israel, he prevailed with God. In his utter helplessness his faith fastened upon Christ, the mighty Deliverer. He was strengthened with the assurance that he would not appear alone before the council. Peace returned to his soul, and he rejoiced that he was permitted to uplift the word of God before the rulers of the nations.

With his mind stayed upon God, Luther prepared for the struggle before him. He thought upon the plan of his answer, examined passages in his own writings, and drew from the Holy Scriptures suitable proofs to sustain his positions. Then, laying his left hand on the Sacred Volume, which was open before him, he lifted his right hand to heaven and vowed "to remain faithful to the gospel, and freely to confess his faith, even should he seal his testimony with his blood."—*Ibid.*, b. 7, ch. 8.

When he was again ushered into the presence of the Diet, his countenance bore no trace of fear or embarrassment. Calm and peaceful, yet grandly brave and noble, he stood as God's witness among the great ones of the earth. The imperial officer now demanded his decision as to whether he desired to retract his doctrines. Luther made his answer in a subdued and humble tone, without violence or passion. His demeanor was diffident and respectful; yet he manifested a confidence and joy that surprised the assembly.

"Most serene emperor, illustrious princes, gracious lords," said Luther, "I appear before you this day, in conformity with the order given

126 [*157-158*]

me yesterday, and by God's mercies I conjure your majesty and your august highnesses to listen graciously to the defense of a cause which I am assured is just and true. If, through ignorance, I should transgress the usages and proprieties of courts, I entreat you to pardon me; for I was not brought up in the palaces of kings, but in the seclusion of a convent."—*Ibid.*, b. 7, ch. 8.

Then, proceeding to the question, he stated that his published works were not all of the same character. In some he had treated of faith and good works, and even his enemies declared them not only harmless but profitable. To retract these would be to condemn truths which all parties confessed. The second class consisted of writings exposing the corruptions and abuses of the papacy. To revoke these works would strengthen the tyranny of Rome and open a wider door to many and great impieties. In the third class of his books he had attacked individuals who had defended existing evils. Concerning these he freely confessed that he had been more violent than was becoming. He did not claim to be free from fault; but even these books he could not revoke, for such a course would embolden the enemies of truth, and they would then take occasion to crush God's people with still greater cruelty.

"Yet I am but a mere man, and not God," he continued; "I shall therefore defend myself as Christ did: 'If I have spoken evil, bear witness of the evil.' . . . By the mercy of God, I conjure you, most serene emperor, and you, most illustrious princes, and all men of every degree, to prove from the writings of the prophets and apostles that I have erred. As soon as I am convinced of this, I will retract every error, and be the first to lay hold of my books and throw them into the fire.

"What I have just said plainly shows, I hope, that I have carefully weighed and considered the dangers to which I expose myself; but far from being dismayed, I rejoice to see that the gospel is now, as in former times, a cause of trouble and dissension. This is the character, this is the destiny, of the word of God. 'I came not to send peace on earth, but a sword,' said Jesus Christ. God is wonderful and terrible in His counsels; beware lest, by presuming to quench dissensions, you should persecute the holy word of God, and draw down upon yourselves a frightful deluge of insurmountable dangers, of present disasters, and eternal desolation. . . . I might quote many examples from the oracles of God. I might speak of the Pharaohs, the kings of Babylon, and those of Israel, whose labors never more effectually contributed to their own destruction than when they sought by counsels, to all appearance most wise, to strengthen their dominion. 'God removeth mountains, and they know it not.' "—*Ibid.,* b. 7, ch. 8.

Luther had spoken in German; he was now requested to repeat the same words in Latin. Though exhausted by the previous effort, he complied, and again delivered his speech, with the same clearness and energy as at the first. God's providence directed in this matter. The minds of many of the princes were so blinded by error and superstition that at the first delivery they did not see the force of Luther's reasoning; but the repetition enabled them to perceive clearly the points presented.

Those who stubbornly closed their eyes to the light, and determined not to be convinced of the truth, were enraged at the power of Luther's words. As he ceased speaking, the spokesman of the Diet said angrily: "You have not answered the question put to you. . . . You are required to give a clear and precise answer. . . . Will you, or will you not, retract?"

The Reformer answered: "Since your most serene majesty and your high mightinesses require from me a clear, simple, and precise answer, I will give you one, and it is this: I cannot submit my faith either to the pope or to the councils, because it is clear as the day that they have frequently erred and contradicted each other. Unless therefore I am convinced by the testimony of Scripture or by the clearest reasoning, unless I am persuaded by means of the passages I have quoted, and unless they thus render my conscience bound by the word of God, *I cannot and I will not retract,* for it is unsafe for a Christian to speak against his conscience.

Here I stand, I can do no other; may God help me. Amen."—*Ibid.*, b. 7, ch. 8.

Thus stood this righteous man upon the sure foundation of the word of God. The light of heaven illuminated his countenance. His greatness and purity of character, his peace and joy of heart, were manifest to all as he testified against the power of error and witnessed to the superiority of that faith that overcomes the world.

The whole assembly were for a time speechless with amazement. At his first answer Luther had spoken in a low tone, with a respectful, almost submissive bearing. The Romanists had interpreted this as evidence that his courage was beginning to fail. They regarded the request for delay as merely the prelude to his recantation. Charles himself, noting, half contemptuously, the monk's worn frame, his plain attire, and the simplicity of his address, had declared: "This monk will never make a heretic of me." The courage and firmness which he now displayed, as well as the power and clearness of his reasoning, filled all parties with surprise. The emperor, moved to admiration, exclaimed: "This monk speaks with an intrepid heart and unshaken courage." Many of the German princes looked with pride and joy upon this representative of their nation.

The partisans of Rome had been worsted; their cause appeared in a most unfavorable light. They sought to maintain their power, not by appealing to the Scriptures, but by a resort to threats, Rome's unfailing argument. Said the spokesman of the Diet: "If you do not retract, the emperor and the states of the empire will consult what course to adopt against an incorrigible heretic."

Luther's friends, who had with great joy listened to his noble defense, trembled at these words; but the doctor himself said calmly: "May God be my helper, for I can retract nothing."—*Ibid.*, b. 7, ch. 8.

He was directed to withdraw from the Diet while the princes consulted together. It was felt that a great crisis had come. Luther's persistent refusal to submit might affect the history of the church for ages. It was decided to give him one more opportunity to retract. For the last time he was brought into the assembly. Again the question was put, whether he would renounce his doctrines. "I have no other reply to make," he said, "than that which I have already made." It was evident that he could not be induced, either by promises or threats, to yield to the mandate of Rome.

The papal leaders were chagrined that their power, which had caused kings and nobles to tremble, should be thus despised by a humble monk;

they longed to make him feel their wrath by torturing his life away. But Luther, understanding his danger, had spoken to all with Christian dignity and calmness. His words had been free from pride, passion, and misrepresentation. He had lost sight of himself, and the great men surrounding him, and felt only that he was in the presence of One infinitely superior to popes, prelates, kings, and emperors. Christ had spoken through Luther's testimony with a power and grandeur that for the time inspired both friends and foes with awe and wonder. The Spirit of God had been present in that council, impressing the hearts of the chiefs of the empire. Several of the princes boldly acknowledged the justice of Luther's cause. Many were convinced of the truth; but with some the impressions received were not lasting. There was another class who did not at the time express their convictions, but who, having searched the Scriptures for themselves, at a future time became fearless supporters of the Reformation.

The elector Frederick had looked forward anxiously to Luther's appearance before the Diet, and with deep emotion he listened to his speech. With joy and pride he witnessed the doctor's courage, firmness, and self-possession, and determined to stand more firmly in his defense. He contrasted the parties in contest, and saw that the wisdom of popes, kings, and prelates had been brought to nought by the power of truth. The papacy had sustained a defeat which would be felt among all nations and in all ages.

As the legate perceived the effect produced by Luther's speech, he feared, as never before, for the security of the Romish power, and resolved to employ every means at his command to effect the Reformer's overthrow. With all the eloquence and diplomatic skill for which he was so eminently distinguished, he represented to the youthful emperor the folly and danger of sacrificing, in the cause of an insignificant monk, the friendship and support of the powerful see of Rome.

His words were not without effect. On the day following Luther's answer, Charles caused a message to be presented to the Diet, announcing his determination to carry out the policy of his predecessors to maintain and protect the Catholic religion. Since Luther had refused to renounce his errors, the most vigorous measures should be employed against him and the heresies he taught. "A single monk, misled by his own folly, has risen against the faith of Christendom. To stay such impiety, I will sacrifice my kingdoms, my treasures, my friends, my body, my blood, my soul, and my life. I am about to dismiss the Augustine

Luther, forbidding him to cause the least disorder among the people; I shall then proceed against him and his adherents as contumacious heretics, by excommunication, by interdict, and by every means calculated to destroy them. I call on the members of the states to behave like faithful Christians."—*Ibid.*, b. 7, ch. 9. Nevertheless the emperor declared that Luther's safe-conduct must be respected, and that before proceedings against him could be instituted, he must be allowed to reach his home in safety.

Two conflicting opinions were now urged by the members of the Diet. The emissaries and representatives of the pope again demanded that the Reformer's safe-conduct should be disregarded. "The Rhine," they said, "should receive his ashes, as it had received those of John Huss a century ago."—*Ibid.*, b. 7, ch. 9. But princes of Germany, though themselves papists and avowed enemies to Luther, protested against such a breach of public faith, as a stain upon the honor of the nation. They pointed to the calamities which had followed the death of Huss, and declared that they dared not call down upon Germany, and upon the head of their youthful emperor, a repetition of those terrible evils.

Charles himself, in answer to the base proposal, said: "Though honor and faith should be banished from all the world, they ought to find a refuge in the hearts of princes."—*Ibid.*, b. 7, ch. 9. He was still further urged by the most bitter of Luther's papal enemies to deal with the Reformer as Sigismund had dealt with Huss—abandon him to the mercies of the church; but recalling the scene when Huss in public assembly had pointed to his chains and reminded the monarch of his plighted faith, Charles V declared: "I should not like to blush like Sigismund."—Lenfant, vol. 1, p. 422.

Yet Charles had deliberately rejected the truths presented by Luther. "I am firmly resolved to imitate the example of my ancestors," wrote the monarch.—D'Aubigné, b. 7, ch. 9. He had decided that he would not step out of the path of custom, even to walk in the ways of truth and righteousness. Because his fathers did, he would uphold the papacy, with all its cruelty and corruption. Thus he took his position, refusing to accept any light in advance of what his fathers had received, or to perform any duty that they had not performed.

There are many at the present day thus clinging to the customs and traditions of their fathers. When the Lord sends them additional light, they refuse to accept it, because, not having been granted to their fathers, it was not received by them. We are not placed where our fathers were;

consequently our duties and responsibilities are not the same as theirs. We shall not be approved of God in looking to the example of our fathers to determine our duty instead of searching the word of truth for ourselves. Our responsibility is greater than was that of our ancestors. We are accountable for the light which they received, and which was handed down as an inheritance for us, and we are accountable also for the additional light which is now shining upon us from the word of God.

Said Christ of the unbelieving Jews: "If I had not come and spoken unto them, they had not had sin: but now they have no cloak for their sin." John 15:22. The same divine power had spoken through Luther to the emperor and princes of Germany. And as the light shone forth from God's word, His Spirit pleaded for the last time with many in that assembly. As Pilate, centuries before, permitted pride and popularity to close his heart against the world's Redeemer; as the trembling Felix bade the messenger of truth, "Go thy way for this time; when I have a convenient season, I will call for thee;" as the proud Agrippa confessed, "Almost thou persuadest me to be a Christian" (Acts 24:25; 26:28), yet turned away from the Heaven-sent message—so had Charles V, yielding to the dictates of worldly pride and policy, decided to reject the light of truth.

Rumors of the designs against Luther were widely circulated, causing great excitement throughout the city. The Reformer had made many friends, who, knowing the treacherous cruelty of Rome toward all who dared expose her corruptions, resolved that he should not be sacrificed. Hundreds of nobles pledged themselves to protect him. Not a few openly denounced the royal message as evincing a weak submission to the controlling power of Rome. On the gates of houses and in public places, placards were posted, some condemning and others sustaining Luther. On one of these were written merely the significant words of the wise man: "Woe to thee, O land, when thy king is a child." Ecclesiastes 10:16. The popular enthusiasm in Luther's favor throughout all Germany convinced both the emperor and the Diet that any injustice shown him would endanger the peace of the empire and even the stability of the throne.

Frederick of Saxony maintained a studied reserve, carefully concealing his real feelings toward the Reformer, while at the same time he guarded him with tireless vigilance, watching all his movements and all those of his enemies. But there were many who made no attempt to conceal their sympathy with Luther. He was visited by princes, counts, barons, and other persons of distinction, both lay and ecclesiastical. "The doctor's little room," wrote Spalatin, "could not contain all the visitors who presented themselves."—Martyn, vol. 1, p. 404. The people gazed upon him as if he were more than human. Even those who had no faith in his doctrines could not but admire that lofty integrity which led him to brave death rather than violate his conscience.

Earnest efforts were made to obtain Luther's consent to a compromise with Rome. Nobles and princes represented to him that if he persisted in setting up his own judgment against that of the church and the councils he would soon be banished from the empire and would have no defense. To this appeal Luther answered: "The gospel of Christ cannot be preached without offense. . . . Why then should the fear or apprehension of danger separate me from the Lord, and from that divine word which alone is truth? No; I would rather give up my body, my blood, and my life."—D'Aubigné, b. 7, ch. 10.

Again he was urged to submit to the judgment of the emperor, and then he would have nothing to fear. "I consent," said he in reply, "with all my heart, that the emperor, the princes, and even the meanest Christian, should examine and judge my works; but on one condition, that they take the word of God for their standard. Men have nothing to do but to obey it. Do not offer violence to my conscience, which is bound and chained up with the Holy Scriptures."—*Ibid.*, b. 7, ch. 10.

To another appeal he said: "I consent to renounce my safe-conduct. I place my person and my life in the emperor's hands, but the word of God—never!"—*Ibid.*, b. 7, ch. 10. He stated his willingness to submit to the decision of a general council, but only on condition that the council be required to decide according to the Scriptures. "In what concerns the word of God and the faith," he added, "every Christian is as good a judge as the pope, though supported by a million councils, can be for him." —Martyn, vol. 1, p. 410. Both friends and foes were at last convinced that further effort for reconciliation would be useless.

Had the Reformer yielded a single point, Satan and his hosts would have gained the victory. But his unwavering firmness was the means of emancipating the church, and beginning a new and better era. The influence of this one man, who dared to think and act for himself in religious matters, was to affect the church and the world, not only in his own time, but in all future generations. His firmness and fidelity would strengthen all, to the close of time, who should pass through a similar experience. The power and majesty of God stood forth above the counsel of men, above the mighty power of Satan.

Luther was soon commanded by the authority of the emperor to return home, and he knew that this notice would be speedily followed by his condemnation. Threatening clouds overhung his path; but as he departed from Worms, his heart was filled with joy and praise. "The devil himself," said he, "guarded the pope's citadel; but Christ has made a wide breach in it, and Satan was constrained to confess that the Lord is mightier than he."—D'Aubigné, b. 7, ch. 11.

After his departure, still desirous that his firmness should not be mistaken for rebellion, Luther wrote to the emperor. "God, who is the searcher of hearts, is my witness," he said, "that I am ready most earnestly to obey your majesty, in honor or in dishonor, in life or in death, and with no exception save the word of God, by which man lives. In all the affairs of this present life, my fidelity shall be unshaken, for here to lose or to gain is of no consequence to salvation. But when eternal interests are concerned, God wills not that man should submit unto man. For such submission in spiritual matters is a real worship, and ought to be rendered solely to the Creator."—*Ibid.*, b. 7, ch. 11.

On the journey from Worms, Luther's reception was even more flattering than during his progress thither. Princely ecclesiastics welcomed the excommunicated monk, and civil rulers honored the man whom the emperor had denounced. He was urged to preach, and, notwithstanding the imperial prohibition, he again entered the pulpit. "I never pledged myself to chain up the word of God," he said, "nor will I."—Martyn, vol. 1, p. 420.

He had not been long absent from Worms, when the papists prevailed upon the emperor to issue an edict against him. In this decree Luther was denounced as "Satan himself under the form of a man and dressed in a monk's frock."—D'Aubigné, b. 7, ch. 11. It was commanded that as soon as his safe-conduct should expire, measures be taken to stop his work. All persons were forbidden to harbor him, to give him food or drink, or by word or act, in public or private, to aid or abet him. He was to be seized wherever he might be, and delivered to the authorities. His adherents also were to be imprisoned and their property confiscated. His writings were to be destroyed, and, finally, all who should dare to act contrary to this decree were included in its condemnation. The elector of Saxony and the princes most friendly to Luther had left Worms soon after his departure, and the emperor's decree received the sanction of the Diet. Now the Romanists were jubilant. They considered the fate of the Reformation sealed.

God had provided a way of escape for His servant in this hour of

Luther's friends, knowing that certain death awaited the Reformer, spirited him away to the safety of Wartburg.

peril. A vigilant eye had followed Luther's movements, and a true and noble heart had resolved upon his rescue. It was plain that Rome would be satisfied with nothing short of his death; only by concealment could he be preserved from the jaws of the lion. God gave wisdom to Frederick of Saxony to devise a plan for the Reformer's preservation. With the co-operation of true friends the elector's purpose was carried out, and Luther was effectually hidden from friends and foes. Upon his homeward journey he was seized, separated from his attendants, and hurriedly conveyed through the forest to the castle of Wartburg, an isolated mountain fortress. Both his seizure and his concealment were so involved in mystery that even Frederick himself for a long time knew not whither he had been conducted. This ignorance was not without design; so long as the elector knew nothing of Luther's whereabouts, he could reveal nothing. He satisfied himself that the Reformer was safe, and with this knowledge he was content.

Spring, summer, and autumn passed, and winter came, and Luther still remained a prisoner. Aleander and his partisans exulted as the light of the gospel seemed about to be extinguished. But instead of this, the Reformer was filling his lamp from the storehouse of truth; and its light was to shine forth with brighter radiance.

In the friendly security of the Wartburg, Luther for a time rejoiced in his release from the heat and turmoil of battle. But he could not long find satisfaction in quiet and repose. Accustomed to a life of activity and stern conflict, he could ill endure to remain inactive. In those solitary days the condition of the church rose up before him, and he cried in despair: "Alas! there is no one in this latter day of His anger, to stand like a wall before the Lord, and save Israel!"—*Ibid.*, b. 9, ch. 2. Again, his thoughts returned to himself, and he feared being charged with cowardice in withdrawing from the contest. Then he reproached himself for his indolence and self-indulgence. Yet at the same time he was daily accomplishing more than it seemed possible for one man to do. His pen was never idle. While his enemies flattered themselves that he was silenced, they were astonished and confused by tangible proof that he was still active. A host of tracts, issuing from his pen, circulated throughout Germany. He also performed a most important service for his countrymen by translating the New Testament into the German tongue. From his rocky Patmos he continued for nearly a whole year to proclaim the gospel and rebuke the sins and errors of the times.

But it was not merely to preserve Luther from the wrath of his enemies, nor even to afford him a season of quiet for these important labors, that God had withdrawn His servant from the stage of public life. There were results more precious than these to be secured. In the solitude and obscurity of his mountain retreat, Luther was removed from earthly supports and shut out from human praise. He was thus saved from the pride and self-confidence that are so often caused by success. By suffering and humiliation he was prepared again to walk safely upon the dizzy heights to which he had been so suddenly exalted.

As men rejoice in the freedom which the truth brings them, they are inclined to extol those whom God has employed to break the chains of error and superstition. Satan seeks to divert men's thoughts and affections from God, and to fix them upon human agencies; he leads them to honor the mere instrument and to ignore the Hand that directs all the events of providence. Too often religious leaders who are thus praised and reverenced lose sight of their dependence upon God and are led to trust in themselves. As a result they seek to control the minds and consciences of the people, who are disposed to look to them for guidance instead of looking to the word of God. The work of reform is often retarded because of this spirit indulged by its supporters. From this danger, God would guard the cause of the Reformation. He desired that work to receive, not the impress of man, but that of God. The eyes of men had been turned to Luther as the expounder of the truth; he was removed that all eyes might be directed to the eternal Author of truth.

chapter 9

Light Kindled in Switzerland

IN THE choice of instrumentalities for the reforming of the church, the same divine plan is seen as
in that for the planting of the church. The heavenly Teacher passed by
the great men of the earth, the titled and wealthy, who were accustomed
to receive praise and homage as leaders of the people. They were so proud
and self-confident in their boasted superiority that they could not be
molded to sympathize with their fellowmen and to become colaborers
with the humble Man of Nazareth. To the unlearned, toiling fishermen
of Galilee was the call addressed: "Follow Me, and I will make you fishers
of men." Matthew 4:19. These disciples were humble and teachable.
The less they had been influenced by the false teaching of their time, the
more successfully could Christ instruct and train them for His service.
So in the days of the Great Reformation. The leading Reformers were
men from humble life—men who were most free of any of their time
from pride of rank and from the influence of bigotry and priestcraft. It
is God's plan to employ humble instruments to accomplish great results.
Then the glory will not be given to men, but to Him who works through
them to will and to do of His own good pleasure.

A few weeks after the birth of Luther in a miner's cabin in Saxony,
Ulric Zwingli was born in a herdsman's cottage among the Alps. Zwingli's
surroundings in childhood, and his early training, were such as to prepare
him for his future mission. Reared amid scenes of natural grandeur,
beauty, and awful sublimity, his mind was early impressed with a sense
of the greatness, the power, and the majesty of God. The history of the

Zwingli's ministry at Zurich, illumi-
nating the truths of God's Word,
aroused the opposition of the monks.

brave deeds achieved upon his native mountains kindled his youthful aspirations. And at the side of his pious grandmother he listened to the few precious Bible stories which she had gleaned from amid the legends and traditions of the church. With eager interest he heard of the grand deeds of patriarchs and prophets, of the shepherds who watched their flocks on the hills of Palestine where angels talked with them, of the Babe of Bethlehem and the Man of Calvary.

Like John Luther, Zwingli's father desired an education for his son, and the boy was early sent from his native valley. His mind rapidly developed, and it soon became a question where to find teachers competent to instruct him. At the age of thirteen he went to Bern, which then possessed the most distinguished school in Switzerland. Here, however, a danger arose which threatened to blight the promise of his life. Determined efforts were put forth by the friars to allure him into a monastery. The Dominican and Franciscan monks were in rivalry for popular favor. This they endeavored to secure by the showy adornments of their churches, the pomp of their ceremonials, and the attractions of famous relics and miracle-working images.

The Dominicans of Bern saw that if they could win this talented young scholar, they would secure both gain and honor. His extreme youth, his natural ability as a speaker and writer, and his genius for music and poetry, would be more effective than all their pomp and display, in attracting the people to their services and increasing the revenues of their order. By deceit and flattery they endeavored to induce Zwingli to enter their convent. Luther, while a student at school, had buried himself in a convent cell, and he would have been lost to the world had not God's providence released him. Zwingli was not permitted to encounter the same peril. Providentially his father received information of the designs of the friars. He had no intention of allowing his son to follow the idle and worthless life of the monks. He saw that his future usefulness was at stake, and directed him to return home without delay.

The command was obeyed; but the youth could not be long content in his native valley, and he soon resumed his studies, repairing, after a time, to Basel. It was here that Zwingli first heard the gospel of God's free grace. Wittembach, a teacher of the ancient languages, had, while studying Greek and Hebrew, been led to the Holy Scriptures, and thus rays of divine light were shed into the minds of the students under his instruction. He declared that there was a truth more ancient, and of infinitely greater worth, than the theories taught by schoolmen and philosophers. This ancient truth was that the death of Christ is the sinner's only ransom. To Zwingli these words were as the first ray of light that precedes the dawn.

Zwingli was soon called from Basel to enter upon his lifework. His first field of labor was in an Alpine parish, not far distant from his native valley. Having received ordination as a priest, he "devoted himself with his whole soul to the search after divine truth; for he was well aware," says a fellow Reformer, "how much he must know to whom the flock of Christ is entrusted."—Wylie, b. 8, ch. 5. The more he searched the Scriptures, the clearer appeared the contrast between their truths and the heresies of Rome. He submitted himself to the Bible as the word of God, the only sufficient, infallible rule. He saw that it must be its own interpreter. He dared not attempt to explain Scripture to sustain a preconceived theory or doctrine, but held it his duty to learn what is its direct and obvious teaching. He sought to avail himself of every help to obtain a full and correct understanding of its meaning, and he invoked the aid of the Holy Spirit, which would, he declared, reveal it to all who sought it in sincerity and with prayer.

"The Scriptures," said Zwingli, "come from God, not from man, and even that God who enlightens will give thee to understand that the speech comes from God. The word of God . . . cannot fail; it is bright, it teaches itself, it discloses itself, it illumines the soul with all salvation and grace, comforts it in God, humbles it, so that it loses and even forfeits itself, and embraces God." The truth of these words Zwingli himself had proved. Speaking of his experience at this time, he afterward wrote: "When . . . I began to give myself wholly up to the Holy Scriptures, philosophy and theology (scholastic) would always keep suggesting quarrels to me. At last I came to this, that I thought, 'Thou must let all that lie, and learn the meaning of God purely out of His own simple word.' Then I began to ask God for His light, and the Scriptures began to be much easier to me."—*Ibid.*, b. 8, ch. 6.

The doctrine preached by Zwingli was not received from Luther. It was the doctrine of Christ. "If Luther preaches Christ," said the Swiss Reformer, "he does what I am doing. Those whom he has brought to Christ are more numerous than those whom I have led. But this matters not. I will bear no other name than that of Christ, whose soldier I am, and who alone is my Chief. Never has one single word been written by me to Luther, nor by Luther to me. And why? . . . That it might be shown how much the Spirit of God is in unison with itself, since both of us,

without any collusion, teach the doctrine of Christ with such uniformity."
—D'Aubigné, b. 8, ch. 9.

In 1516 Zwingli was invited to become a preacher in the convent at Einsiedeln. Here he was to have a closer view of the corruptions of Rome and was to exert an influence as a Reformer that would be felt far beyond his native Alps. Among the chief attractions of Einsiedeln was an image of the Virgin which was said to have the power of working miracles. Above the gateway of the convent was the inscription, "Here a plenary remission of sins may be obtained."—*Ibid.*, b. 8, ch. 5. Pilgrims at all seasons resorted to the shrine of the Virgin; but at the great yearly festival of its consecration multitudes came from all parts of Switzerland, and even from France and Germany. Zwingli, greatly afflicted at the sight, seized the opportunity to proclaim liberty through the gospel to these bondslaves of superstition.

"Do not imagine," he said, "that God is in this temple more than in any other part of creation. Whatever be the country in which you dwell, God is around you, and hears you. . . . Can unprofitable works, long pilgrimages, offerings, images, the invocation of the Virgin or of the saints, secure for you the grace of God? . . . What avails the multitude of words with which we embody our prayers? What efficacy has a glossy cowl, a smooth-shorn head, a long and flowing robe, or gold-embroidered slippers? . . . God looks at the heart, and our hearts are far from Him." "Christ," he said, "who was once offered upon the cross, is the sacrifice and victim, that had made satisfaction for the sins of believers to all eternity."—*Ibid.*, b. 8, ch. 5.

To many listeners these teachings were unwelcome. It was a bitter disappointment to them to be told that their toilsome journey had been made in vain. The pardon freely offered to them through Christ they could not comprehend. They were satisfied with the old way to heaven which Rome had marked out for them. They shrank from the perplexity of searching for anything better. It was easier to trust their salvation to the priests and the pope than to seek for purity of heart.

But another class received with gladness the tidings of redemption through Christ. The observances enjoined by Rome had failed to bring peace of soul, and in faith they accepted the Saviour's blood as their propitiation. These returned to their homes to reveal to others the precious light which they had received. The truth was thus carried from hamlet to hamlet, from town to town, and the number of pilgrims to the Virgin's shrine greatly lessened. There was a falling off in the offerings, and consequently in the salary of Zwingli, which was drawn from them. But this caused him only joy as he saw that the power of fanaticism and superstition was being broken.

The authorities of the church were not blind to the work which Zwingli was accomplishing; but for the present they forbore to interfere. Hoping yet to secure him to their cause, they endeavored to win him by flatteries; and meanwhile the truth was gaining a hold upon the hearts of the people.

Zwingli's labors at Einsiedeln had prepared him for a wider field, and this he was soon to enter. After three years here he was called to the office of preacher in the cathedral at Zurich. This was then the most important town of the Swiss confederacy, and the influence exerted here would be widely felt. The ecclesiastics by whose invitation he came to Zurich were, however, desirous of preventing any innovations, and they accordingly proceeded to instruct him as to his duties.

"You will make every exertion," they said, "to collect the revenues of the chapter, without overlooking the least. You will exhort the faithful, both from the pulpit and in the confessional, to pay all tithes and dues, and to show by their offerings their affection to the church. You will be diligent in increasing the income arising from the sick, from masses, and in general from every ecclesiastical ordinance." "As for the administration of the sacraments, the preaching, and the care of the flock," added his instructors, "these are also the duties of the chaplain. But for these you may employ a substitute, and particularly in preaching. You should administer the sacraments to none but persons of note, and only when called upon; you are forbidden to do so without distinction of persons." —*Ibid.*, b. 8, ch. 6.

Zwingli listened in silence to this charge, and in reply, after expressing his gratitude for the honor of a call to this important station, he proceeded to explain the course which he proposed to adopt. "The life of Christ," he said, "has been too long hidden from the people. I shall preach upon the whole of the Gospel of St. Matthew, . . . drawing solely from the fountains of Scripture, sounding its depths, comparing one passage with another, and seeking for understanding by constant and earnest prayer. It is to God's glory, to the praise of His only Son, to the real salvation of souls, and to their edification in the true faith, that I shall consecrate my ministry."—*Ibid.*, b. 8, ch. 6. Though some of the ecclesiastics disapproved his plan, and endeavored to dissuade him from it, Zwingli remained steadfast. He declared that he was about to introduce no new method, but the old method employed by the church in earlier and purer times.

Already an interest had been awakened in the truths he taught; and the people flocked in great numbers to listen to his preaching. Many who had long since ceased to attend service were among his hearers. He began his ministry by opening the Gospels and reading and explaining to his hearers the inspired narrative of the life, teachings, and death of Christ. Here, as at Einsiedeln, he presented the word of God as the only infallible authority and the death of Christ as the only complete sacrifice. "It is to Christ," he said, "that I desire to lead you—to Christ, the true source of salvation."—*Ibid.*, b. 8, ch. 6. Around the preacher crowded the people of all classes, from statesmen and scholars to the artisan and the peasant. With deep interest they listened to his words. He not only proclaimed the offer of a free salvation, but fearlessly rebuked the evils and corruptions of the times. Many returned from the cathedral praising God. "This man," they said, "is a preacher of the truth. He will be our Moses, to lead us forth from this Egyptian darkness." —*Ibid.*, b. 8, ch. 6.

But though at first his labors were received with great enthusiasm, after a time opposition arose. The monks set themselves to hinder his work and condemn his teachings. Many assailed him with gibes and sneers; others resorted to insolence and threats. But Zwingli bore all with patience, saying: "If we desire to gain over the wicked to Jesus Christ, we must shut our eyes against many things."—*Ibid.*, b. 8, ch. 6.

About this time a new agency came in to advance the work of reform. One Lucian was sent to Zurich with some of Luther's writings, by a friend of the reformed faith at Basel, who suggested that the sale of these books might be a powerful means of scattering the light. "Ascertain," he wrote to Zwingli, "whether this man possesses sufficient prudence and skill; if so, let him carry from city to city, from town to town, from village to village, and even from house to house, among the Swiss, the works of Luther, and especially his exposition of the Lord's Prayer written for the laity. The more they are known, the more purchasers they will find."—*Ibid.*, b. 8, ch. 6. Thus the light found entrance.

At the time when God is preparing to break the shackles of ignorance and superstition, then it is that Satan works with greatest power to enshroud men in darkness and to bind their fetters still more firmly. As men were rising up in different lands to present to the people forgiveness and justification through the blood of Christ, Rome proceeded with renewed energy to open her market throughout Christendom, offering pardon for money.

Every sin had its price, and men were granted free license for crime if the treasury of the church was kept well filled. Thus the two movements advanced—one offering forgiveness of sin for money, the other forgiveness through Christ—Rome licensing sin and making it her source of revenue; the Reformers condemning sin and pointing to Christ as the propitiation and deliverer.

In Germany the sale of indulgences had been committed to the Dominican friars and was conducted by the infamous Tetzel. In Switzerland the traffic was put into the hands of the Franciscans, under the control of Samson, an Italian monk. Samson had already done good service to the church, having secured immense sums from Germany and Switzerland to fill the papal treasury. Now he traversed Switzerland, attracting great crowds, despoiling the poor peasants of their scanty earnings, and exacting rich gifts from the wealthy classes. But the influence of the reform already made itself felt in curtailing, though it could not stop, the traffic. Zwingli was still at Einsiedeln when Samson, soon after entering Switzerland, arrived with his wares at a neighboring town. Being apprised of his mission, the Reformer immediately set out to oppose him. The two did not meet, but such was Zwingli's success in exposing the friar's pretensions that he was obliged to leave for other quarters.

At Zurich, Zwingli preached zealously against the pardon-mongers; and when Samson approached the place, he was met by a messenger from the council with an intimation that he was expected to pass on. He finally secured an entrance by stratagem, but was sent away without the sale of a single pardon, and he soon after left Switzerland.

A strong impetus was given to the reform by the appearance of the plague, or Great Death, which swept over Switzerland in the year 1519. As men were thus brought face to face with the destroyer, many were led to feel how vain and worthless were the pardons which they had so lately purchased; and they longed for a surer foundation for their faith. Zwingli at Zurich was smitten down; he was brought so low that all hope of his recovery was relinquished, and the report was widely circulated that he was dead. In that trying hour his hope and courage were unshaken. He looked in faith to the cross of Calvary, trusting in the all-sufficient propitiation for sin. When he came back from the gates of death, it was to preach the gospel with greater fervor than ever before; and his words exerted an unwonted power. The people welcomed with joy their beloved pastor, returned to them from the brink of the grave. They themselves had come from attending upon the sick and the dying, and they felt, as never before, the value of the gospel.

Zwingli had arrived at a clearer understanding of its truths, and had more fully experienced in himself its renewing power. The fall of man and the plan of redemption were the subjects upon which he dwelt. "In Adam," he said, "we are all dead, sunk in corruption and condemnation." —Wylie, b. 8, ch. 9. "Christ . . . has purchased for us a never-ending redemption. . . . His passion is . . . an eternal sacrifice, and everlastingly effectual to heal; it satisfies the divine justice forever in behalf of all those who rely upon it with firm and unshaken faith." Yet he clearly taught that men are not, because of the grace of Christ, free to continue in sin. "Wherever there is faith in God, there God is; and wherever God abideth, there a zeal exists urging and impelling men to good works."—D'Aubigné, b. 8, ch. 9.

Such was the interest in Zwingli's preaching that the cathedral was filled to overflowing with the crowds that came to listen to him. Little by little, as they could bear it, he opened the truth to his hearers. He was careful not to introduce, at first, points which would startle them and create prejudice. His work was to win their hearts to the teachings of Christ, to soften them by His love, and keep before them His example; and as they should receive the principles of the gospel, their superstitious beliefs and practices would inevitably be overthrown.

Step by step the Reformation advanced in Zurich. In alarm its enemies aroused to active opposition. One year before, the monk of Wittenberg had uttered his No to the pope and the emperor at Worms, and now everything seemed to indicate a similar withstanding of the papal claims at Zurich. Repeated attacks were made upon Zwingli. In the papal cantons, from time to time, disciples of the gospel were brought to the stake, but this was not enough; the teacher of heresy must be silenced. Accordingly the bishop of Constance dispatched three deputies to the Council of Zurich, accusing Zwingli of teaching the people to transgress the laws of the church, thus endangering the peace and good order of society. If the authority of the church were to be set aside, he urged, universal anarchy would result. Zwingli replied that he had been for four years teaching the gospel in Zurich, "which was more quiet and peaceful than any other town in the confederacy." "Is not, then," he said, "Christianity the best safeguard of the general security?"—Wylie, b. 8, ch. 11.

The deputies had admonished the councilors to continue in the church, out of which, they declared, there was no salvation. Zwingli responded: "Let not this accusation move you. The foundation of the church is the same Rock, the same Christ, that gave Peter his name because he confessed Him faithfully. In every nation whosoever believes with all his heart in the Lord Jesus is accepted of God. Here, truly, is the church, out of which no one can be saved."—D'Aubigné, London ed., b. 8, ch. 11. As a result of the conference, one of the bishop's deputies accepted the reformed faith.

The council declined to take action against Zwingli, and Rome prepared for a fresh attack. The Reformer, when apprised of the plots of his enemies, exclaimed: "Let them come on; I fear them as the beetling cliff fears the waves that thunder at its feet."—Wylie, b. 8, ch. 11. The efforts of the ecclesiastics only furthered the cause which they sought to overthrow. The truth continued to spread. In Germany its adherents, cast down by Luther's disappearance, took heart again, as they saw the progress of the gospel in Switzerland.

As the Reformation became established in Zurich, its fruits were more fully seen in the suppression of vice and the promotion of order and harmony. "Peace has her habitation in our town," wrote Zwingli; "no quarrel, no hypocrisy, no envy, no strife. Whence can such union come but from the Lord, and our doctrine, which fills us with the fruits of peace and piety?"—*Ibid.*, b. 8, ch. 15.

The victories gained by the Reformation stirred the Romanists to still more determined efforts for its overthrow. Seeing how little had been accomplished by persecution in suppressing Luther's work in Germany, they decided to meet the reform with its own weapons. They would hold a disputation with Zwingli, and having the arrangement of matters, they would make sure of victory by choosing, themselves, not only the place of the combat, but the judges that should decide between the disputants. And if they could once get Zwingli into their power, they would take care that he did not escape them. The leader silenced, the movement could speedily be crushed. This purpose, however, was carefully concealed.

The disputation was appointed to be held at Baden; but Zwingli was not present. The Council of Zurich, suspecting the designs of the papists, and warned by the burning piles kindled in the papal cantons for confessors of the gospel, forbade their pastor to expose himself to this peril. At Zurich he was ready to meet all the partisans that Rome might send; but to go to Baden, where the blood of martyrs for the truth had just been shed, was to go to certain death. Oecolampadius and Haller were chosen to represent the Reformers, while the famous Dr. Eck, supported by a host of learned doctors and prelates, was the champion of Rome.

Though Zwingli was not present at the conference, his influence was felt. The secretaries were all chosen by the papists, and others were forbidden to take notes, on pain of death. Notwithstanding this, Zwingli received daily a faithful account of what was said at Baden. A student in attendance at the disputation made a record each evening of the arguments that day presented. These papers two other students undertook to deliver, with the daily letters of Oecolampadius, to Zwingli at Zurich. The Reformer answered, giving counsel and suggestions. His letters were written by night, and the students returned with them to Baden in the morning. To elude the vigilance of the guard stationed at the city gates, these messengers brought baskets of poultry on their heads, and they were permitted to pass without hindrance.

Thus Zwingli maintained the battle with his wily antagonists. He "has labored more," said Myconius, "by his meditations, his sleepless nights, and the advice which he transmitted to Baden, than he would have done by discussing in person in the midst of his enemies."—D'Aubigné, b. 11, ch. 13.

The Romanists, flushed with anticipated triumph, had come to Baden attired in their richest robes and glittering with jewels. They fared luxuriously, their tables spread with the most costly delicacies and the choicest wines. The burden of their ecclesiastical duties was lightened by gaiety and reveling. In marked contrast appeared the Reformers, who were looked upon by the people as little better than a company of beggars, and whose frugal fare kept them but short time at table. Oecolampadius's landlord, taking occasion to watch him in his room, found him always engaged in study or at prayer, and greatly wondering, reported that the heretic was at least "very pious."

At the conference, "Eck haughtily ascended a pulpit splendidly decorated, while the humble Oecolampadius, meanly clothed, was forced to take his seat in front of his opponent on a rudely carved stool."—*Ibid.*, b. 11, ch. 13. Eck's stentorian voice and unbounded assurance never failed him. His zeal was stimulated by the hope of gold as well as fame; for the defender of the faith was to be rewarded by a handsome fee. When better arguments failed, he had resort to insults, and even to oaths.

Oecolampadius, modest and self-distrustful, had shrunk from the combat, and he entered upon it with the solemn avowal: "I acknowledge no other standard of judgment than the word of God."—*Ibid.*, b. 11, ch. 13. Though gentle and courteous in demeanor, he proved himself able and unflinching. While the Romanists, according to their wont, appealed for authority to the customs of the church, the Reformer adhered steadfastly to the Holy Scriptures. "Custom," he said, "has no force in our Switzerland, unless it be according to the constitution; now, in matters of faith, the Bible is our constitution."—*Ibid.*, b. 11, ch. 13.

The contrast between the two disputants was not without effect. The calm, clear reasoning of the Reformer, so gently and modestly presented, appealed to minds that turned in disgust from Eck's boastful and boisterous assumptions.

The discussion continued eighteen days. At its close the papists with great confidence claimed the victory. Most of the deputies sided with Rome, and the Diet pronounced the Reformers vanquished and declared that they, together with Zwingli, their leader, were cut off from the church. But the fruits of the conference revealed on which side the advantage lay. The contest resulted in a strong impetus to the Protestant cause, and it was not long afterward that the important cities of Bern and Basel declared for the Reformation.

chapter 10

Progress in Spite of Difficulty

LUTHER'S mysterious disappearance excited consternation throughout all Germany. Inquiries concerning him were heard everywhere. The wildest rumors were circulated, and many believed that he had been murdered. There was great
lamentation, not only by his avowed friends, but by thousands who had
not openly taken their stand with the Reformation. Many bound themselves by a solemn oath to avenge his death.

The Romish leaders saw with terror to what a pitch had risen the
feeling against them. Though at first exultant at the supposed death of
Luther, they soon desired to hide from the wrath of the people. His
enemies had not been so troubled by his most daring acts while among
them as they were at his removal. Those who in their rage had sought
to destroy the bold Reformer were filled with fear now that he had
become a helpless captive. "The only remaining way of saving ourselves,"
said one, "is to light torches, and hunt for Luther through the whole
world, to restore him to the nation that is calling for him."—D'Aubigné,
b. 9, ch. 1. The edict of the emperor seemed to fall powerless. The papal
legates were filled with indignation as they saw that it commanded far
less attention than did the fate of Luther.

The tidings that he was safe, though a prisoner, calmed the fears of
the people, while it still further aroused their enthusiasm in his favor.
His writings were read with greater eagerness than ever before. Increasing numbers joined the cause of the heroic man who had, at such fearful
odds, defended the word of God. The Reformation was constantly gaining in strength. The seed which Luther had sown sprang up everywhere.

Enemies of the Lutheran Reformation
in Germany employed the most stringent measure against its adherents.

[*185-186*] 151

© P.P.P.A. JOHN STEEL, ARTIST

His absence accomplished a work which his presence would have failed to do. Other laborers felt a new responsibility, now that their great leader was removed. With new faith and earnestness they pressed forward to do all in their power, that the work so nobly begun might not be hindered.

But Satan was not idle. He now attempted what he has attempted in every other reformatory movement—to deceive and destroy the people by palming off upon them a counterfeit in place of the true work. As there were false christs in the first century of the Christian church, so there arose false prophets in the sixteenth century.

A few men, deeply affected by the excitement in the religious world, imagined themselves to have received special revelations from Heaven, and claimed to have been divinely commissioned to carry forward to its completion the Reformation which, they declared, had been but feebly begun by Luther. In truth, they were undoing the very work which he had accomplished. They rejected the great principle which was the very foundation of the Reformation—that the word of God is the all-sufficient rule of faith and practice; and for that unerring guide they substituted the changeable, uncertain standard of their own feelings and impressions. By this act of setting aside the great detector of error and falsehood the way was opened for Satan to control minds as best pleased himself.

One of these prophets claimed to have been instructed by the angel Gabriel. A student who united with him forsook his studies, declaring that he had been endowed by God Himself with wisdom to expound His word. Others who were naturally inclined to fanaticism united with them. The proceedings of these enthusiasts created no little excitement. The preaching of Luther had aroused the people everywhere to feel the necessity of reform, and now some really honest persons were misled by the pretensions of the new prophets.

The leaders of the movement proceeded to Wittenberg and urged their claims upon Melanchthon and his colaborers. Said they: "We are sent by God to instruct the people. We have held familiar conversations with the Lord; we know what will happen; in a word, we are apostles and prophets, and appeal to Dr. Luther."—*Ibid.*, b. 9, ch. 7.

The Reformers were astonished and perplexed. This was such an element as they had never before encountered, and they knew not what course to pursue. Said Melanchthon: "There are indeed extraordinary spirits in these men; but what spirits? . . . On the one hand, let us beware of quenching the Spirit of God, and on the other, of being led astray by the spirit of Satan."—*Ibid.*, b. 9, ch. 7.

The fruit of the new teaching soon became apparent. The people were led to neglect the Bible or to cast it wholly aside. The schools were thrown into confusion. Students, spurning all restraint, abandoned their studies and withdrew from the university. The men who thought themselves competent to revive and control the work of the Reformation succeeded only in bringing it to the verge of ruin. The Romanists now regained their confidence and exclaimed exultingly: "One last struggle, and all will be ours."—*Ibid.*, b. 9, ch. 7.

Luther at the Wartburg, hearing of what had occurred, said with deep concern: "I always expected that Satan would send us this plague." —*Ibid.*, b. 9, ch. 7. He perceived the true character of those pretended prophets and saw the danger that threatened the cause of truth. The opposition of the pope and the emperor had not caused him so great perplexity and distress as he now experienced. From the professed friends of the Reformation had risen its worst enemies. The very truths which had brought him so great joy and consolation were being employed to stir up strife and create confusion in the church.

In the work of reform, Luther had been urged forward by the Spirit of God, and had been carried beyond himself. He had not purposed to take such positions as he did, or to make so radical changes. He had been but the instrument in the hand of Infinite Power. Yet he often trembled for the result of his work. He had once said: "If I knew that my doctrine injured one man, one single man, however lowly and obscure,—which it cannot, for it is the gospel itself,—I would rather die ten times than not retract it."—*Ibid.*, b. 9, ch. 7.

And now Wittenberg itself, the very center of the Reformation, was fast falling under the power of fanaticism and lawlessness. This terrible condition had not resulted from the teachings of Luther; but throughout Germany his enemies were charging it upon him. In bitterness of soul he sometimes asked: "Can such, then, be the end of this great work of the Reformation?"—*Ibid.*, b. 9, ch. 7. Again, as he wrestled with God in prayer, peace flowed into his heart. "The work is not mine, but Thine own," he said; "Thou wilt not suffer it to be corrupted by superstition or fanaticism." But the thought of remaining longer from the conflict in such a crisis, became insupportable. He determined to return to Wittenberg.

Without delay he set out on his perilous journey. He was under the ban of the empire. Enemies were at liberty to take his life; friends were forbidden to aid or shelter him. The imperial government was adopting the most stringent measures against his adherents. But he saw that the work of the gospel was imperiled, and in the name of the Lord he went out fearlessly to battle for the truth.

In a letter to the elector, after stating his purpose to leave the Wartburg, Luther said: "Be it known to your highness that I am going to Wittenberg under a protection far higher than that of princes and electors. I think not of soliciting your highness's support, and far from desiring your protection, I would rather protect you myself. If I knew that your highness could or would protect me, I would not go to Wittenberg at all. There is no sword that can further this cause. God alone must do everything, without the help or concurrence of man. He who has the greatest faith is he who is most able to protect."—*Ibid.*, b. 9, ch. 8.

In a second letter, written on the way to Wittenberg, Luther added: "I am ready to incur the displeasure of your highness and the anger of the whole world. Are not the Wittenbergers my sheep? Has not God entrusted them to me? And ought I not, if necessary, to expose myself to death for their sakes? Besides, I fear to see a terrible outbreak in Germany, by which God will punish our nation."—*Ibid.*, b. 9, ch. 7.

With great caution and humility, yet with decision and firmness, he entered upon his work. "By the word," said he, "must we overthrow and destroy what has been set up by violence. I will not make use of force against the superstitious and unbelieving. . . . No one must be constrained. Liberty is the very essence of faith."—*Ibid.*, b. 9, ch. 8.

It was soon noised through Wittenberg that Luther had returned and that he was to preach. The people flocked from all directions, and the church was filled to overflowing. Ascending the pulpit, he with great wisdom and gentleness instructed, exhorted, and reproved. Touching the course of some who had resorted to violent measures in abolishing the mass, he said:

"The mass is a bad thing; God is opposed to it; it ought to be abolished; and I would that throughout the whole world it were replaced by the supper of the gospel. But let no one be torn from it by force. We must leave the matter in God's hands. His word must act, and not we. And why so? you will ask. Because I do not hold men's hearts in my hand, as the potter holds the clay. We have a right to speak: we have *not* the right to act. Let us preach; the rest belongs unto God. Were I to employ force, what should I gain? Grimace, formality, apings, human ordinances, and hypocrisy. . . . But there would be no sincerity of heart, nor faith, nor charity. Where these three are wanting, all is wanting, and I would not give a pear stalk for such a result. . . . God does more by His word alone than you and I and all the world by our united strength. God lays hold upon the heart; and when the heart is taken, all is won. . . .

"I will preach, discuss, and write; but I will constrain none, for faith is a voluntary act. See what I have done. I stood up against the pope, indulgences, and papists, but without violence or tumult. I put forward God's word; I preached and wrote—this was all I did. And yet while I was asleep, . . . the word that I had preached overthrew popery, so that neither prince nor emperor has done it so much harm. And yet I did nothing; the word alone did all. If I had wished to appeal to force, the whole of Germany would perhaps have been deluged with blood. But what would have been the result? Ruin and desolation both to body and soul. I therefore kept quiet, and left the word to run through the world alone."—*Ibid.*, b. 9, ch. 8.

Day after day, for a whole week, Luther continued to preach to eager crowds. The word of God broke the spell of fanatical excitement. The power of the gospel brought back the misguided people into the way of truth.

Luther had no desire to encounter the fanatics whose course had been productive of so great evil. He knew them to be men of unsound judgment and undisciplined passions, who, while claiming to be specially illuminated from heaven, would not endure the slightest contradiction or even the kindest reproof or counsel. Arrogating to themselves supreme authority, they required everyone, without a question, to acknowledge their claims. But, as they demanded an interview with him, he consented to meet them; and so successfully did he expose their pretensions that the impostors at once departed from Wittenberg.

The fanaticism was checked for a time; but several years later it broke out with greater violence and more terrible results. Said Luther, concerning the leaders in this movement: "To them the Holy Scriptures were but a dead letter, and they all began to cry, 'The Spirit! the Spirit!' But most assuredly I will not follow where their spirit leads them. May God of His mercy preserve me from a church in which there are none but saints. I desire to dwell with the humble, the feeble, the sick, who know and feel their sins, and who groan and cry continually to God from the bottom of their hearts to obtain His consolation and support."—*Ibid.*, b. 10, ch. 10.

Thomas Münzer, the most active of the fanatics, was a man of considerable ability, which, rightly directed, would have enabled him to do good; but he had not learned the first principles of true religion. "He was possessed with a desire of reforming the world, and forgot, as all enthusiasts do, that the reformation should begin with himself."—*Ibid.*, b. 9, ch. 8. He was ambitious to obtain position and influence, and was unwilling to be second, even to Luther. He declared that the Reformers, in substituting the authority of Scripture for that of the pope, were only establishing a different form of popery. He himself, he claimed, had been divinely commissioned to introduce the true reform. "He who possesses this spirit," said Münzer, "possesses the true faith, although he should never see the Scriptures in his life."—*Ibid.*, b. 10, ch. 10.

The fanatical teachers gave themselves up to be governed by impressions, regarding every thought and impulse as the voice of God; consequently they went to great extremes. Some even burned their Bibles, exclaiming: "The letter killeth, but the Spirit giveth life." Münzer's teaching appealed to men's desire for the marvelous, while it gratified their pride by virtually placing human ideas and opinions above the word of God. His doctrines were received by thousands. He soon denounced all order in public worship, and declared that to obey princes was to attempt to serve both God and Belial.

The minds of the people, already beginning to throw off the yoke of the papacy, were also becoming impatient under the restraints of civil authority. Münzer's revolutionary teachings, claiming divine sanction, led them to break away from all control and give the rein to their prejudices and passions. The most terrible scenes of sedition and strife followed, and the fields of Germany were drenched with blood.

The agony of soul which Luther had so long before experienced at Erfurt now pressed upon him with redoubled power as he saw the results of fanaticism charged upon the Reformation. The papist princes declared —and many were ready to credit the statement—that the rebellion was the legitimate fruit of Luther's doctrines. Although this charge was without the slightest foundation, it could not but cause the Reformer great distress. That the cause of truth should be thus disgraced by being ranked with the basest fanaticism, seemed more than he could endure. On the other hand, the leaders in the revolt hated Luther because he had not only opposed their doctrines and denied their claims to divine inspiration, but had pronounced them rebels against the civil authority. In retaliation they denounced him as a base pretender. He seemed to have brought upon himself the enmity of both princes and people.

The Romanists exulted, expecting to witness the speedy downfall of the Reformation; and they blamed Luther, even for the errors which he had been most earnestly endeavoring to correct. The fanatical party, by falsely claiming to have been treated with great injustice, succeeded in gaining the sympathies of a large class of the people, and, as is often the case with those who take the wrong side, they came to be regarded as martyrs. Thus the ones who were exerting every energy in opposition to the Reformation were pitied and lauded as the victims of cruelty and oppression. This was the work of Satan, prompted by the same spirit of rebellion which was first manifested in heaven.

Satan is constantly seeking to deceive men and lead them to call sin righteousness, and righteousness sin. How successful has been his work! How often censure and reproach are cast upon God's faithful servants because they will stand fearlessly in defense of the truth! Men who are but agents of Satan are praised and flattered, and even looked upon as martyrs, while those who should be respected and sustained for their fidelity to God, are left to stand alone, under suspicion and distrust.

Counterfeit holiness, spurious sanctification, is still doing its work of deception. Under various forms it exhibits the same spirit as in the days of Luther, diverting minds from the Scriptures and leading men to follow their own feelings and impressions rather than to yield obedience to the law of God. This is one of Satan's most successful devices to cast reproach upon purity and truth.

Fearlessly did Luther defend the gospel from the attacks which came from every quarter. The word of God proved itself a weapon mighty in every conflict. With that word he warred against the usurped authority of the pope, and the rationalistic philosophy of the schoolmen, while he stood firm as a rock against the fanaticism that sought to ally itself with the Reformation.

Each of these opposing elements was in its own way setting aside the Holy Scriptures and exalting human wisdom as the source of religious truth and knowledge. Rationalism idolizes reason and makes this the criterion for religion. Romanism, claiming for her sovereign pontiff an inspiration descended in unbroken line from the apostles, and unchangeable through all time, gives ample opportunity for every species of extravagance and corruption to be concealed under the sanctity of the apostolic commission. The inspiration claimed by Münzer and his associates proceeded from no higher source than the vagaries of the imagination, and its influence was subversive of all authority, human or divine. True Christianity receives the word of God as the great treasure house of inspired truth and the test of all inspiration.

Upon his return from the Wartburg, Luther completed his translation of the New Testament, and the gospel was soon after given to the people of Germany in their own language. This translation was received with great joy by all who loved the truth; but it was scornfully rejected by those who chose human traditions and the commandments of men.

The priests were alarmed at the thought that the common people would now be able to discuss with them the precepts of God's word, and that their own ignorance would thus be exposed. The weapons of their carnal reasoning were powerless against the sword of the Spirit. Rome summoned all her authority to prevent the circulation of the Scriptures; but decrees, anathemas, and tortures were alike in vain. The more she condemned and prohibited the Bible, the greater was the anxiety of the people to know what it really taught. All who could read were eager to study the word of God for themselves. They carried it about with them, and read and reread, and could not be satisfied until they had committed large portions to memory. Seeing the favor with which the New Testament was received, Luther immediately began the translation of the Old, and published it in parts as fast as completed.

Luther's writings were welcomed alike in city and in hamlet. "What Luther and his friends composed, others circulated. Monks, convinced of the unlawfulness of monastic obligations, desirous of exchanging a long life of slothfulness for one of active exertion, but too ignorant to proclaim the word of God, traveled through the provinces, visiting hamlets and cottages, where they sold the books of Luther and his friends. Germany soon swarmed with these bold colporteurs."—*Ibid.*, b. 9, ch. 11.

These writings were studied with deep interest by rich and poor, the learned and the ignorant. At night the teachers of the village schools read them aloud to little groups gathered at the fireside. With every effort some souls would be convicted of the truth and, receiving the word with gladness, would in their turn tell the good news to others.

The words of Inspiration were verified: "The entrance of Thy words giveth light; it giveth understanding unto the simple." Psalm 119:130. The study of the Scriptures was working a mighty change in the minds and hearts of the people. The papal rule had placed upon its subjects an iron yoke which held them in ignorance and degradation. A superstitious observance of forms had been scrupulously maintained; but in all their service the heart and intellect had had little part. The preaching of Luther, setting forth the plain truths of God's word, and then the word itself, placed in the hands of the common people, had aroused their dormant powers, not only purifying and ennobling the spiritual nature, but imparting new strength and vigor to the intellect.

Persons of all ranks were to be seen with the Bible in their hands, defending the doctrines of the Reformation. The papists who had left the study of the Scriptures to the priests and monks now called upon them to come forward and refute the new teachings. But, ignorant alike of the Scriptures and of the power of God, priests and friars were totally defeated by those whom they had denounced as unlearned and heretical. "Unhappily," said a Catholic writer, "Luther had persuaded his followers to put no faith in any other oracle than the Holy Scriptures."—D'Aubigné, b. 9, ch. 11. Crowds would gather to hear the truth advocated by men of little education, and even discussed by them with learned and eloquent theologians. The shameful ignorance of these great men was made apparent as their arguments were met by the simple teachings of God's word. Laborers, soldiers, women, and even children, were better acquainted with the Bible teachings than were the priests and learned doctors.

The contrast between the disciples of the gospel and the upholders of popish superstition was no less manifest in the ranks of scholars than among the common people. "Opposed to the old champions of the hierarchy, who had neglected the study of languages and the cultivation of literature, . . . were generous-minded youth, devoted to study, investigating Scripture, and familiarizing themselves with the masterpieces of antiquity. Possessing an active mind, an elevated soul, and intrepid heart, these young men soon acquired such knowledge that for a long period none could compete with them. . . . Accordingly, when these youthful defenders of the Reformation met the Romish doctors in any assembly, they attacked them with such ease and confidence that these ignorant men hesitated, became embarrassed, and fell into a contempt merited in the eyes of all."—*Ibid.*, b. 9, ch. 11.

As the Romish clergy saw their congregations diminishing, they invoked the aid of the magistrates, and by every means in their power endeavored to bring back their hearers. But the people had found in the new teachings that which supplied the wants of their souls, and they turned away from those who had so long fed them with the worthless husks of superstitious rites and human traditions.

When persecution was kindled against the teachers of the truth, they gave heed to the words of Christ: "When they persecute you in this city, flee ye into another." Matthew 10:23. The light penetrated everywhere. The fugitives would find somewhere a hospitable door opened to them, and there abiding, they would preach Christ, sometimes in the church, or, if denied that privilege, in private houses or in the open air. Wherever they could obtain a hearing was a consecrated temple. The truth, proclaimed with such energy and assurance, spread with irresistible power.

In vain both ecclesiastical and civil authorities were invoked to crush the heresy. In vain they resorted to imprisonment, torture, fire, and sword. Thousands of believers sealed their faith with their blood, and yet the work went on. Persecution served only to extend the truth, and the fanaticism which Satan endeavored to unite with it resulted in making more clear the contrast between the work of Satan and the work of God.

chapter 11

The Protest of the Princes

ONE of the noblest testimonies ever uttered for the Reformation was the Protest offered by the Christian princes of Germany at the Diet of Spires in 1529. The courage, faith, and firmness of those men of God gained for succeeding ages liberty of thought and of conscience. Their Protest gave to the reformed church the name of Protestant; its principles are "the very essence of Protestantism."—D'Aubigné, b. 13, ch. 6.

A dark and threatening day had come for the Reformation. Notwithstanding the Edict of Worms, declaring Luther to be an outlaw and forbidding the teaching or belief of his doctrines, religious toleration had thus far prevailed in the empire. God's providence had held in check the forces that opposed the truth. Charles V was bent on crushing the Reformation, but often as he raised his hand to strike he had been forced to turn aside the blow. Again and again the immediate destruction of all who dared to oppose themselves to Rome appeared inevitable; but at the critical moment the armies of the Turk appeared on the eastern frontier, or the king of France, or even the pope himself, jealous of the increasing greatness of the emperor, made war upon him; and thus, amid the strife and tumult of nations, the Reformation had been left to strengthen and extend.

At last, however, the papal sovereigns had stifled their feuds, that they might make common cause against the Reformers. The Diet of Spires in 1526 had given each state full liberty in matters of religion until the meeting of a general council; but no sooner had the dangers passed which secured this concession, than the emperor summoned a second Diet to convene at Spires in 1529 for the purpose of crushing heresy. The princes were to be induced, by peaceable means if possible, to side against the Reformation; but if these failed, Charles was prepared to resort to the sword.

The papists were exultant. They appeared at Spires in great numbers, and openly manifested their hostility toward the Reformers and all who favored them. Said Melanchthon: "We are the execration and the sweepings of the world; but Christ will look down on His poor people, and will preserve them."—*Ibid.*, b. 13, ch. 5. The evangelical princes in attendance at the Diet were forbidden even to have the gospel preached in their dwellings. But the people of Spires thirsted for the word of God, and, notwithstanding the prohibition, thousands flocked to the services held in the chapel of the elector of Saxony.

This hastened the crisis. An imperial message announced to the Diet that as the resolution granting liberty of conscience had given rise to great disorders, the emperor required that it be annulled. This arbitrary act excited the indignation and alarm of the evangelical Christians. Said one: "Christ has again fallen into the hands of Caiaphas and Pilate." The Romanists became more violent. A bigoted papist declared: "The Turks are better than the Lutherans; for the Turks observe fast days, and the Lutherans violate them. If we must choose between the Holy Scriptures of God and the old errors of the church, we should reject the former." Said Melanchthon: "Every day, in full assembly, Faber casts some new stone at us gospelers."—*Ibid.*, b. 13, ch. 5.

Religious toleration had been legally established, and the evangelical states were resolved to oppose the infringement of their rights. Luther, being still under the ban imposed by the Edict of Worms, was not permitted to be present at Spires; but his place was supplied by his colaborers and the princes whom God had raised up to defend His cause in this emergency. The noble Frederick of Saxony, Luther's former protector, had been removed by death; but Duke John, his brother and successor, had joyfully welcomed the Reformation, and while a friend of peace, he displayed great energy and courage in all matters relating to the interests of the faith.

The priests demanded that the states which had accepted the Reformation submit implicitly to Romish jurisdiction. The Reformers, on the other hand, claimed the liberty which had previously been granted. They could not consent that Rome should again bring under her control those states that had with so great joy received the word of God.

As a compromise it was finally proposed that where the Reformation had not become established, the Edict of Worms should be rigorously enforced; and that "in those where the people had deviated from it, and where they could not conform to it without danger of revolt, they should at least effect no new reform, they should touch upon no controverted point, they should not oppose the celebration of the mass, they should permit no Roman Catholic to embrace Lutheranism."—*Ibid.*, b. 13, ch. 5. This measure passed the Diet, to the great satisfaction of the popish priests and prelates.

If this edict were enforced, "the Reformation could neither be extended . . . where as yet it was unknown, nor be established on solid foundations . . . where it already existed."—*Ibid.*, b. 13, ch. 5. Liberty of speech would be prohibited. No conversions would be allowed. And to these restrictions and prohibitions the friends of the Reformation were required at once to submit. The hopes of the world seemed about to be extinguished. "The re-establishment of the Romish hierarchy . . . would infallibly bring back the ancient abuses;" and an occasion would readily be found for "completing the destruction of a work already so violently shaken" by fanaticism and dissension.—*Ibid.*, b. 13, ch. 5.

As the evangelical party met for consultation, one looked to another in blank dismay. From one to another passed the inquiry: "What is to be done?" Mighty issues for the world were at stake. "Shall the chiefs of the Reformation submit, and accept the edict? How easily might the Reformers at this crisis, which was truly a tremendous one, have argued themselves into a wrong course! How many plausible pretexts and fair reasons might they have found for submission! The Lutheran princes were guaranteed the free exercise of their religion. The same boon was extended to all those of their subjects who, prior to the passing of the measure, had embraced the reformed views. Ought not this to content them? How many perils would submission avoid! On what unknown hazards and conflicts would opposition launch them! Who knows what opportunities the future may bring? Let us embrace peace; let us seize the olive branch Rome holds out, and close the wounds of Germany. With arguments like these might the Reformers have justified their adoption of a course which would have assuredly issued in no long time in the overthrow of their cause.

"Happily they looked at the principle on which this arrangement was based, and they acted in faith. What was that principle? It was the right of Rome to coerce conscience and forbid free inquiry. But were not themselves and their Protestant subjects to enjoy religious freedom? Yes, as a favor specially stipulated for in the arrangement, but not as a right. As to all outside that arrangement, the great principle of authority was to rule; conscience was out of court; Rome was infallible judge, and must be obeyed. The acceptance of the proposed arrangement would have been a virtual admission that religious liberty ought to be confined to reformed Saxony; and as to all the rest of Christendom, free inquiry and the profession of the reformed faith were crimes, and must be visited with the dungeon and the stake. Could they consent to localize religious liberty? to have it proclaimed that the Reformation had made its last convert? had subjugated its last acre? and that wherever Rome bore sway at this hour, there her dominion was to be perpetuated? Could the Reformers have pleaded that they were innocent of the blood of those hundreds and thousands who, in pursuance of this arrangement, would have to yield up their lives in popish lands? This would have been to betray, at that supreme hour, the cause of the gospel and the liberties of Christendom."—Wylie, b. 9, ch. 15. Rather would they "sacrifice everything, even their states, their crowns, and their lives."—D'Aubigné, b. 13, ch. 5.

"Let us reject this decree," said the princes. "In matters of conscience the majority has no power." The deputies declared: "It is to the decree of 1526 that we are indebted for the peace that the empire enjoys: its abolition would fill Germany with troubles and divisions. The Diet is incompetent to do more than preserve religious liberty until the council meets."—*Ibid.*, b. 13, ch. 5. To protect liberty of conscience is the duty of the state, and this is the limit of its authority in matters of religion. Every secular government that attempts to regulate or enforce religious observances by civil authority is sacrificing the very principle for which the evangelical Christians so nobly struggled.

The papists determined to put down what they termed "daring obstinacy." They began by endeavoring to cause divisions among the supporters of the Reformation and to intimidate all who had not openly declared in its favor. The representatives of the free cities were at last summoned before the Diet and required to declare whether they would accede to the terms of the proposition. They pleaded for delay, but in vain. When brought to the test, nearly one half their number sided with the Reformers. Those who thus refused to sacrifice liberty of conscience and the right of individual judgment well knew that their position marked them for future criticism, condemnation, and persecution. Said one of the delegates: "We must either deny the word of God, or—be burnt."—*Ibid.*, b. 13, ch. 5.

King Ferdinand, the emperor's representative at the Diet, saw that the decree would cause serious divisions unless the princes could be induced to accept and sustain it. He therefore tried the art of persuasion, well knowing that to employ force with such men would only render them the more determined. He "begged the princes to accept the decree, assuring them that the emperor would be exceedingly pleased with them." But these faithful men acknowledged an authority above that of earthly rulers, and they answered calmly: "We will obey the emperor in everything that may contribute to maintain peace and the honor of God."—*Ibid.*, b. 13, ch. 5.

In the presence of the Diet the king at last announced to the elector and his friends that the edict "was about to be drawn up in the form of an imperial decree," and that "their only remaining course was to submit to the majority." Having thus spoken, he withdrew from the assembly, giving the Reformers no opportunity for deliberation or reply. "To no purpose they sent a deputation entreating the king to return." To their remonstrances he answered only: "It is a settled affair; submission is all that remains."—*Ibid.*, b. 13, ch. 5.

The imperial party were convinced that the Christian princes would adhere to the Holy Scriptures as superior to human doctrines and requirements; and they knew that wherever this principle was accepted, the papacy would eventually be overthrown. But, like thousands since their time, looking only "at the things which are seen," they flattered themselves that the cause of the emperor and the pope was strong, and that of the Reformers weak. Had the Reformers depended upon human aid alone, they would have been as powerless as the papists supposed. But though weak in numbers, and at variance with Rome, they had their strength. They appealed "from the report of the Diet to the word of God, and from the emperor Charles to Jesus Christ, the King of kings and Lord of lords."—*Ibid.*, b. 13, ch. 6.

As Ferdinand had refused to regard their conscientious convictions, the princes decided not to heed his absence, but to bring their Protest before the national council without delay. A solemn declaration was therefore drawn up and presented to the Diet:

"We protest by these presents, before God, our only Creator, Preserver, Redeemer, and Saviour, and who will one day be our Judge, as

well as before all men and all creatures, that we, for us and for our people, neither consent nor adhere in any manner whatsoever to the proposed decree, in anything that is contrary to God, to His holy word, to our right conscience, to the salvation of our souls."

"What! we ratify this edict! We assert that when Almighty God calls a man to His knowledge, this man nevertheless cannot receive the knowledge of God!" "There is no sure doctrine but such as is conformable to the word of God. . . . The Lord forbids the teaching of any other doctrine. . . . The Holy Scriptures ought to be explained by other and clearer texts; . . . this Holy Book is, in all things necessary for the Christian, easy of understanding, and calculated to scatter the darkness. We are resolved, with the grace of God, to maintain the pure and exclusive preaching of His only word, such as it is contained in the biblical books of the Old and New Testaments, without adding anything thereto that may be contrary to it. This word is the only truth; it is the sure rule of all doctrine and of all life, and can never fail or deceive us. He who builds on this foundation shall stand against all the powers of hell, while all the human vanities that are set up against it shall fall before the face of God."

"For this reason we reject the yoke that is imposed on us." "At the same time we are in expectation that his imperial majesty will behave toward us like a Christian prince who loves God above all things; and we declare ourselves ready to pay unto him, as well as unto you, gracious lords, all the affection and obedience that are our just and legitimate duty."—*Ibid.*, b. 13, ch. 6.

A deep impression was made upon the Diet. The majority were filled with amazement and alarm at the boldness of the protesters. The future appeared to them stormy and uncertain. Dissension, strife, and bloodshed seemed inevitable. But the Reformers, assured of the justice of their cause, and relying upon the arm of Omnipotence, were "full of courage and firmness."

"The principles contained in this celebrated Protest . . . constitute the very essence of Protestantism. Now this Protest opposes two abuses of man in matters of faith: the first is the intrusion of the civil magistrate, and the second the arbitrary authority of the church. Instead of these abuses, Protestantism sets the power of conscience above the magistrate, and the authority of the word of God above the visible church. In the first place, it rejects the civil power in divine things, and says with the prophets and apostles, '*We must obey God rather than man.*' In presence of the crown of Charles the Fifth, it uplifts the crown of Jesus Christ.

The protest of the princes against the emperor's edict to restrict religious liberty coined the word Protestant.

But it goes farther: it lays down the principle that all human teaching should be subordinate to the oracles of God."—*Ibid.*, b. 13, ch. 6. The protesters had moreover affirmed their right to utter freely their convictions of truth. They would not only believe and obey, but teach what the word of God presents, and they denied the right of priest or magistrate to interfere. The Protest of Spires was a solemn witness against religious intolerance, and an assertion of the right of all men to worship God according to the dictates of their own consciences.

The declaration had been made. It was written in the memory of thousands and registered in the books of heaven, where no effort of man could erase it. All evangelical Germany adopted the Protest as the expression of its faith. Everywhere men beheld in this declaration the promise of a new and better era. Said one of the princes to the Protestants of Spires: "May the Almighty, who has given you grace to confess energetically, freely, and fearlessly, preserve you in that Christian firmness until the day of eternity."—*Ibid.*, b. 13, ch. 6.

Had the Reformation, after attaining a degree of success, consented to temporize to secure favor with the world, it would have been untrue to God and to itself, and would thus have ensured its own destruction. The experience of these noble Reformers contains a lesson for all succeeding ages. Satan's manner of working against God and His word has not changed; he is still as much opposed to the Scriptures being made the guide of life as in the sixteenth century. In our time there is a wide departure from their doctrines and precepts, and there is need of a return to the great Protestant principle—the Bible, and the Bible only, as the rule of faith and duty. Satan is still working through every means which he can control to destroy religious liberty. The antichristian power which the protesters of Spires rejected is now with renewed vigor seeking to re-establish its lost supremacy. The same unswerving adherence to the word of God manifested at that crisis of the Reformation is the only hope of reform today.

There appeared tokens of danger to the Protestants; there were tokens, also, that the divine hand was stretched out to protect the faithful. It was about this time that "Melanchthon hastily conducted through the streets of Spires toward the Rhine his friend Simon Grynaeus, pressing him to cross the river. The latter was astonished at such precipitation. 'An old man of grave and solemn air, but who is unknown to me,' said Melanchthon, 'appeared before me and said, In a minute officers of justice will be sent by Ferdinand to arrest Grynaeus.'"

During the day, Grynaeus had been scandalized at a sermon by Faber, a leading papal doctor; and at the close, remonstrated with him for defending "certain detestable errors." "Faber dissembled his anger, but immediately after repaired to the king, from whom he had obtained an order against the importunate professor of Heidelberg. Melanchthon doubted not that God had saved his friend by sending one of His holy angels to forewarn him.

"Motionless on the banks of the Rhine, he waited until the waters of that stream had rescued Grynaeus from his persecutors. 'At last,' cried Melanchthon, as he saw him on the opposite side, 'at last he is torn from the cruel jaws of those who thirst for innocent blood.' When he returned to his house, Melanchthon was informed that officers in search of Grynaeus had ransacked it from top to bottom."—*Ibid.*, b. 13, ch. 6.

The Reformation was to be brought into greater prominence before the mighty ones of the earth. The evangelical princes had been denied a hearing by King Ferdinand; but they were to be granted an opportunity to present their cause in the presence of the emperor and the assembled dignitaries of church and state. To quiet the dissensions which disturbed the empire, Charles V, in the year following the Protest of Spires, convoked a diet at Augsburg, over which he announced his intention to preside in person. Thither the Protestant leaders were summoned.

Great dangers threatened the Reformation; but its advocates still trusted their cause with God, and pledged themselves to be firm to the gospel. The elector of Saxony was urged by his councilors not to appear at the Diet. The emperor, they said, required the attendance of the princes in order to draw them into a snare. "Is it not risking everything to go and shut oneself up within the walls of a city with a powerful enemy?" But others nobly declared, "Let the princes only comport themselves with courage, and God's cause is saved." "God is faithful; He will not abandon us," said Luther.—*Ibid.*, b. 14, ch. 2. The elector set out, with his retinue, for Augsburg. All were acquainted with the dangers that menaced him, and many went forward with gloomy countenance and troubled heart. But Luther, who accompanied them as far as Coburg, revived their sinking faith by singing the hymn, written on that journey, "A strong tower is our God." Many an anxious foreboding was banished, many a heavy heart lightened, at the sound of the inspiring strains.

The reformed princes had determined upon having a statement of their views in systematic form, with the evidence from the Scriptures, to present before the Diet; and the task of its preparation was committed to Luther, Melanchthon, and their associates. This Confession was accepted by the Protestants as an exposition of their faith, and they assembled to affix their names to the important document. It was a solemn and trying time. The Reformers were solicitous that their cause should not be confounded with political questions; they felt that the Reformation should exercise no other influence than that which proceeds from the word of God. As the Christian princes advanced to sign the Confession, Melanchthon interposed, saying: "It is for the theologians and ministers to propose these things; let us reserve for other matters the authority of the mighty ones of the earth." "God forbid," replied John of Saxony, "that you should exclude me. I am resolved to do what is right, without troubling myself about my crown. I desire to confess the Lord. My electoral hat and my ermine are not so precious to me as the cross of Jesus Christ." Having thus spoken, he wrote down his name. Said another of the princes as he took the pen: "If the honor of my Lord Jesus Christ requires it, I am ready . . . to leave my goods and life behind." "I would rather renounce my subjects and my states, rather quit the country of my fathers staff in hand," he continued, "than receive any other doctrine than that which is contained in this Confession."— *Ibid.*, b. 14, ch. 6. Such was the faith and daring of those men of God.

The appointed time came to appear before the emperor. Charles V, seated upon his throne, surrounded by the electors and the princes, gave audience to the Protestant Reformers. The confession of their faith was read. In that august assembly the truths of the gospel were clearly set forth, and the errors of the papal church were pointed out. Well has that day been pronounced "the greatest day of the Reformation, and one of the most glorious in the history of Christianity and of mankind."— *Ibid.*, b. 14, ch. 7.

But a few years had passed since the monk of Wittenberg stood alone at Worms before the national council. Now in his stead were the noblest and most powerful princes of the empire. Luther had been forbidden to appear at Augsburg, but he had been present by his words and prayers. "I am overjoyed," he wrote, "that I have lived until this hour, in which Christ has been publicly exalted by such illustrious confessors, and in so glorious an assembly."—*Ibid.*, b. 14, ch. 7. Thus was fulfilled what the Scripture says: "I will speak of Thy testimonies . . . before kings." Psalm 119:46.

In the days of Paul the gospel for which he was imprisoned was thus brought before the princes and nobles of the imperial city. So on this occasion, that which the emperor had forbidden to be preached from the pulpit was proclaimed from the palace; what many had regarded as unfit even for servants to listen to was heard with wonder by the masters and lords of the empire. Kings and great men were the auditory, crowned princes were the preachers, and the sermon was the royal truth of God. "Since the apostolic age," says a writer, "there has never been a greater work or a more magnificent confession."—D'Aubigné b. 14, ch. 7.

"All that the Lutherans have said is true; we cannot deny it," declared a papist bishop. "Can you refute by sound reasons the Confession made by the elector and his allies?" asked another of Dr. Eck. "With the writings of the apostles and prophets—no!" was the reply; "but with those of the Fathers and of the councils—yes!" "I understand," responded the questioner. "The Lutherans, according to you, are in Scripture, and we are outside."—*Ibid.*, b. 14, ch. 8.

Some of the princes of Germany were won to the reformed faith. The emperor himself declared that the Protestant articles were but the truth. The Confession was translated into many languages and circulated through all Europe, and it has been accepted by millions in succeeding generations as the expression of their faith.

God's faithful servants were not toiling alone. While principalities and powers and wicked spirits in high places were leagued against them, the Lord did not forsake His people. Could their eyes have been opened, they would have seen as marked evidence of divine presence and aid as was granted to a prophet of old. When Elisha's servant pointed his master to the hostile army surrounding them and cutting off all opportunity for escape, the prophet prayed: "Lord, I pray Thee, open his eyes, that he may see." 2 Kings 6:17. And, lo, the mountain was filled with chariots and horses of fire, the army of heaven stationed to protect the man of God. Thus did angels guard the workers in the cause of the Reformation.

One of the principles most firmly maintained by Luther was that there should be no resort to secular power in support of the Reformation, and no appeal to arms for its defense. He rejoiced that the gospel was confessed by princes of the empire; but when they proposed to unite in a defensive league, he declared that "the doctrine of the gospel should be defended by *God* alone. . . . The less man meddled in the work, the more striking would be God's intervention in its behalf. All the politic precautions suggested were, in his view, attributable to unworthy fear and sinful mistrust."—D'Aubigné, London ed., b. 10, ch. 14.

When powerful foes were uniting to overthrow the reformed faith, and thousands of swords seemed about to be unsheathed against it, Luther wrote: "Satan is putting forth his fury; ungodly pontiffs are conspiring; and we are threatened with war. Exhort the people to contend valiantly before the throne of the Lord, by faith and prayer, so that our enemies, vanquished by the Spirit of God, may be constrained to peace. Our chief want, our chief labor, is prayer; let the people know that they are now exposed to the edge of the sword and to the rage of Satan, and let them pray."—D'Aubigné, b. 10, ch. 14.

Again, at a later date, referring to the league contemplated by the reformed princes, Luther declared that the only weapon employed in this warfare should be "the sword of the Spirit." He wrote to the elector of Saxony: "We cannot on our conscience approve the proposed alliance. We would rather die ten times than see our gospel cause one drop of blood to be shed. Our part is to be like lambs of the slaughter. The cross of Christ must be borne. Let your highness be without fear. We shall do more by our prayers than all our enemies by their boastings. Only let not your hands be stained with the blood of your brethren. If the emperor requires us to be given up to his tribunals, we are ready to appear. You cannot defend our faith: each one should believe at his own risk and peril."—*Ibid.*, b. 14, ch. 1.

From the secret place of prayer came the power that shook the world in the Great Reformation. There, with holy calmness, the servants of the Lord set their feet upon the rock of His promises. During the struggle at Augsburg, Luther "did not pass a day without devoting three hours at least to prayer, and they were hours selected from those the most favorable to study." In the privacy of his chamber he was heard to pour out his soul before God in words "full of adoration, fear, and hope, as when one speaks to a friend." "I know that Thou art our Father and our God," he said, "and that Thou wilt scatter the persecutors of Thy children; for Thou art Thyself endangered with us. All this matter is Thine, and it is only by Thy constraint that we have put our hands to it. Defend us, then, O Father!"—*Ibid.*, b. 14, ch. 6.

To Melanchthon, who was crushed under the burden of anxiety and fear, he wrote: "Grace and peace in Christ—in Christ, I say, and not in the world. Amen. I hate with exceeding hatred those extreme cares which consume you. If the cause is unjust, abandon it; if the cause is just, why should we belie the promises of Him who commands us to sleep without fear? . . . Christ will not be wanting to the work of justice and truth. He lives, He reigns; what fear, then, can we have?"—*Ibid.*, b. 14, ch. 6.

God did listen to the cries of His servants. He gave to princes and ministers grace and courage to maintain the truth against the rulers of the darkness of this world. Saith the Lord: "Behold, I lay in Zion a chief cornerstone, elect, precious: and he that believeth on Him shall not be confounded." 1 Peter 2:6. The Protestant Reformers had built on Christ, and the gates of hell could not prevail against them.

chapter 12

Daybreak in France

THE Protest of Spires and the Confession at Augsburg, which marked the triumph of the Reformation in Germany, were followed by years of conflict and darkness. Weakened by divisions among its supporters, and assailed by powerful foes, Protestantism seemed destined to be utterly destroyed. Thousands sealed their testimony with their blood. Civil war broke out; the Protestant cause was betrayed by one of its leading adherents; the noblest of the reformed princes fell into the hands of the emperor and were dragged as captives from town to town. But in the moment of his apparent triumph, the emperor was smitten with defeat. He saw the prey wrested from his grasp, and he was forced at last to grant toleration to the doctrines which it had been the ambition of his life to destroy. He had staked his kingdom, his treasures, and life itself upon the crushing out of the heresy. Now he saw his armies wasted by battle, his treasuries drained, his many kingdoms threatened by revolt, while everywhere the faith which he had vainly endeavored to suppress, was extending. Charles V had been battling against omnipotent power. God had said, "Let there be light," but the emperor had sought to keep the darkness unbroken. His purposes had failed; and in premature old age, worn out with the long struggle, he abdicated the throne and buried himself in a cloister.

In Switzerland, as in Germany, there came dark days for the Reformation. While many cantons accepted the reformed faith, others clung with blind persistence to the creed of Rome. Their persecution of those who desired to receive the truth finally gave rise to civil war. Zwingli

In Paris the victims were put to
death with cruel torture, the fire being
lowered in order to prolong the agony.

© P.P.P.A. JOHN STEEL, ARTIST

and many who had united with him in reform fell on the bloody field of Cappel. Oecolampadius, overcome by these terrible disasters, soon after died. Rome was triumphant, and in many places seemed about to recover all that she had lost. But He whose counsels are from everlasting had not forsaken His cause or His people. His hand would bring deliverance for them. In other lands He had raised up laborers to carry forward the reform.

In France, before the name of Luther had been heard as a Reformer, the day had already begun to break. One of the first to catch the light was the aged Lefevre, a man of extensive learning, a professor in the University of Paris, and a sincere and zealous papist. In his researches into ancient literature his attention was directed to the Bible, and he introduced its study among his students.

Lefevre was an enthusiastic adorer of the saints, and he had undertaken to prepare a history of the saints and martyrs as given in the legends of the church. This was a work which involved great labor; but he had already made considerable progress in it, when, thinking that he might obtain useful assistance from the Bible, he began its study with this object. Here indeed he found saints brought to view, but not such as figured in the Roman calendar. A flood of divine light broke in upon his mind. In amazement and disgust he turned away from his self-appointed task and devoted himself to the word of God. The precious truths which he there discovered he soon began to teach.

In 1512, before either Luther or Zwingli had begun the work of reform, Lefevre wrote: "It is God who gives us, by faith, that righteousness which by grace alone justifies to eternal life."—Wylie, b. 13, ch. 1. Dwelling upon the mysteries of redemption, he exclaimed: "Oh, the unspeakable greatness of that exchange,—the Sinless One is condemned, and he who is guilty goes free; the Blessing bears the curse, and the cursed is brought into blessing; the Life dies, and the dead live; the Glory is whelmed in darkness, and he who knew nothing but confusion of face is clothed with glory."—D'Aubigné, London ed., b. 12, ch. 2.

And while teaching that the glory of salvation belongs solely to God, he also declared that the duty of obedience belongs to man. "If thou art a member of Christ's church," he said, "thou art a member of His body; if thou art of His body, then thou art full of the divine nature. . . . Oh, if men could but enter into the understanding of this privilege, how purely, chastely, and holily would they live, and how contemptible, when compared with the glory within them—that glory which the eye of flesh cannot see—would they deem all the glory of this world."—*Ibid.*, b. 12, ch. 2.

There were some among Lefevre's students who listened eagerly to his words, and who, long after the teacher's voice should be silenced, were to continue to declare the truth. Such was William Farel. The son of pious parents, and educated to accept with implicit faith the teachings of the church, he might, with the apostle Paul, have declared concerning himself: "After the most straitest sect of our religion I lived a Pharisee." Acts 26:5. A devoted Romanist, he burned with zeal to destroy all who should dare to oppose the church. "I would gnash my teeth like a furious wolf," he afterward said, referring to this period of his life, "when I heard anyone speaking against the pope."—Wylie, b. 13, ch. 2. He had been untiring in his adoration of the saints, in company with Lefevre making the round of the churches of Paris, worshiping at the altars, and adorning with gifts the holy shrines. But these observances could not bring peace of soul. Conviction of sin fastened upon him, which all the acts of penance that he practiced failed to banish. As to a voice from heaven he listened to the Reformer's words: "Salvation is of grace." "The Innocent One is condemned, and the criminal is acquitted." "It is the cross of Christ alone that openeth the gates of heaven, and shutteth the gates of hell."—*Ibid.*, b. 13, ch. 2.

Farel joyfully accepted the truth. By a conversion like that of Paul he turned from the bondage of tradition to the liberty of the sons of God. "Instead of the murderous heart of a ravening wolf," he came back, he says, "quietly like a meek and harmless lamb, having his heart entirely withdrawn from the pope, and given to Jesus Christ."—D'Aubigné, b. 12, ch. 3.

While Lefevre continued to spread the light among his students, Farel, as zealous in the cause of Christ as he had been in that of the pope, went forth to declare the truth in public. A dignitary of the church, the bishop of Meaux, soon after united with them. Other teachers who ranked high for their ability and learning joined in proclaiming the gospel, and it won adherents among all classes, from the homes of artisans and peasants to the palace of the king. The sister of Francis I, then the reigning monarch, accepted the reformed faith. The king himself, and the queen mother, appeared for a time to regard it with favor, and with high hopes the Reformers looked forward to the time when France should be won to the gospel.

But their hopes were not to be realized. Trial and persecution awaited the disciples of Christ. This, however, was mercifully veiled from their eyes. A time of peace intervened, that they might gain strength to meet the tempest; and the Reformation made rapid progress. The bishop of Meaux labored zealously in his own diocese to instruct both the clergy and the people. Ignorant and immoral priests were removed, and, so far as possible, replaced by men of learning and piety. The bishop greatly desired that his people might have access to the word of God for themselves, and this was soon accomplished. Lefevre undertook the translation of the New Testament; and at the very time when Luther's German Bible was issuing from the press in Wittenberg, the French New Testament was published at Meaux. The bishop spared no labor or expense to circulate it in his parishes, and soon the peasants of Meaux were in possession of the Holy Scriptures.

As travelers perishing from thirst welcome with joy a living water spring, so did these souls receive the message of heaven. The laborers in the field, the artisans in the workshop, cheered their daily toil by talking of the precious truths of the Bible. At evening, instead of resorting to the wineshops, they assembled in one another's homes to read God's word and join in prayer and praise. A great change was soon manifest in these communities. Though belonging to the humblest class, an unlearned and hard-working peasantry, the reforming, uplifting power of divine grace was seen in their lives. Humble, loving, and holy, they stood as witnesses to what the gospel will accomplish for those who receive it in sincerity.

The light kindled at Meaux shed its beams afar. Every day the number of converts was increasing. The rage of the hierarchy was for a time held in check by the king, who despised the narrow bigotry of the monks; but the papal leaders finally prevailed. Now the stake was set up. The bishop of Meaux, forced to choose between the fire and recantation, accepted the easier path; but notwithstanding the leader's fall, his flock remained steadfast. Many witnessed for the truth amid the flames. By their courage and fidelity at the stake, these humble Christians spoke to thousands who in days of peace had never heard their testimony.

It was not alone the humble and the poor that amid suffering and scorn dared to bear witness for Christ. In the lordly halls of the castle and the palace there were kingly souls by whom truth was valued above wealth or rank or even life. Kingly armor concealed a loftier and more steadfast spirit than did the bishop's robe and miter. Louis de Berquin was of noble birth. A brave and courtly knight, he was devoted to study, polished in manners, and of blameless morals. "He was," says a writer, "a great follower of the papistical constitutions, and a great hearer of masses and sermons; . . . and he crowned all his other virtues by holding Lutheranism in special abhorrence." But, like so many others, providentially guided to the Bible, he was amazed to find there, "not the doctrines of Rome, but the doctrines of Luther."—Wylie, b. 13, ch. 9. Henceforth he gave himself with entire devotion to the cause of the gospel.

"The most learned of the nobles of France," his genius and eloquence, his indomitable courage and heroic zeal, and his influence at court—for he was a favorite with the king—caused him to be regarded by many as one destined to be the Reformer of his country. Said Beza: "Berquin would have been a second Luther, had he found in Francis I a second elector." "He is worse than Luther," cried the papists.—*Ibid.*, b. 13, ch. 9. More dreaded he was indeed by the Romanists of France. They thrust him into prison as a heretic, but he was set at liberty by the king. For years the struggle continued. Francis, wavering between Rome and the Reformation, alternately tolerated and restrained the fierce zeal of the monks. Berquin was three times imprisoned by the papal authorities, only to be released by the monarch, who, in admiration of his genius and his nobility of character, refused to sacrifice him to the malice of the hierarchy.

Berquin was repeatedly warned of the danger that threatened him in France, and urged to follow the steps of those who had found safety in voluntary exile. The timid and time-serving Erasmus, who with all the splendor of his scholarship failed of that moral greatness which holds life and honor subservient to truth, wrote to Berquin: "Ask to be sent as ambassador to some foreign country; go and travel in Germany. You know Beda and such as he—he is a thousand-headed monster, darting venom on every side. Your enemies are named legion. Were your cause better than that of Jesus Christ, they will not let you go till they have miserably destroyed you. Do not trust too much to the king's protection. At all events, *do not compromise me* with the faculty of theology."—*Ibid.*, b. 13, ch. 9.

But as dangers thickened, Berquin's zeal only waxed the stronger. So far from adopting the politic and self-serving counsel of Erasmus, he determined upon still bolder measures. He would not only stand in defense of the truth, but he would attack error. The charge of heresy which the Romanists were seeking to fasten upon him, he would rivet upon them. The most active and bitter of his opponents were the learned doctors and monks of the theological department in the great University of Paris, one of the highest ecclesiastical authorities both in the city and the nation. From the writings of these doctors, Berquin drew twelve propositions which he publicly declared to be "opposed to the Bible, and heretical;" and he appealed to the king to act as judge in the controversy.

The monarch, not loath to bring into contrast the power and acuteness of the opposing champions, and glad of an opportunity of humbling the pride of these haughty monks, bade the Romanists defend their cause by the Bible. This weapon, they well knew, would avail them little; imprisonment, torture, and the stake were arms which they better understood how to wield. Now the tables were turned, and they saw themselves about to fall into the pit into which they had hoped to plunge Berquin. In amazement they looked about them for some way of escape.

"Just at that time an image of the Virgin at the corner of one of the streets, was mutilated." There was great excitement in the city. Crowds of people flocked to the place, with expressions of mourning and indignation. The king also was deeply moved. Here was an advantage which the monks could turn to good account, and they were quick to improve it. "These are the fruits of the doctrines of Berquin," they cried. "All is about to be overthrown—religion, the laws, the throne itself—by this Lutheran conspiracy."—*Ibid.*, b. 13, ch. 9.

Again Berquin was apprehended. The king withdrew from Paris, and the monks were thus left free to work their will. The Reformer was tried and condemned to die, and lest Francis should even yet interpose to save him, the sentence was executed on the very day it was pronounced. At noon Berquin was conducted to the place of death. An immense throng gathered to witness the event, and there were many who saw with astonishment and misgiving that the victim had been chosen from the best and bravest of the noble families of France. Amazement, indignation, scorn, and bitter hatred darkened the faces of that surging crowd; but upon one face no shadow rested. The martyr's thoughts were far from that scene of tumult; he was conscious only of the presence of his Lord.

The wretched tumbrel upon which he rode, the frowning faces of his persecutors, the dreadful death to which he was going—these he heeded not; He who liveth and was dead, and is alive for evermore, and hath the keys of death and of hell, was beside him. Berquin's countenance was radiant with the light and peace of heaven. He had attired himself in goodly raiment, wearing "a cloak of velvet, a doublet of satin and damask, and golden hose."—D'Aubigné, *History of the Reformation in Europe in the Time of Calvin*, b. 2, ch. 16. He was about to testify to his faith in the presence of the King of kings and the witnessing universe, and no token of mourning should belie his joy.

As the procession moved slowly through the crowded streets, the people marked with wonder the unclouded peace, the joyous triumph, of his look and bearing. "He is," they said, "like one who sits in a temple, and meditates on holy things."—Wylie, b. 13, ch. 9.

At the stake, Berquin endeavored to address a few words to the people; but the monks, fearing the result, began to shout, and the soldiers to clash their arms, and their clamor drowned the martyr's voice. Thus in 1529 the highest literary and ecclesiastical authority of cultured Paris "set the populace of 1793 the base example of stifling on the scaffold the sacred words of the dying."—*Ibid.*, b. 13, ch. 9.

Berquin was strangled, and his body was consumed in the flames. The tidings of his death caused sorrow to the friends of the Reformation throughout France. But his example was not lost. "We, too, are ready," said the witnesses for the truth, "to meet death cheerfully, setting our eyes on the life that is to come."—D'Aubigné, *History of the Reformation in Europe in the Time of Calvin*, b. 2, ch. 16.

During the persecution at Meaux, the teachers of the reformed faith were deprived of their license to preach, and they departed to other fields. Lefevre after a time made his way to Germany. Farel returned to his native town in eastern France, to spread the light in the home of his childhood. Already tidings had been received of what was going on at Meaux, and the truth, which he taught with fearless zeal, found listeners. Soon the authorities were roused to silence him, and he was banished from the city. Though he could no longer labor publicly, he traversed the plains and villages, teaching in private dwellings and in secluded meadows, and finding shelter in the forests and among the rocky caverns which had been his haunts in boyhood. God was preparing him for greater trials. "The crosses, persecutions, and machinations of Satan, of which I was forewarned, have not been wanting," he said; "they are even much severer than I could have borne of myself; but God is my Father; He has provided and always will provide me the strength which I require."—D'Aubigné, *History of the Reformation of the Sixteenth Century,* b. 12, ch. 9.

As in apostolic days, persecution had "fallen out rather unto the furtherance of the gospel." Philippians 1:12. Driven from Paris and Meaux, "they that were scattered abroad went everywhere preaching the word." Acts 8:4. And thus the light found its way into many of the remote provinces of France.

God was still preparing workers to extend His cause. In one of the schools of Paris was a thoughtful, quiet youth, already giving evidence of a powerful and penetrating mind, and no less marked for the blamelessness of his life than for intellectual ardor and religious devotion. His genius and application soon made him the pride of the college, and it was confidently anticipated that John Calvin would become one of the ablest and most honored defenders of the church. But a ray of divine light penetrated even within the walls of scholasticism and superstition by which Calvin was enclosed. He heard of the new doctrines with a shudder, nothing doubting that the heretics deserved the fire to which they were given. Yet all unwittingly he was brought face to face with the heresy and forced to test the power of Romish theology to combat the Protestant teaching.

A cousin of Calvin's, who had joined the Reformers, was in Paris. The two kinsmen often met and discussed together the matters that were disturbing Christendom. "There are but two religions in the world," said Olivetan, the Protestant. "The one class of religions are those which men have invented, in all of which man saves himself by ceremonies and good works; the other is that one religion which is revealed in the Bible, and which teaches man to look for salvation solely from the free grace of God."

"I will have none of your new doctrines," exclaimed Calvin; "think you that I have lived in error all my days?"—Wylie, b. 13, ch. 7.

But thoughts had been awakened in his mind which he could not banish at will. Alone in his chamber he pondered upon his cousin's words.

Conviction of sin fastened upon him; he saw himself, without an intercessor, in the presence of a holy and just Judge. The mediation of saints, good works, the ceremonies of the church, all were powerless to atone for sin. He could see before him nothing but the blackness of eternal despair. In vain the doctors of the church endeavored to relieve his woe. Confession, penance, were resorted to in vain; they could not reconcile the soul with God.

While still engaged in these fruitless struggles, Calvin, chancing one day to visit one of the public squares, witnessed there the burning of a heretic. He was filled with wonder at the expression of peace which rested upon the martyr's countenance. Amid the tortures of that dreadful death, and under the more terrible condemnation of the church, he manifested a faith and courage which the young student painfully contrasted with his own despair and darkness, while living in strictest obedience to the church. Upon the Bible, he knew, the heretics rested their faith. He determined to study it, and discover, if he could, the secret of their joy.

In the Bible he found Christ. "O Father," he cried, "His sacrifice has appeased Thy wrath; His blood has washed away my impurities; His cross has borne my curse; His death has atoned for me. We had devised for ourselves many useless follies, but Thou hast placed Thy word before me like a torch, and Thou hast touched my heart, in order that I may hold in abomination all other merits save those of Jesus."—Martyn, vol. 3, ch. 13.

Calvin had been educated for the priesthood. When only twelve years of age he had been appointed to the chaplaincy of a small church, and his head had been shorn by the bishop in accordance with the canon of the church. He did not receive consecration, nor did he fulfill the duties of a priest, but he became a member of the clergy, holding the title of his office, and receiving an allowance in consideration thereof.

Now, feeling that he could never become a priest, he turned for a time to the study of law, but finally abandoned this purpose and determined to devote his life to the gospel. But he hesitated to become a public teacher. He was naturally timid, and was burdened with a sense of the weighty responsibility of the position, and he desired still to devote himself to study. The earnest entreaties of his friends, however, at last won his consent. "Wonderful it is," he said, "that one of so lowly an origin should be exalted to so great a dignity."—Wylie, b. 13, ch. 9.

Quietly did Calvin enter upon his work, and his words were as the dew falling to refresh the earth. He had left Paris, and was now in a provincial town under the protection of the princess Margaret, who, loving the gospel, extended her protection to its disciples. Calvin was still a youth, of gentle, unpretentious bearing. His work began with the people at their homes. Surrounded by the members of the household, he read the Bible and opened the truths of salvation. Those who heard the message carried the good news to others, and soon the teacher passed beyond the city to the outlying towns and hamlets. To both the castle and the cabin he found entrance, and he went forward, laying the foundation of churches that were to yield fearless witnesses for the truth.

A few months and he was again in Paris. There was unwonted agitation in the circle of learned men and scholars. The study of the ancient languages had led men to the Bible, and many whose hearts were untouched by its truths were eagerly discussing them and even giving battle to the champions of Romanism. Calvin, though an able combatant in the fields of theological controversy, had a higher mission to accomplish than that of these noisy schoolmen. The minds of men were stirred, and now was the time to open to them the truth. While the halls of the universities were filled with the clamor of theological disputation, Calvin was making his way from house to house, opening the Bible to the people, and speaking to them of Christ and Him crucified.

In God's providence, Paris was to receive another invitation to accept the gospel. The call of Lefevre and Farel had been rejected, but again the message was to be heard by all classes in that great capital. The king, influenced by political considerations, had not yet fully sided with Rome against the Reformation. Margaret still clung to the hope that Protestantism was to triumph in France. She resolved that the reformed faith should be preached in Paris. During the absence of the king, she ordered a Protestant minister to preach in the churches of the city. This being forbidden by the papal dignitaries, the princess threw open the palace. An apartment was fitted up as a chapel, and it was announced that every day, at a specified hour, a sermon would be preached, and the people of every rank and station were invited to attend. Crowds flocked to the service. Not only the chapel, but the antechambers and halls were thronged. Thousands every day assembled—nobles, statesmen, lawyers, merchants, and artisans. The king, instead of forbidding the assemblies, ordered that two of the churches of Paris should be opened. Never before had the city been so moved by the word of God. The spirit of life from heaven seemed to be breathed upon the people. Temperance, purity, order, and industry were taking the place of drunkenness, licentiousness, strife, and idleness.

But the hierarchy were not idle. The king still refused to interfere to stop the preaching, and they turned to the populace. No means were spared to excite the fears, the prejudices, and the fanaticism of the ignorant and superstitious multitude. Yielding blindly to her false teachers, Paris, like Jerusalem of old, knew not the time of her visitation nor the things which belonged unto her peace. For two years the word of God was preached in the capital; but, while there were many who accepted the gospel, the majority of the people rejected it. Francis had made a show of toleration, merely to serve his own purposes, and the papists succeeded in regaining the ascendancy. Again the churches were closed, and the stake was set up.

Calvin was still in Paris, preparing himself by study, meditation, and prayer for his future labors, and continuing to spread the light. At last, however, suspicion fastened upon him. The authorities determined to bring him to the flames. Regarding himself as secure in his seclusion, he had no thought of danger, when friends came hurrying to his room with the news that officers were on their way to arrest him. At that instant a loud knocking was heard at the outer entrance. There was not a moment to be lost. Some of his friends detained the officers at the door, while others assisted the Reformer to let himself down from a window, and he rapidly made his way to the outskirts of the city. Finding shelter in the cottage of a laborer who was a friend to the reform, he disguised himself in the garments of his host, and, shouldering a hoe, started on his journey. Traveling southward, he again found refuge in the dominions of Margaret. (See D'Aubigné, *History of the Reformation in Europe in the Time of Calvin,* b. 2, ch. 30.)

Here for a few months he remained, safe under the protection of powerful friends, and engaged as before in study. But his heart was set upon the evangelization of France, and he could not long remain inactive. As soon as the storm had somewhat abated, he sought a new field of labor in Poitiers, where was a university, and where already the new opinions had found favor. Persons of all classes gladly listened to the gospel. There was no public preaching, but in the home of the chief magistrate, in his own lodgings, and sometimes in a public garden, Calvin opened the words of eternal life to those who desired to listen. After a time, as the number of hearers increased, it was thought safer to assemble outside the city. A cave in the side of a deep and narrow gorge, where trees and overhanging rocks made the seclusion still more complete, was chosen as the place of meeting. Little companies, leaving the city by different routes, found their way hither. In this retired spot the Bible was read aloud and explained. Here the Lord's Supper was celebrated for the first time by the Protestants of France. From this little church several faithful evangelists were sent out.

Once more Calvin returned to Paris. He could not even yet relinquish the hope that France as a nation would accept the Reformation. But he found almost every door of labor closed. To teach the gospel was to take the direct road to the stake, and he at last determined to depart to Germany. Scarcely had he left France when a storm burst over the Protestants, that, had he remained, must surely have involved him in the general ruin.

The French Reformers, eager to see their country keeping pace with Germany and Switzerland, determined to strike a bold blow against the superstitions of Rome, that should arouse the whole nation. Accordingly placards attacking the mass were in one night posted all over France. Instead of advancing the reform, this zealous but ill-judged movement brought ruin, not only upon its propagators, but upon the friends of the reformed faith throughout France. It gave the Romanists what they had long desired—a pretext for demanding the utter destruction of the heretics as agitators dangerous to the stability of the throne and the peace of the nation.

By some secret hand—whether of indiscreet friend or wily foe was never known—one of the placards was attached to the door of the king's private chamber. The monarch was filled with horror. In this paper, superstitions that had received the veneration of ages were attacked with an unsparing hand. And the unexampled boldness of obtruding these plain and startling utterances into the royal presence aroused the wrath of the king. In his amazement he stood for a little time trembling and speechless. Then his rage found utterance in the terrible words: "Let all be seized without distinction who are suspected of Lutheresy. I will exterminate them all."—*Ibid.*, b. 4, ch. 10. The die was cast. The king had determined to throw himself fully on the side of Rome.

Measures were at once taken for the arrest of every Lutheran in Paris. A poor artisan, an adherent of the reformed faith, who had been accustomed to summon the believers to their secret assemblies, was seized and, with the threat of instant death at the stake, was commanded to conduct the papal emissary to the home of every Protestant

186 [*224-225*]

Enemies of the Reformation ferreted out every Protestant in France, putting to death all they could find.

in the city. He shrank in horror from the base proposal, but at last fear of the flames prevailed, and he consented to become the betrayer of his brethren. Preceded by the host, and surrounded by a train of priests, incense bearers, monks, and soldiers, Morin, the royal detective, with the traitor, slowly and silently passed through the streets of the city. The demonstration was ostensibly in honor of the "holy sacrament," an act of expiation for the insult put upon the mass by the protesters. But beneath this pageant a deadly purpose was concealed. On arriving opposite the house of a Lutheran, the betrayer made a sign, but no word was uttered. The procession halted, the house was entered, the family were dragged forth and chained, and the terrible company went forward in search of fresh victims. They "spared no house, great or small, not even the colleges of the University of Paris. . . . Morin made all the city quake. . . . It was a reign of terror."—*Ibid.*, b. 4, ch. 10.

The victims were put to death with cruel torture, it being specially ordered that the fire should be lowered in order to prolong their agony. But they died as conquerors. Their constancy was unshaken, their peace unclouded. Their persecutors, powerless to move their inflexible firmness, felt themselves defeated. "The scaffolds were distributed over all the quarters of Paris, and the burnings followed on successive days, the design being to spread the terror of heresy by spreading the executions. The advantage, however, in the end, remained with the gospel. All Paris was enabled to see what kind of men the new opinions could produce. There was no pulpit like the martyr's pile. The serene joy that lighted up the faces of these men as they passed along . . . to the place of execution, their heroism as they stood amid the bitter flames, their meek forgiveness of injuries, transformed, in instances not a few, anger into pity, and hate into love, and pleaded with resistless eloquence in behalf of the gospel."—Wylie, b. 13, ch. 20.

The priests, bent upon keeping the popular fury at its height, circulated the most terrible accusations against the Protestants. They were charged with plotting to massacre the Catholics, to overthrow the government, and to murder the king. Not a shadow of evidence could be produced in support of the allegations. Yet these prophecies of evil were to have a fulfillment; under far different circumstances, however, and from causes of an opposite character. The cruelties that were inflicted upon the innocent Protestants by the Catholics accumulated in a weight of retribution, and in after centuries wrought the very doom they had predicted to be impending, upon the king, his government, and his subjects; but it was brought about by infidels and by the papists themselves. It was not the establishment, but the suppression, of Protestantism, that, three hundred years later, was to bring upon France these dire calamities.

Suspicion, distrust, and terror now pervaded all classes of society. Amid the general alarm it was seen how deep a hold the Lutheran teaching had gained upon the minds of men who stood highest for education, influence, and excellence of character. Positions of trust and honor were suddenly found vacant. Artisans, printers, scholars, professors in the universities, authors, and even courtiers, disappeared. Hundreds fled from Paris, self-constituted exiles from their native land, in many cases thus giving the first intimation that they favored the reformed faith. The papists looked about them in amazement at thought of the unsuspected heretics that had been tolerated among them. Their rage spent itself upon the multitudes of humbler victims who were within their power. The prisons were crowded, and the very air seemed darkened with the smoke of burning piles, kindled for the confessors of the gospel.

Francis I had gloried in being a leader in the great movement for the revival of learning which marked the opening of the sixteenth century. He had delighted to gather at his court men of letters from every country. To his love of learning and his contempt for the ignorance and superstition of the monks was due, in part at least, the degree of toleration that had been granted to the reform. But, inspired with zeal to stamp out heresy, this patron of learning issued an edict declaring printing abolished all over France! Francis I presents one among the many examples on record showing that intellectual culture is not a safeguard against religious intolerance and persecution.

France by a solemn and public ceremony was to commit herself fully to the destruction of Protestantism. The priests demanded that the affront offered to High Heaven in the condemnation of the mass be expiated in blood, and that the king, in behalf of his people, publicly give his sanction to the dreadful work.

The 21st of January, 1535, was fixed upon for the awful ceremonial. The superstitious fears and bigoted hatred of the whole nation had been roused. Paris was thronged with the multitudes that from all the surrounding country crowded her streets. The day was to be ushered in by a vast and imposing procession. "The houses along the line of march were hung with mourning drapery, and altars rose at intervals." Before every door was a lighted torch in honor of the "holy sacrament." Before daybreak the procession formed at the palace of the king. "First came the banners and crosses of the several parishes; next appeared the citizens, walking two and two, and bearing torches." The four orders of friars followed, each in its own peculiar dress. Then came a vast collection of famous relics. Following these rode lordly ecclesiastics in their purple and scarlet robes and jeweled adornings, a gorgeous and glittering array.

"The host was carried by the bishop of Paris under a magnificent canopy, . . . supported by four princes of the blood. . . . After the host walked the king. . . . Francis I on that day wore no crown, nor robe of state." With "head uncovered, his eyes cast on the ground, and in his hand a lighted taper," the king of France appeared "in the character of a penitent."—*Ibid.*, b. 13, ch. 21. At every altar he bowed down in humiliation, not for the vices that defiled his soul, nor the innocent blood that stained his hands, but for the deadly sin of his subjects who had dared to condemn the mass. Following him came the queen and the dignitaries of state, also walking two and two, each with a lighted torch.

As a part of the services of the day the monarch himself addressed the high officials of the kingdom in the great hall of the bishop's palace. With a sorrowful countenance he appeared before them and in words of moving eloquence bewailed "the crime, the blasphemy, the day of sorrow and disgrace," that had come upon the nation. And he called upon every loyal subject to aid in the extirpation of the pestilent heresy that threatened France with ruin. "As true, messieurs, as I am your king," he said, "if I knew one of my own limbs spotted or infected with this detestable rottenness, I would give it you to cut off. . . . And further, if I saw one of my children defiled by it, I would not spare him. . . . I would deliver him up myself, and would sacrifice him to God." Tears choked his utterance, and the whole assembly wept, with one accord exclaiming: "We will live and die for the Catholic religion!"—D'Aubigné, *History of the Reformation in Europe in the Time of Calvin*, b. 4, ch. 12.

Terrible had become the darkness of the nation that had rejected the light of truth. The grace "that bringeth salvation" had appeared; but France, after beholding its power and holiness, after thousands had been drawn by its divine beauty, after cities and hamlets had been illuminated by its radiance, had turned away, choosing darkness rather than light. They had put from them the heavenly gift when it was offered them. They had called evil good, and good evil, till they had fallen victims to their willful self-deception. Now, though they might actually believe that they were doing God service in persecuting His people, yet their sincerity did not render them guiltless. The light that would have saved them from deception, from staining their souls with blood-guiltiness, they had willfully rejected.

A solemn oath to extirpate heresy was taken in the great cathedral where, nearly three centuries later, the Goddess of Reason was to be enthroned by a nation that had forgotten the living God. Again the procession formed, and the representatives of France set out to begin the work which they had sworn to do. "At short distances scaffolds had been erected, on which certain Protestant Christians were to be burned alive, and it was arranged that the fagots should be lighted at the moment the king approached, and that the procession should halt to witness the execution."—Wylie, b. 13, ch. 21. The details of the tortures endured by these witnesses for Christ are too harrowing for recital; but there was no wavering on the part of the victims. On being urged to recant, one answered: "I only believe in what the prophets and the apostles formerly preached, and what all the company of saints believed. My faith has a confidence in God which will resist all the powers of hell."—D'Aubigné, *History of the Reformation in Europe in the Time of Calvin*, b. 4, ch. 12.

Again and again the procession halted at the places of torture. Upon reaching their starting point at the royal palace, the crowd dispersed, and the king and the prelates withdrew, well satisfied with the day's proceedings and congratulating themselves that the work now begun would be continued to the complete destruction of heresy.

The gospel of peace which France had rejected was to be only too surely rooted out, and terrible would be the results. On the 21st of January, 1793, two hundred and fifty-eight years from the very day that fully committed France to the persecution of the Reformers, another procession, with a far different purpose, passed through the streets of Paris. "Again the king was the chief figure; again there were tumult and shouting; again there was heard the cry for more victims; again there were black scaffolds; and again the scenes of the day were closed by horrid executions; Louis XVI, struggling hand to hand with his jailers and executioners, was dragged forward to the block, and there held down by main force till the ax had fallen, and his disservered head rolled on the scaffold."—Wylie, b. 13, ch. 21. Nor was the king the only victim; near the same spot two thousand and eight hundred human beings perished by the guillotine during the bloody days of the Reign of Terror.

The Reformation had presented to the world an open Bible, unsealing the precepts of the law of God and urging its claims upon the consciences of the people. Infinite Love had unfolded to men the statutes and principles of heaven. God had said: "Keep therefore and do them; for this is your wisdom and your understanding in the sight of the nations, which shall hear all these statutes, and say, Surely this great nation is a wise and understanding people." Deuteronomy 4:6. When France rejected the gift of heaven, she sowed the seeds of anarchy and ruin; and the inevitable outworking of cause and effect resulted in the Revolution and the Reign of Terror.

Long before the persecution excited by the placards, the bold and ardent Farel had been forced to flee from the land of his birth. He repaired to Switzerland, and by his labors, seconding the work of Zwingli, he helped to turn the scale in favor of the Reformation. His later years were to be spent here, yet he continued to exert a decided influence upon the reform in France. During the first years of his exile, his efforts were especially directed to spreading the gospel in his native country. He spent considerable time in preaching among his countrymen near the frontier, where with tireless vigilance he watched the conflict and aided by his words of encouragement and counsel. With the assistance of other exiles, the writings of the German Reformers were translated into the French language and, together with the French Bible, were printed in large quantities. By colporteurs these works were sold extensively in France. They were furnished to the colporteurs at a low price, and thus the profits of the work enabled them to continue it.

Farel entered upon his work in Switzerland in the humble guise of a schoolmaster. Repairing to a secluded parish, he devoted himself to the instruction of children. Besides the usual branches of learning, he cautiously introduced the truths of the Bible, hoping through the children to reach the parents. There were some who believed, but the priests came forward to stop the work, and the superstitious country people were roused to oppose it. "That cannot be the gospel of Christ," urged the priests, "seeing the preaching of it does not bring peace, but war." —Wylie, b. 14, ch. 3. Like the first disciples, when persecuted in one city he fled to another. From village to village, from city to city, he went, traveling on foot, enduring hunger, cold, and weariness, and everywhere in peril of his life. He preached in the market places, in the churches, sometimes in the pulpits of the cathedrals. Sometimes he found the church empty of hearers; at times his preaching was interrupted by shouts and jeers; again he was pulled violently out of the pulpit. More than once he was set upon by the rabble and beaten almost to death. Yet he pressed forward. Though often repulsed, with unwearying persistence he returned to the attack; and, one after another, he saw towns and cities which had been strongholds of popery, opening their gates to the gospel. The little parish where he had first labored soon accepted the reformed faith. The cities of Morat and Neuchâtel also renounced the Romish rites and removed the idolatrous images from their churches.

Farel had long desired to plant the Protestant standard in Geneva. If this city could be won, it would be a center for the Reformation in France, in Switzerland, and in Italy. With this object before him, he had continued his labors until many of the surrounding towns and hamlets had been gained. Then with a single companion he entered Geneva. But only two sermons was he permitted to preach. The priests, having vainly endeavored to secure his condemnation by the civil authorities, summoned him before an ecclesiastical council, to which they came with arms concealed under their robes, determined to take his life. Outside the hall, a furious mob, with clubs and swords, was gathered to make sure of his death if he should succeed in escaping the council. The presence of magistrates and an armed force, however, saved him. Early next morning he was conducted, with his companion, across the lake to a place of safety. Thus ended his first effort to evangelize Geneva.

For the next trial a lowlier instrument was chosen—a young man, so humble in appearance that he was coldly treated even by the professed friends of reform. But what could such a one do where Farel had been rejected? How could one of little courage and experience withstand the tempest before which the strongest and bravest had been forced to flee? "Not by might, nor by power, but by My Spirit, saith the Lord." Zechariah 4:6. "God hath chosen the weak things of the world to confound the things which are mighty." "Because the foolishness of God is wiser than men; and the weakness of God is stronger than men." 1 Corinthians 1:27, 25.

Froment began his work as a schoolmaster. The truths which he taught the children at school they repeated at their homes. Soon the parents came to hear the Bible explained, until the schoolroom was filled with attentive listeners. New Testaments and tracts were freely distributed, and they reached many who dared not come openly to listen to the new doctrines. After a time this laborer also was forced to flee; but the truths he taught had taken hold upon the minds of the people.

[231-233] 193

The Reformation had been planted, and it continued to strengthen and extend. The preachers returned, and through their labors the Protestant worship was finally established in Geneva.

The city had already declared for the Reformation when Calvin, after various wanderings and vicissitudes, entered its gates. Returning from a last visit to his birthplace, he was on his way to Basel, when, finding the direct road occupied by the armies of Charles V, he was forced to take the circuitous route by Geneva.

In this visit Farel recognized the hand of God. Though Geneva had accepted the reformed faith, yet a great work remained to be accomplished here. It is not as communities but as individuals that men are converted to God; the work of regeneration must be wrought in the heart and conscience by the power of the Holy Spirit, not by the decrees of councils. While the people of Geneva had cast off the authority of Rome, they were not so ready to renounce the vices that had flourished under her rule. To establish here the pure principles of the gospel and to prepare this people to fill worthily the position to which Providence seemed calling them were not light tasks.

Farel was confident that he had found in Calvin one whom he could unite with himself in this work. In the name of God he solemnly adjured the young evangelist to remain and labor here. Calvin drew back in alarm. Timid and peace-loving, he shrank from contact with the bold, independent, and even violent spirit of the Genevese. The feebleness of his health, together with his studious habits, led him to seek retirement. Believing that by his pen he could best serve the cause of reform, he desired to find a quiet retreat for study, and there, through the press, instruct and build up the churches. But Farel's solemn admonition came to him as a call from Heaven, and he dared not refuse. It seemed to him, he said, "that the hand of God was stretched down from heaven, that it lay hold of him, and fixed him irrevocably to the place he was so impatient to leave."—D'Aubigné, *History of the Reformation in Europe in the Time of Calvin,* b. 9, ch. 17.

At this time great perils surrounded the Protestant cause. The anathemas of the pope thundered against Geneva, and mighty nations threatened it with destruction. How was this little city to resist the powerful hierarchy that had so often forced kings and emperors to submission? How could it stand against the armies of the world's great conquerors?

Throughout Christendom, Protestantism was menaced by formidable foes. The first triumphs of the Reformation past, Rome summoned new forces, hoping to accomplish its destruction. At this time the order of the Jesuits was created, the most cruel, unscrupulous, and powerful of all the champions of popery. Cut off from earthly ties and human interests, dead to the claims of natural affection, reason and conscience wholly silenced, they knew no rule, no tie, but that of their order, and no duty but to extend its power. (See Appendix.) The gospel of Christ had enabled its adherents to meet danger and endure suffering, undismayed by cold, hunger, toil, and poverty, to uphold the banner of truth in face of the rack, the dungeon, and the stake. To combat these forces, Jesuitism inspired its followers with a fanaticism that enabled them to endure like dangers, and to oppose to the power of truth all the weapons of deception. There was no crime too great for them to commit, no deception too base for them to practice, no disguise too difficult for them to assume. Vowed to perpetual poverty and humility, it was their studied aim to secure wealth and power, to be devoted to the overthrow of Protestantism, and the re-establishment of the papal supremacy.

When appearing as members of their order, they wore a garb of sanctity, visiting prisons and hospitals, ministering to the sick and the poor, professing to have renounced the world, and bearing the sacred name of Jesus, who went about doing good. But under this blameless exterior the most criminal and deadly purposes were often concealed. It was a fundamental principle of the order that the end justifies the means. By this code, lying, theft, perjury, assassination, were not only pardonable but commendable, when they served the interests of the church. Under various disguises the Jesuits worked their way into offices of state, climbing up to be the counselors of kings, and shaping the policy of nations. They became servants to act as spies upon their masters. They established colleges for the sons of princes and nobles, and schools for the common people; and the children of Protestant parents were drawn into an observance of popish rites. All the outward pomp and display of the Romish worship was brought to bear to confuse the mind and dazzle and captivate the imagination, and thus the liberty for which the fathers had toiled and bled was betrayed by the sons. The Jesuits rapidly spread themselves over Europe, and wherever they went, there followed a revival of popery.

To give them greater power, a bull was issued re-establishing the inquisition. (See Appendix.) Notwithstanding the general abhorrence with which it was regarded, even in Catholic countries, this terrible tribunal was again set up by popish rulers, and atrocities too terrible to bear the light of day were repeated in its secret dungeons. In many countries, thousands upon thousands of the very flower of the nation, the purest and noblest, the most intellectual and highly educated, pious and devoted pastors, industrious and patriotic citizens, brilliant scholars, talented artists, skillful artisans, were slain or forced to flee to other lands.

Such were the means which Rome had invoked to quench the light of the Reformation, to withdraw from men the Bible, and to restore the ignorance and superstition of the Dark Ages. But under God's blessing and the labors of those noble men whom He had raised up to succeed Luther, Protestantism was not overthrown. Not to the favor or arms of princes was it to owe its strength. The smallest countries, the humblest and least powerful nations, became its strongholds. It was little Geneva in the midst of mighty foes plotting her destruction; it was Holland on her sandbanks by the northern sea, wrestling against the tyranny of Spain, then the greatest and most opulent of kingdoms; it was bleak, sterile Sweden, that gained victories for the Reformation.

For nearly thirty years Calvin labored at Geneva, first to establish there a church adhering to the morality of the Bible, and then for the advancement of the Reformation throughout Europe. His course as a public leader was not faultless, nor were his doctrines free from error. But he was instrumental in promulgating truths that were of special importance in his time, in maintaining the principles of Protestantism against the fast-returning tide of popery, and in promoting in the reformed churches simplicity and purity of life, in place of the pride and corruption fostered under the Romish teaching.

From Geneva, publications and teachers went out to spread the reformed doctrines. To this point the persecuted of all lands looked for instruction, counsel, and encouragement. The city of Calvin became a refuge for the hunted Reformers of all Western Europe. Fleeing from the awful tempests that continued for centuries, the fugitives came to the gates of Geneva. Starving, wounded, bereft of home and kindred, they were warmly welcomed and tenderly cared for; and finding a home here, they blessed the city of their adoption by their skill, their learning, and their piety. Many who sought here a refuge returned to their own countries to resist the tyranny of Rome. John Knox, the brave Scotch Reformer, not a few of the English Puritans, the Protestants of Holland and of Spain, and the Huguenots of France carried from Geneva the torch of truth to lighten the darkness of their native lands.

chapter 13

Heroes for Truth in the Netherlands and Scandinavia

IN THE Netherlands the papal tyranny very early called forth resolute protest. Seven hundred years before Luther's time the Roman pontiff was thus fearlessly impeached by two bishops, who, having been sent on an embassy to Rome, had learned the true character of the "holy see": God "has made His queen and spouse, the church, a noble and everlasting provision for her family, with a dowry that is neither fading nor corruptible, and given her an eternal crown and scepter; . . . all which benefits you like a thief intercept. You set up yourself in the temple of God; instead of a pastor, you are become a wolf to the sheep; . . . you would make us believe you are a supreme bishop, but you rather behave like a tyrant. . . . Whereas you ought to be a servant of servants, as you call yourself, you endeavor to become a lord of lords. . . . You bring the commands of God into contempt. . . . The Holy Ghost is the builder of all churches as far as the earth extends. . . . The city of our God, of which we are the citizens, reaches to all the regions of the heavens; and it is greater than the city, by the holy prophets named Babylon, which pretends to be divine, wins herself to heaven, and brags that her wisdom is immortal; and finally, though without reason, that she never did err, nor ever can."—Gerard Brandt, *History of the Reformation in and About the Low Countries,* b. 1, p. 6.

Others arose from century to century to echo this protest. And those early teachers who, traversing different lands and known by various names, bore the character of the Vaudois missionaries, and spread everywhere the knowledge of the gospel, penetrated to the Netherlands. Their doctrines spread rapidly. The Waldensian Bible they translated in verse into the Dutch language. They declared "that there was great advantage in it; no jests, no fables, no trifles, no deceits, but the words of truth; that indeed there was here and there a hard crust, but that the marrow and sweetness of what was good and holy might be easily discovered in it." —*Ibid.*, b. 1, p. 14. Thus wrote the friends of the ancient faith, in the twelfth century.

Now began the Romish persecutions; but in the midst of fagots and torture the believers continued to multiply, steadfastly declaring that the Bible is the only infallible authority in religion, and that "no man should be coerced to believe, but should be won by preaching."—Martyn, vol. 2, p. 87.

The teachings of Luther found a congenial soil in the Netherlands, and earnest and faithful men arose to preach the gospel. From one of the provinces of Holland came Menno Simons. Educated a Roman Catholic and ordained to the priesthood, he was wholly ignorant of the Bible, and he would not read it for fear of being beguiled into heresy. When a doubt concerning the doctrine of transubstantiation forced itself upon him, he regarded it as a temptation from Satan, and by prayer and confession sought to free himself from it; but in vain. By mingling in scenes of dissipation he endeavored to silence the accusing voice of conscience; but without avail. After a time he was led to the study of the New Testament, and this, with Luther's writings, caused him to accept the reformed faith. He soon after witnessed in a neighboring village the beheading of a man who was put to death for having been rebaptized. This led him to study the Bible in regard to infant baptism. He could find no evidence for it in the Scriptures, but saw that repentance and faith are everywhere required as the condition of receiving baptism.

Menno withdrew from the Roman Church and devoted his life to teaching the truths which he had received. In both Germany and the Netherlands a class of fanatics had risen, advocating absurd and seditious doctrines, outraging order and decency, and proceeding to violence and insurrection. Menno saw the horrible results to which these movements would inevitably lead, and he strenuously opposed the erroneous teachings and wild schemes of the fanatics. There were many, however, who had been misled by these fanatics, but who had renounced their pernicious doctrines; and there were still remaining many descendants of the ancient Christians, the fruits of the Waldensian teaching. Among these classes Menno labored with great zeal and success.

For twenty-five years he traveled, with his wife and children, enduring great hardships and privations, and frequently in peril of his life. He traversed the Netherlands and northern Germany, laboring chiefly among the humbler classes, but exerting a widespread influence. Naturally eloquent, though possessing a limited education, he was a man of unwavering integrity, of humble spirit and gentle manners, and of sincere and earnest piety, exemplifying in his own life the precepts which he taught, and he commanded the confidence of the people. His followers were scattered and oppressed. They suffered greatly from being confounded with the fanatical Munsterites. Yet great numbers were converted under his labors.

Nowhere were the reformed doctrines more generally received than in the Netherlands. In few countries did their adherents endure more terrible persecution. In Germany Charles V had banned the Reformation, and he would gladly have brought all its adherents to the stake; but the princes stood up as a barrier against his tyranny. In the Netherlands his power was greater, and persecuting edicts followed each other in quick succession. To read the Bible, to hear or preach it, or even to speak concerning it, was to incur the penalty of death by the stake. To pray to God in secret, to refrain from bowing to an image, or to sing a psalm, was also punishable with death. Even those who should abjure their errors were condemned, if men, to die by the sword; if women, to be buried alive. Thousands perished under the reign of Charles and of Philip II.

At one time a whole family was brought before the inquisitors, charged with remaining away from mass and worshiping at home. On his examination as to their practices in secret the youngest son answered: "We fall on our knees, and pray that God may enlighten our minds and pardon our sins; we pray for our sovereign, that his reign may be prosperous and his life happy; we pray for our magistrates, that God may preserve them."—Wylie, b. 18, ch. 6. Some of the judges were deeply moved, yet the father and one of his sons were condemned to the stake.

The rage of the persecutors was equaled by the faith of the martyrs. Not only men but delicate women and young maidens displayed unflinching courage. "Wives would take their stand by their husband's stake, and while he was enduring the fire they would whisper words of solace, or sing psalms to cheer him." "Young maidens would lie down in their living grave as if they were entering into their chamber of nightly sleep; or go forth to the scaffold and the fire, dressed in their best apparel, as if they were going to their marriage."—*Ibid.*, b. 18, ch. 6.

As in the days when paganism sought to destroy the gospel, the blood of the Christians was seed. (See Tertullian, *Apology*, paragraph 50.) Persecution served to increase the number of witnesses for the truth. Year after year the monarch, stung to madness by the unconquerable determination of the people, urged on his cruel work; but in vain. Under the noble William of Orange the Revolution at last brought to Holland freedom to worship God.

In the mountains of Piedmont, on the plains of France and the shores of Holland, the progress of the gospel was marked with the blood of its disciples. But in the countries of the North it found a peaceful entrance. Students at Wittenberg, returning to their homes, carried the reformed faith to Scandinavia. The publication of Luther's writings also spread the light. The simple, hardy people of the North turned from the corruption, the pomp, and the superstitions of Rome, to welcome the purity, the simplicity, and the life-giving truths of the Bible.

Tausen, "the Reformer of Denmark," was a peasant's son. The boy early gave evidence of vigorous intellect; he thirsted for an education; but this was denied him by the circumstances of his parents, and he entered a cloister. Here the purity of his life, together with his diligence and fidelity, won the favor of his superior. Examination showed him to possess talent that promised at some future day good service to the church. It was determined to give him an education at some one of the universities of Germany or the Netherlands. The young student was granted permission to choose a school for himself, with one proviso, that he must not go to Wittenberg. The scholar of the church was not to be endangered by the poison of heresy. So said the friars.

Tausen went to Cologne, which was then, as now, one of the strongholds of Romanism. Here he soon became disgusted with the mysticisms of the schoolmen. About the same time he obtained Luther's writings. He read them with wonder and delight, and greatly desired to enjoy the personal instruction of the Reformer. But to do so he must risk giving offense to his monastic superior and forfeiting his support. His decision was soon made, and erelong he was enrolled as a student at Wittenberg.

On returning to Denmark, he again repaired to his cloister. No one as yet suspected him of Lutheranism; he did not reveal his secret, but endeavored, without exciting the prejudices of his companions, to lead them to a purer faith and a holier life. He opened the Bible, and explained its true meaning, and at last preached Christ to them as the sinner's righteousness and his only hope of salvation. Great was the wrath of the prior, who had built high hopes upon him as a valiant defender of Rome. He was at once removed from his own monastery to another and confined to his cell under strict supervision.

To the terror of his new guardians several of the monks soon declared themselves converts to Protestantism. Through the bars of his cell Tausen had communicated to his companions a knowledge of the truth. Had those Danish fathers been skilled in the church's plan of dealing with heresy, Tausen's voice would never again have been heard; but instead of consigning him to a tomb in some underground dungeon, they expelled him from the monastery. Now they were powerless. A royal edict, just issued, offered protection to the teachers of the new doctrine. Tausen began to preach. The churches were opened to him, and the people thronged to listen. Others also were preaching the word of God. The New Testament, translated into the Danish tongue, was widely circulated. The efforts made by the papists to overthrow the work resulted in extending it, and erelong Denmark declared its acceptance of the reformed faith.

In Sweden, also, young men who had drunk from the well of Wittenberg carried the water of life to their countrymen. Two of the leaders in the Swedish Reformation, Olaf and Laurentius Petri, the sons of a blacksmith of Orebro, studied under Luther and Melanchthon, and the truths which they thus learned they were diligent to teach. Like the great Reformer, Olaf aroused the people by his zeal and eloquence, while Laurentius, like Melanchthon, was learned, thoughtful, and calm. Both were men of ardent piety, of high theological attainments, and of unflinching courage in advancing the truth. Papist opposition was not lacking. The Catholic priests stirred up the ignorant and superstitious people. Olaf Petri was often assailed by the mob, and upon several occasions barely escaped with his life. These Reformers were, however, favored and protected by the king.

Under the rule of the Roman Church the people were sunken in poverty and ground down by oppression. They were destitute of the Scriptures; and having a religion of mere signs and ceremonies, which conveyed no light to the mind, they were returning to the superstitious beliefs and pagan practices of their heathen ancestors. The nation was divided into contending factions, whose perpetual strife increased the misery of all. The king determined upon a reformation in the state and the church, and he welcomed these able assistants in the battle against Rome.

In the presence of the monarch and the leading men of Sweden, Olaf Petri with great ability defended the doctrines of the reformed faith against the Romish champions. He declared that the teachings of the Fathers are to be received only when in accordance with the Scriptures; that the essential doctrines of the faith are presented in the Bible in a clear and simple manner, so that all men may understand them. Christ said, "My doctrine is not Mine, but His that sent Me" (John 7:16); and Paul declared that should he preach any other gospel than that which he had received, he would be accursed (Galatians 1:8). "How, then," said the Reformer, "shall others presume to enact dogmas at their pleasure, and impose them as things necessary to salvation?"—Wylie, b. 10, ch. 4. He showed that the decrees of the church are of no authority when in opposition to the commands of God, and maintained the great Protestant principle that "the Bible and the Bible only" is the rule of faith and practice.

This contest, though conducted upon a stage comparatively obscure, serves to show us "the sort of men that formed the rank and file of the army of the Reformers. They were not illiterate, sectarian, noisy controversialists—far from it; they were men who had studied the word of God, and knew well how to wield the weapons with which the armory of the Bible supplied them. In respect of erudition they were ahead of their age. When we confine our attention to such brilliant centers as Wittenberg and Zurich, and to such illustrious names as those of Luther and Melanchthon, of Zwingli and Oecolampadius, we are apt to be told, these were the leaders of the movement, and we should naturally expect in them prodigious power and vast acquisitions; but the subordinates were not like these. Well, we turn to the obscure theater of Sweden, and the humble names of Olaf and Laurentius Petri—from the masters to the disciples—what do we find? . . . Scholars and theologians; men who have thoroughly mastered the whole system of gospel truth, and who win an easy victory over the sophists of the schools and the dignitaries of Rome."—*Ibid.*, b. 10, ch. 4.

As the result of this disputation the king of Sweden accepted the Protestant faith, and not long afterward the national assembly declared in its favor. The New Testament had been translated by Olaf Petri into the Swedish language, and at the desire of the king the two brothers undertook the translation of the whole Bible. Thus for the first time the people of Sweden received the word of God in their native tongue. It was ordered by the Diet that throughout the kingdom, ministers should explain the Scriptures and that the children in the schools should be taught to read the Bible.

Steadily and surely the darkness of ignorance and superstition was dispelled by the blessed light of the gospel. Freed from Romish oppression, the nation attained to a strength and greatness it had never before reached. Sweden became one of the bulwarks of Protestantism. A century later, at a time of sorest peril, this small and hitherto feeble nation—the only one in Europe that dared lend a helping hand—came to the deliverance of Germany in the terrible struggle of the Thirty Years' War. All Northern Europe seemed about to be brought again under the tyranny of Rome. It was the armies of Sweden that enabled Germany to turn the tide of popish success, to win toleration for the Protestants—Calvinists as well as Lutherans—and to restore liberty of conscience to those countries that had accepted the Reformation.

Truth Advances in the British Isles

WHILE Luther was opening a closed Bible to the people of Germany, Tyndale was impelled by the Spirit of God to do the same for England. Wycliffe's Bible had been translated from the Latin text, which contained many errors. It had never been printed, and the cost of manuscript copies was so great that few but wealthy men or nobles could procure it; and, furthermore, being strictly proscribed by the church, it had had a comparatively narrow circulation. In 1516, a year before the appearance of Luther's theses, Erasmus had published his Greek and Latin version of the New Testament. Now for the first time the word of God was printed in the original tongue. In this work many errors of former versions were corrected, and the sense was more clearly rendered. It led many among the educated classes to a better knowledge of the truth, and gave a new impetus to the work of reform. But the common people were still, to a great extent, debarred from God's word. Tyndale was to complete the work of Wycliffe in giving the Bible to his countrymen.

A diligent student and an earnest seeker for truth, he had received the gospel from the Greek Testament of Erasmus. He fearlessly preached his convictions, urging that all doctrines be tested by the Scriptures. To the papist claim that the church had given the Bible, and the church alone could explain it, Tyndale responded: "Do you know who taught the eagles to find their prey? Well, that same God teaches His hungry children to find their Father in His word. Far from having given us the Scriptures, it is you who have hidden them from us; it is you who burn

Protestants in England were often arrested as they worshiped in secret, sometimes in the woods at midnight.

those who teach them, and if you could, you would burn the Scriptures themselves."—D'Aubigné, *History of the Reformation of the Sixteenth Century,* b. 18, ch. 4.

Tyndale's preaching excited great interest; many accepted the truth. But the priests were on the alert, and no sooner had he left the field than they by their threats and misrepresentations endeavored to destroy his work. Too often they succeeded. "What is to be done?" he exclaimed. "While I am sowing in one place, the enemy ravages the field I have just left. I cannot be everywhere. Oh! if Christians possessed the Holy Scriptures in their own tongue, they could of themselves withstand these sophists. Without the Bible it is impossible to establish the laity in the truth."—*Ibid.*, b. 18, ch. 4.

A new purpose now took possession of his mind. "It was in the language of Israel," said he, "that the psalms were sung in the temple of Jehovah; and shall not the gospel speak the language of England among us? . . . Ought the church to have less light at noonday than at the dawn? . . . Christians must read the New Testament in their mother tongue." The doctors and teachers of the church disagreed among themselves. Only by the Bible could men arrive at the truth. "One holdeth this doctor, another that. . . . Now each of these authors contradicts the other. How then can we distinguish him who says right from him who says wrong? . . . How? . . . Verily by God's word."—*Ibid.*, b. 18, ch. 4.

It was not long after that a learned Catholic doctor, engaging in controversy with him, exclaimed: "We were better to be without God's laws than the pope's." Tyndale replied: "I defy the pope and all his laws; and if God spare my life, ere many years I will cause a boy that driveth the plow to know more of the Scripture than you do."—Anderson, *Annals of the English Bible,* page 19.

The purpose which he had begun to cherish, of giving to the people the New Testament Scriptures in their own language, was now confirmed, and he immediately applied himself to the work. Driven from his home by persecution, he went to London, and there for a time pursued his labors undisturbed. But again the violence of the papists forced him to flee. All England seemed closed against him, and he resolved to seek shelter in Germany. Here he began the printing of the English New Testament. Twice the work was stopped; but when forbidden to print in one city, he went to another. At last he made his way to Worms, where, a few years before, Luther had defended the gospel before the Diet. In that ancient city were many friends of the Reformation, and Tyndale there prosecuted his work without further hindrance. Three thousand copies of the New Testament were soon finished, and another edition followed in the same year.

With great earnestness and perseverance he continued his labors. Notwithstanding the English authorities had guarded their ports with the strictest vigilance, the word of God was in various ways secretly conveyed to London and thence circulated throughout the country. The papists attempted to suppress the truth, but in vain. The bishop of Durham at one time bought of a bookseller who was a friend of Tyndale his whole stock of Bibles, for the purpose of destroying them, supposing that this would greatly hinder the work. But, on the contrary, the money thus furnished, purchased material for a new and better edition, which, but for this, could not have been published. When Tyndale was afterward made a prisoner, his liberty was offered him on condition that he would reveal the names of those who had helped him meet the expense of printing his Bibles. He replied that the bishop of Durham had done more than any other person; for by paying a large price for the books left on hand, he had enabled him to go on with good courage.

Tyndale was betrayed into the hands of his enemies, and at one time suffered imprisonment for many months. He finally witnessed for his faith by a martyr's death; but the weapons which he prepared have enabled other soldiers to do battle through all the centuries even to our time.

Latimer maintained from the pulpit that the Bible ought to be read in the language of the people. The Author of Holy Scripture, said he, "is God Himself;" and this Scripture partakes of the might and eternity of its Author. "There is no king, emperor, magistrate, and ruler . . . but are bound to obey . . . His holy word." "Let us not take any bywalks, but let God's word direct us: let us not walk after . . . our forefathers, nor seek not what they did, but what they should have done."—Hugh Latimer, "First Sermon Preached Before King Edward VI."

Barnes and Frith, the faithful friends of Tyndale, arose to defend the truth. The Ridleys and Cranmer followed. These leaders in the English Reformation were men of learning, and most of them had been highly esteemed for zeal or piety in the Romish communion. Their opposition to the papacy was the result of their knowledge of the errors of the "holy see." Their acquaintance with the mysteries of Babylon gave greater power to their testimonies against her.

"Now I would ask a strange question," said Latimer. "Who is the most diligent bishop and prelate in all England? . . . I see you listening and hearkening that I should name him. . . . I will tell you: it is the devil. . . . He is never out of his diocese; call for him when you will, he is ever at home; . . . he is ever at his plow. . . . Ye shall never find him idle, I warrant you. . . . Where the devil is resident, . . . there away with books, and up with candles; away with Bibles, and up with beads; away with the light of the gospel, and up with the light of candles, yea, at noondays; . . . down with Christ's cross, up with purgatory pickpurse; . . . away with clothing the naked, the poor, and impotent, up with decking of images and gay garnishing of stocks and stones; up with man's traditions and his laws, down with God's traditions and His most holy word. . . . O that our prelates would be as diligent to sow the corn of good doctrine, as Satan is to sow cockle and darnel!"—*Ibid.*, "Sermon of the Plough."

The grand principle maintained by these Reformers—the same that had been held by the Waldenses, by Wycliffe, by John Huss, by Luther, Zwingli, and those who united with them—was the infallible authority of the Holy Scriptures as a rule of faith and practice. They denied the right of popes, councils, Fathers, and kings, to control the conscience in matters of religion. The Bible was their authority, and by its teaching they tested all doctrines and all claims. Faith in God and His word sustained these holy men as they yielded up their lives at the stake. "Be of good comfort," exclaimed Latimer to his fellow martyr as the flames were about to silence their voices, "we shall this day light such a candle, by God's grace, in England, as I trust shall never be put out."—*Works of Hugh Latimer*, vol. 1, p. xiii.

In Scotland the seeds of truth scattered by Columba and his colaborers had never been wholly destroyed. For hundreds of years after the churches of England submitted to Rome, those of Scotland maintained their freedom. In the twelfth century, however, popery became established here, and in no country did it exercise a more absolute sway. Nowhere was the darkness deeper. Still there came rays of light to pierce the gloom and give promise of the coming day. The Lollards, coming from England with the Bible and the teachings of Wycliffe, did much to preserve the knowledge of the gospel, and every century had its witnesses and martyrs.

With the opening of the Great Reformation came the writings of Luther, and then Tyndale's English New Testament. Unnoticed by the hierarchy, these messengers silently traversed the mountains and valleys, kindling into new life the torch of truth so nearly extinguished in Scotland, and undoing the work which Rome for four centuries of oppression had done.

Then the blood of martyrs gave fresh impetus to the movement. The papist leaders, suddenly awakening to the danger that threatened their cause, brought to the stake some of the noblest and most honored of the sons of Scotland. They did but erect a pulpit, from which the words of these dying witnesses were heard throughout the land, thrilling the souls of the people with an undying purpose to cast off the shackles of Rome.

Hamilton and Wishart, princely in character as in birth, with a long line of humbler disciples, yielded up their lives at the stake. But from the burning pile of Wishart there came one whom the flames were not to silence, one who under God was to strike the death knell of popery in Scotland.

John Knox had turned away from the traditions and mysticisms of the church, to feed upon the truths of God's word; and the teaching of Wishart had confirmed his determination to forsake the communion of Rome and join himself to the persecuted Reformers.

Urged by his companions to take the office of preacher, he shrank with trembling from its responsibility, and it was only after days of seclusion and painful conflict with himself that he consented. But having once accepted the position, he pressed forward with inflexible determination and undaunted courage as long as life continued. This truehearted Reformer feared not the face of man. The fires of martyrdom, blazing around him, served only to quicken his zeal to greater intensity. With the tyrant's ax held menacingly over his head, he stood his ground, striking sturdy blows on the right hand and on the left to demolish idolatry.

When brought face to face with the queen of Scotland, in whose presence the zeal of many a leader of the Protestants had abated, John Knox bore unswerving witness for the truth. He was not to be won by caresses; he quailed not before threats. The queen charged him with heresy. He had taught the people to receive a religion prohibited by the state, she declared, and had thus transgressed God's command enjoining subjects to obey their princes. Knox answered firmly:

"As right religion took neither original strength nor authority from worldly princes, but from the eternal God alone, so are not subjects bound to frame their religion according to the appetites of their princes. For oft it is that princes are the most ignorant of all others in God's true religion. . . . If all the seed of Abraham had been of the religion of Pharaoh, whose subjects they long were, I pray you, madam, what religion would there

[*249-251*] 209

have been in the world? Or if all men in the days of the apostles had been of the religion of the Roman emperors, what religion would there have been upon the face of the earth? . . . And so, madam, ye may perceive that subjects are not bound to the religion of their princes, albeit they are commanded to give them obedience."

Said Mary: "Ye interpret the Scriptures in one manner, and they [the Roman Catholic teachers] interpret in another; whom shall I believe, and who shall be judge?"

"Ye shall believe God, that plainly speaketh in His word," answered the Reformer; "and farther than the word teaches you, ye neither shall believe the one nor the other. The word of God is plain in itself; and if there appear any obscurity in one place, the Holy Ghost, which is never contrary to Himself, explains the same more clearly in other places, so that there can remain no doubt but unto such as obstinately remain ignorant."—David Laing, *The Collected Works of John Knox,* vol. 2, pp. 281, 284.

Such were the truths that the fearless Reformer, at the peril of his life, spoke in the ear of royalty. With the same undaunted courage he kept to his purpose, praying and fighting the battles of the Lord, until Scotland was free from popery.

In England the establishment of Protestantism as the national religion diminished, but did not wholly stop, persecution. While many of the doctrines of Rome had been renounced, not a few of its forms were retained. The supremacy of the pope was rejected, but in his place the monarch was enthroned as the head of the church. In the service of the church there was still a wide departure from the purity and simplicity of the gospel. The great principle of religious liberty was not yet understood. Though the horrible cruelties which Rome employed against heresy were resorted to but rarely by Protestant rulers, yet the right of every man to worship God according to the dictates of his own conscience was not acknowledged. All were required to accept the doctrines and observe the forms of worship prescribed by the established church. Dissenters suffered persecution, to a greater or less extent, for hundreds of years.

In the seventeenth century thousands of pastors were expelled from their positions. The people were forbidden, on pain of heavy fines, imprisonment, and banishment, to attend any religious meetings except such as were sanctioned by the church. Those faithful souls who could not refrain from gathering to worship God were compelled to meet in dark alleys, in obscure garrets, and at some seasons in the woods at midnight. In the sheltering depths of the forest, a temple of God's own building, those scattered and persecuted children of the Lord assembled to pour out their souls in prayer and praise. But despite all their precautions, many suffered for their faith. The jails were crowded. Families were broken up. Many were banished to foreign lands. Yet God was with His people, and persecution could not prevail to silence their testimony. Many were driven across the ocean to America and here laid the foundations of civil and religious liberty which have been the bulwark and glory of this country.

Again, as in apostolic days, persecution turned out to the furtherance of the gospel. In a loathsome dungeon crowded with profligates and felons, John Bunyan breathed the very atmosphere of heaven; and there he wrote his wonderful allegory of the pilgrim's journey from the land of destruction to the celestial city. For over two hundred years that voice from Bedford jail has spoken with thrilling power to the hearts of men. Bunyan's *Pilgrim's Progress* and *Grace Abounding to the Chief of Sinners* have guided many feet into the path of life.

Baxter, Flavel, Alleine, and other men of talent, education, and deep Christian experience stood up in valiant defense of the faith which was once delivered to the saints. The work accomplished by these men, proscribed and outlawed by the rulers of this world, can never perish. Flavel's *Fountain of Life* and *Method of Grace* have taught thousands how to commit the keeping of their souls to Christ. Baxter's *Reformed Pastor* has proved a blessing to many who desire a revival of the work of God, and his *Saints' Everlasting Rest* has done its work in leading souls to the "rest" that remaineth for the people of God.

A hundred years later, in a day of great spiritual darkness, Whitefield and the Wesleys appeared as light bearers for God. Under the rule of the established church the people of England had lapsed into a state of religious declension hardly to be distinguished from heathenism. Natural religion was the favorite study of the clergy, and included most of their theology. The higher classes sneered at piety, and prided themselves on being above what they called its fanaticism. The lower classes were grossly ignorant and abandoned to vice, while the church had no courage or faith any longer to support the downfallen cause of truth.

The great doctrine of justification by faith, so clearly taught by Luther, had been almost wholly lost sight of; and the Romish principle of trusting to good works for salvation, had taken its place. Whitefield and the Wesleys, who were members of the established church, were sincere seekers for the favor of God, and this they had been taught was to be secured by a virtuous life and an observance of the ordinances of religion.

When Charles Wesley at one time fell ill, and anticipated that death was approaching, he was asked upon what he rested his hope of eternal life. His answer was: "I have used my best endeavors to serve God." As the friend who had put the question seemed not to be fully satisfied with his answer, Wesley thought: "What! are not my endeavors a sufficient ground of hope? Would he rob me of my endeavors? I have nothing else to trust to."—John Whitehead, *Life of the Rev. Charles Wesley*, page 102. Such was the dense darkness that had settled down on the church, hiding the atonement, robbing Christ of His glory, and turning the minds of men from their only hope of salvation—the blood of the crucified Redeemer.

Wesley and his associates were led to see that true religion is seated in the heart, and that God's law extends to the thoughts as well as to the words and actions. Convinced of the necessity of holiness of heart, as well as correctness of outward deportment, they set out in earnest upon a new life. By the most diligent and prayerful efforts they endeavored to subdue the evils of the natural heart. They lived a life of self-denial, charity, and humiliation, observing with great rigor and exactness every measure which they thought could be helpful to them in obtaining what they most desired—that holiness which could secure the favor of God. But they did not obtain the object which they sought. In vain were their endeavors to free themselves from the condemnation of sin or to break its power. It was the same struggle which Luther had experienced in his cell at Erfurt. It was the same question which had tortured his soul—"How should man be just before God?" Job 9:2.

The fires of divine truth, well-nigh extinguished upon the altars of Protestantism, were to be rekindled from the ancient torch handed down the ages by the Bohemian Christians. After the Reformation, Protestantism in Bohemia had been trampled out by the hordes of Rome. All who refused to renounce the truth were forced to flee. Some of these, finding refuge in Saxony, there maintained the ancient faith. It was from the descendants of these Christians that light came to Wesley and his associates.

John and Charles Wesley, after being ordained to the ministry, were sent on a mission to America. On board the ship was a company of Moravians. Violent storms were encountered on the passage, and John Wesley, brought face to face with death, felt that he had not the assurance of peace with God. The Germans, on the contrary, manifested a calmness and trust to which he was a stranger.

"I had long before," he says, "observed the great seriousness of their behavior. Of their humility they had given a continual proof, by performing those servile offices for the other passengers which none of the English would undertake; for which they desired and would receive no pay, saying it was good for their proud hearts, and their loving Saviour had done more for them. And every day had given them occasion of showing a meekness which no injury could move. If they were pushed, struck, or thrown about, they rose again and went away; but no complaint was found in their mouth. There was now an opportunity of trying whether they were delivered from the spirit of fear, as well as from that of pride, anger, and revenge. In the midst of the psalm wherewith their service began, the sea broke over, split the mainsail in pieces, covered the ship, and poured in between the decks as if the great deep had already swallowed us up. A terrible screaming began among the English. The Germans calmly sang on. I asked one of them afterwards, 'Were you not afraid?' He answered, 'I thank God, no.' I asked, 'But were not your women and children afraid?' He replied mildly, 'No; our women and children are not afraid to die.'"—Whitehead, *Life of the Rev. John Wesley*, page 10.

Upon arriving in Savannah, Wesley for a short time abode with the Moravians, and was deeply impressed with their Christian deportment. Of one of their religious services, in striking contrast to the lifeless formalism of the Church of England, he wrote: "The great simplicity as well as solemnity of the whole almost made me forget the seventeen hundred years between, and imagine myself in one of those assemblies where form and state were not; but Paul, the tentmaker, or Peter, the fisherman, presided; yet with the demonstration of the Spirit and of power."—*Ibid.*, pages 11, 12.

On his return to England, Wesley, under the instruction of a Moravian preacher, arrived at a clearer understanding of Bible faith. He was convinced that he must renounce all dependence upon his own works for salvation and must trust wholly to "the Lamb of God, which taketh away the sin of the world." At a meeting of the Moravian society in London a statement was read from Luther, describing the change which the Spirit of God works in the heart of the believer. As Wesley listened, faith was kindled in his soul. "I felt my heart strangely warmed," he says. "I felt I did trust in Christ, Christ alone, for salvation: and an assurance was given me, that He had taken away *my* sins, even *mine,* and saved *me* from the law of sin and death."—*Ibid.*, page 52.

Through long years of wearisome and comfortless striving—years of rigorous self-denial, of reproach and humiliation—Wesley had steadfastly adhered to his one purpose of seeking God. Now he had found Him; and he found that the grace which he had toiled to win by prayers and fasts, by almsdeeds and self-abnegation, was a gift, "without money and without price."

Once established in the faith of Christ, his whole soul burned with the desire to spread everywhere a knowledge of the glorious gospel of God's free grace. "I look upon all the world as my parish," he said; "in whatever part of it I am, I judge it meet, right, and my bounden duty, to declare unto all that are willing to hear, the glad tidings of salvation."—*Ibid.*, page 74.

He continued his strict and self-denying life, not now as the *ground,* but the *result* of faith; not the *root,* but the *fruit* of holiness. The grace of God in Christ is the foundation of the Christian's hope, and that grace will be manifested in obedience. Wesley's life was devoted to the preaching of the great truths which he had received—justification through faith in the atoning blood of Christ, and the renewing power of the Holy Spirit upon the heart, bringing forth fruit in a life conformed to the example of Christ.

Whitefield and the Wesleys had been prepared for their work by long and sharp personal convictions of their own lost condition; and that they might be able to endure hardness as good soldiers of Christ, they had been subjected to the fiery ordeal of scorn, derision, and persecution, both in the university and as they were entering the ministry. They and a few others who sympathized with them were contemptuously called Methodists by their ungodly fellow students—a name which is at the present time regarded as honorable by one of the largest denominations in England and America.

As members of the Church of England they were strongly attached to her forms of worship, but the Lord had presented before them in His word a higher standard. The Holy Spirit urged them to preach Christ and Him crucified. The power of the Highest attended their labors. Thousands were convicted and truly converted. It was necessary that these sheep be protected from ravening wolves. Wesley had no thought of forming a new denomination, but he organized them under what was called the Methodist Connection.

Mysterious and trying was the opposition which these preachers encountered from the established church; yet God, in His wisdom, had overruled events to cause the reform to begin within the church itself. Had it come wholly from without, it would not have penetrated where it was so much needed. But as the revival preachers were churchmen, and labored within the pale of the church wherever they could find opportunity, the truth had an entrance where the doors would otherwise have remained closed. Some of the clergy were roused from their moral stupor and became zealous preachers in their own parishes. Churches that had been petrified by formalism were quickened into life.

In Wesley's time, as in all ages of the church's history, men of different gifts performed their appointed work. They did not harmonize upon every point of doctrine, but all were moved by the Spirit of God, and united in the absorbing aim to win souls to Christ. The differences between Whitefield and the Wesleys threatened at one time to create alienation; but as they learned meekness in the school of Christ, mutual forbearance and charity reconciled them. They had no time to dispute, while error and iniquity were teaming everywhere, and sinners were going down to ruin.

The servants of God trod a rugged path. Men of influence and learning employed their powers against them. After a time many of the clergy manifested determined hostility, and the doors of the churches were closed against a pure faith and those who proclaimed it. The course of the clergy in denouncing them from the pulpit aroused the elements of darkness, ignorance, and iniquity. Again and again did John Wesley escape death by a miracle of God's mercy. When the rage of the mob was excited against him, and there seemed no way of escape, an angel in human form came to his side, the mob fell back, and the servant of Christ passed in safety from the place of danger.

Of his deliverance from the enraged mob on one of these occasions, Wesley said: "Many endeavored to throw me down while we were going down hill on a slippery path to the town; as well judging that if I was once on the ground, I should hardly rise any more. But I made no stumble at all, nor the least slip, till I was entirely out of their hands. . . . Although many strove to lay hold on my collar or clothes, to pull me down, they could not fasten at all: only one got fast hold of the flap of my waistcoat, which was soon left in his hand; the other flap, in the pocket of which was a bank note, was torn but half off. . . . A lusty man just behind, struck at me several times, with a large oaken stick; with which if he had struck me once on the back part of my head, it would have saved him all further trouble. But every time, the blow was turned aside, I know not how; for I could not move to the right hand or left. . . . Another came rushing through the press, and raising his arm to strike, on a sudden let it drop, and only stroked my head, saying, 'What soft hair he has!' . . . The very first men whose hearts were turned were the heroes of the town, the captains of the rabble on all occasions, one of them having been a prize fighter at the bear gardens. . . .

"By how gentle degrees does God prepare us for His will! Two years ago, a piece of brick grazed my shoulders. It was a year after that the stone struck me between the eyes. Last month I received one blow, and this evening two, one before we came into the town, and one after we were gone out; but both were as nothing: for though one man struck me on the breast with all his might, and the other on the mouth with such force that the blood gushed out immediately, I felt no more pain from either of the blows than if they had touched me with a straw."—John Wesley, *Works,* vol. 3, pp. 297, 298.

The Methodists of those early days—people as well as preachers—endured ridicule and persecution, alike from church members and from the openly irreligious who were inflamed by their misrepresentations. They were arraigned before courts of justice—such only in name, for justice was rare in the courts of that time. Often they suffered violence from their persecutors. Mobs went from house to house, destroying furniture and goods, plundering whatever they chose, and brutally abusing men, women, and children. In some instances, public notices were posted, calling upon those who desired to assist in breaking the windows and robbing the houses of the Methodists, to assemble at a given time and place. These open violations of both human and divine law were allowed to pass without a reprimand. A systematic persecution was carried on against a people whose only fault was that of seeking to turn the feet of sinners from the path of destruction to the path of holiness.

Said John Wesley, referring to the charges against himself and his associates: "Some allege that the doctrines of these men are false, erroneous, and enthusiastic; that they are new and unheard-of till of late; that they are Quakerism, fanaticism, popery. This whole pretense has been already cut up by the roots, it having been shown at large that every branch of this doctrine is the plain doctrine of Scripture interpreted by our own church. Therefore it cannot be either false or erroneous, provided the Scripture be true." "Others allege, 'Their doctrine is too strict; they make the way to heaven too narrow.' And this is in truth the original objection, (as it was almost the only one for some time,) and is secretly at the bottom of a thousand more, which appear in various forms. But do they make the way to heaven any narrower than our Lord and His apostles made it? Is their doctrine stricter than that of the Bible? Consider only a few plain texts: 'Thou shalt love the Lord thy God with all thy heart, and with all thy mind, and with all thy soul, and with all thy strength.' 'For every idle word which men shall speak, they shall give an account in the day of judgment.' 'Whether ye eat, or drink, or whatever ye do, do all to the glory of God.'

"If their doctrine is stricter than this, they are to blame; but you know in your conscience it is not. And who can be one jot less strict without corrupting the word of God? Can any steward of the mysteries of God be found faithful if he change any part of that sacred depositum? No. He can abate nothing, he can soften nothing; he is constrained to declare to all men, 'I may not bring down the Scripture to your taste. You must come up to it, or perish forever.' This is the real ground of that other popular cry concerning 'the uncharitableness of these men.' Uncharitable, are they? In what respect? Do they not feed the hungry and clothe the naked? 'No; that is not the thing: they are not wanting in this: but they are so uncharitable in judging! they think none can be saved but those of their own way.' "—*Ibid.*, vol. 3, pp. 152, 153.

The spiritual declension which had been manifest in England just before the time of Wesley was in great degree the result of antinomian teaching. Many affirmed that Christ had abolished the moral law and that Christians are therefore under no obligation to observe it; that a believer is freed from the "bondage of good works." Others, though admitting the perpetuity of the law, declared that it was unnecessary for ministers to exhort the people to obedience of its precepts, since those whom God had elected to salvation would, "by the irresistible impulse of divine grace, be led to the practice of piety and virtue," while those who were doomed to eternal reprobation "did not have power to obey the divine law."

Others, also holding that "the elect cannot fall from grace nor forfeit the divine favor," arrived at the still more hideous conclusion that "the wicked actions they commit are not really sinful, nor to be considered as instances of their violation of the divine law, and that, consequently, they have no occasion either to confess their sins or to break them off by repentance."—McClintock and Strong, *Cyclopedia,* art. "Antinomians." Therefore, they declared that even one of the vilest of sins, "considered universally an enormous violation of the divine law, is not a sin in the sight of God," if committed by one of the elect, "because it is one of the essential and distinctive characteristics of the elect, that they cannot do anything that is either displeasing to God or prohibited by the law."

These monstrous doctrines are essentially the same as the later teaching of popular educators and theologians—that there is no unchangeable divine law as the standard of right, but that the standard of morality is indicated by society itself, and has constantly been subject to change. All these ideas are inspired by the same master spirit—by him who, even among the sinless inhabitants of heaven, began his work of seeking to break down the righteous restraints of the law of God.

The doctrine of the divine decrees, unalterably fixing the character of men, had led many to a virtual rejection of the law of God. Wesley steadfastly opposed the errors of the antinomian teachers and showed that this doctrine which led to antinomianism was contrary to the Scriptures. "The grace of God that bringeth salvation hath appeared to *all men.*" "This is good and acceptable in the sight of God our Saviour; who will have *all men* to be saved, and to come unto the knowledge of the truth. For there is one God, and one mediator between God and men, the man Christ Jesus; who gave Himself a ransom for *all.*" Titus 2:11; 1 Timothy 2:3-6. The Spirit of God is freely bestowed to enable every man to lay hold upon the means of salvation. Thus Christ, "the true Light," "lighteth every man that cometh into the world." John 1:9. Men fail of salvation through their own willful refusal of the gift of life.

In answer to the claim that at the death of Christ the precepts of the Decalogue had been abolished with the ceremonial law, Wesley said: "The moral law, contained in the Ten Commandments and enforced by the prophets, He did not take away. It was not the design of His coming to revoke any part of this. This is a law which never can be broken, which 'stands fast as the faithful witness in heaven.' . . . This was from the beginning of the world, being 'written not on tables of stone,' but on the hearts of all the children of men, when they came out of the hands of the Creator. And however the letters once wrote by the finger of God are now in a great measure defaced by sin, yet can they not wholly be blotted out, while we have any consciousness of good and evil. Every part of this law must remain in force upon all mankind, and in all ages; as not depending either on time or place, or any other circumstances liable to change, but on the nature of God, and the nature of man, and their unchangeable relation to each other.

" 'I am not come to destroy, but to fulfill.' . . . Without question, His meaning in this place is (consistently with all that goes before and follows after)—I am come to establish it in its fullness, in spite of all the glosses of men: I am come to place in a full and clear view whatsoever was dark or obscure therein: I am come to declare the true and full import of every part of it; to show the length and breadth, the entire extent, of every commandment contained therein, and the height and depth, the inconceivable purity and spirituality of it in all its branches." —Wesley, sermon 25.

Wesley declared the perfect harmony of the law and the gospel.

"There is, therefore, the closest connection that can be conceived, between the law and the gospel. On the one hand, the law continually makes way for, and points us to, the gospel; on the other, the gospel continually leads us to a more exact fulfilling of the law. The law, for instance, requires us to love God, to love our neighbor, to be meek, humble, or holy. We feel that we are not sufficient for these things; yea, that 'with man this is impossible;' but we see a promise of God to give us that love, and to make us humble, meek, and holy: we lay hold of this gospel, of these glad tidings; it is done unto us according to our faith; and 'the righteousness of the law is fulfilled in us,' through faith which is in Christ Jesus. . . .

"In the highest rank of the enemies of the gospel of Christ," said Wesley, "are they who openly and explicitly 'judge the law' itself, and 'speak evil of the law;' who teach men to break (to dissolve, to loose, to untie the obligation of) not one only, whether of the least or of the greatest, but all the commandments at a stroke. . . . The most surprising of all the circumstances that attend this strong delusion, is that they who are given up to it, really believe that they honor Christ by overthrowing His law, and that they are magnifying His office while they are destroying His doctrine! Yea, they honor Him just as Judas did when he said, 'Hail, Master, and kissed Him.' And He may as justly say to every one of them, 'Betrayest thou the Son of man with a kiss?' It is no other than betraying Him with a kiss, to talk of His blood, and take away His crown; to set light by any part of His law, under pretense of advancing His gospel. Nor indeed can anyone escape this charge, who preaches faith in any such a manner as either directly or indirectly tends to set aside any branch of obedience: who preaches Christ so as to disannul, or weaken in any wise, the least of the commandments of God."—*Ibid.*

To those who urged that "the preaching of the gospel answers all the ends of the law," Wesley replied: "This we utterly deny. It does not answer the very first end of the law, namely, the convincing men of sin, the awakening those who are still asleep on the brink of hell." The apostle Paul declares that "by the law is the knowledge of sin;" "and not until man is convicted of sin, will he truly feel his need of the atoning blood of Christ. . . . 'They that be whole,' as our Lord Himself observes, 'need not a physician, but they that are sick.' It is absurd, therefore, to offer a physician to them that are whole, or that at least imagine themselves so to be. You are first to convince them that they are sick; otherwise they will not thank you for your labor. It is equally absurd to offer Christ to them whose heart is whole, having never yet been broken."—*Ibid.*, sermon 35.

Thus while preaching the gospel of the grace of God, Wesley, like his Master, sought to "magnify the law, and make it honorable." Faithfully did he accomplish the work given him of God, and glorious were the results which he was permitted to behold. At the close of his long life of more than fourscore years—above half a century spent in itinerant ministry—his avowed adherents numbered more than half a million souls. But the multitude that through his labors had been lifted from the ruin and degradation of sin to a higher and a purer life, and the number who by his teaching had attained to a deeper and richer experience, will never be known till the whole family of the redeemed shall be gathered into the kingdom of God. His life presents a lesson of priceless worth to every Christian. Would that the faith and humility, the untiring zeal, self-sacrifice, and devotion of this servant of Christ might be reflected in the churches of today!

chapter 15

Terror and Retribution
in France

IN THE sixteenth century the Reformation, presenting an open Bible to the people, had sought admission to all the countries of Europe. Some nations welcomed it with gladness, as a messenger of Heaven. In other lands the papacy succeeded to a great extent in preventing its entrance; and the light of Bible knowledge, with its elevating influences, was almost wholly excluded. In one country, though the light found entrance, it was not comprehended by the darkness. For centuries, truth and error struggled for the mastery. At last the evil triumphed, and the truth of Heaven was thrust out. "This is the condemnation, that light is come into the world, and men loved darkness rather than light." John 3:19. The nation was left to reap the results of the course which she had chosen. The restraint of God's Spirit was removed from a people that had despised the gift of His grace. Evil was permitted to come to maturity. And all the world saw the fruit of willful rejection of the light.

The war against the Bible, carried forward for so many centuries in France, culminated in the scenes of the Revolution. That terrible outbreaking was but the legitimate result of Rome's suppression of the Scriptures. (See Appendix.) It presented the most striking illustration which the world has ever witnessed of the working out of the papal policy—an illustration of the results to which for more than a thousand years the teaching of the Roman Church had been tending.

The suppression of the Scriptures during the period of papal su-

France went so far in opposing truth
as to exalt the Goddess of Reason
as an object of national worship.

premacy was foretold by the prophets; and the Revelator points also to the terrible results that were to accrue especially to France from the domination of the "man of sin."

Said the angel of the Lord: "The holy city shall they tread underfoot forty and two months. And I will give power unto My two witnesses, and they shall prophecy a thousand two hundred and threescore days, clothed in sackcloth. . . . And when they shall have finished their testimony, the beast that ascendeth out of the bottomless pit shall make war against them, and shall overcome them, and kill them. And their dead bodies shall lie in the street of the great city, which spiritually is called Sodom and Egypt, where also our Lord was crucified. . . . And they that dwell upon the earth shall rejoice over them, and make merry, and shall send gifts one to another; because these two prophets tormented them that dwelt on the earth. And after three days and a half the Spirit of life from God entered into them, and they stood upon their feet; and great fear fell upon them which saw them." Revelation 11:2-11.

The periods here mentioned—"forty and two months," and "a thousand two hundred and threescore days"—are the same, alike representing the time in which the church of Christ was to suffer oppression from Rome. The 1260 years of papal supremacy began in A.D. 538, and would therefore terminate in 1798. (See Appendix note for page 33.) At that time a French army entered Rome and made the pope a prisoner, and he died in exile. Though a new pope was soon afterward elected, the papal hierarchy has never since been able to wield the power which it before possessed.

The persecution of the church did not continue throughout the entire period of the 1260 years. God in mercy to His people cut short the time of their fiery trial. In foretelling the "great tribulation" to befall the church, the Saviour said: "Except those days should be shortened, there should no flesh be saved: but for the elect's sake those days shall be shortened." Matthew 24:22. Through the influence of the Reformation the persecution was brought to an end prior to 1798.

Concerning the two witnesses the prophet declares further: "These are the two olive trees, and the two candlesticks standing before the God of the earth." "Thy word," said the psalmist, "is a lamp unto my feet, and a light unto my path." Revelation 11:4; Psalm 119:105. The two witnesses represent the Scriptures of the Old and the New Testament. Both are important testimonies to the origin and perpetuity of the law of God. Both are witnesses also to the plan of salvation. The types, sacrifices, and prophecies of the Old Testament point forward to a Saviour to come. The Gospels and Epistles of the New Testament tell of a Saviour who has come in the exact manner foretold by type and prophecy.

"They shall prophecy a thousand two hundred and threescore days, clothed in sackcloth." During the greater part of this period, God's witnesses remained in a state of obscurity. The papal power sought to hide from the people the word of truth, and set before them false witnesses to contradict its testimony. (See Appendix.) When the Bible was proscribed by religious and secular authority; when its testimony was perverted, and every effort made that men and demons could invent to turn the minds of the people from it; when those who dared proclaim its sacred truths were hunted, betrayed, tortured, buried in dungeon cells, martyred for their faith, or compelled to flee to mountain fastnesses, and to dens and caves of the earth—then the faithful witnesses prophesied in sackcloth. Yet they continued their testimony throughout the entire period of 1260 years. In the darkest times there were faithful men who loved God's word and were jealous for His honor. To these loyal servants were given wisdom, power, and authority to declare His truth during the whole of this time.

"And if any man will hurt them, fire proceedeth out of their mouth, and devoureth their enemies: and if any man will hurt them, he must in this manner be killed." Revelation 11:5. Men cannot with impunity trample upon the word of God. The meaning of this fearful denunciation is set forth in the closing chapter of the Revelation: "I testify unto every man that heareth the words of the prophecy of this book, If any man shall add unto these things, God shall add unto him the plagues that are written in this book: and if any man shall take away from the words of the book of this prophecy, God shall take away his part out of the book of life, and out of the holy city, and from the things which are written in this book." Revelation 22:18, 19.

Such are the warnings which God has given to guard men against changing in any manner that which He has revealed or commanded. These solemn denunciations apply to all who by their influence lead men to regard lightly the law of God. They should cause those to fear and tremble who flippantly declare it a matter of little consequence whether we obey God's law or not. All who exalt their own opinions above divine revelation, all who would change the plain meaning of Scripture to suit their own convenience, or for the sake of conforming to the world, are taking upon themselves a fearful responsibility. The written word, the law of God, will measure the character of every man and condemn all whom this unerring test shall declare wanting.

"When they shall have finished [are finishing] their testimony." The period when the two witnesses were to prophesy clothed in sackcloth, ended in 1798. As they were approaching the termination of their work in obscurity, war was to be made upon them by the power represented as "the beast that ascendeth out of the bottomless pit." In many of the nations of Europe the powers that ruled in church and state had for centuries been controlled by Satan through the medium of the papacy. But here is brought to view a new manifestation of satanic power.

It had been Rome's policy, under a profession of reverence for the Bible, to keep it locked up in an unknown tongue and hidden away from the people. Under her rule the witnesses prophesied "clothed in sackcloth." But another power—the beast from the bottomless pit—was to arise to make open, avowed war upon the word of God.

"The great city" in whose streets the witnesses are slain, and where their dead bodies lie, is "spiritually" Egypt. Of all nations presented in Bible history, Egypt most boldly denied the existence of the living God and resisted His commands. No monarch ever ventured upon more open and highhanded rebellion against the authority of Heaven than did the king of Egypt. When the message was brought him by Moses, in the name of the Lord, Pharaoh proudly answered: "Who is Jehovah, that I should hearken unto His voice to let Israel go? I know not Jehovah, and moreover I will not let Israel go." Exodus 5:2, A.R.V. This is atheism, and the nation represented by Egypt would give voice to a similar denial of the claims of the living God and would manifest a like spirit of unbelief and defiance. "The great city" is also compared, "spiritually," to Sodom. The corruption of Sodom in breaking the law of God was especially manifested in licentiousness. And this sin was also to be a pre-eminent characteristic of the nation that should fulfill the specifications of this scripture.

According to the words of the prophet, then, a little before the year 1798 some power of satanic origin and character would rise to make war upon the Bible. And in the land where the testimony of God's two witnesses should thus be silenced, there would be manifest the atheism of the Pharaoh and the licentiousness of Sodom.

This prophecy has received a most exact and striking fulfillment in the history of France. During the Revolution, in 1793, "the world for the first time heard an assembly of men, born and educated in civilization, and assuming the right to govern one of the finest of the European nations, uplift their united voice to deny the most solemn truth which man's soul receives, and renounce unanimously the belief and worship of a Deity."—Sir Walter Scott, *Life of Napoleon*, vol. 1, ch. 17. "France is the only nation in the world concerning which the authentic record survives, that as a nation she lifted her hand in open rebellion against the Author of the universe. Plenty of blasphemers, plenty of infidels, there have been, and still continue to be, in England, Germany, Spain, and elsewhere; but France stands apart in the world's history as the single state which, by the decree of her Legislative Assembly, pronounced that there was no God, and of which the entire population of the capital, and a vast majority elsewhere, women as well as men, danced and sang with joy in accepting the announcement."—*Blackwood's Magazine*, November, 1870.

France presented also the characteristics which especially distinguished Sodom. During the Revolution there was manifest a state of moral debasement and corruption similar to that which brought destruction upon the cities of the plain. And the historian presents together the atheism and the licentiousness of France, as given in the prophecy: "Intimately connected with these laws affecting religion, was that which reduced the union of marriage—the most sacred engagement which human beings can form, and the permanence of which leads most strongly to the consolidation of society—to the state of a mere civil contract of a transitory character, which any two persons might engage in and cast loose at pleasure. . . . If fiends had set themselves to work to discover a mode of most effectually destroying whatever is venerable, graceful, or permanent in domestic life, and of obtaining at the same time an assurance that the mischief which it was their object to create should be perpetuated from one generation to another, they could not have invented a more effectual plan than the degradation of marriage. . . . Sophie Arnoult, an actress famous for the witty things she said, described the republican marriage as 'the sacrament of adultery.' "—Scott, vol. 1, ch. 17.

"Where also our Lord was crucified." This specification of the prophecy was also fulfilled by France. In no land had the spirit of enmity against Christ been more strikingly displayed. In no country had the truth encountered more bitter and cruel opposition. In the persecution which France had visited upon the confessors of the gospel, she had crucified Christ in the person of His disciples.

Century after century the blood of the saints had been shed. While the Waldenses laid down their lives upon the mountains of Piedmont "for the word of God, and for the testimony of Jesus Christ," similar witness to the truth had been borne by their brethren, the Albigenses of France. In the days of the Reformation its disciples had been put to death with horrible tortures. King and nobles, highborn women and delicate maidens, the pride and chivalry of the nation, had feasted their eyes upon the agonies of the martyrs of Jesus. The brave Huguenots, battling for those rights which the human heart holds most sacred, had poured out their blood on many a hard-fought field. The Protestants were counted as outlaws, a price was set upon their heads, and they were hunted down like wild beasts.

The "Church in the Desert," the few descendants of the ancient Christians that still lingered in France in the eighteenth century, hiding away in the mountains of the south, still cherished the faith of their fathers. As they ventured to meet by night on mountainside or lonely moor, they were chased by dragoons and dragged away to lifelong slavery in the galleys. The purest, the most refined, and the most intelligent of the French were chained, in horrible torture, amidst robbers and assassins. (See Wylie, b. 22, ch. 6.) Others, more mercifully dealt with, were shot down in cold blood, as, unarmed and helpless, they fell upon their knees in prayer. Hundreds of aged men, defenseless women, and innocent children were left dead upon the earth at their place of meeting. In traversing the mountainside or the forest, where they had been accustomed to assemble, it was not unusual to find "at every four paces, dead bodies dotting the sward, and corpses hanging suspended from the trees." Their country, laid waste with the sword, the ax, the fagot, "was converted into one vast, gloomy wilderness." "These atrocities were enacted . . . in no dark age, but in the brilliant era of Louis XIV. Science was then cultivated, letters flourished, the divines of the court and of the capital were learned and eloquent men, and greatly affected the graces of meekness and charity."—*Ibid.*, b. 22, ch. 7.

But blackest in the black catalogue of crime, most horrible among the fiendish deeds of all the dreadful centuries, was the St. Bartholomew Massacre. The world still recalls with shuddering horror the scenes of that most cowardly and cruel onslaught. The king of France, urged on by Romish priests and prelates, lent his sanction to the dreadful work. A bell, tolling at dead of night, was a signal for the slaughter. Protestants by thousands, sleeping quietly in their homes, trusting to the plighted honor of their king, were dragged forth without a warning and murdered in cold blood.

As Christ was the invisible leader of His people from Egyptian bondage, so was Satan the unseen leader of his subjects in this horrible work of multiplying martyrs. For seven days the massacre was continued in Paris, the first three with inconceivable fury. And it was not confined to the city itself, but by special order of the king was extended to all the provinces and towns where Protestants were found. Neither age nor sex was respected. Neither the innocent babe nor the man of gray hairs was spared. Noble and peasant, old and young, mother and child, were cut down together. Throughout France the butchery continued for two months. Seventy thousand of the very flower of the nation perished.

"When the news of the massacre reached Rome, the exultation among the clergy knew no bounds. The cardinal of Lorraine rewarded the messenger with a thousand crowns; the cannon of St. Angelo thundered forth a joyous salute; and bells rang out from every steeple; bonfires turned night into day; and Gregory XIII, attended by the cardinals and other ecclesiastical dignitaries, went in long procession to the church of St. Louis, where the cardinal of Lorraine chanted a *Te Deum.* . . . A medal was struck to commemorate the massacre, and in the Vatican may still be seen three frescoes of Vasari, describing the attack upon the admiral, the king in council plotting the massacre, and the massacre itself. Gregory sent Charles the Golden Rose; and four months after the massacre, . . . he listened complacently to the sermon of a French priest, . . . who spoke of 'that day so full of happiness and joy, when the most holy father received the news, and went in solemn state to render thanks to God and St. Louis.' "—Henry White, *The Massacre of St. Bartholomew,* ch. 14, par. 34.

The same master spirit that urged on the St. Bartholomew Massacre led also in the scenes of the Revolution. Jesus Christ was declared to be an impostor, and the rallying cry of the French infidels was, "Crush the Wretch," meaning Christ. Heaven-daring blasphemy and abominable wickedness went hand in hand, and the basest of men, the most abandoned monsters of cruelty and vice, were most highly exalted. In all this, supreme homage was paid to Satan; while Christ, in His characteristics of truth, purity, and unselfish love, was crucified.

"The beast that ascendeth out of the bottomless pit shall make war against them, and shall overcome them, and kill them." The atheistical power that ruled in France during the Revolution and the Reign of Terror, did wage such a war against God and His holy word as the world had never witnessed. The worship of the Deity was abolished by the National Assembly. Bibles were collected and publicly burned with every possible manifestation of scorn. The law of God was trampled underfoot. The institutions of the Bible were abolished. The weekly rest day was set aside, and in its stead every tenth day was devoted to reveling and blasphemy. Baptism and the Communion were prohibited. And announcements posted conspicuously over the burial places declared death to be an eternal sleep.

The fear of God was said to be so far from the beginning of wisdom that it was the beginning of folly. All religious worship was prohibited, except that of liberty and the country. The "constitutional bishop of Paris was brought forward to play the principal part in the most impudent and scandalous farce ever acted in the face of a national representation. . . . He was brought forward in full procession, to declare to the Convention that the religion which he had taught so many years was, in every respect, a piece of priestcraft, which had no foundation either in history or sacred truth. He disowned, in solemn and explicit terms, the existence of the Deity to whose worship he had been consecrated, and devoted himself in future to the homage of liberty, equality, virtue, and morality. He then laid on the table his episcopal decorations, and received a fraternal embrace from the president of the Convention. Several apostate priests followed the example of this prelate."—Scott, vol. 1, ch. 17.

"And they that dwell upon the earth shall rejoice over them, and make merry, and shall send gifts one to another; because these two prophets tormented them that dwelt on the earth." Infidel France had silenced the reproving voice of God's two witnesses. The word of truth lay dead in her streets, and those who hated the restrictions and requirements of God's law were jubilant. Men publicly defied the King of heaven. Like the sinners of old, they cried: "How doth God know? and is there knowledge in the Most High?" Psalm 73:11.

With blasphemous boldness almost beyond belief, one of the priests of the new order said: "God, if You exist, avenge Your injured name. I bid You defiance! You remain silent; You dare not launch Your thunders. Who after this will believe in Your existence?"—Lacretelle, *History*, vol. 11, p. 309; in Sir Archibald Alison, *History of Europe,* vol.1, ch. 10. What an echo is this of the Pharaoh's demand: "Who is Jehovah, that I should obey His voice?" "I know not Jehovah!"

"The fool hath said in his heart, There is no God." Psalm 14:1. And the Lord declares concerning the perverters of the truth: "Their folly shall be manifest unto all." 2 Timothy 3:9. After France had renounced the worship of the living God, "the high and lofty One that inhabiteth eternity," it was only a little time till she descended to degrading idolatry, by the worship of the Goddess of Reason, in the person of a profligate woman. And this in the representative assembly of the nation, and by its highest civil and legislative authorities! Says the historian: "One of the ceremonies of this insane time stands unrivaled for absurdity combined with impiety. The doors of the Convention were thrown open to a band of musicians, preceded by whom, the members of the municipal body entered in solemn procession, singing a hymn in praise of liberty, and escorting, as the object of their future worship, a veiled female, whom they termed the Goddess of Reason. Being brought within the bar, she was unveiled with great form, and placed on the right of the president, when she was generally recognized as a dancing girl of the opera. . . . To this person, as the fittest representative of that reason whom they worshiped, the National Convention of France rendered public homage.

"This impious and ridiculous mummery had a certain fashion; and the installation of the Goddess of Reason was renewed and imitated throughout the nation, in such places where the inhabitants desired to show themselves equal to all the heights of the Revolution."—Scott, vol. 1, ch. 17.

Said the orator who introduced the worship of Reason: "Legislators! Fanaticism has given way to reason. Its bleared eyes could not endure

the brilliancy of the light. This day an immense concourse has assembled beneath those gothic vaults, which, for the first time, re-echoed the truth. There the French have celebrated the only true worship—that of Liberty, that of Reason. There we have formed wishes for the prosperity of the arms of the Republic. There we have abandoned inanimate idols for Reason, for that animated image, the masterpiece of nature."—M. A. Thiers, *History of the French Revolution*, vol. 2, pp. 370, 371.

When the goddess was brought into the Convention, the orator took her by the hand, and turning to the assembly said: "Mortals, cease to tremble before the powerless thunders of a God whom your fears have created. Henceforth acknowledge no divinity but Reason. I offer you its noblest and purest image; if you must have idols, sacrifice only to such as this. . . . Fall before the august Senate of Freedom, oh! Veil of Reason!"

"The goddess, after being embraced by the president, was mounted on a magnificent car, and conducted, amid an immense crowd, to the cathedral of Notre Dame, to take the place of the Deity. There she was elevated on the high altar, and received the adoration of all present."—Alison, vol. 1, ch. 10.

This was followed, not long afterward, by the public burning of the Bible. On one occasion "the Popular Society of the Museum" entered the hall of the municipality, exclaiming, *"Vive la Raison!"* and carrying on the top of a pole the half-burned remains of several books, among others breviaries, missals, and the Old and New Testaments, which "expiated in a great fire," said the president, "all the fooleries which they have made the human race commit."—*Journal of Paris*, 1793, No. 318. Quoted in Buchez-Roux, *Collection of Parliamentary History*, vol. 30, pp. 200, 201.

It was popery that had begun the work which atheism was completing. The policy of Rome had wrought out those conditions, social, political, and religious, that were hurrying France on to ruin. Writers, in referring to the horrors of the Revolution, say that these excesses are to be charged upon the throne and the church. (See Appendix.) In strict justice they are to be charged upon the church. Popery had poisoned the minds of kings against the Reformation, as an enemy to the crown, an element of discord that would be fatal to the peace and harmony of the nation. It was the genius of Rome that by this means inspired the direst cruelty and the most galling oppression which proceeded from the throne.

The spirit of liberty went with the Bible. Wherever the gospel was received, the minds of the people were awakened. They began to cast off the shackles that had held them bondslaves of ignorance, vice, and

Repudiation of true worship by the French during the Revolution included public vilification of the Bible.

superstition. They began to think and act as men. Monarchs saw it and trembled for their despotism.

Rome was not slow to inflame their jealous fears. Said the pope to the regent of France in 1525: "This mania [Protestantism] will not only confound and destroy religion, but all principalities, nobility, laws, orders, and ranks besides."—G. de Félice, *History of the Protestants of France,* b. 1, ch. 2, par. 8. A few years later a papal nuncio warned the king: "Sire, be not deceived. The Protestants will upset all civil as well as religious order. . . . The throne is in as much danger as the altar. . . . The introduction of a new religion must necessarily introduce a new government." —D'Aubigné, *History of the Reformation in Europe in the Time of Calvin,* b. 2, ch. 36. And theologians appealed to the prejudices of the people by declaring that the Protestant doctrine "entices men away to novelties and folly; it robs the king of the devoted affection of his subjects, and devastates both church and state." Thus Rome succeeded in arraying France against the Reformation. "It was to uphold the throne, preserve the nobles, and maintain the laws, that the sword of persecution was first unsheathed in France."—Wylie, b. 13, ch. 4.

Little did the rulers of the land foresee the results of that fateful policy. The teaching of the Bible would have implanted in the minds and hearts of the people those principles of justice, temperance, truth, equity, and benevolence which are the very cornerstone of a nation's prosperity. "Righteousness exalteth a nation." Thereby "the throne is established." Proverbs 14:34; 16:12. "The work of righteousness shall be peace;" and the effect, "quietness and assurance forever." Isaiah 32:17. He who obeys the divine law will most truly respect and obey the laws of his country. He who fears God will honor the king in the exercise of all just and legitimate authority. But unhappy France prohibited the Bible and banned its disciples. Century after century, men of principle and integrity, men of intellectual acuteness and moral strength, who had the courage to avow their convictions and the faith to suffer for the truth—for centuries these men toiled as slaves in the galleys, perished at the stake, or rotted in dungeon cells. Thousands upon thousands found safety in flight; and this continued for two hundred and fifty years after the opening of the Reformation.

"Scarcely was there a generation of Frenchmen during that long period that did not witness the disciples of the gospel fleeing before the insane fury of the persecutor, and carrying with them the intelligence, the arts, the industry, the order, in which, as a rule, they pre-eminently excelled, to enrich the lands in which they found an asylum. And in proportion as they replenished other countries with these good gifts, did they empty their own of them. If all that was now driven away had been retained in France; if, during these three hundred years, the industrial skill of the exiles had been cultivating her soil; if, during these three hundred years, their artistic bent had been improving her manufactures; if, during these three hundred years, their creative genius and analytic power had been enriching her literature and cultivating her science; if their wisdom had been guiding her councils, their bravery fighting her battles, their equity framing her laws, and the religion of the Bible strengthening the intellect and governing the conscience of her people, what a glory would at this day have encompassed France! What a great, prosperous, and happy country—a pattern to the nations—would she have been!

"But a blind and inexorable bigotry chased from her soil every teacher of virtue, every champion of order, every honest defender of the throne; it said to the men who would have made their country a 'renown and glory' in the earth, Choose which you will have, a stake or exile. At last the ruin of the state was complete; there remained no more conscience to be proscribed; no more religion to be dragged to the stake; no more patriotism to be chased into banishment."—Wylie, b. 13, ch. 20. And the Revolution, with all its horrors, was the dire result.

"With the flight of the Huguenots a general decline settled upon France. Flourishing manufacturing cities fell into decay; fertile districts returned to their native wildness; intellectual dullness and moral declension succeeded a period of unwonted progress. Paris became one vast almshouse, and it is estimated that, at the breaking out of the Revolution, two hundred thousand paupers claimed charity from the hands of the king. The Jesuits alone flourished in the decaying nation, and ruled with dreadful tyranny over churches and schools, the prisons and the galleys."

The gospel would have brought to France the solution of those political and social problems that baffled the skill of her clergy, her king, and her legislators, and finally plunged the nation into anarchy and ruin. But under the domination of Rome the people had lost the Saviour's blessed lessons of self-sacrifice and unselfish love. They had been led away from the practice of self-denial for the good of others. The rich had found no rebuke for their oppression of the poor, the poor no help for their servitude and degradation. The selfishness of the wealthy and powerful grew more and more apparent and oppressive. For centuries the greed and profligacy of the noble resulted in grinding extortion toward the peasant. The rich wronged the poor, and the poor hated the rich.

In many provinces the estates were held by the nobles, and the laboring classes were only tenants; they were at the mercy of their landlords and were forced to submit to their exorbitant demands. The burden of supporting both the church and the state fell upon the middle and lower classes, who were heavily taxed by the civil authorities and by the clergy. "The pleasure of the nobles was considered the supreme law; the farmers and the peasants might starve, for aught their oppressors cared. . . . The people were compelled at every turn to consult the exclusive interest of the landlord. The lives of the agricultural laborers were lives of incessant work and unrelieved misery; their complaints, if they ever dared to complain, were treated with insolent contempt. The courts of justice would always listen to a noble as against a peasant; bribes were notoriously accepted by the judges; and the merest caprice of the aristocracy had the force of law, by virtue of this system of universal corruption. Of the taxes wrung from the commonalty, by the secular magnates on the one hand, and the clergy on the other, not half ever found its way into the royal or episcopal treasury; the rest was squandered in profligate self-indulgence. And the men who thus impoverished their fellow subjects were themselves exempt from taxation, and entitled by law or custom to all the appointments of the state. The privileged classes numbered a hundred and fifty thousand, and for their gratification millions were condemned to hopeless and degrading lives." (See Appendix.)

The court was given up to luxury and profligacy. There was little confidence existing between the people and the rulers. Suspicion fastened upon all the measures of the government as designing and selfish. For more than half a century before the time of the Revolution the throne was occupied by Louis XV, who, even in those evil times, was distinguished as an indolent, frivolous, and sensual monarch. With a depraved and cruel aristocracy and an impoverished and ignorant lower class, the state financially embarrassed and the people exasperated, it needed no prophet's eye to foresee a terrible impending outbreak. To the warnings of his counselors the king was accustomed to reply: "Try to make things go on as long as I am likely to live; after my death it may be as it will." It was in vain that the necessity of reform was urged. He saw the evils, but had neither the courage nor the power to meet them. The doom awaiting France was but too truly pictured in his indolent and selfish answer, "After me, the deluge!"

By working upon the jealousy of the kings and the ruling classes, Rome had influenced them to keep the people in bondage, well knowing that the state would thus be weakened, and purposing by this means to fasten both rulers and people in her thrall. With farsighted policy she perceived that in order to enslave men effectually, the shackles must be bound upon their souls; that the surest way to prevent them from escaping their bondage was to render them incapable of freedom. A thousand-fold more terrible than the physical suffering which resulted from her policy, was the moral degradation. Deprived of the Bible, and abandoned to the teachings of bigotry and selfishness, the people were shrouded in ignorance and superstition, and sunken in vice, so that they were wholly unfitted for self-government.

But the outworking of all this was widely different from what Rome had purposed. Instead of holding the masses in a blind submission to her dogmas, her work resulted in making them infidels and revolutionists. Romanism they despised as priestcraft. They beheld the clergy as a party to their oppression. The only god they knew was the god of Rome; her teaching was their only religion. They regarded her greed and cruelty as the legitimate fruit of the Bible, and they would have none of it.

Rome had misrepresented the character of God and perverted His requirements, and now men rejected both the Bible and its Author. She had required a blind faith in her dogmas, under the pretended sanction of the Scriptures. In the reaction, Voltaire and his associates cast aside God's word altogether and spread everywhere the poison of infidelity. Rome had ground down the people under her iron heel; and now the masses, degraded and brutalized, in their recoil from her tryranny, cast off all restraint. Enraged at the glittering cheat to which they had so long paid homage, they rejected truth and falsehood together; and mistaking license for liberty, the slaves of vice exulted in their imagined freedom.

At the opening of the Revolution, by a concession of the king, the people were granted a representation exceeding that of the nobles and the clergy combined. Thus the balance of power was in their hands; but they were not prepared to use it with wisdom and moderation. Eager to redress the wrongs they had suffered, they determined to undertake the reconstruction of society. An outraged populace, whose minds were filled with bitter and long-treasured memories of wrong, resolved to revolutionize the state of misery that had grown unbearable and to avenge themselves upon those whom they regarded as the authors of their sufferings. The oppressed wrought out the lesson they had learned under tyranny and became the oppressors of those who had oppressed them.

Unhappy France reaped in blood the harvest she had sown. Terrible were the results of her submission to the controlling power of Rome. Where France, under the influence of Romanism, had set up the first stake at the opening of the Reformation, there the Revolution set up its first guillotine. On the very spot where the first martyrs to the Protestant faith were burned in the sixteenth century, the first victims were guillotined in the eighteenth. In repelling the gospel, which would have brought her healing, France had opened the door to infidelity and ruin. When the restraints of God's law were cast aside, it was found that the laws of man were inadequate to hold in check the powerful tides of human passion; and the nation swept on to revolt and anarchy. The war against the Bible inaugurated an era which stands in the world's history as the Reign of Terror. Peace and happiness were banished from the homes and hearts of men. No one was secure. He who triumphed today was suspected, condemned, tomorrow. Violence and lust held undisputed sway.

King, clergy, and nobles were compelled to submit to the atrocities of an excited and maddened people. Their thirst for vengeance was only stimulated by the execution of the king; and those who had decreed his death soon followed him to the scaffold. A general slaughter of all suspected of hostility to the Revolution was determined. The prisons were crowded, at one time containing more than two hundred thousand captives. The cities of the kingdom were filled with scenes of horror. One party of revolutionists was against another party, and France became a vast field for contending masses, swayed by the fury of their passions. "In Paris one tumult succeeded another, and the citizens were divided into a medley of factions, that seemed intent on nothing but mutual extermination." And to add to the general misery, the nation became involved in a prolonged and devastating war with the great powers of Europe. "The country was nearly bankrupt, the armies were clamoring for arrears of pay, the Parisians were starving, the provinces were laid waste by brigands, and civilization was almost extinguished in anarchy and license."

All too well the people had learned the lessons of cruelty and torture which Rome had so diligently taught. A day of retribution at last had come. It was not now the disciples of Jesus that were thrust into dungeons and dragged to the stake. Long ago these had perished or been driven into exile. Unsparing Rome now felt the deadly power of those whom she had trained to delight in deeds of blood. "The example of persecution which the clergy of France had exhibited for so many ages, was now retorted upon them with signal vigor. The scaffolds ran red with the blood of the priests. The galleys and the prisons, once crowded with Huguenots, were now filled with their persecutors. Chained to the bench and toiling at the oar, the Roman Catholic clergy experienced all those woes which their church had so freely inflicted on the gentle heretics." (See Appendix.)

"Then came those days when the most barbarous of all codes was administered by the most barbarous of all tribunals; when no man could greet his neighbors or say his prayers . . . without danger of committing a capital crime; when spies lurked in every corner; when the guillotine was long and hard at work every morning; when the jails were filled as close as the holds of a slave ship; when the gutters ran foaming with blood into the Seine. . . . While the daily wagonloads of victims were carried to their doom through the streets of Paris, the proconsuls, whom the sovereign committee had sent forth to the departments, reveled in an extravagance of cruelty unknown even in the capital. The knife of the deadly machine rose and fell too slow for their work of slaughter. Long rows of captives were mowed down with grapeshot. Holes were made in the bottom of crowded barges. Lyons was turned into a desert. At Arras even the cruel mercy of a speedy death was denied to the prisoners. All down the Loire, from Saumur to the sea, great flocks of crows and kites feasted on naked corpses, twined together in hideous embraces. No mercy was shown to sex or age. The number of young lads and of girls of seventeen who were murdered by that execrable government, is to be reckoned by hundreds. Babies torn from the breast were tossed from pike to pike along the Jacobin ranks." (See Appendix.) In the short space of ten years, multitudes of human beings perished.

All this was as Satan would have it. This was what for ages he had been working to secure. His policy is deception from first to last, and his steadfast purpose is to bring woe and wretchedness upon men, to deface and defile the workmanship of God, to mar the divine purposes of benevolence and love, and thus cause grief in heaven. Then by his deceptive arts he blinds the minds of men, and leads them to throw back the blame of his work upon God, as if all this misery were the result of the Creator's plan. In like manner, when those who have been degraded and brutalized through his cruel power achieve their freedom, he urges them on to excesses and atrocities. Then this picture of unbridled license is pointed out by tyrants and oppressors as an illustration of the results of liberty.

When error in one garb has been detected, Satan only masks it in a different disguise, and multitudes receive it as eagerly as at the first. When the people found Romanism to be a deception, and he could not through this agency lead them to transgression of God's law, he urged them to regard all religion as a cheat, and the Bible as a fable; and, casting aside the divine statutes, they gave themselves up to unbridled iniquity.

The fatal error which wrought such woe for the inhabitants of France was the ignoring of this one great truth: that true freedom lies within the proscriptions of the law of God. "O that thou hadst hearkened to My commandments! then had thy peace been as a river, and thy righteousness as the waves of the sea." "There is no peace, saith the Lord, unto the wicked." "But whoso hearkeneth unto Me shall dwell safely, and shall be quiet from fear of evil." Isaiah 48:18, 22; Proverbs 1:33.

Atheists, infidels, and apostates oppose and denounce God's law; but the results of their influence prove that the well-being of man is bound up with his obedience of the divine statutes. Those who will not read the lesson from the book of God are bidden to read it in the history of nations.

When Satan wrought through the Roman Church to lead men away from obedience, his agency was concealed, and his work was so disguised that the degradation and misery which resulted were not seen to be the fruit of transgression. And his power was so far counteracted by the working of the Spirit of God that his purposes were prevented from reaching their full fruition. The people did not trace the effect to its cause and discover the source of their miseries. But in the Revolution the law of God was openly set aside by the National Council. And in the Reign of Terror which followed, the working of cause and effect could be seen by all.

When France publicly rejected God and set aside the Bible, wicked men and spirits of darkness exulted in their attainment of the object so long desired—a kingdom free from the restraints of the law of God. Because sentence against an evil work was not speedily executed, therefore the heart of the sons of men was "fully set in them to do evil." Ecclesiastes 8:11. But the transgression of a just and righteous law must inevitably result in misery and ruin. Though not visited at once with judgments, the wickedness of men was nevertheless surely working out their doom. Centuries of apostasy and crime had been treasuring up wrath against the day of retribution; and when their iniquity was full, the despisers of God learned too late that it is a fearful thing to have worn out the divine patience. The restraining Spirit of God, which imposes a check upon the cruel power of Satan, was in a great measure removed, and he whose only delight is the wretchedness of men was permitted to work his will. Those who had chosen the service of rebellion were left to reap its fruits until the land was filled with crimes too horrible for pen to trace. From devastated provinces and ruined cities a terrible cry was heard—a cry of bitterest anguish. France was shaken as if by an earthquake. Religion, law, social order, the family, the state, and the church—all were smitten down by the impious hand that had been lifted against the law of God. Truly spoke the wise man: "The wicked shall fall by his own wickedness." "Though a sinner do evil a hundred times, and his days be prolonged, yet surely I know that it shall be well with them that fear God, which fear before Him: but it shall not be well with the wicked." Proverbs 11:5; Ecclesiastes 8:12, 13. "They hated knowledge, and did not choose the fear of the Lord;" "therefore shall they eat of the fruit of their own way, and be filled with their own devices." Proverbs 1:29, 31.

God's faithful witnesses, slain by the blasphemous power that "ascendeth out of the bottomless pit," were not long to remain silent. "After three days and a half the Spirit of life from God entered into them, and they stood upon their feet; and great fear fell upon them which saw them." Revelation 11:11. It was in 1793 that the decrees which abolished the Christian religion and set aside the Bible passed the French Assembly. Three years and a half later a resolution rescinding these decrees, thus granting toleration to the Scriptures, was adopted by the same body. The world stood aghast at the enormity of guilt which had resulted from a rejection of the Sacred Oracles, and men recognized the necessity of faith in God and His word as the foundation of virtue and morality. Saith the Lord: "Whom hast thou reproached and blasphemed? and against whom hast thou exalted thy voice, and lifted up thine eyes on high? even against the Holy One of Israel." Isaiah 37:23. "Therefore, behold, I will cause them to know, this once will I cause them to know My hand and My might; and they shall know that My name is Jehovah." Jeremiah 16:21, A.R.V.

Concerning the two witnesses the prophet declares further: "And they heard a great voice from heaven saying unto them, Come up hither. And they ascended up to heaven in a cloud; and their enemies beheld them." Revelation 11:12. Since France made war upon God's two witnesses, they have been honored as never before. In 1804 the British and Foreign Bible Society was organized. This was followed by similar organizations, with numerous branches, upon the continent of Europe. In 1816 the American Bible Society was founded. When the British Society was formed, the Bible had been printed and circulated in fifty tongues. It has since been translated into many hundreds of languages and dialects. (See Appendix.)

For the fifty years preceding 1792, little attention was given to the work of foreign missions. No new societies were formed, and there were but few churches that made any effort for the spread of Christianity in heathen lands. But toward the close of the eighteenth century a great change took place. Men became dissatisfied with the results of rationalism and realized the necessity of divine revelation and experimental religion. From this time the work of foreign missions attained an unprecedented growth. (See Appendix.)

The improvements in printing have given an impetus to the work of circulating the Bible. The increased facilities for communication between different countries, the breaking down of ancient barriers of prejudice and national exclusiveness, and the loss of secular power by the pontiff of Rome have opened the way for the entrance of the word of God. For some years the Bible has been sold without restraint in the streets of Rome, and it has now been carried to every part of the habitable globe.

The infidel Voltaire once boastingly said: "I am weary of hearing people repeat that twelve men established the Christian religion. I will prove that one man may suffice to overthrow it." Generations have passed since his death. Millions have joined in the war upon the Bible. But it is so far from being destroyed, that where there were a hundred in Voltaire's time, there are now ten thousand, yes, a hundred thousand copies of the book of God. In the words of an early Reformer concerning the Christian church, "The Bible is an anvil that has worn out many hammers." Saith the Lord: "No weapon that is formed against thee shall prosper; and every tongue that shall rise against thee in judgment thou shalt condemn." Isaiah 54:17.

"The word of our God shall stand forever." "All His commandments are sure. They stand fast for ever and ever, and are done in truth and uprightness." Isaiah 40:8; Psalm 111:7, 8. Whatever is built upon the authority of man will be overthrown; but that which is founded upon the rock of God's immutable word shall stand forever.

chapter 16

Seeking Freedom in a New World

THE English Reformers, while renouncing the doctrines of Romanism, had retained many of its forms. Thus though the authority and the creed of Rome were rejected, not a few of her customs and ceremonies were incorporated into the worship of the Church of England. It was claimed that these things were not matters of conscience; that though they were not commanded in Scripture, and hence were nonessential, yet not being forbidden, they were not intrinsically evil. Their observance tended to narrow the gulf which separated the reformed churches from Rome, and it was urged that they would promote the acceptance of the Protestant faith by Romanists.

To the conservative and compromising, these arguments seemed conclusive. But there was another class that did not so judge. The fact that these customs "tended to bridge over the chasm between Rome and the Reformation" (Martyn, volume 5, page 22), was in their view a conclusive argument against retaining them. They looked upon them as badges of the slavery from which they had been delivered and to which they had no disposition to return. They reasoned that God has in His word established the regulations governing His worship, and that men are not at liberty to add to these or to detract from them. The very beginning of the great apostasy was in seeking to supplement the authority of God by that of the church. Rome began by enjoining what God had not forbidden, and she ended by forbidding what He had explicitly enjoined.

Many earnestly desired to return to the purity and simplicity which

The Pilgrim Fathers left England for sake of liberty of conscience and founded a new nation on this principle.

[289-290] 245

© P.P.P.A. JOHN STEEL, ARTIST

characterized the primitive church. They regarded many of the established customs of the English Church as monuments of idolatry, and they could not in conscience unite in her worship. But the church, being supported by the civil authority, would permit no dissent from her forms. Attendance upon her service was required by law, and unauthorized assemblies for religious worship were prohibited, under penalty of imprisonment, exile, and death.

At the opening of the seventeenth century the monarch who had just ascended the throne of England declared his determination to make the Puritans "conform, or . . . harry them out of the land, or else worse." —George Bancroft, History of the United States of America, pt. 1, ch. 12, par. 6. Hunted, persecuted, and imprisoned, they could discern in the future no promise of better days, and many yielded to the conviction that for such as would serve God according to the dictates of their conscience, "England was ceasing forever to be a habitable place."—J. G. Palfrey, *History of New England*, ch. 3, par. 43. Some at last determined to seek refuge in Holland. Difficulties, losses, and imprisonment were encountered. Their purposes were thwarted, and they were betrayed into the hands of their enemies. But steadfast perseverance finally conquered, and they found shelter on the friendly shores of the Dutch Republic.

In their flight they had left their houses, their goods, and their means of livelihood. They were strangers in a strange land, among a people of different language and customs. They were forced to resort to new and untried occupations to earn their bread. Middle-aged men, who had spent their lives in tilling the soil, had now to learn mechanical trades. But they cheerfully accepted the situation and lost no time in idleness or repining. Though often pinched with poverty, they thanked God for the blessings which were still granted them and found their joy in unmolested spiritual communion. "They knew they were pilgrims, and looked not much on those things, but lifted up their eyes to heaven, their dearest country, and quieted their spirits."—Bancroft, pt. 1, ch. 12, par. 15.

In the midst of exile and hardship their love and faith waxed strong. They trusted the Lord's promises, and He did not fail them in time of need. His angels were by their side, to encourage and support them. And when God's hand seemed pointing them across the sea, to a land where they might found for themselves a state, and leave to their children the precious heritage of religious liberty, they went forward, without shrinking, in the path of providence.

God had permitted trials to come upon His people to prepare them

246 [*290-291*]

for the accomplishment of His gracious purpose toward them. The church had been brought low, that she might be exalted. God was about to display His power in her behalf, to give to the world another evidence that He will not forsake those who trust in Him. He had overruled events to cause the wrath of Satan and the plots of evil men to advance His glory and to bring His people to a place of security. Persecution and exile were opening the way to freedom.

When first constrained to separate from the English Church, the Puritans had joined themselves together by a solemn covenant, as the Lord's free people, "to walk together in all His ways made known or to be made known to them."—J. Brown, *The Pilgrim Fathers*, page 74. Here was the true spirit of reform, the vital principle of Protestantism. It was with this purpose that the Pilgrims departed from Holland to find a home in the New World. John Robinson, their pastor, who was providentially prevented from accompanying them, in his farewell address to the exiles said:

"Brethren, we are now erelong to part asunder, and the Lord knoweth whether I shall live ever to see your faces more. But whether the Lord hath appointed it or not, I charge you before God and His blessed angels to follow me no farther than I have followed Christ. If God should reveal anything to you by any other instrument of His, be as ready to receive it as ever you were to receive any truth of my ministry; for I am very confident the Lord hath more truth and light yet to break forth out of His holy word."—Martyn, vol. 5, p. 70.

"For my part, I cannot sufficiently bewail the condition of the reformed churches, who are come to a period in religion, and will go at present no farther than the instruments of their reformation. The Lutherans cannot be drawn to go beyond what Luther saw; . . . and the Calvinists, you see, stick fast where they were left by that great man of God, who yet saw not all things. This is a misery much to be lamented; for though they were burning and shining lights in their time, yet they penetrated not into the whole counsel of God, but were they now living, would be as willing to embrace further light as that which they first received."—D. Neal, *History of the Puritans*, vol. 1, p. 269.

"Remember your church covenant, in which you have agreed to walk in all the ways of the Lord, made or to be made known unto you. Remember your promise and covenant with God and with one another, to receive whatever light and truth shall be made known to you from His written word; but withal, take heed, I beseech you, what you receive for truth, and compare it and weigh it with other scriptures of truth before you accept it; for it is not possible the Christian world should come so lately out of such thick antichristian darkness, and that full perfection of knowledge should break forth at once."—Martyn, vol. 5, pp. 70, 71.

It was the desire for liberty of conscience that inspired the Pilgrims to brave the perils of the long journey across the sea, to endure the hardships and dangers of the wilderness, and with God's blessing to lay, on the shores of America, the foundation of a mighty nation. Yet honest and God-fearing as they were, the Pilgrims did not yet comprehend the great principle of religious liberty. The freedom which they sacrificed so much to secure for themselves, they were not equally ready to grant to others. "Very few, even of the foremost thinkers and moralists of the seventeenth century, had any just conception of that grand principle, the outgrowth of the New Testament, which acknowledges God as the sole judge of human faith."—*Ibid.*, vol. 5, p. 297. The doctrine that God has committed to the church the right to control the conscience, and to define and punish heresy, is one of the most deeply rooted of papal errors. While the Reformers rejected the creed of Rome, they were not entirely free from her spirit of intolerance. The dense darkness in which, through the long ages of her rule, popery had enveloped all Christendom, had not even yet been wholly dissipated. Said one of the leading ministers in the colony of Massachusetts Bay: "It was toleration that made the world antichristian; and the church never took harm by the punishment of heretics."—*Ibid.*, vol. 5, p. 335. The regulation was adopted by the colonists that only church members should have a voice in the civil government. A kind of state church was formed, all the people being required to contribute to the support of the clergy, and the magistrates being authorized to suppress heresy. Thus the secular power was in the hands of the church. It was not long before these measures led to the inevitable result —persecution.

Eleven years after the planting of the first colony, Roger Williams came to the New World. Like the early Pilgrims he came to enjoy religious freedom; but, unlike them, he saw—what so few in his time had yet seen—that this freedom was the inalienable right of all, whatever might be their creed. He was an earnest seeker for truth, with Robinson holding it impossible that all the light from God's word had yet been received. Williams "was the first person in modern Christendom to establish civil government on the doctrine of the liberty of conscience, the equality of opinions before the law."—Bancroft, pt. 1, ch. 15, par. 16. He declared it to be the duty of the magistrate to restrain crime, but never to control the conscience. "The public or the magistrates may decide," he said, "what is due from man to man; but when they attempt to prescribe a man's duties to God, they are out of place, and there can be no safety; for it is clear that if the magistrate has the power, he may decree one set of opinions or beliefs today and another tomorrow; as has been done in England by different kings and queens, and by different popes and councils in the Roman Church; so that belief would become a heap of confusion."—Martyn, vol. 5, p. 340.

Attendance at the services of the established church was required under a penalty of fine or imprisonment. "Williams reprobated the law; the worst statute in the English code was that which did but enforce attendance upon the parish church. To compel men to unite with those of a different creed, he regarded as an open violation of their natural rights; to drag to public worship the irreligious and the unwilling, seemed only like requiring hypocrisy. . . . 'No one should be bound to worship, or,' he added, 'to maintain a worship, against his own consent.' 'What!' exclaimed his antagonists, amazed at his tenets, 'is not the laborer worthy of his hire?' 'Yes,' replied he, 'from them that hire him.' "—Bancroft, pt. 1, ch. 15, par. 2.

Roger Williams was respected and beloved as a faithful minister, a man of rare gifts, of unbending integrity and true benevolence; yet his steadfast denial of the right of civil magistrates to authority over the church, and his demand for religious liberty, could not be tolerated. The application of this new doctrine, it was urged, would "subvert the fundamental state and government of the country."—*Ibid.*, pt. 1, ch. 15, par. 10. He was sentenced to banishment from the colonies, and, finally, to avoid arrest, he was forced to flee, amid the cold and storms of winter, into the unbroken forest.

"For fourteen weeks," he says, "I was sorely tossed in a bitter season, not knowing what bread or bed did mean." But "the ravens fed me in the wilderness," and a hollow tree often served him for a shelter.—Martyn, vol. 5, pp. 349, 350. Thus he continued his painful flight through the snow and the trackless forest, until he found refuge with an Indian tribe whose confidence and affection he had won while endeavoring to teach them the truths of the gospel.

Making his way at last, after months of change and wandering, to the shores of Narragansett Bay, he there laid the foundation of the first state of modern times that in the fullest sense recognized the right of religious freedom. The fundamental principle of Roger Williams's colony was "that every man should have liberty to worship God according to the light of his own conscience."—*Ibid.*, vol. 5, p. 354. His little state, Rhode Island, became the asylum of the oppressed, and it increased and prospered until its foundation principles—civil and religious liberty—became the cornerstones of the American Republic.

In that grand old document which our forefathers set forth as their bill of rights—the Declaration of Independence—they declared: "We hold these truths to be self-evident, that all men are created equal; that they are endowed by their Creator with certain unalienable rights; that among these are life, liberty, and the pursuit of happiness." And the Constitution guarantees, in the most explicit terms, the inviolability of conscience: "No religious test shall ever be required as a qualification to any office of public trust under the United States." "Congress shall make no law respecting an establishment of religion, or prohibiting the free exercise thereof."

"The framers of the Constitution recognized the eternal principle that man's relation with his God is above human legislation, and his rights of conscience inalienable. Reasoning was not necessary to establish this truth; we are conscious of it in our own bosoms. It is this consciousness which, in defiance of human laws, has sustained so many martyrs in tortures and flames. They felt that their duty to God was superior to human enactments, and that man could exercise no authority over their consciences. It is an inborn principle which nothing can eradicate."—Congressional documents (U.S.A.), serial No. 200, document No. 271.

As the tidings spread through the countries of Europe, of a land where every man might enjoy the fruit of his own labor and obey the convictions of his own conscience, thousands flocked to the shores of the New World. Colonies rapidly multiplied. "Massachusetts, by special law, offered free welcome and aid, at the public cost, to Christians of any nationality who might fly beyond the Atlantic 'to escape from wars or famine, or the oppression of their persecutors.' Thus the fugitive and the downtrodden were, by statute, made the guests of the commonwealth."—Martyn, vol. 5, p. 417. In twenty years from the first landing at Plymouth, as many thousand Pilgrims were settled in New England.

To secure the object which they sought, "they were content to earn a bare subsistence by a life of frugality and toil. They asked nothing from the soil but the reasonable returns of their own labor. No golden vision threw a deceitful halo around their path. . . . They were content with the slow but steady progress of their social polity. They patiently endured the privations of the wilderness, watering the tree of liberty with their tears, and with the sweat of their brow, till it took deep root in the land."

The Bible was held as the foundation of faith, the source of wisdom, and the charter of liberty. Its principles were diligently taught in the home, in the school, and in the church, and its fruits were manifest in thrift, intelligence, purity, and temperance. One might be for years a dweller in the Puritan settlement, "and not see a drunkard, or hear an oath, or meet a beggar."—Bancroft, pt. 1, ch. 19, par. 25. It was demonstrated that the principles of the Bible are the surest safeguards of national greatness. The feeble and isolated colonies grew to a confederation of powerful states, and the world marked with wonder the peace and prosperity of "a church without a pope, and a state without a king."

But continually increasing numbers were attracted to the shores of America, actuated by motives widely different from those of the first Pilgrims. Though the primitive faith and purity exerted a widespread and molding power, yet its influence became less and less as the numbers increased of those who sought only worldly advantage.

The regulation adopted by the early colonists, of permitting only members of the church to vote or to hold office in the civil government, led to most pernicious results. This measure had been accepted as a means of preserving the purity of the state, but it resulted in the corruption of the church. A profession of religion being the condition of suffrage and officeholding, many, actuated solely by motives of worldly policy, united with the church without a change of heart. Thus the churches came to consist, to a considerable extent, of unconverted persons; and even in the ministry were those who not only held errors of doctrine, but who were ignorant of the renewing power of the Holy Spirit. Thus again was demonstrated the evil results, so often witnessed in the history of the church from the days of Constantine to the present, of attempting to build up the church by the aid of the state, of appealing to the secular power in support of the gospel of Him who declared: "My kingdom is not of this world." John 18:36. The union of the church with the state, be the degree never so slight, while it may appear to bring the world nearer to the church, does in reality but bring the church nearer to the world.

The great principle so nobly advocated by Robinson and Roger Williams, that truth is progressive, that Christians should stand ready to accept all the light which may shine from God's holy word, was lost sight of by their descendants. The Protestant churches of America—and those of Europe as well—so highly favored in receiving the blessings of the Reformation, failed to press forward in the path of reform. Though a few faithful men arose, from time to time, to proclaim new truth and expose long-cherished error, the majority, like the Jews in Christ's day or the papists in the time of Luther, were content to believe as their fathers had believed and to live as they had lived. Therefore religion again degenerated into formalism; and errors and superstitions which would have been cast aside had the church continued to walk in the light of God's word, were retained and cherished. Thus the spirit inspired by the Reformation gradually died out, until there was almost as great need of reform in the Protestant churches as in the Roman Church in the time of Luther. There was the same worldliness and spiritual stupor, a similar reverence for the opinions of men, and substitution of human theories for the teachings of God's word.

The wide circulation of the Bible in the early part of the nineteenth century, and the great light thus shed upon the world, was not followed by a corresponding advance in knowledge of revealed truth, or in experimental religion. Satan could not, as in former ages, keep God's word from the people; it had been placed within the reach of all; but in order still to accomplish his object, he led many to value it but lightly. Men ne-

Roger Williams, banished from his home colony for his views on liberty, found refuge with friendly Indians.

© S.P.A. ROBERT TEMPLE AYRES, ARTIST

glected to search the Scriptures, and thus they continued to accept false interpretations, and to cherish doctrines which had no foundation in the Bible.

Seeing the failure of his efforts to crush out the truth by persecution, Satan had again resorted to the plan of compromise which led to the great apostasy and the formation of the Church of Rome. He had induced Christians to ally themselves, not now with pagans, but with those who, by their devotion to the things of this world, had proved themselves to be as truly idolaters as were the worshipers of graven images. And the results of this union were no less pernicious now than in former ages; pride and extravagance were fostered under the guise of religion, and the churches became corrupted. Satan continued to pervert the doctrines of the Bible, and traditions that were to ruin millions were taking deep root. The church was upholding and defending these traditions, instead of contending for "the faith which was once delivered unto the saints." Thus were degraded the principles for which the Reformers had done and suffered so much.

chapter 17

Promises of Christ's Return

ONE of the most solemn and yet most glorious truths revealed in the Bible is that of Christ's second coming to complete the great work of redemption. To God's pilgrim people, so long left to sojourn in "the region and shadow of death," a precious, joy-inspiring hope is given in the promise of His appearing, who is "the resurrection and the life," to "bring home again His banished." The doctrine of the second advent is the very keynote of the Sacred Scriptures. From the day when the first pair turned their sorrowing steps from Eden, the children of faith have waited the coming of the Promised One to break the destroyer's power and bring them again to the lost Paradise. Holy men of old looked forward to the advent of the Messiah in glory, as the consummation of their hope. Enoch, only the seventh in descent from them that dwelt in Eden, he who for three centuries on earth walked with his God, was permitted to behold from afar the coming of the Deliverer. "Behold," he declared, "the Lord cometh with ten thousands of His saints, to execute judgment upon all." Jude 14, 15. The patriarch Job in the night of his affliction exclaimed with unshaken trust: "I know that my Redeemer liveth, and that He shall stand at the latter day upon the earth: . . . in my flesh shall I see God: whom I shall see for myself, and mine eyes shall behold, and not another." Job 19:25-27.

The coming of Christ to usher in the reign of righteousness has inspired the most sublime and impassioned utterances of the sacred writers. The poets and prophets of the Bible have dwelt upon it in words glowing with celestial fire. The psalmist sang of the power and majesty of Israel's

King: "Out of Zion, the perfection of beauty, God hath shined. Our God shall come, and shall not keep silence. . . . He shall call to the heavens from above, and to the earth, that He may judge His people." Psalm 50:2-4. "Let the heavens rejoice, and let the earth be glad . . . before the Lord: for He cometh, for He cometh to judge the earth: He shall judge the world with righteousness, and the people with His truth." Psalm 96:11-13.

Said the prophet Isaiah: "Awake and sing, ye that dwell in dust: for thy dew is as the dew of herbs, and the earth shall cast out the dead." "Thy dead men shall live, together with my dead body shall they arise." "He will swallow up death in victory; and the Lord God will wipe away tears from off all faces; and the rebuke of His people shall He take away from off all the earth: for the Lord hath spoken it. And it shall be said in that day, Lo, this is our God; we have waited for Him, and He will save us: this is the Lord; we have waited for Him, we will be glad and rejoice in His salvation." Isaiah 26:19; 25:8, 9.

And Habakkuk, rapt in holy vision, beheld His appearing. "God came from Teman, and the Holy One from Mount Paran. His glory covered the heavens, and the earth was full of His praise. And His brightness was as the light." "He stood, and measured the earth: He beheld, and drove asunder the nations; and the everlasting mountains were scattered, the perpetual hills did bow: His ways are everlasting." "Thou didst ride upon Thine horses and Thy chariots of salvation." "The mountains saw Thee, and they trembled: . . . the deep uttered his voice, and lifted up his hands on high. The sun and moon stood still in their habitation: at the light of Thine arrows they went, and at the shining of Thy glittering spear." "Thou wentest forth for the salvation of Thy people, even for salvation with Thine anointed." Habakkuk 3:3, 4, 6, 8, 10, 11, 13.

When the Saviour was about to be separated from His disciples, He comforted them in their sorrow with the assurance that He would come again: "Let not your heart be troubled. . . . In My Father's house are many mansions. . . . I go to prepare a place for you. And if I go and prepare a place for you, I will come again, and receive you unto Myself." John 14:1-3. "The Son of man shall come in His glory, and all the holy angels with Him." "Then shall He sit upon the throne of His glory: and before Him shall be gathered all nations." Matthew 25:31, 32.

The angels who lingered upon Olivet after Christ's ascension repeated to the disciples the promise of His return: "This *same* Jesus, which is taken up from you into heaven, shall *so* come in like manner as ye have seen Him go into heaven." Acts 1:11. And the apostle Paul, speaking by the Spirit of Inspiration, testified: "The Lord *Himself* shall descend from heaven with a shout, with the voice of the Archangel, and with the trump of God." 1 Thessalonians 4:16. Says the prophet of Patmos: "Behold, He cometh with clouds; and every eye shall see Him." Revelation 1:7.

About His coming cluster the glories of that "restitution of all things, which God hath spoken by the mouth of all His holy prophets since the world began." Acts 3:21. Then the long-continued rule of evil shall be broken; "the kingdoms of this world" will become "the kingdoms of our Lord, and of His Christ; and He shall reign for ever and ever." Revelation 11:15. "The glory of the Lord shall be revealed, and all flesh shall see it together." "The Lord God will cause righteousness and praise to spring forth before all the nations." He shall be "for a crown of glory, and for a diadem of beauty, unto the residue of His people." Isaiah 40:5; 61:11; 28:5.

It is then that the peaceful and long-desired kingdom of the Messiah shall be established under the whole heaven. "The Lord shall comfort Zion: He will comfort all her waste places; and He will make her wilderness like Eden, and her desert like the garden of the Lord." "The glory of Lebanon shall be given unto it, the excellency of Carmel and Sharon." "Thou shalt no more be termed Forsaken; neither shall thy land any more be termed Desolate: but thou shalt be called My Delight, and thy land Beulah." "As the bridegroom rejoiceth over the bride, so shall thy God rejoice over thee." Isaiah 51:3; 35:2; 62:4, 5, margin.

The coming of the Lord has been in all ages the hope of His true followers. The Saviour's parting promise upon Olivet, that He would come again, lighted up the future for His disciples, filling their hearts with joy and hope that sorrow could not quench nor trials dim. Amid suffering and persecution, the "appearing of the great God and our Saviour Jesus Christ" was the "blessed hope." When the Thessalonian Christians were filled with grief as they buried their loved ones, who had hoped to live to witness the coming of the Lord, Paul, their teacher, pointed them to the resurrection, to take place at the Saviour's advent. Then the dead in Christ should rise, and together with the living be caught up to meet the Lord in the air. "And so," he said, "shall we ever be with the Lord. Wherefore comfort one another with these words." 1 Thessalonians 4:16-18.

On rocky Patmos the beloved disciple hears the promise, "Surely I come quickly," and his longing response voices the prayer of the church in all her pilgrimage, "Even so, come, Lord Jesus." Revelation 22:20.

From the dungeon, the stake, the scaffold, where saints and martyrs witnessed for the truth, comes down the centuries the utterance of their faith and hope. Being "assured of His personal resurrection, and consequently of their own at His coming, for this cause," says one of these Christians, "they despised death, and were found to be above it."—Daniel T. Taylor, *The Reign of Christ on Earth: or, The Voice of the Church in All Ages,* page 33. They were willing to go down to the grave, that they might "rise free."—*Ibid.,* page 54. They looked for the "Lord to come from heaven in the clouds with the glory of His Father," "bringing to the just the times of the kingdom." The Waldenses cherished the same faith. —*Ibid.,* pages 129-132. Wycliffe looked forward to the Redeemer's appearing as the hope of the church.—*Ibid.,* pages 132-134.

Luther declared: "I persuade myself verily, that the day of judgment will not be absent full three hundred years. God will not, cannot, suffer this wicked world much longer." "The great day is drawing near in which the kingdom of abominations shall be overthrown."—*Ibid.,* pages 158, 134.

"This aged world is not far from its end," said Melanchthon. Calvin bids Christians "not to hesitate, ardently desiring the day of Christ's coming as of all events most auspicious;" and declares that "the whole family of the faithful will keep in view that day." "We must hunger after Christ, we must seek, contemplate," he says, "till the dawning of that great day, when our Lord will fully manifest the glory of His kingdom."—*Ibid.,* pages 158, 134.

"Has not the Lord Jesus carried up our flesh into heaven?" said Knox, the Scotch Reformer, "and shall He not return? We know that He shall return, and that with expedition." Ridley and Latimer, who laid down their lives for the truth, looked in faith for the Lord's coming. Ridley wrote: "The world without doubt—this I do believe, and therefore I say it—draws to an end. Let us with John, the servant of God, cry in our hearts unto our Saviour Christ, Come, Lord Jesus, come."—*Ibid.,* pages 151, 145.

"The thoughts of the coming of the Lord," said Baxter, "are most sweet and joyful to me."—Richard Baxter, *Works,* vol. 17, p. 555. "It is the work of faith and the character of His saints to love His appearing and to look for that blessed hope." "If death be the last enemy to be destroyed at the resurrection, we may learn how earnestly believers should long and pray for the second coming of Christ, when this full and final conquest shall be made."—*Ibid.*, vol. 17, p. 500. "This is the day that all believers should long, and hope, and wait for, as being the accomplishment of all the work of their redemption, and all the desires and endeavors of their souls." "Hasten, O Lord, this blessed day!"—*Ibid.*, vol. 17, pp. 182, 183. Such was the hope of the apostolic church, of the "church in the wilderness," and of the Reformers.

Prophecy not only foretells the manner and object of Christ's coming, but presents tokens by which men are to know when it is near. Said Jesus: "There shall be signs in the sun, and in the moon, and in the stars." Luke 21:25. "The sun shall be darkened, and the moon shall not give her light, and the stars of heaven shall fall, and the powers that are in heaven shall be shaken. And then shall they see the Son of man coming in the clouds with great power and glory." Mark 13:24-26. The revelator thus describes the first of the signs to precede the second advent: "There was a great earthquake; and the sun became black as sackcloth of hair, and the moon became as blood." Revelation 6:12.

These signs were witnessed before the opening of the nineteenth century. In fulfillment of this prophecy there occurred, in the year 1755, the most terrible earthquake that has ever been recorded. Though commonly known as the earthquake of Lisbon, it extended to the greater part of Europe, Africa, and America. It was felt in Greenland, in the West Indies, in the island of Madeira, in Norway and Sweden, Great Britain and Ireland. It pervaded an extent of not less than four million square miles. In Africa the shock was almost as severe as in Europe. A great part of Algiers was destroyed; and a short distance from Morocco, a village containing eight or ten thousand inhabitants was swallowed up. A vast wave swept over the coast of Spain and Africa engulfing cities and causing great destruction.

It was in Spain and Portugal that the shock manifested its extreme violence. At Cadiz the inflowing wave was said to be sixty feet high. Mountains, "some of the largest in Portugal, were impetuously shaken, as it were, from their very foundations, and some of them opened at their summits, which were split and rent in a wonderful manner, huge masses of them being thrown down into the adjacent valleys. Flames are related to have issued from these mountains."—Sir Charles Lyell, *Principles of Geology*, page 495.

At Lisbon "a sound of thunder was heard underground, and immediately afterwards a violent shock threw down the greater part of that city. In the course of about six minutes sixty thousand persons perished.

The sea first retired, and laid the bar dry; it then rolled in, rising fifty feet or more above its ordinary level." "Among other extraordinary events related to have occurred at Lisbon during the catastrophe, was the subsidence of a new quay, built entirely of marble, at an immense expense. A great concourse of people had collected there for safety, as a spot where they might be beyond the reach of falling ruins; but suddenly the quay sank down with all the people on it, and not one of the dead bodies ever floated to the surface."—*Ibid.*, page 495.

"The shock" of the earthquake "was instantly followed by the fall of every church and convent, almost all the large public buildings, and more than one fourth of the houses. In about two hours after the shock, fires broke out in different quarters, and raged with such violence for the space of nearly three days, that the city was completely desolated. The earthquake happened on a holyday, when the churches and convents were full of people, very few of whom escaped."—*Encyclopedia Americana*, art. "Lisbon," note (ed. 1831). "The terror of the people was beyond description. Nobody wept; it was beyond tears. They ran hither and thither, delirious with horror and astonishment, beating their faces and breasts, cying, '*Misericordia! the world's at an end!*' Mothers forgot their children, and ran about loaded with crucifixed images. Unfortunately, many ran to the churches for protection; but in vain was the sacrament exposed; in vain did the poor creatures embrace the altars; images, priests, and people were buried in one common ruin." It has been estimated that ninety thousand persons lost their lives on that fatal day.

Twenty-five years later appeared the next sign mentioned in the prophecy—the darkening of the sun and moon. What rendered this more striking was the fact that the time of its fulfillment had been definitely pointed out. In the Saviour's conversation with His disciples upon Olivet, after describing the long period of trial for the church—the 1260 years of papal persecution, concerning which He had promised that the tribulation should be shortened—He thus mentioned certain events to precede His coming, and fixed the time when the first of these should be witnessed: "In those days, after that tribulation, the sun shall be darkened, and the moon shall not give her light." Mark 13:24. The 1260 days, or years, terminated in 1798. A quarter of a century earlier, persecution had almost wholly ceased. Following this persecution, according to the words of Christ, the sun was to be darkened. On the 19th of May, 1780, this prophecy was fulfilled.

The 1755 Lisbon earthquake stands as a striking instance of fulfilling prophecy, heralding Christ's soon return.

THE TRIUMPH OF GOD'S LOVE

"Almost, if not altogether alone, as the most mysterious and as yet unexplained phenomenon of its kind, . . . stands the dark day of May 19, 1780—a most unaccountable darkening of the whole visible heavens and atmosphere in New England."—R. M. Devens, *Our First Century,* page 89.

An eyewitness living in Massachusetts describes the event as follows: "In the morning the sun rose clear, but was soon overcast. The clouds became lowery, and from them, black and ominous, as they soon appeared, lightning flashed, thunder rolled, and a little rain fell. Toward nine o'clock, the clouds became thinner, and assumed a brassy or coppery appearance, and earth, rocks, trees, buildings, water, and persons were changed by this strange, unearthly light. A few minutes later, a heavy black cloud spread over the entire sky except a narrow rim at the horizon, and it was as dark as it usually is at nine o'clock on a summer evening. . . .

"Fear, anxiety, and awe gradually filled the minds of the people. Women stood at the door, looking out upon the dark landscape; men returned from their labor in the fields; the carpenter left his tools, the blacksmith his forge, the tradesman his counter. Schools were dismissed, and tremblingly the children fled homeward. Travelers put up at the nearest farmhouse. 'What is coming?' queried every lip and heart. It seemed as if a hurricane was about to dash across the land, or as if it was the day of the consummation of all things.

"Candles were used; and hearth fires shone as brightly as on a moonless evening in autumn. . . . Fowls retired to their roosts and went to sleep, cattle gathered at the pasture bars and lowed, frogs peeped, birds sang their evening songs, and bats flew about. But the human knew that night had not come. . . .

"Dr. Nathanael Whittaker, pastor of the Tabernacle church in Salem, held religious services in the meetinghouse, and preached a sermon in which he maintained that the darkness was supernatural. Congregations came together in many other places. The texts for the extemporaneous sermons were invariably those that seemed to indicate that the darkness was consonant with Scriptural prophecy. . . . The darkness was most dense shortly after eleven o'clock."—*The Essex Antiquarian,* April, 1899, vol. 3, No. 4, pp. 53, 54. "In most parts of the country it was so great in the daytime, that the people could not tell the hour by either watch or clock, nor dine, nor manage their domestic business, without the light of candles. . . .

"The extent of this darkness was extraordinary. It was observed as far east as Falmouth. To the westward it reached to the farthest part of Connecticut, and to Albany. To the southward, it was observed along the seacoasts; and to the north as far as the American settlements extend." —William Gordon, *History of the Rise, Progress, and Establishment of the Independence of the U.S.A.*, vol. 3, p. 57.

The intense darkness of the day was succeeded, an hour or two before evening, by a partially clear sky, and the sun appeared, though it was still obscured by the black, heavy mist. "After sundown, the clouds came again overhead, and it grew dark very fast." "Nor was the darkness of the night less uncommon and terrifying than that of the day; notwithstanding there was almost a full moon, no object was discernible but by the help of some artificial light, which, when seen from the neighboring houses and other places at a distance, appeared through a kind of Egyptian darkness which seemed almost impervious to the rays."—Isaiah Thomas, *Massachusetts Spy; or, American Oracle of Liberty*, vol. 10, No. 472 (May 25, 1780). Said an eyewitness of the scene: "I could not help conceiving at the time, that if every luminous body in the universe had been shrouded in impenetrable shades, or struck out of existence, the darkness could not have been more complete."—Letter by Dr. Samuel Tenney, of Exeter, New Hampshire, December, 1785 (in *Massachusetts Historical Society Collections*, 1792, 1st series, vol. 1, p. 97). Though at nine o'clock that night the moon rose to the full, "it had not the least effect to dispel the deathlike shadows." After midnight the darkness disappeared, and the moon, when first visible, had the appearance of blood.

May 19, 1780, stands in history as "The Dark Day." Since the time of Moses no period of darkness of equal density, extent, and duration, has ever been recorded. The description of this event, as given by eyewitnesses, is but an echo of the words of the Lord, recorded by the prophet Joel, twenty-five hundred years previous to their fulfillment: "The sun shall be turned into darkness, and the moon into blood, before the great and terrible day of the Lord come." Joel 2:31.

Christ had bidden His people watch for the signs of His advent and rejoice as they should behold the tokens of their coming King. "When these things begin to come to pass," He said, "then look up, and lift up your heads; for your redemption draweth nigh." He pointed His followers to the budding trees of spring, and said: "When they now shoot forth, ye see and know of your own selves that summer is now nigh at hand.

So likewise ye, when ye see these things come to pass, know ye that the kingdom of God is nigh at hand." Luke 21:28, 30, 31.

But as the spirit of humility and devotion in the church had given place to pride and formalism, love for Christ and faith in His coming had grown cold. Absorbed in worldliness and pleasure seeking, the professed people of God were blinded to the Saviour's instructions concerning the signs of His appearing. The doctrine of the second advent had been neglected; the scriptures relating to it were obscured by misinterpretation, until it was, to a great extent, ignored and forgotten. Especially was this the case in the churches of America. The freedom and comfort enjoyed by all classes of society, the ambitious desire for wealth and luxury, begetting an absorbing devotion to money-making, the eager rush for popularity and power, which seemed to be within the reach of all, led men to center their interests and hopes on the things of this life, and to put far in the future that solemn day when the present order of things should pass away.

When the Saviour pointed out to His followers the signs of His return, He foretold the state of backsliding that would exist just prior to His second advent. There would be, as in the days of Noah, the activity and stir of worldly business and pleasure seeking—buying, selling, planting, building, marrying, and giving in marriage—with forgetfulness of God and the future life. For those living at this time, Christ's admonition is: "Take heed to yourselves, lest at any time your hearts be overcharged with surfeiting, and drunkenness, and cares of this life, and so that day come upon you unawares." "Watch ye therefore, and pray always, that ye may be accounted worthy to escape all these things that shall come to pass, and to stand before the Son of man." Luke 21:34, 36.

The condition of the church at this time is pointed out in the Saviour's words in the Revelation: "Thou hast a name that thou livest, and art dead." And to those who refuse to arouse from their careless security, the solemn warning is addressed: "If therefore thou shalt not watch, I will come on thee as a thief, and thou shalt not know what hour I will come upon thee." Revelation 3:1, 3.

It was needful that men should be awakened to their danger; that they should be roused to prepare for the solemn events connected with the close of probation. The prophet of God declares: "The day of the Lord is great and very terrible; and who can abide it?" Who shall stand when He appeareth who is "of purer eyes than to behold evil," and cannot "look on iniquity"? Joel 2:11; Habakkuk 1:13. To them that cry, "My

God, we know Thee," yet have transgressed His covenant, and hastened after another god, hiding iniquity in their hearts, and loving the paths of unrighteousness—to these the day of the Lord is "darkness, and not light, even very dark, and no brightness in it." Hosea 8:2, 1; Psalm 16:4; Amos 5:20. "It shall come to pass at that time," saith the Lord, "that I will search Jerusalem with candles, and punish the men that are settled on their lees: that say in their heart, The Lord will not do good, neither will He do evil." Zephaniah 1:12. "I will punish the world for their evil, and the wicked for their iniquity; and I will cause the arrogancy of the proud to cease, and will lay low the haughtiness of the terrible." Isaiah 13:11. "Neither their silver nor their gold shall be able to deliver them;" "their goods shall become a booty, and their houses a desolation." Zephaniah 1:18, 13.

The prophet Jeremiah, looking forward to this fearful time, exclaimed: "I am pained at my very heart. . . . I cannot hold my peace, because thou hast heard, O my soul, the sound of the trumpet, the alarm of war. Destruction upon destruction is cried." Jeremiah 4:19, 20.

"That day is a day of wrath, a day of trouble and distress, a day of wasteness and desolation, a day of darkness and gloominess, a day of clouds and thick darkness, a day of the trumpet and alarm." Zephaniah 1:15, 16. "Behold, the day of the Lord cometh, . . . to lay the land desolate: and He shall destroy the sinners thereof out of it." Isaiah 13:9.

In view of that great day the word of God, in the most solemn and impressive language, calls upon His people to arouse from their spiritual lethargy and to seek His face with repentance and humiliation: "Blow ye the trumpet in Zion, and sound an alarm in My holy mountain: let all the inhabitants of the land tremble: for the day of the Lord cometh, for it is nigh at hand." "Sanctify a fast, call a solemn assembly: gather the people, sanctify the congregation, assemble the elders, gather the children: . . . let the bridegroom go forth of his chamber, and the bride out of her closet. Let the priests, the ministers of the Lord, weep between the porch and the altar." "Turn ye even to Me with all your heart, and with fasting, and with weeping, and with mourning: and rend your heart, and not your garments, and turn unto the Lord your God: for He is gracious and merciful, slow to anger, and of great kindness." Joel 2:1, 15-17, 12, 13.

To prepare a people to stand in the day of God, a great work of reform was to be accomplished. God saw that many of His professed people were not building for eternity, and in His mercy He was about to send a message of warning to arouse them from their stupor and lead them to make ready for the coming of the Lord.

This warning is brought to view in Revelation 14. Here is a threefold message represented as proclaimed by heavenly beings and immediately followed by the coming of the Son of man to reap "the harvest of the earth." The first of these warnings announces the approaching judgment. The prophet beheld an angel flying "in the midst of heaven, having the everlasting gospel to preach unto them that dwell on the earth, and to every nation, and kindred, and tongue, and people, saying with a loud voice, Fear God, and give glory to Him; for the hour of His judgment is come: and worship Him that made heaven, and earth, and the sea, and the fountains of waters." Revelation 14:6, 7.

This message is declared to be a part of "the everlasting gospel." The work of preaching the gospel has not been committed to angels, but has been entrusted to men. Holy angels have been employed in directing this work, they have in charge the great movements for the salvation of men; but the actual proclamation of the gospel is performed by the servants of Christ upon the earth.

Faithful men, who were obedient to the promptings of God's spirit and the teachings of His word, were to proclaim this warning to the world. They were those who had taken heed to the "sure word of prophecy," the "light that shineth in a dark place, until the day dawn, and the daystar arise." 2 Peter 1:19. They had been seeking the knowledge of God more than all hid treasures, counting it "better than the merchandise of silver, and the gain thereof than fine gold." Proverbs 3:14. And the Lord revealed to them the great things of the kingdom. "The secret of the Lord is with them that fear Him; and He will show them His covenant." Psalm 25:14.

It was not the scholarly theologians who had an understanding of this truth, and engaged in its proclamation. Had these been faithful watchmen, diligently and prayerfully searching the Scriptures, they would have known the time of night; the prophecies would have opened to them the events about to take place. But they did not occupy this position, and the message was given by humbler men. Said Jesus: "Walk while ye have the light, lest darkness come upon you." John 12:35. Those who turn away from the light which God has given, or who neglect to seek it when it is within their reach, are left in darkness. But the Saviour declares: "He that followeth Me shall not walk in darkness, but shall have the light of life." John 8:12. Whoever is with singleness of purpose seeking to do God's will, earnestly heeding the light already given, will receive greater light; to that soul some star of heavenly radiance will be sent to guide him into all truth.

At the time of Christ's first advent the priests and scribes of the Holy City, to whom were entrusted the oracles of God, might have discerned the signs of the times and proclaimed the coming of the Promised One. The prophecy of Micah designated His birthplace; Daniel specified the time of His advent. Micah 5:2; Daniel 9:25. God committed these prophecies to the Jewish leaders; they were without excuse if they did not know and declare to the people that the Messiah's coming was at hand. Their ignorance was the result of sinful neglect. The Jews were building monuments for the slain prophets of God, while by their deference to the great men of earth they were paying homage to the servants of Satan. Absorbed in their ambitious strife for place and power among men, they lost sight of the divine honors proffered them by the King of heaven.

With profound and reverent interest the elders of Israel should have been studying the place, the time, the circumstances, of the greatest event in the world's history—the coming of the Son of God to accomplish the redemption of man. All the people should have been watching and waiting that they might be among the first to welcome the world's Redeemer. But, lo, at Bethlehem two weary travelers from the hills of Nazareth traverse the whole length of the narrow street to the eastern extremity of the town, vainly seeking a place of rest and shelter for the night. No doors are open to receive them. In a wretched hovel prepared for cattle, they at last find refuge, and there the Saviour of the world is born.

Heavenly angels had seen the glory which the Son of God shared with the Father before the world was, and they had looked forward with intense interest to His appearing on earth as an event fraught with the greatest joy to all people. Angels were appointed to carry the glad tidings to those who were prepared to receive it and who would joyfully make it known to the inhabitants of the earth. Christ had stooped to take upon Himself man's nature; He was to bear an infinite weight of woe as He should make His soul an offering for sin; yet angels desired that even in His humiliation the Son of the Highest might appear before men with a dignity and glory befitting His character. Would the great men of earth assemble at Israel's capital to greet His coming? Would legions of angels present Him to the expectant company?

An angel visits the earth to see who are prepared to welcome Jesus. But he can discern no tokens of expectancy. He hears no voice of praise and triumph that the period of Messiah's coming is at hand. The angel hovers for a time over the chosen city and the temple where the divine presence has been manifested for ages; but even here is the same indifference. The priests, in their pomp and pride, are offering polluted sacrifices in the temple. The Pharisees are with loud voices addressing the people or making boastful prayers at the corners of the streets. In the palaces of kings, in the assemblies of philosophers, in the schools of the rabbis, all are alike unmindful of the wondrous fact which has filled all heaven with joy and praise—that the Redeemer of men is about to appear upon the earth.

There is no evidence that Christ is expected, and no preparation for the Prince of life. In amazement the celestial messenger is about to return to heaven with the shameful tidings, when he discovers a group of shepherds who are watching their flocks by night, and, as they gaze into the starry heavens, are contemplating the prophecy of a Messiah to come to earth, and longing for the advent of the world's Redeemer. Here is a company that is prepared to receive the heavenly message. And suddenly the angel of the Lord appears, declaring the good tidings of great joy. Celestial glory floods all the plain, an innumerable company of angels is revealed, and as if the joy were too great for one messenger to bring from heaven, a multitude of voices break forth in the anthem which all the nations of the saved shall one day sing: "Glory to God in the highest, and on earth peace, good will toward men." Luke 2:14.

Oh, what a lesson is this wonderful story of Bethlehem! How it rebukes our unbelief, our pride and self-sufficiency. How it warns us to beware, lest by our criminal indifference we also fail to discern the signs of the times, and therefore know not the day of our visitation.

It was not alone upon the hills of Judea, not among the lowly shepherds only, that angels found the watchers for Messiah's coming. In the land of the heathen also were those that looked for Him; they were wise men, rich and noble, the philosophers of the East. Students of nature, the Magi had seen God in His handiwork. From the Hebrew Scriptures they had learned of the Star to arise out of Jacob, and with eager desire they awaited His coming, who should be not only the "Consolation of Israel," but a "Light to lighten the Gentiles," and "for salvation unto the ends of the earth." Luke 2:25, 32; Acts 13:47. They were seekers for light, and light from the throne of God illumined the path for their feet. While the priests and rabbis of Jerusalem, the appointed guardians and expounders of the truth, were shrouded in darkness, the Heaven-sent star guided these Gentile strangers to the birthplace of the newborn King.

It is "unto them that look for Him" that Christ is to "appear the second time without sin unto salvation." Hebrews 9:28. Like the tidings of the Saviour's birth, the message of the second advent was not committed to the religious leaders of the people. They had failed to preserve their connection with God, and had refused light from heaven; therefore they were not of the number described by the apostle Paul: "But ye, brethren, are not in darkness, that that day should overtake you as a thief. Ye are all the children of light, and the children of the day: we are not of the night, nor of darkness." 1 Thessalonians 5:4, 5.

The watchmen upon the walls of Zion should have been the first to catch the tidings of the Saviour's advent, the first to lift their voices to proclaim Him near, the first to warn the people to prepare for His coming. But they were at ease, dreaming of peace and safety, while the people were asleep in their sins. Jesus saw His church, like the barren fig tree, covered with pretentious leaves, yet destitute of precious fruit. There was a boastful observance of the forms of religion, while the spirit of true humility, penitence, and faith—which alone could render the service acceptable to God—was lacking. Instead of the graces of the Spirit there were manifested pride, formalism, vainglory, selfishness, oppression. A backsliding church closed their eyes to the signs of the times. God did not forsake them, or suffer His faithfulness to fail; but they departed from Him, and separated themselves from His love. As they refused to comply with the conditions, His promises were not fulfilled to them.

Such is the sure result of neglect to appreciate and improve the light and privileges which God bestows. Unless the church will follow on in

His opening providence, accepting every ray of light, performing every duty which may be revealed, religion will inevitably degenerate into the observance of forms, and the spirit of vital godliness will disappear. This truth has been repeatedly illustrated in the history of the church. God requires of His people works of faith and obedience corresponding to the blessings and privileges bestowed. Obedience requires a sacrifice and involves a cross; and this is why so many of the professed followers of Christ refused to receive the light from heaven, and, like the Jews of old, knew not the time of their visitation. Luke 19:44. Because of their pride and unbelief the Lord passed them by and revealed His truth to those who, like the shepherds of Bethlehem and the Eastern Magi, had given heed to all the light they had received.

chapter 18

New Light in the New World

AN UPRIGHT, honest-hearted farmer, who had
been led to doubt the divine authority of the
Scriptures, yet who sincerely desired to know the truth, was the man
specially chosen of God to lead out in the proclamation of Christ's second
coming. Like many other reformers, William Miller had in early life
battled with poverty and had thus learned the great lessons of energy
and self-denial. The members of the family from which he sprang were
characterized by an independent, liberty-loving spirit, by capability of
endurance, and ardent patriotism—traits which were also prominent in
his character. His father was a captain in the army of the Revolution, and
to the sacrifices which he made in the struggles and sufferings of that
stormy period may be traced the straitened circumstances of Miller's
early life.

He had a sound physical constitution, and even in childhood gave
evidence of more than ordinary intellectual strength. As he grew older,
this became more marked. His mind was active and well developed, and
he had a keen thirst for knowledge. Though he did not enjoy the advan-
tages of a collegiate education, his love of study and a habit of careful
thought and close criticism rendered him a man of sound judgment and
comprehensive views. He possessed an irreproachable moral character
and an enviable reputation, being generally esteemed for integrity, thrift,
and benevolence. By dint of energy and application he early acquired a
competence, though his habits of study were still maintained. He filled

various civil and military offices with credit, and the avenues to wealth and honor seemed wide open to him.

His mother was a woman of sterling piety, and in childhood, he had been subject to religious impressions. In early manhood, however, he was thrown into the society of deists, whose influence was the stronger from the fact that they were mostly good citizens and men of humane and benevolent disposition. Living, as they did, in the midst of Christian institutions, their characters had been to some extent molded by their surroundings. For the excellencies which won them respect and confidence they were indebted to the Bible; and yet these good gifts were so perverted as to exert an influence against the word of God. By association with these men, Miller was led to adopt their sentiments. The current interpretations of Scripture presented difficulties which seemed to him insurmountable; yet his new belief, while setting aside the Bible, offered nothing better to take its place, and he remained far from satisfied. He continued to hold these views, however, for about twelve years. But at the age of thirty-four the Holy Spirit impressed his heart with a sense of his condition as a sinner. He found in his former belief no assurance of happiness beyond the grave. The future was dark and gloomy. Referring afterward to his feelings at this time, he said:

"Annihilation was a cold and chilling thought, and accountability was sure destruction to all. The heavens were as brass over my head, and the earth as iron under my feet. Eternity—what was it? And death—why was it? The more I reasoned, the further I was from demonstration. The more I thought, the more scattered were my conclusions. I tried to stop thinking, but my thoughts would not be controlled. I was truly wretched, but did not understand the cause. I murmured and complained, but knew not of whom. I knew that there was a wrong, but knew not how or where to find the right. I mourned, but without hope."

In this state he continued for some months. "Suddenly," he says, "the character of a Saviour was vividly impressed upon my mind. It seemed that there might be a being so good and compassionate as to himself atone for our transgressions, and thereby save us from suffering the penalty of sin. I immediately felt how lovely such a being must be, and imagined that I could cast myself into the arms of, and trust in the mercy of, such a one. But the question arose, How can it be proved that such a being does exist? Aside from the Bible, I found that I could get no evidence of the existence of such a Saviour, or even of a future state. . . .

"I saw that the Bible did bring to view just such a Saviour as I needed;

and I was perplexed to find how an uninspired book should develop principles so perfectly adapted to the wants of a fallen world. I was constrained to admit that the Scriptures must be a revelation from God. They became my delight; and in Jesus I found a friend. The Saviour became to me the chiefest among ten thousand; and the Scriptures, which before were dark and contradictory, now became the lamp to my feet and light to my path. My mind became settled and satisfied. I found the Lord God to be a Rock in the midst of the ocean of life. The Bible now became my chief study, and I can truly say, I searched it with great delight. I found the half was never told me. I wondered why I had not seen its beauty and glory before, and marveled that I could have ever rejected it. I found everything revealed that my heart could desire, and a remedy for every disease of the soul. I lost all taste for other reading, and applied my heart to get wisdom from God."—S. Bliss, *Memoirs of Wm. Miller*, pages 65-67.

Miller publicly professed his faith in the religion which he had despised. But his infidel associates were not slow to bring forward all those arguments which he himself had often urged against the divine authority of the Scriptures. He was not then prepared to answer them; but he reasoned that if the Bible is a revelation from God, it must be consistent with itself; and that as it was given for man's instruction, it must be adapted to his understanding. He determined to study the Scriptures for himself, and ascertain if every apparent contradiction could not be harmonized.

Endeavoring to lay aside all preconceived opinions, and dispensing with commentaries, he compared scripture with scripture by the aid of the marginal references and the concordance. He pursued his study in a regular and methodical manner; beginning with Genesis, and reading verse by verse, he proceeded no faster than the meaning of the several passages so unfolded as to leave him free from all embarrassment. When he found anything obscure, it was his custom to compare it with every other text which seemed to have any reference to the matter under consideration. Every word was permitted to have its proper bearing upon the subject of the text, and if his view of it harmonized with every collateral passage, it ceased to be a difficulty. Thus whenever he met with a passage hard to be understood he found an explanation in some other portion of the Scriptures. As he studied with earnest prayer for divine enlightenment, that which had before appeared dark to his understanding was made clear. He experienced the truth of the psalmist's words: "The entrance of Thy words giveth light; it giveth understanding unto the simple." Psalm 119:130.

With intense interest he studied the books of Daniel and the Revelation, employing the same principles of interpretation as in the other scriptures, and found, to his great joy, that the prophetic symbols could be understood. He saw that the prophecies, so far as they had been fulfilled, had been fulfilled literally; that all the various figures, metaphors, parables, similitudes, etc., were either explained in their immediate connection, or the terms in which they were expressed were defined in other scriptures, and when thus explained, were to be literally understood. "I was thus satisfied," he says, "that the Bible is a system of revealed truths, so clearly and simply given that the wayfaring man, though a fool, need not err therein."—Bliss, page 70. Link after link of the chain of truth rewarded his efforts, as step by step he traced down the great lines of prophecy. Angels of heaven were guiding his mind and opening the Scriptures to his understanding.

Taking the manner in which the prophecies had been fulfilled in the past as a criterion by which to judge of the fulfillment of those which were still future, he became satisfied that the popular view of the spiritual reign of Christ—a temporal millennium before the end of the world —was not sustained by the word of God. This doctrine, pointing to a thousand years of righteousness and peace before the personal coming of the Lord, put far off the terrors of the day of God. But, pleasing though it may be, it is contrary to the teachings of Christ and His apostles, who declared that the wheat and the tares are to grow together until the harvest, the end of the world; that "evil men and seducers shall wax worse and worse;" that "in the last days perilous times shall come;" and that the kingdom of darkness shall continue until the advent of the Lord and shall be consumed with the spirit of His mouth and be destroyed with the brightness of His coming. Matthew 13:30, 38-41; 2 Timothy 3:13, 1; 2 Thessalonians 2:8.

The doctrine of the world's conversion and the spiritual reign of Christ was not held by the apostolic church. It was not generally accepted by Christians until about the beginning of the eighteenth century. Like every other error, its results were evil. It taught men to look far in the future for the coming of the Lord and prevented them from giving heed to the signs heralding His approach. It induced a feeling of confidence and security that was not well founded and led many to neglect the preparation necessary in order to meet their Lord.

Miller found the literal, personal coming of Christ to be plainly taught in the Scriptures. Says Paul: "The Lord Himself shall descend from heaven with a shout, with the voice of the Archangel, and with the trump of God." 2 Thessalonians 4:16. And the Saviour declares: "They shall *see* the Son of man coming in the clouds of heaven with power and great glory." "For as the lightning cometh out of the east, and shineth even unto the west; so shall also the coming of the Son of man be." Matthew 24:30, 27. He is to be accompanied by all the hosts of heaven. "The Son of man shall come in His glory, and all the holy angels with Him." Matthew 25:31. "And He shall send His angels with a great sound of a trumpet, and they shall gather together His elect." Matthew 24:31.

At His coming the righteous dead will be raised, and the righteous living will be changed. "We shall not all sleep," says Paul, "but we shall all be changed, in a moment, in the twinkling of an eye, at the last trump: for the trumpet shall sound, and the dead shall be raised incorruptible, and we shall be changed. For this corruptible must put on incorruption, and this mortal must put on immortality." 1 Corinthians 15:51-53. And in his letter to the Thessalonians, after describing the coming of the Lord, he says: "The dead in Christ shall rise first: then we which are alive and remain shall be caught up together with them in the clouds, to meet the Lord in the air: and so shall we ever be with the Lord." 1 Thessalonians 4:16, 17.

Not until the personal advent of Christ can His people receive the kingdom. The Saviour said: "When the Son of man shall come in His glory, and all the holy angels with Him, then shall He sit upon the throne of His glory: and before Him shall be gathered all nations: and He shall separate them one from another, as a shepherd divideth his sheep from the goats: and He shall set the sheep on His right hand, but the goats on the left. Then shall the King say unto them on His right hand, Come, ye blessed of My Father, inherit the kingdom prepared for you from the foundation of the world." Matthew 25:31-34. We have seen by the scriptures just given that when the Son of man comes, the dead are raised incorruptible and the living are changed. By this great change they are prepared to receive the kingdom; for Paul says: "Flesh and blood cannot inherit the kingdom of God; neither doth corruption inherit incorruption." 1 Corinthians 15:50. Man in his present state is mortal, corruptible; but the kingdom of God will be incorruptible, enduring forever. Therefore man in his present state cannot enter into the kingdom of God. But when Jesus comes, He confers immortality upon His people; and then He calls them to inherit the kingdom of which they have hitherto been only heirs.

These and other scriptures clearly proved to Miller's mind that the events which were generally expected to take place before the coming of Christ, such as the universal reign of peace and the setting up of the kingdom of God upon the earth, were to be subsequent to the second advent. Furthermore, all the signs of the times and the condition of the world corresponded to the prophetic description of the last days. He was forced to the conclusion, from the study of Scripture alone, that the period allotted for the continuance of the earth in its present state was about to close.

"Another kind of evidence that vitally affected my mind," he says, "was the chronology of the Scriptures. . . . I found that predicted events, which had been fulfilled in the past, often occurred within a given time. The one hundred and twenty years to the flood (Genesis 6:3); the seven days that were to precede it, with forty days of predicted rain (Genesis 7:4); the four hundred years of the sojourn of Abraham's seed (Genesis 15:13); the three days of the butler's and baker's dreams (Genesis 40: 12-20); the seven years of Pharaoh's (Genesis 41:28-54); the forty years in the wilderness (Numbers 14:34); the three and a half years of famine (1 Kings 17:1) [see Luke 4:25;] . . . the seventy years' captivity (Jeremiah 25:11); Nebuchadnezzar's seven times (Daniel 4:13-16); and the seven weeks, threescore and two weeks, and the one week, making seventy weeks, determined upon the Jews (Daniel 9:24-27)—the events limited by these times were all once only a matter of prophecy, and were fulfilled in accordance with the predictions."—Bliss, pages 74, 75.

When, therefore, he found, in his study of the Bible, various chronological periods that, according to his understanding of them, extended to the second coming of Christ, he could not but regard them as the "times before appointed," which God had revealed unto His servants. "The secret things," says Moses, "belong unto the Lord our God: but those things which are revealed belong unto us and to our children forever;" and the Lord declares by the prophet Amos, that He "will do nothing, but He revealeth His secret unto His servants the prophets." Deuteronomy 29:29; Amos 3:7. The students of God's word may, then, confidently expect to find the most stupendous event to take place in human history clearly pointed out in the Scriptures of truth.

"As I was fully convinced," says Miller, "that all Scripture given by inspiration of God is profitable (2 Timothy 3:16); that it came not at any time by the will of man, but was written as holy men were moved by the Holy Ghost (2 Peter 1:21), and was written 'for our learning, that we through patience and comfort of the Scriptures might have hope' (Romans 15:4), I could but regard the chronological portions of the Bible as being as much a portion of the word of God, and as much entitled to our serious consideration, as any other portion of the Scriptures. I therefore felt that in endeavoring to comprehend what God had in His mercy seen fit to reveal to us, I had no right to pass over the prophetic periods."—Bliss, page 75.

The prophecy which seemed most clearly to reveal the *time* of the second advent was that of Daniel 8:14: "Unto two thousand and three hundred days; then shall the sanctuary be cleansed." Following his rule of making Scripture its own interpreter, Miller learned that a day in symbolic prophecy represents a year (Numbers 14:34; Ezekiel 4:6); he saw that the period of 2300 prophetic days, or literal years, would extend far beyond the close of the Jewish dispensation, hence it could not refer to the sanctuary of that dispensation. Miller accepted the generally received view that in the Christian age the earth is the sanctuary, and he therefore understood that the cleansing of the sanctuary foretold in Daniel 8:14 represented the purification of the earth by fire at the second coming of Christ. If, then, the correct starting point could be found for the 2300 days, he concluded that the time of the second advent could be readily ascertained. Thus would be revealed the time of that great consummation, the time when the present state, with "all its pride and power, pomp and vanity, wickedness and oppression, would come to an end;" when the curse would be "removed from off the earth, death be

THE TRIUMPH OF GOD'S LOVE

destroyed, reward be given to the servants of God, the prophets and saints, and them who fear His name, and those be destroyed that destroy the earth."—Bliss, page 76.

With a new and deeper earnestness, Miller continued the examination of the prophecies, whole nights as well as days being devoted to the study of what now appeared of such stupendous importance and all-absorbing interest. In the eighth chapter of Daniel he could find no clue to the starting point of the 2300 days; the angel Gabriel, though commanded to make Daniel understand the vision, gave him only a partial explanation. As the terrible persecution to befall the church was unfolded to the prophet's vision, physical strength gave way. He could endure no more, and the angel left him for a time. Daniel "fainted, and was sick certain days." "And I was astonished at the vision," he says, "but none understood it."

Yet God had bidden His messenger: "Make this man to understand the vision." That commission must be fulfilled. In obedience to it, the angel, some time afterward, returned to Daniel, saying: "I am now come forth to give thee skill and understanding;" "therefore understand the matter, and consider the vision." Daniel 8:27, 16; 9:22, 23, 25-27. There was one important point in the vision of chapter 8 which had been left unexplained, namely, that relating to time—the period of the 2300 days; therefore the angel, in resuming his explanation, dwells chiefly upon the subject of time:

"Seventy weeks are determined upon thy people and upon thy Holy City. . . . Know therefore and understand, that from the going forth of the commandment to restore and to build Jerusalem unto the Messiah the Prince shall be seven weeks, and threescore and two weeks: the street shall be built again, and the wall, even in troublous times. And after three-score and two weeks shall Messiah be cut off, but not for Himself. . . . And He shall confirm the covenant with many for one week: and in the midst of the week He shall cause the sacrifice and the oblation to cease."

The angel had been sent to Daniel for the express purpose of explaining to him the point which he had failed to understand in the vision of the eighth chapter, the statement relative to time—"unto two thousand and three hundred days; then shall the sanctuary be cleansed." After bidding Daniel "understand the matter, and consider the vision," the very first words of the angel are: "Seventy weeks are determined upon thy people and upon thy Holy City." The word here translated "determined" literally signifies "cut off." Seventy weeks, representing 490 years, are declared by the angel to be cut off, as specially pertaining to the Jews. But from what were they cut off? As the 2300 days was the only period of time mentioned in chapter 8, it must be the period from which the seventy weeks were cut off; the seventy weeks must therefore be a part of the 2300 days, and the two periods must begin together. The seventy weeks were declared by the angel to date from the going forth of the commandment to restore and build Jerusalem. If the date of this commandment could be found, then the starting point for the great period of the 2300 days would be ascertained.

In the seventh chapter of Ezra the decree is found. Verses 12-26. In its completest form it was issued by Artaxerxes, king of Persia, 457 B.C. But in Ezra 6:14 the house of the Lord at Jerusalem is said to have been built "according to the commandment ["decree," margin] of Cyrus, and Darius, and Artaxerxes king of Persia." These three kings, in originating, reaffirming, and completing the decree, brought it to the perfection required by the prophecy to mark the beginning of the 2300 years. Taking 457 B.C., the time when the decree was completed, as the date of the commandment, every specification of the prophecy concerning the seventy weeks was seen to have been fulfilled.

"From the going forth of the commandment to restore and to build Jerusalem unto the Messiah the Prince shall be seven weeks, and three-score and two weeks"—namely, sixty-nine weeks, or 483 years. The decree of Artaxerxes went into effect in the autumn of 457 B.C. From this date, 483 years extend to the autumn of A.D. 27. (See Appendix.) At that time this prophecy was fulfilled. The word "Messiah" signifies "the Anointed One." In the autumn of A.D. 27 Christ was baptized by John and received the anointing of the Spirit. The apostle Peter testifies that "God anointed Jesus of Nazareth with the Holy Ghost and with power." Acts 10:38. And the Saviour Himself declared: "The Spirit of the Lord is upon Me, because He hath anointed Me to preach the gospel to the poor." Luke 4:18. After His baptism He went into Galilee, "preaching the gospel of the kingdom of God, and saying, *The time* is fulfilled." Mark 1:14, 15.

"And He shall confirm the covenant with many for one week." The "week" here brought to view is the last one of the seventy; it is the last seven years of the period allotted especially to the Jews. During this time, extending from A.D. 27 to A.D. 34, Christ, at first in person and afterward by His disciples, extended the gospel invitation especially to the Jews. As the apostles went forth with the good tidings of the kingdom, the

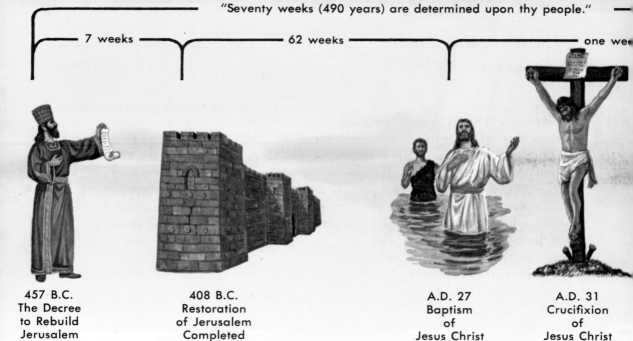

"Seventy weeks (490 years) are determined upon thy people."

7 weeks — 62 weeks — one week

457 B.C.	408 B.C.	A.D. 27	A.D. 31
The Decree to Rebuild Jerusalem	Restoration of Jerusalem Completed	Baptism of Jesus Christ	Crucifixion of Jesus Christ

Saviour's direction was: "Go not into the way of the Gentiles, and into any city of the Samaritans enter ye not: but go rather to the lost sheep of the house of Israel." Matthew 10:5, 6.

"In the midst of the week He shall cause the sacrifice and the oblation to cease." In A.D. 31, three and a half years after His baptism, our Lord was crucified. With the great sacrifice offered upon Calvary, ended that system of offerings which for four thousand years had pointed forward to the Lamb of God. Type had met antitype, and all the sacrifices and oblations of the ceremonial system were there to cease.

The seventy weeks, or 490 years, especially allotted to the Jews, ended, as we have seen, in A.D. 34. At that time, through the action of the Jewish Sanhedrin, the nation sealed its rejection of the gospel by the martyrdom of Stephen and the persecution of the followers of Christ. Then the message of salvation, no longer restricted to the chosen people, was given to the world. The disciples, forced by persecution to flee from Jerusalem, "went everywhere preaching the word." "Philip went down to the city of Samaria, and preached Christ unto them." Peter, divinely guided, opened the gospel to the centurion of Caesarea, the God-fearing Cornelius; and the ardent Paul, won to the faith of Christ, was commissioned to carry the glad tidings "far hence unto the Gentiles." Acts 8:4, 5; 22:21.

Thus far every specification of the prophecies is strikingly fulfilled, and the beginning of the seventy weeks is fixed beyond question at 457 B.C., and their expiration in A.D. 34. From this data there is no difficulty in finding the termination of the 2300 days. The seventy weeks—490 days

The 2300 Days (Years) of Amazing Bible Prophecy

A.D. 34
Stoning
of
Stephen

A.D. 1844
Cleansing
of
Heavenly Sanctuary

—having been cut off from the 2300, there were 1810 days remaining. After the end of 490 days, the 1810 days were still to be fulfilled. From A.D. 34, 1810 years extend to 1844. Consequently the 2300 days of Daniel 8:14 terminate in 1844. At the expiration of this great prophetic period, upon the testimony of the angel of God, "the sanctuary shall be cleansed." Thus the time of the cleansing of the sanctuary—which was almost universally believed to take place at the second advent—was definitely pointed out.

Miller and his associates at first believed that the 2300 days would terminate in the *spring* of 1844, whereas the prophecy points to the *autumn* of that year. (See Appendix.) The misapprehension of this point brought disappointment and perplexity to those who had fixed upon the earlier date as the time of the Lord's coming. But this did not in the least affect the strength of the argument showing that the 2300 days terminated in the year 1844, and that the great event represented by the cleansing of the sanctuary must then take place.

Entering upon the study of the Scriptures as he had done, in order to prove that they were a revelation from God, Miller had not, at the outset, the slightest expectation of reaching the conclusion at which he had now arrived. He himself could hardly credit the results of his investigation. But the Scripture evidence was too clear and forcible to be set aside.

He had devoted two years to the study of the Bible, when, in 1818, he reached the solemn conviction that in about twenty-five years Christ would appear for the redemption of His people. "I need not speak," says Miller, "of the joy that filled my heart in view of the delightful prospect, nor of the ardent longings of my soul for a participation in the joys of the redeemed. The Bible was now to me a new book. It was indeed a feast of reason; all that was dark, mystical, or obscure to me in its teachings, had been dissipated from my mind before the clear light that now dawned from its sacred pages; and, oh, how bright and glorious the truth appeared! All the contradictions and inconsistencies I had before found in the word were gone; and although there were many portions of which I was not satisfied I had a full understanding, yet so much light had emanated from it to the illumination of my before darkened mind, that I felt a delight in studying the Scripture which I had not before supposed could be derived from its teachings."—Bliss, pages 76, 77.

"With the solemn conviction that such momentous events were predicted in the Scriptures to be fulfilled in so short a space of time, the question came home to me with mighty power regarding my duty to the world, in view of the evidence that had affected my own mind."—*Ibid.*, page 81. He could not but feel that it was his duty to impart to others the light which he had received. He expected to encounter opposition from the ungodly, but was confident that all Christians would rejoice in the hope of meeting the Saviour whom they professed to love. His only fear was that in their great joy at the prospect of glorious deliverance, so soon to be consummated, many would receive the doctrine without sufficiently examining the Scriptures in demonstration of its truth. He therefore hesitated to present it, lest he should be in error and be the means of misleading others. He was thus led to review the evidences in support of the conclusions at which he had arrived, and to consider carefully every difficulty which presented itself to his mind. He found that objections vanished before the light of God's word, as mist before the rays of the sun. Five years spent thus left him fully convinced of the correctness of his position.

And now the duty of making known to others what he believed to be so clearly taught in the Scriptures, urged itself with new force upon him. "When I was about my business," he said, "it was continually ringing in my ears, 'Go and tell the world of their danger.' This text was constantly occurring to me: 'When I say unto the wicked, O wicked man, thou shalt surely die; if thou dost not speak to warn the wicked from his way, that wicked man shall die in his iniquity; but his blood will I require at thine hand. Nevertheless, if thou warn the wicked of his way to turn from it; if he do not turn from his way, he shall die in his iniquity; but thou hast delivered thy soul.' Ezekiel 33:8, 9. I felt that if the wicked could be effectually warned, multitudes of them would repent; and that if they were not warned, their blood might be required at my hand."—Bliss, page 92.

He began to present his views in private as he had opportunity, praying that some minister might feel their force and devote himself to their promulgation. But he could not banish the conviction that he had a personal duty to perform in giving the warning. The words were ever recurring to his mind: "Go and tell it to the world; their blood will I require at thy hand." For nine years he waited, the burden still pressing upon his soul, until in 1831 he for the first time publicly gave the reasons of his faith.

As Elisha was called from following his oxen in the field, to receive the mantle of consecration to the prophetic office, so was William Miller called to leave his plow and open to the people the mysteries of the kingdom of God. With trembling he entered upon his work, leading his hearers down, step by step, through the prophetic periods to the second appearing of Christ. With every effort he gained strength and courage as he saw the widespread interest excited by his words.

It was only at the solicitation of his brethren, in whose words he heard the call of God, that Miller consented to present his views in public. He was now fifty years of age, unaccustomed to public speaking, and burdened with a sense of unfitness for the work before him. But from the first his labors were blessed in a remarkable manner to the salvation of souls. His first lecture was followed by a religious awakening in which thirteen entire families, with the exception of two persons, were converted. He was immediately urged to speak in other places, and in nearly every place has labor resulted in a revival of the work of God. Sinners were converted, Christians were roused to greater consecration, and deists and infidels were led to acknowledge the truth of the Bible and the Christian religion. The testimony of those among whom he labored was: "A class of minds are reached by him not within the influence of other men."—*Ibid.*, page 138. His preaching was calculated to arouse the public mind to the great things of religion and to check the growing worldliness and sensuality of the age.

In nearly every town there were scores, in some, hundreds, converted as a result of his preaching. In many places Protestant churches of nearly all denominations were thrown open to him, and the invitations to labor

usually came from the ministers of the several congregations. It was his invariable rule not to labor in any place to which he had not been invited, yet he soon found himself unable to comply with half the requests that poured in upon him. Many who did not accept his views as to the exact time of the second advent were convinced of the certainty and nearness of Christ's coming and their need of preparation. In some of the large cities his work produced a marked impression. Liquor dealers abandoned the traffic and turned their shops into meeting rooms; gambling dens were broken up; infidels, deists, Universalists, and even the most abandoned profligates were reformed, some of whom had not entered a house of worship for years. Prayer meetings were established by the various denominations, in different quarters, at almost every hour, businessmen assembling at midday for prayer and praise. There was no extravagant excitement, but an almost universal solemnity on the minds of the people. His work, like that of the early Reformers, tended rather to convince the understanding and arouse the conscience than merely to excite the emotions.

In 1833 Miller received a license to preach, from the Baptist Church, of which he was a member. A large number of the ministers of his denomination also approved his work, and it was with their formal sanction that he continued his labors. He traveled and preached unceasingly, though his personal labors were confined principally to the New England and Middle States. For several years his expenses were met wholly from his own private purse, and he never afterward received enough to meet the expense of travel to the places where he was invited. Thus his public labors, so far from being a pecuniary benefit, were a heavy tax upon his property, which gradually diminished during this period of his life. He was the father of a large family, but as they were all frugal and industrious, his farm sufficed for their maintenance as well as his own.

In 1833, two years after Miller began to present in public the evidences of Christ's soon coming, the last of the signs appeared which were promised by the Saviour as tokens of His second advent. Said Jesus: "The stars shall fall from heaven." Matthew 24:29. And John in the Revelation declared, as he beheld in vision the scenes that should herald the day of God: "The stars of heaven fell unto the earth, even as a fig tree casteth her untimely figs, when she is shaken of a mighty wind." Revelation 6:13. This prophecy received a striking and impressive fulfillment in the great meteoric shower of November 13, 1833. That was the most extensive and wonderful display of falling stars which has ever been re-

The historic meteoric shower of November 13, 1833, alerted men's minds to the prophecies of the second advent.

corded; "the whole firmament, over all the United States, being then, for hours, in fiery commotion! No celestial phenomenon has ever occurred in this country, since its first settlement, which was viewed with such intense admiration by one class in the community, or with so much dread and alarm by another." "Its sublimity and awful beauty still linger in many minds. . . . Never did rain fall much thicker than the meteors fell toward the earth; east, west, north, and south, it was the same. In a word, the whole heavens seemed in motion. . . . The display, as described in Professor Silliman's *Journal*, was seen all over North America. . . . From two o'clock until broad daylight, the sky being perfectly serene and cloudless, an incessant play of dazzlingly brilliant luminosities was kept up in the whole heavens."—R. M. Devens, *American Progress; or, The Great Events of the Greatest Century*, ch. 28, pars. 1-5.

"No language, indeed, can come up to the splendor of that magnificent display; . . . no one who did not witness it can form an adequate conception of its glory. It seemed as if the whole starry heavens had congregated at one point near the zenith, and were simultaneously shooting forth, with the velocity of lightning, to every part of the horizon; and yet they were not exhausted—thousands swiftly followed in the tracks of thousands, as if created for the occasion."—F. Reed, in the *Christian Advocate and Journal*, Dec. 13, 1833. "A more correct picture of a fig tree casting its figs when blown by a mighty wind, it was not possible to behold." —"The Old Countryman," in Portland *Evening Advertiser*, Nov. 26, 1833.

In the New York *Journal of Commerce* of November 14, 1833, appeared a long article regarding this wonderful phenomenon, containing this statement: "No philosopher or scholar has told or recorded an event, I suppose, like that of yesterday morning. A prophet eighteen hundred years ago foretold it exactly, if we will be at the trouble of understanding stars falling to mean falling stars, . . . in the only sense in which it is possible to be literally true."

Thus was displayed the last of those signs of His coming, concerning which Jesus bade His disciples: "When ye shall see all these things, *know* that it is near, even at the doors." Matthew 24:33. After these signs, John beheld, as the great event next impending, the heavens departing as a scroll, while the earth quaked, mountains and islands removed out of their places, and the wicked in terror sought to flee from the presence of the Son of man. Revelation 6:12-17.

Many who witnessed the falling of the stars, looked upon it as a herald of the coming judgment, "an awful type, a sure forerunner, a merciful sign, of that great and dreadful day."—"The Old Countryman," in Portland *Evening Advertiser*, Nov. 26, 1833. Thus the attention of the people was directed to the fulfillment of prophecy, and many were led to give heed to the warning of the second advent.

In the year 1840 another remarkable fulfillment of prophecy excited widespread interest. Two years before, Josiah Litch, one of the leading ministers preaching the second advent, published an exposition of Revelation 9, predicting the fall of the Ottoman Empire. According to his calculations, this power was to be overthrown "in A.D. 1840, sometime in the month of August;" and only a few days previous to its accomplishment he wrote: "Allowing the first period, 150 years, to have been exactly fulfilled before Deacozes ascended the throne by permission of the Turks, and that the 391 years, fifteen days, commenced at the close of the first period, it will end on the 11th of August, 1840, when the Ottoman power in Constantinople may be expected to be broken. And this, I believe, will be found to be the case."—Josiah Litch, in *Signs of the Times, and Expositor of Prophecy*, Aug. 1, 1840.

At the very time specified, Turkey, through her ambassadors, accepted the protection of the allied powers of Europe, and thus placed herself under the control of Christian nations. The event exactly fulfilled the prediction. (See Appendix.) When it became known, multitudes were convinced of the correctness of the principles of prophetic interpretation adopted by Miller and his associates, and a wonderful impetus was given to the advent movement. Men of learning and position united with Miller, both in preaching and in publishing his views, and from 1840 to 1844 the work rapidly extended.

William Miller possessed strong mental powers, disciplined by thought and study; and he added to these the wisdom of heaven by connecting himself with the Source of wisdom. He was a man of sterling worth, who could not but command respect and esteem wherever integrity of character and moral excellence were valued. Uniting true kindness of heart with Christian humility and the power of self-control, he was attentive and affable to all, ready to listen to the opinions of others and to weigh their arguments. Without passion or excitement he tested all theories and doctrines by the word of God, and his sound reasoning and thorough knowledge of the Scriptures enabled him to refute error and expose falsehood.

Yet he did not prosecute his work without bitter opposition. As with earlier Reformers, the truths which he presented were not received with favor by popular religious teachers. As these could not maintain their position by the Scriptures, they were driven to resort to the sayings and doctrines of men, to the traditions of the Fathers. But the word of God was the only testimony accepted by the preachers of the advent truth. "The Bible, and the Bible only," was their watchword. The lack of Scripture argument on the part of their opponents was supplied by ridicule and scoffing. Time, means, and talents were employed in maligning those whose only offense was that they looked with joy for the return of their Lord and were striving to live holy lives and to exhort others to prepare for His appearing.

Earnest were the efforts put forth to draw away the minds of the people from the subject of the second advent. It was made to appear a sin, something of which men should be ashamed, to study the prophecies which relate to the coming of Christ and the end of the world. Thus the popular ministry undermined faith in the word of God. Their teaching made men infidels, and many took license to walk after their own ungodly lusts. Then the authors of the evil charged it all upon Adventists.

While drawing crowded houses of intelligent and attentive hearers, Miller's name was seldom mentioned by the religious press except by way of ridicule or denunciation. The careless and ungodly emboldened by the position of religious teachers, resorted to opprobrious epithets, to base and blasphemous witticisms, in their efforts to heap contumely upon him and his work. The gray-headed man who had left a comfortable home to travel at his own expense from city to city, from town to town, toiling unceasingly to bear to the world the solemn warning of the judgment near, was sneeringly denounced as a fanatic, a liar, a speculating knave.

The ridicule, falsehood, and abuse heaped upon him called forth indignant remonstrance, even from the secular press. "To treat a subject of such overwhelming majesty and fearful consequences," with lightness and ribaldry was declared by worldly men to be "not merely to sport with the feelings of its propagators and advocates," but "to make a jest of the day of judgment, to scoff at the Deity Himself, and contemn the terrors of His judgment bar."—Bliss, page 183.

The instigator of all evil sought not only to counteract the effect of the advent message, but to destroy the messenger himself. Miller made a practical application of Scripture truth to the hearts of his hearers, reproving their sins and disturbing their self-satisfaction, and his plain and cutting words aroused their enmity. The opposition manifested by church members toward his message emboldened the baser classes to go to greater lengths; and enemies plotted to take his life as he should leave the place of meeting. But holy angels were in the throng, and one of these, in the form of a man, took the arm of this servant of the Lord and led him in safety from the angry mob. His work was not yet done, and Satan and his emissaries were disappointed in their purpose.

Despite all opposition, the interest in the advent movement had continued to increase. From scores and hundreds, the congregations had grown to as many thousands. Large accessions had been made to the various churches, but after a time the spirit of opposition was manifested even against these converts, and the churches began to take disciplinary steps with those who had embraced Miller's views. This action called forth a response from his pen, in an address to Christians of all denominations, urging that if his doctrines were false, he should be shown his error from the Scriptures.

"What have we believed," he said, "that we have not been commanded to believe by the word of God, which you yourselves allow is the rule, and only rule, of our faith and practice? What have we done that should call down such virulent denunciations against us from pulpit and press, and give you just cause to exclude us [Adventists] from your churches and fellowship?" "If we are wrong, pray show us wherein consists our wrong. Show us from the word of God that we are in error; we have had ridicule enough; that can never convince us that we are in the wrong; the word of God alone can change our views. Our conclusions have been formed deliberately and prayerfully, as we have seen the evidence in the Scriptures."—*Ibid.*, pages 250, 252.

From age to age the warnings which God has sent to the world by His servants have been received with like incredulity and unbelief. When the iniquity of the antediluvians moved Him to bring a flood of waters upon the earth, He first made known to them His purpose, that they might have opportunity to turn from their evil ways. For a hundred and twenty years was sounded in their ears the warning to repent, lest the wrath of God be manifested in their destruction. But the message seemed to them an idle tale, and they believed it not. Emboldened in their wickedness they mocked the messenger of God, made light of his entreaties, and even accused him of presumption. How dare one man stand up against all the great men of the earth? If Noah's message were true, why did not all the world see it and believe it? One man's assertion against the wisdom of thousands! They would not credit the warning, nor would they seek shelter in the ark.

Scoffers pointed to the things of nature—to the unvarying succession of the seasons, to the blue skies that had never poured out rain, to the green fields refreshed by the soft dews of night—and they cried out: "Doth he not speak parables?" In contempt they declared the preacher of righteousness to be a wild enthusiast; and they went on, more eager in their pursuit of pleasure, more intent upon their evil ways, than before. But their unbelief did not hinder the predicted event. God bore long with their wickedness, giving them ample opportunity for repentance; but at the appointed time His judgments were visited upon the rejecters of His mercy.

Christ declares that there will exist similar unbelief concerning His second coming. As the people of Noah's day "knew not until the Flood came, and took them all away; so," in the words of our Saviour, "shall also the coming of the Son of man be." Matthew 24:39. When the professed people of God are uniting with the world, living as they live, and joining with them in forbidden pleasures; when the luxury of the world becomes the luxury of the church; when the marriage bells are chiming, and all are looking forward to many years of worldly prosperity—then, suddenly as the lightning flashes from the heavens, will come the end of their bright visions and delusive hopes.

As God sent His servant to warn the world of the coming Flood, so He sent chosen messengers to make known the nearness of the final judgment. And as Noah's contemporaries laughed to scorn the predictions of the preacher of righteousness, so in Miller's day many, even of the professed people of God, scoffed at the words of warning.

And why were the doctrine and preaching of Christ's second coming so unwelcome to the churches? While to the wicked the advent of the Lord brings woe and desolation, to the righteous it is fraught with joy and hope. This great truth had been the consolation of God's faithful ones through all the ages; why had it become, like its Author, "a stone of stumbling" and "a rock of offense" to His professed people? It was our Lord Himself who promised His disciples: "If I go and prepare a place for you, I will come again, and receive you unto Myself." John 14:3. It was the compassionate Saviour, who, anticipating the loneliness and sorrow of His followers, commissioned angels to comfort them with the assurance that He would come again in person, even as He went into heaven. As the disciples stood gazing intently upward to catch the last glimpse of Him whom they loved, their attention was arrested by the words: "Ye men of Galilee, why stand ye gazing up into heaven? this same Jesus, which is taken up from you into heaven, shall so come in like manner as ye have seen Him go into heaven." Acts 1:11. Hope was kindled afresh by the angels' message. The disciples "returned to Jerusalem with great joy: and were continually in the temple, praising and blessing God." Luke 24:52, 53. They were not rejoicing because Jesus had been separated from them and they were left to struggle with the trials and temptations of the world, but because of the angels' assurance that He would come again.

The proclamation of Christ's coming should now be, as when made by the angels to the shepherds of Bethlehem, good tidings of great joy. Those who really love the Saviour cannot but hail with gladness the announcement founded upon the word of God that He in whom their hopes of eternal life are centered is coming again, not to be insulted, despised, and rejected, as at His first advent, but in power and glory, to redeem His people. It is those who do not love the Saviour that desire Him to remain away, and there can be no more conclusive evidence that the churches have departed from God than the irritation and animosity excited by this Heaven-sent message.

Those who accepted the advent doctrine were roused to the necessity of repentance and humiliation before God. Many had long been halting between Christ and the world; now they felt that it was time to take a stand. "The things of eternity assumed to them an unwonted reality. Heaven was brought near, and they felt themselves guilty before

God."—Bliss, page 146. Christians were quickened to new spiritual life. They were made to feel that time was short, that what they had to do for their fellow men must be done quickly. Earth receded, eternity seemed to open before them, and the soul, with all that pertained to its immortal weal or woe, was felt to eclipse every temporal object. The Spirit of God rested upon them and gave power to their earnest appeals to their brethren, as well as to sinners, to prepare for the day of God. The silent testimony of their daily life was a constant rebuke to formal and unconsecrated church members. These did not wish to be disturbed in their pursuit of pleasure, their devotion to money-making, and their ambition for worldly honor. Hence the enmity and opposition excited against the advent faith and those who proclaimed it.

As the arguments from the prophetic periods were found to be impregnable, opposers endeavored to discourage investigation of the subject by teaching that the prophecies were sealed. Thus Protestants followed in the steps of Romanists. While the papal church withholds the Bible (see Appendix) from the people,* Protestant churches claimed that an important part of the Sacred Word—and that the part which brings to view truths specially applicable to our time—could not be understood.

Ministers and people declared that the prophecies of Daniel and the Revelation were incomprehensible mysteries. But Christ directed His disciples to the words of the prophet Daniel concerning events to take place in their time, and said: "Whoso readeth, let him *understand.*" Matthew 24:15. And the assertion that the Revelation is a mystery, not to be understood, is contradicted by the very title of the book: "The Revelation of Jesus Christ, which God gave unto Him, to show unto His servants things which must shortly come to pass. . . . *Blessed* is he that *readeth,* and they that *hear* the words of this prophecy, and *keep* those things which are written therein: for the time is at hand." Revelation 1:1-3.

Says the prophet: "Blessed is he that readeth"—there are those who will not read; the blessing is not for them. "And they that hear"—there are some, also, who refuse to hear anything concerning the prophecies; the blessing is not for this class. "And keep those things which are written therein"—many refuse to heed the warnings and instructions contained in the Revelation; none of these can claim the blessing promised. All who ridicule the subjects of the prophecy and mock at the symbols here

*Published in 1888 and 1911.

solemnly given, all who refuse to reform their lives and to prepare for the coming of the Son of man, will be unblessed.

In view of the testimony of Inspiration, how dare men teach that the Revelation is a mystery beyond the reach of human understanding? It is a mystery revealed, a book opened. The study of the Revelation directs the mind to the prophecies of Daniel, and both present most important instruction, given of God to men, concerning events to take place at the close of this world's history.

To John were opened scenes of deep and thrilling interest in the experience of the church. He saw the position, dangers, conflicts, and final deliverance of the people of God. He records the closing messages which are to ripen the harvest of the earth, either as sheaves for the heavenly garner or as fagots for the fires of destruction. Subjects of vast importance were revealed to him, especially for the last church, that those who should turn from error to truth might be instructed concerning the perils and conflicts before them. None need be in darkness in regard to what is coming upon the earth.

Why, then, this widespread ignorance concerning an important part of Holy Writ? Why this general reluctance to investigate its teachings? It is the result of a studied effort of the prince of darkness to conceal from men that which reveals his deceptions. For this reason, Christ the Revelator, foreseeing the warfare that would be waged against the study of the Revelation, pronounced a blessing upon all who should read, hear, and observe the words of the prophecy.

chapter 19

Light Through Darkness

THE work of God in the earth presents, from age to age, a striking similarity in every great reformation or religious movement. The principles of God's dealing with men are ever the same. The important movements of the present have their parallel in those of the past, and the experience of the church in former ages has lessons of great value for our own time.

No truth is more clearly taught in the Bible than that God by His Holy Spirit especially directs His servants on earth in the great movements for the carrying forward of the work of salvation. Men are instruments in the hand of God, employed by Him to accomplish His purposes of grace and mercy. Each has his part to act; to each is granted a measure of light, adapted to the necessities of his time, and sufficient to enable him to perform the work which God has given him to do. But no man, however honored of Heaven, has ever attained to a full understanding of the great plan of redemption, or even to a perfect appreciation of the divine purpose in the work for his own time. Men do not fully understand what God would accomplish by the work which He gives them to do; they do not comprehend, in all its bearings, the message which they utter in His name.

"Canst thou by searching find out God? canst thou find out the Almighty unto perfection?" "My thoughts are not your thoughts, neither are your ways My ways, saith the Lord. For as the heavens are higher than the earth, so are My ways higher than your ways, and My thoughts

Even as after Christ's resurrection, doubts were cleared up by a restudy of prophecy, so it happened following 1844.

than your thoughts." "I am God, and there is none like Me, declaring the end from the beginning, and from ancient times the things that are not yet done." Job 11:7; Isaiah 55:8, 9; 46:9, 10.

Even the prophets who were favored with the special illumination of the Spirit did not fully comprehend the import of the revelations committed to them. The meaning was to be unfolded from age to age, as the people of God should need the instruction therein contained.

Peter, writing of the salvation brought to light through the gospel, says: Of this salvation "the prophets have inquired and searched diligently, who prophesied of the grace that should come unto you: searching *what,* or *what manner of time* the Spirit of Christ which was in them did signify, when it testified beforehand the sufferings of Christ, and the glory that should follow. Unto whom it was revealed, that not unto *themselves,* but unto *us* they did minister." 1 Peter 1:10-12.

Yet while it was not given to the prophets to understand fully the things revealed to them, they earnestly sought to obtain all the light which God had been pleased to make manifest. They "inquired and searched diligently," "searching what, or what manner of time the Spirit of Christ which was in them did signify." What a lesson to the people of God in the Christian age, for whose benefit these prophecies were given to His servants! "Unto whom it was revealed, that not unto themselves, but unto us they did minister." Witness these holy men of God as they "inquired and searched diligently" concerning revelations given them from generations that were yet unborn. Contrast their holy zeal with the listless unconcern with which the favored ones of later ages treat this gift of Heaven. What a rebuke to the ease-loving, world-loving indifference which is content to declare that the prophecies cannot be understood!

Though the finite minds of men are inadequate to enter into the counsels of the Infinite One, or to understand fully the working out of His purposes, yet often it is because of some error or neglect on their own part that they so dimly comprehend the messages of Heaven. Not infrequently the minds of the people, and even of God's servants, are so blinded by human opinions, the traditions and false teaching of men, that they are able only partially to grasp the great things which He has revealed in His word. Thus it was with the disciples of Christ, even when the Saviour was with them in person. Their minds had become imbued with the popular conception of the Messiah as a temporal prince, who was to exalt Israel to the throne of the universal empire, and they could not understand the meaning of His words foretelling His sufferings and death.

Christ Himself had sent them forth with the message: "The time is fulfilled, and the kingdom of God is at hand: repent ye, and believe the gospel." Mark 1:15. That message was based on the prophecy of Daniel 9. The sixty-nine weeks were declared by the angel to extend to "the Messiah the Prince," and with high hopes and joyful anticipations the disciples looked forward to the establishment of Messiah's kingdom at Jerusalem to rule over the whole earth.

They preached the message which Christ had committed to them, though they themselves misapprehended its meaning. While their announcement was founded on Daniel 9:25, they did not see, in the next verse of the same chapter, that Messiah was to be cut off. From their very birth their hearts had been set upon the anticipated glory of an earthly empire, and this blinded their understanding alike to the specifications of the prophecy and to the words of Christ.

They performed their duty in presenting to the Jewish nation the invitation of mercy, and then, at the very time when they expected to see their Lord ascend the throne of David, they beheld Him seized as a malefactor, scourged, derided, and condemned, and lifted up on the cross of Calvary. What despair and anguish wrung the hearts of those disciples during the days while their Lord was sleeping in the tomb!

Christ had come at the exact time and in the manner foretold by prophecy. The testimony of Scripture had been fulfilled in every detail of His ministry. He had preached the message of salvation, and "His word was with power." The hearts of His hearers had witnessed that it was of Heaven. The word and the Spirit of God attested the divine commission of His Son.

The disciples still clung with undying affection to their beloved Master. And yet their minds were shrouded in uncertainty and doubt. In their anguish they did not then recall the words of Christ pointing forward to His suffering and death. If Jesus of Nazareth had been the true Messiah, would they have been thus plunged in grief and disappointment? This was the question that tortured their souls while the Saviour lay in His sepulcher during the hopeless hours of that Sabbath which intervened between His death and His resurrection.

Though the night of sorrow gathered dark about these followers of Jesus, yet were they not forsaken. Saith the prophet: "When I sit in darkness, the Lord shall be a light unto me. . . . He will bring me forth to the light, and I shall behold His righteousness." "Yea, the darkness hideth not from Thee; but the night shineth as the day: the darkness and the light are both alike to Thee." God hath spoken: "Unto the upright there ariseth light in the darkness." "I will bring the blind by a way that they knew not; I will lead them in paths that they have not known: I will make darkness light before them, and crooked things straight. These things will I do unto them, and not forsake them." Micah 7:8, 9; Psalms 139:12; 112:4; Isaiah 42:16.

The announcement which had been made by the disciples in the name of the Lord was in every particular correct, and the events to which it pointed were even then taking place. "The time is fulfilled, the kingdom of God is at hand," had been their message. At the expiration of "the time"—the sixty-nine weeks of Daniel 9, which were to extend to the Messiah, "the Anointed One"—Christ had received the anointing of the Spirit after His baptism by John in Jordan. And the "kingdom of God" which they had declared to be at hand was established by the death of Christ. This kingdom was not, as they had been taught to believe, an earthly empire. Nor was it that future, immortal kingdom which shall be set up when "the kingdom and dominion, and the greatness of the kingdom under the whole heaven, shall be given to the people of the saints of the Most High;" that everlasting kingdom, in which "all dominions shall serve and obey Him." Daniel 7:27. As used in the Bible, the expression "kingdom of God" is employed to designate both the kingdom of grace and the kingdom of glory. The kingdom of grace is brought to view by Paul in the Epistle to the Hebrews. After pointing to Christ, the compassionate intercessor who is "touched with the feeling of our infirmities," the apostle says: "Let us therefore come boldly unto *the throne of grace,* that we may obtain mercy, and find grace." Hebrews 4:15, 16. The throne of grace represents the kingdom of grace; for the existence of a throne implies the existence of a kingdom. In many of His parables Christ uses the expression "the kingdom of heaven" to designate the work of divine grace upon the hearts of men.

So the throne of glory represents the kingdom of glory; and this kingdom is referred to in the Saviour's words: "When the Son of man shall come in His glory, and all the holy angels with Him, then shall He sit upon the throne of His glory: and before Him shall be gathered all nations." Matthew 25:31, 32. This kingdom is yet future. It is not to be set up until the second advent of Christ.

The kingdom of grace was instituted immediately after the fall of man, when a plan was devised for the redemption of the guilty race. It then existed in the purpose and by the promise of God; and through faith, men could become its subjects. Yet it was not actually established until the death of Christ. Even after entering upon His earthly mission, the Saviour, wearied with the stubbornness and ingratitude of men, might have drawn back from the sacrifice of Calvary. In Gethsemane the cup of woe trembled in His hand. He might even then have wiped the blood-sweat from His brow and have left the guilty race to perish in their iniquity. Had He done this, there could have been no redemption for fallen men. But when the Saviour yielded up His life, and with His expiring breath cried out, "It is finished," then the fulfillment of the plan of redemption was assured. The promise of salvation made to the sinful pair in Eden was ratified. The kingdom of grace, which had before existed by the promise of God, was then established.

Thus the death of Christ—the very event which the disciples had looked upon as the final destruction of their hope—was that which made it forever sure. While it had brought them a cruel disappointment, it was the climax of proof that their belief had been correct. The event that had filled them with mourning and despair was that which opened the door of hope to every child of Adam, and in which centered the future life and eternal happiness of all God's faithful ones in all the ages.

Purposes of infinite mercy were reaching their fulfillment, even through the disappointment of the disciples. While their hearts had been won by the divine grace and power of His teaching, who "spake as never man spake," yet intermingled with the pure gold of their love for Jesus, was the base alloy of worldly pride and selfish ambitions. Even in the Passover chamber, at that solemn hour when their Master was already entering the shadow of Gethsemane, there was "a strife among them, which of them should be accounted the greatest." Luke 22:24. Their vision was filled with the throne, the crown, and the glory, while just before them lay the shame and agony of the garden, the judgment hall, the cross of Calvary. It was their pride of heart, their thirst for worldly glory, that had led them to cling so tenaciously to the false teaching of their time, and to pass unheeded the Saviour's words showing the true nature of His kingdom, and pointing forward to His agony and death. And these errors resulted in the trial—sharp but needful—which was permitted for their correction. Though the disciples had mistaken the meaning of their message, and had failed to realize their expectations, yet they had preached the warning given them of God, and the Lord would reward their faith and honor their obedience. To them was to be entrusted the work of heralding to all nations the glorious gospel of their risen Lord. It was to prepare them for this work that the experience which seemed to them so bitter had been permitted.

After His resurrection Jesus appeared to His disciples on the way to Emmaus, and, "beginning at Moses and all the prophets, He expounded unto them in all the Scriptures the things concerning Himself." Luke 24:27. The hearts of the disciples were stirred. Faith was kindled. They were "begotten again into a lively hope" even before Jesus revealed Himself to them. It was His purpose to enlighten their understanding and to fasten their faith upon the "sure word of prophecy." He wished the truth to take firm root in their minds, not merely because it was supported by His personal testimony, but because of the unquestionable evidence presented by the symbols and shadows of the typical law, and by the prophecies of the Old Testament. It was needful for the followers of Christ to have an intelligent faith, not only in their own behalf, but that they might carry the knowledge of Christ to the world. And as the very first step in imparting this knowledge, Jesus directed the disciples to "Moses and all the prophets." Such was the testimony given by the risen Saviour to the value and importance of the Old Testament Scriptures.

What a change was wrought in the hearts of the disciples as they looked once more on the loved countenance of their Master! Luke 24:32. In a more complete and perfect sense than ever before they had "found Him, of whom Moses in the law, and the prophets, did write." The uncertainty, the anguish, the despair, gave place to perfect assurance, to unclouded faith. What marvel that after His ascension they "were continually in the temple praising and blessing God." The people, knowing only of the Saviour's ignominious death, looked to see in their faces the expression of sorrow, confusion, and defeat; but they saw there gladness and triumph. What a preparation these disciples had received for the work before them! They had passed through the deepest trial which it was possible for them to experience, and had seen how, when to human vision all was lost, the word of God had been triumphantly accomplished. Henceforward what could daunt their faith or chill the ardor of their love? In the keenest sorrow they had "strong consolation," a hope which was as "an anchor of the soul, both sure and steadfast." Hebrews 6:18, 19. They had been witness to the wisdom and power of God, and they were "persuaded, that neither death, nor life, nor angels, nor principalities, nor powers, nor things present, nor things to come, nor height, nor depth, nor any other creature," would be able to separate them from "the love of God, which is in Christ Jesus our Lord." "In all these things," they said, "we are more than conquerors through Him that loved us." Romans 8:38, 39, 37. "The word of the Lord endureth forever." 1 Peter 1:25. And "who is he that condemneth? It is Christ that died, yea rather, that is *risen again,* who is even at the right hand of God, who also maketh intercession for us." Romans 8:34.

Saith the Lord: "My people shall never be ashamed." Joel 2:26. "Weeping may endure for a night, but joy cometh in the morning." Psalm 30:5. When on His resurrection day these disciples met the Saviour, and their hearts burned within them as they listened to His words; when they looked upon the head and hands and feet that had been bruised for them; when, before His ascension, Jesus led them out as far as Bethany, and lifting up His hands in blessing, bade them, "Go ye into all the world, and preach the gospel," adding, "Lo, I am with you alway" (Mark 16:15; Matthew 28:20); when on the Day of Pentecost the promised Comforter descended and the power from on high was given and the souls of the believers thrilled with the conscious presence of their ascended Lord—then, even though, like His, their pathway led through sacrifice and martyrdom, would they have exchanged the ministry of the gospel of His grace, with the "crown of righteousness" to be received at His coming, for the glory of an earthly throne, which had been the hope of their earlier discipleship? He who is "able to do exceeding abundantly above all that we ask or think," had granted them, with the fellowship of His sufferings, the communion of His joy—the joy of "bringing many sons unto glory," joy unspeakable, an "eternal weight of glory," to which, says Paul, "our light affliction, which is but for a moment," is "not worthy to be compared."

The experience of the disciples who preached the "gospel of the kingdom" at the first advent of Christ, had its counterpart in the experience of those who proclaimed the message of His second advent. As the disciples went out preaching, "The time is fulfilled, the kingdom of God is at hand," so Miller and his associates proclaimed that the longest and last prophetic period brought to view in the Bible was about to expire, that the judgment was at hand, and the everlasting kingdom was to be ushered in. The preaching of the disciples in regard to time was based on the seventy weeks of Daniel 9. The message given by Miller and his associates announced the termination of the 2300 days of Daniel 8:14, of which the seventy weeks form a part. The preaching of each was based upon the fulfillment of a different portion of the same great prophetic period.

Like the first disciples, William Miller and his associates did not, themselves, fully comprehend the import of the message which they bore. Errors that had been long established in the church prevented them from arriving at a correct interpretation of an important point in the prophecy. Therefore, though they proclaimed the message which God had committed to them to be given to the world, yet through a misapprehension of its meaning they suffered disappointment.

In explaining Daniel 8:14, "Unto two thousand and three hundred days; then shall the sanctuaray be cleansed," Miller, as has been stated, adopted the generally received view that the earth is the sanctuary, and he believed that the cleansing of the sanctuary represented the purification of the earth by fire at the coming of the Lord. When, therefore, he found that the close of the 2300 days was definitely foretold, he concluded that this revealed the time of the second advent. His error resulted from accepting the popular view as to what constitutes the sanctuary.

In the typical system, which was a shadow of the sacrifice and priesthood of Christ, the cleansing of the sanctuary was the last service performed by the high priest in the yearly round of ministration. It was the closing work of the atonement—a removal or putting away of sin from Israel. It prefigured the closing work in the ministration of our High Priest in heaven, in the removal or blotting out of the sins of His people, which are registered in the heavenly records. This service involves a work of investigation, a work of judgment; and it immediately precedes the coming of Christ in the clouds of heaven with power and great glory; for when He comes, every case has been decided. Says Jesus: "My reward is with Me, to give every man according as his work shall be." Revelation 22:12. It is this work of judgment, immediately preceding the second advent, that is announced in the first angel's message of Revelation 14:7: "Fear God, and give glory to Him; for the hour of His judgment is come."

Those who proclaimed this warning gave the right message at the right time. But as the early disciples declared, "The time is fulfilled, and the kingdom of God is at hand," based on the prophecy of Daniel 9, while they failed to perceive that the death of the Messiah was foretold in the same scripture, so Miller and his associates preached the message based on Daniel 8:14 and Revelation 14:7, and failed to see that there were still other messages brought to view in Revelation 14, which were also to be given before the advent of the Lord. As the disciples were mistaken in regard to the kingdom to be set up at the end of the seventy weeks, so Adventists were mistaken in regard to the event to take place at the expiration of the 2300 days. In both cases there was an acceptance of, or rather an adherence to, popular errors that blinded the mind to the truth. Both classes fulfilled the will of God in delivering the message which He desired to be given, and both, through their own misapprehension of their message, suffered disappointment.

Yet God accomplished His own beneficent purpose in permitting the warning of the judgment to be given just as it was. The great day was at hand, and in His providence the people were brought to the test of a definite time, in order to reveal to them what was in their hearts. The message was designed for the testing and purification of the church. They were to be led to see whether their affections were set upon this world or upon Christ and heaven. They professed to love the Saviour; now they were to prove their love. Were they ready to renounce their worldly hopes and ambitions, and welcome with joy the advent of their Lord? The message was designed to enable them to discern their true spiritual state; it was sent in mercy to arouse them to seek the Lord with repentance and humiliation.

The disappointment also, though the result of their own misapprehension of the message which they gave, was to be overruled for good. It would test the hearts of those who had professed to receive the warning. In the face of their disappointment would they rashly give up their experience and cast away their confidence in God's word? or would they, in prayer and humility, seek to discern where they had failed to comprehend the significance of the prophecy? How many had moved from fear, or from impulse and excitement? How many were halfhearted and unbelieving? Multitudes professed to love the appearing of the Lord. When called to endure the scoffs and reproach of the world, and the test of delay and disappointment, would they renounce the faith? Because they did not immediately understand the dealings of God with them, would they cast aside truths sustained by the clearest testimony of His word?

This test would reveal the strength of those who with real faith had obeyed what they believed to be the teaching of the word and the Spirit of God. It would teach them, as only such an experience could, the danger of accepting the theories and interpretations of men, instead of making the Bible its own interpreter. To the children of faith the perplexity and sorrow resulting from their error would work the needed correction. They would be led to a closer study of the prophetic word. They would be taught to examine more carefully the foundation of their faith, and to reject everything, however widely accepted by the Christian world, that was not founded upon the Scriptures of truth.

With these believers, as with the first disciples, that which in the hour of trial seemed dark to their understanding would afterward be made plain. When they should see the "end of the Lord" they would know that, notwithstanding the trial resulting from their errors, His purposes of love toward them had been steadily fulfilling. They would learn by a blessed experience that He is "very pitiful, and of tender mercy;" that all His paths "are mercy and truth unto such as keep His covenant and His testimonies."

chapter 20

A Global Religious Awakening

A GREAT religious awakening under the proclamation of Christ's soon coming is foretold in the
prophecy of the first angel's message of Revelation 14. An angel is seen
flying "in the midst of heaven, having the everlasting gospel to preach
unto them that dwell on the earth, and to every nation, and kindred, and
tongue, and people." "With a loud voice" he proclaims the message:
"Fear God, and give glory to Him; for the hour of His judgment is come:
and worship Him that made heaven, and earth, and the sea, and the
fountains of waters." Verses 6, 7.

The fact that an angel is said to be the herald of this warning is significant. By the purity, the glory, and the power of the heavenly messenger,
divine wisdom has been pleased to represent the exalted character of
the work to be accomplished by the message and the power and glory
that were to attend it. And the angel's flight "in the midst of heaven,"
the "loud voice" with which the warning is uttered, and its promulgation
to all "that dwell on the earth"—"to every nation, and kindred, and
tongue, and people"—give evidence of the rapidity and world-wide extent of the movement.

The message itself sheds light as to the time when this movement is
to take place. It is declared to be a part of the "everlasting gospel;" and
it announces the opening of the judgment. The message of salvation has
been preached in all ages; but this message is a part of the gospel which
could be proclaimed only in the last days, for only then would it be true
that the hour of judgment *had come.* The prophecies present a succession of events leading down to the opening of the judgment. This is espe-

cially true of the book of Daniel. But that part of his prophecy which related to the last days, Daniel was bidden to close up and seal "to the time of the end." Not till we reach this time could a message concerning the judgment be proclaimed, based on a fulfillment of these prophecies. But at the time of the end, says the prophet, "many shall run to and fro, and knowledge shall be increased." Daniel 12:4.

The apostle Paul warned the church not to look for the coming of Christ in his day. "That day shall not come," he says, "except there come a falling away first, and that man of sin be revealed." 2 Thessalonians 2:3. Not till after the great apostasy, and the long period of the reign of the "man of sin," can we look for the advent of our Lord. The "man of sin," which is also styled "the mystery of iniquity," "the son of perdition," and "that wicked," represents the papacy, which, as foretold in prophecy, was to maintain its supremacy for 1260 years. This period ended in 1798. The coming of Christ could not take place before that time. Paul covers with his caution the whole of the Christian dispensation down to the year 1798. It is this side of that time that the message of Christ's second coming is to be proclaimed.

No such message has ever been given in past ages. Paul, as we have seen, did not preach it; he pointed his brethren into the then far-distant future for the coming of the Lord. The Reformers did not proclaim it. Martin Luther placed the judgment about three hundred years in the future from his day. But since 1798 the book of Daniel has been unsealed, knowledge of the prophecies has increased, and many have proclaimed the solemn message of the judgment near.

Like the great Reformation of the sixteenth century, the advent movement appeared in different countries of Christendom at the same time. In both Europe and America men of faith and prayer were led to the study of the prophecies, and, tracing down the inspired record, they saw convincing evidence that the end of all things was at hand. In different lands there were isolated bodies of Christians who, solely by the study of the Scriptures, arrived at the belief that the Saviour's advent was near.

In 1821, three years after Miller had arrived at his exposition of the prophecies pointing to the time of the judgment, Dr. Joseph Wolff, "the missionary to the world," began to proclaim the Lord's soon coming. Wolff was born in Germany, of Hebrew parentage, his father being a Jewish rabbi. While very young he was convinced of the truth of the Christian religion. Of an active, inquiring mind, he had been an eager listener to the conversations that took place in his father's house as de-

Study of the prophecies about the second advent lighted men's minds everywhere during the nineteenth century.

vout Hebrews daily assembled to recount the hopes and anticipations of their people, the glory of the coming Messiah, and the restoration of Israel. One day hearing Jesus of Nazareth mentioned, the boy inquired who He was. "A Jew of the greatest talent," was the answer; "but as He pretended to be the Messiah, the Jewish tribunal sentenced Him to death." "Why," rejoined the questioner, "is Jerusalem destroyed, and why are we in captivity?" "Alas, alas!" answered his father, "because the Jews murdered the prophets." The thought was at once suggested to the child: "Perhaps Jesus was also a prophet, and the Jews killed Him when He was innocent."—*Travels and Adventures of the Rev. Joseph Wolff*, vol. 1, p. 6. So strong was this feeling that, though forbidden to enter a Christian church, he would often linger outside to listen to the preaching.

When only seven years old he was boasting to an aged Christian neighbor of the future triumph of Israel at the advent of the Messiah, when the old man said kindly: "Dear boy, I will tell you who the real Messiah was: He was Jesus of Nazareth, . . . whom your ancestors have crucified, as they did the prophets of old. Go home and read the fifty-third chapter of Isaiah, and you will be convinced that Jesus Christ is the Son of God." —*Ibid.*, vol. 1, p. 7. Conviction at once fastened upon him. He went home and read the scripture, wondering to see how perfectly it had been fulfilled in Jesus of Nazareth. Were the words of the Christian true? The boy asked of his father an explanation of the prophecy, but was met with a silence so stern that he never again dared to refer to the subject. This, however, only increased his desire to know more of the Christian religion.

The knowledge he sought was studiously kept from him in his Jewish home; but, when only eleven years old, he left his father's house and went out into the world to gain for himself an education, to choose his religion and his lifework. He found a home for a time with kinsmen, but was soon driven from them as an apostate, and alone and penniless he had to make his own way among strangers. He went from place to place, studying diligently and maintaining himself by teaching Hebrew. Through the influence of a Catholic instructor he was led to accept the Romish faith and formed the purpose of becoming a missionary to his own people. With this object he went, a few years later, to pursue his studies in the College of the Propaganda at Rome. Here his habit of independent thought and candid speech brought upon him the imputation of heresy. He openly attacked the abuses of the church and urged the necessity of reform. Though at first treated with special favor by the papal dignitaries, he was after a time removed from Rome. Under the surveillance of the church he went from place to place, until it became evident that he could never be brought to submit to the bondage of Romanism. He was declared to be incorrigible and was left at liberty to go where he pleased. He now made his way to England and, professing the Protestant faith, united with the English Church. After two years' study he set out, in 1821, upon his mission.

While Wolff accepted the great truth of Christ's first advent as "a Man of Sorrows, and acquainted with grief," he saw that the prophecies bring to view with equal clearness His second advent with power and glory. And while he sought to lead his people to Jesus of Nazareth as the Promised One, and to point them to His first coming in humiliation as a sacrifice for the sins of men, he taught them also of His second coming as a king and deliverer.

"Jesus of Nazareth, the true Messiah," he said, "whose hands and feet were pierced, who was brought like a lamb to the slaughter, who was the Man of Sorrows and acquainted with grief, who after the scepter was taken from Judah, and the legislative power from between his feet, came the first time; shall come the second time in the clouds of heaven, and with the trump of the Archangel" (Joseph Wolff, *Researches and Missionary Labors,* page 62) "and shall stand upon the Mount of Olives; and that dominion, once consigned to Adam over the creation, and forfeited by him (Genesis 1:26; 3:17), shall be given to Jesus. He shall be king over all the earth. The groanings and lamentations of the creation shall cease, but songs of praises and thanksgivings shall be heard. . . . When Jesus comes in the glory of His Father, with the holy angels, . . . the dead believers shall rise first. 1 Thessalonians 4:16; 1 Corinthians 15:32. This is what we Christians call the first resurrection. Then the animal kingdom shall change its nature (Isaiah 11:6-9), and be subdued unto Jesus. Psalm 8. Universal peace shall prevail."—*Journal of the Rev. Joseph Wolff,* pages 378, 379. "The Lord again shall look down upon the earth, and say, 'Behold, it is very good.' "—*Ibid.,* page 294.

Wolff believed the coming of the Lord to be at hand, his interpretation of the prophetic periods placing the great consummation within a very few years of the time pointed out by Miller. To those who urged from the scripture, "Of that day and hour knoweth no man," that men are to know nothing concerning the nearness of the advent, Wolff replied: "Did our Lord say that that day and hour should *never* be known? Did He not give us signs of the times, in order that we may know at least the *approach* of His coming, as one knows the approach of the summer by the fig tree putting forth its leaves? Matthew 24:32. Are we never to know that period, whilst He Himself exhorteth us not only to read Daniel the prophet, but to understand it? and in that very Daniel, where it is said that the words were shut up to the time of the end (which was the case in his time), and that 'many shall run to and fro' (a Hebrew expression for observing and thinking upon the time), 'and *knowledge*' (regarding that time) 'shall be increased.' Daniel 12:4. Besides this, our Lord does not intend to say by this, that the *approach* of the time shall not be known, but that the *exact 'day* and *hour* knoweth no man.' Enough, He does say, shall be known by the signs of the times, to induce us to prepare for His coming, as Noah prepared the ark."—Wolff, *Researches and Missionary Labors,* pages 404, 405.

Concerning the popular system of interpreting, or misinterpreting, the Scriptures, Wolff wrote: "The greater part of the Christian church have swerved from the plain sense of Scripture, and have turned to the phantomizing system of the Buddhists, who believe that the future happiness of mankind will consist in moving about in the air, and suppose that when they are reading *Jews* they must understand *Gentiles;* and when they read *Jerusalem,* they must understand the *church;* and if it is said *earth,* it means *sky;* and for the coming of the *Lord* they must understand the progress of the *missionary societies;* and going up to the mountain of the Lord's house, signifies a grand *class meeting of Methodists.*"—*Journal of the Rev. Joseph Wolff,* page 96.

During the twenty-four years from 1821 to 1845, Wolff traveled extensively: in Africa, visiting Egypt and Abyssinia; in Asia, traversing Palestine, Syria, Persia, Bokhara, and India. He also visited the United States, on the journey thither preaching on the island of Saint Helena. He arrived in New York in August, 1837; and, after speaking in that city, he preached in Philadelphia and Baltimore, and finally proceeded to Washington. Here, he says, "on a motion brought forward by the ex-President, John Quincy Adams, in one of the houses of Congress, the House unanimously granted to me the use of the Congress Hall for a lecture, which I delivered on a Saturday, honored with the presence of all the members of Congress, and also of the bishop of Virginia, and of the clergy and citizens of Washington. The same honor was granted to me by the members of the government of New Jersey and Pennsylvania, in whose presence I delivered lectures on my researches in Asia, and also on the personal reign of Jesus Christ."—*Ibid.,* pages 398, 399.

Dr. Wolff traveled in the most barbarous countries without the protection of any European authority, enduring many hardships and surrounded with countless perils. He was bastinadoed and starved, sold as a slave, and three times condemned to death. He was beset by robbers, and sometimes nearly perished from thirst. Once he was stripped of all that he possessed and left to travel hundreds of miles on foot through the mountains, the snow beating in his face and his naked feet benumbed by contact with the frozen ground.

When warned against going unarmed among savage and hostile tribes, he declared himself "provided with arms"—"prayer, zeal for Christ, and confidence in His help." "I am also," he said, "provided with the love of God and my neighbor in my heart, and the Bible is in my hand."—W. H. D. Adams, *In Perils Oft*, page 192. The Bible in Hebrew and English he carried with him wherever he went. Of one of his later journeys he says: "I . . . kept the Bible open in my hand. I felt my power was in the Book, and that its might would sustain me."—*Ibid.*, page 201.

Thus he persevered in his labors until the message of the judgment had been carried to a large part of the habitable globe. Among Jews, Turks, Parsees, Hindus, and many other nationalities and races he distributed the word of God in these various tongues and everywhere heralded the approaching reign of the Messiah.

In his travels in Bokhara he found the doctrine of the Lord's soon coming held by a remote and isolated people. The Arabs of Yemen, he says, "are in possession of a book called *Seera*, which gives notice of the second coming of Christ and His reign in glory; and they expect great events to take place in the year 1840."—*Journal of the Rev. Joseph Wolff,* page 377. "In Yemen . . . I spent six days with the children of Rechab. They drink no wine, plant no vineyard, sow no seed, and live in tents, and remember good old Jonadab, the son of Rechab; and I found in their company children of Israel, of the tribe of Dan, . . . who expect, with the children of Rechab, the speedy arrival of the Messiah in the clouds of heaven."—*Ibid.*, page 389.

A similar belief was found by another missionary to exist in Tatary. A Tatar priest put the question to the missionary as to when Christ would come the second time. When the missionary answered that he knew nothing about it, the priest seemed greatly surprised at such ignorance in one who professed to be a Bible teacher, and stated his own belief, founded on prophecy, that Christ would come about 1844.

As early as 1826 the advent message began to be preached in England. The movement here did not take so definite a form as in America; the exact time of the advent was not so generally taught, but the great truth of Christ's soon coming in power and glory was extensively proclaimed. And this not among the dissenters and nonconformists only. Mourant Brock, an English writer, states that about seven hundred ministers of the Church of England were engaged in preaching "this gospel of the kingdom." The message pointing to 1844 as the time of the Lord's coming was also given in Great Britain. Advent publications from the United States were widely circulated. Books and journals were republished in England. And in 1842 Robert Winter, an Englishman by birth, who had received the advent faith in America, returned to his native country to herald the coming of the Lord. Many united with him in the work, and the message of the judgment was proclaimed in various parts of England.

In South America, in the midst of barbarism and priestcraft, Lacunza, a Spaniard and a Jesuit, found his way to the Scriptures and thus received the truth of Christ's speedy return. Impelled to give the warning, yet desiring to escape the censures of Rome, he published his views under the assumed name of "Rabbi Ben-Ezra," representing himself as a converted Jew. Lacunza lived in the eighteenth century, but it was about 1825 that his book, having found its way to London, was translated into the English language. Its publication served to deepen the interest already awakening in England in the subject of the second advent.

In Germany the doctrine had been taught in the eighteenth century by Bengel, a minister in the Lutheran Church and a celebrated Biblical scholar and critic. Upon completing his education, Bengel had "devoted himself to the study of theology, to which the grave and religious tone of his mind, deepened by his early training and discipline, naturally inclined him. Like other young men of thoughtful character, before and since, he had to struggle with doubts and difficulties of a religious nature, and he alludes, with much feeling, to the 'many arrows which pierced his poor heart, and made his youth hard to bear.'" Becoming a member of the consistory of Württemberg, he advocated the cause of religious liberty. "While maintaining the rights and privileges of the church, he was an advocate for all reasonable freedom being accorded to those who felt themselves bound, on grounds of conscience, to withdraw from her communion."—*Encyclopaedia Britannica*, 9th ed., art. "Bengel." The good effects of this policy are still felt in his native province.

It was while preparing a sermon from Revelation 21 for advent Sunday that the light of Christ's second coming broke in upon Bengel's mind. The prophecies of the Revelation unfolded to his understanding as never before. Overwhelmed with a sense of the stupendous importance and surpassing glory of the scenes presented by the prophet, he was forced to turn for a time from the contemplation of the subject. In the pulpit it again presented itself to him with all its vividness and power. From that time he devoted himself to the study of the prophecies, especially those of the Apocalypse, and soon arrived at the belief that they pointed to the coming of Christ as near. The date which he fixed upon as the time of the second advent was within a very few years of that afterward held by Miller.

Bengel's writings have been spread throughout Christendom. His views of prophecy were quite generally received in his own state of Württemberg, and to some extent in other parts of Germany. The movement continued after his death, and the advent message was heard in Germany at the same time that it was attracting attention in other lands. At an early date some of the believers went to Russia and there formed colonies, and the faith of Christ's soon coming is still held by the German churches of that country.

The light shone also in France and Switzerland. At Geneva where Farel and Calvin had spread the truth of the Reformation, Gaussen preached the message of the second advent. While a student at school, Gaussen had encountered that spirit of rationalism which pervaded all Europe during the latter part of the eighteenth and the opening of the nineteenth century; and when he entered the ministry he was not only ignorant of true faith, but inclined to skepticism. In his youth he had become interested in the study of prophecy. After reading Rollin's *An-*

cient History, his attention was called to the second chapter of Daniel, and he was struck with the wonderful exactness with which the prophecy had been fulfilled, as seen in the historian's record. Here was a testimony to the inspiration of the Scriptures, which served as an anchor to him amid the perils of later years. He could not rest satisfied with the teachings of rationalism, and in studying the Bible and searching for clearer light he was, after a time, led to a positive faith.

As he pursued his investigation of the prophecies he arrived at the belief that the coming of the Lord was at hand. Impressed with the solemnity and importance of this great truth, he desired to bring it before the people; but the popular belief that the prophecies of Daniel are mysteries and cannot be understood was a serious obstacle in his way. He finally determined—as Farel had done before him in evangelizing Geneva—to begin with the children, through whom he hoped to interest the parents.

"I desire this to be understood," he afterward said, speaking of his object in this undertaking, "it is not because of its small importance, but on the contrary because of its great value, that I wished to present it in this familiar form, and that I addressed it to the children. I desired to be heard, and I feared that I would not be if I addressed myself to the grown people first." "I determined therefore to go to the youngest. I gather an audience of children; if the group enlarges, if it is seen that they listen, are pleased, interested, that they understand and explain the subject, I am sure to have a second circle soon, and in their turn, grown people will see that it is worth their while to sit down and study. When this is done, the cause is gained."—L. Gaussen, *Daniel the Prophet,* vol. 2, Preface.

The effort was successful. As he addressed the children, older persons came to listen. The galleries of his church were filled with attentive hearers. Among them were men of rank and learning, and strangers and foreigners visiting Geneva; and thus the message was carried to other parts.

Encouraged by this success, Gaussen published his lessons, with the hope of promoting the study of the prophetic books in the churches of the French-speaking people. "To publish instruction given to the children," says Gaussen, "is to say to adults, who too often neglect such books under the false pretense that they are obscure, 'How can they be obscure, since your children understand them?'" "I had a great desire," he adds, "to render a knowledge of the prophecies popular in our flocks, if possible." "There is no study, indeed, which it seems to me answers the needs of the time better." "It is by this that we are to prepare for the tribulation near at hand, and watch and wait for Jesus Christ."

Though one of the most distinguished and beloved of preachers in the French language, Gaussen was after a time suspended from the ministry, his principal offense being that instead of the church's catechism, a tame and rationalistic manual, almost destitute of positive faith, he had used the Bible in giving instruction to the youth. He afterward became teacher in a theological school, while on Sunday he continued his work as catechist, addressing the children and instructing them in the Scriptures. His works on prophecy also excited much interest. From the professor's chair, through the press, and in his favorite occupation as teacher of children he continued for many years to exert an extensive influence and was instrumental in calling the attention of many to the study of the prophecies which showed that the coming of the Lord was near.

In Scandinavia also the advent message was proclaimed, and a widespread interest was kindled. Many were roused from their careless security to confess and forsake their sins, and seek pardon in the name of Christ. But the clergy of the state church opposed the movement, and through their influence some who preached the message were thrown into prison. In many places where the preachers of the Lord's soon coming were thus silenced, God was pleased to send the message, in a miraculous manner, through little children. As they were under age, the law of the state could not restrain them, and they were permitted to speak unmolested.

The movement was chiefly among the lower class, and it was in the humble dwellings of the laborers that the people assembled to hear the warning. The child-preachers themselves were mostly poor cottagers. Some of them were not more than six or eight years of age; and while their lives testified that they loved the Saviour, and were trying to live in obedience to God's holy requirements, they ordinarily manifested only the intelligence and ability usually seen in children of that age. When standing before the people, however, it was evident that they were moved by an influence beyond their own natural gifts. Tone and manner changed, and with solemn power they gave the warning of the judgment, employing the very words of Scripture: "Fear God, and give glory to Him; for the hour of His judgment is come." They reproved the sins of the people, not only condemning immorality and vice, but rebuking worldliness and backsliding, and warning their hearers to make haste to flee from the wrath to come.

The people heard with trembling. The convicting Spirit of God spoke to their hearts. Many were led to search the Scriptures with new and deeper interest, the intemperate and immoral were reformed, others abandoned their dishonest practices, and a work was done so marked that even ministers of the state church were forced to acknowledge that the hand of God was in the movement.

It was God's will that the tidings of the Saviour's coming should be given in the Scandinavian countries; and when the voices of His servants were silenced, He put His Spirit upon the children, that the work might be accomplished. When Jesus drew near to Jerusalem attended by the rejoicing multitudes that, with shouts of triumph and the waving of palm branches, heralded Him as the Son of David, the jealous Pharisees called upon Him to silence them; but Jesus answered that all this was in fulfillment of prophecy, and if these should hold their peace, the very stones would cry out. The people, intimidated by the threats of the priests and rulers, ceased their joyful proclamation as they entered the gates of Jerusalem; but the children in the temple courts afterward took up the refrain, and, waving their branches of palm, they cried: "Hosanna to the Son of David!" Matthew 21:8-16. When the Pharisees, sorely displeased, said unto Him, "Hearest Thou what these say?" Jesus answered, "Yea; have ye never read, Out of the mouth of babes and sucklings Thou hast perfected praise?" As God wrought through children at the time of Christ's first advent, so He wrought through them in giving the message of His second advent. God's word must be fulfilled, that the proclamation of the Saviour's coming should be given to all peoples, tongues, and nations.

To William Miller and his colaborers it was given to preach the warning in America. This country became the center of the great advent movement. It was here that the prophecy of the first angel's message had its most direct fulfillment. The writings of Miller and his associates were carried to distant lands. Wherever missionaries had penetrated in all the world, were sent the glad tidings of Christ's speedy return. Far and wide spread the message of the everlasting gospel: "Fear God, and give glory to Him; for the hour of His judgment is come."

The testimony of the prophecies which seemed to point to the coming of Christ in the spring of 1844 took deep hold of the minds of the people. As the message went from state to state, there was everywhere awakened widespread interest. Many were convinced that the arguments from the prophetic periods were correct, and, sacrificing their pride of opinion, they joyfully received the truth. Some ministers laid aside their sectarian views and feelings, left their salaries and their churches, and united in proclaiming the coming of Jesus. There were comparatively few ministers, however, who would accept this message; therefore it was largely committed to humble laymen. Farmers left their fields, mechanics their tools, traders their merchandise, professional men their positions; and yet the number of workers was small in comparison with the work to be accomplished. The condition of an ungodly church and a world lying in wickedness, burdened the souls of the true watchmen, and they willingly endured toil, privation, and suffering, that they might call men to repentance unto salvation. Though opposed by Satan, the work went steadily forward, and the advent truth was accepted by many thousands.

Everywhere the searching testimony was heard, warning sinners, both worldlings and church members, to flee from the wrath to come. Like John the Baptist, the forerunner of Christ, the preachers laid the ax at the root of the tree and urged all to bring forth fruit meet for repentance. Their stirring appeals were in marked contrast to the assurances of peace and safety that were heard from popular pulpits; and wherever the message was given, it moved the people. The simple, direct testimony of the Scriptures, set home by the power of the Holy Spirit, brought a weight of conviction which few were able wholly to resist. Professors of religion were roused from their false security. They saw their backslidings, their worldliness and unbelief, their pride and selfishness. Many sought the Lord with repentance and humiliation. The affections that had so long clung to earthly things they now fixed upon heaven. The Spirit of God rested upon them, and with hearts softened and subdued they joined to sound the cry: "Fear God, and give glory to Him; for the hour of His judgment is come."

THE TRIUMPH OF GOD'S LOVE

Sinners inquired with weeping: "What must I do to be saved?" Those whose lives had been marked with dishonesty were anxious to make restitution. All who found peace in Christ longed to see others share the blessing. The hearts of parents were turned to their children, and the hearts of children to their parents. The barriers of pride and reserve were swept away. Heartfelt confessions were made, and the members of the household labored for the salvation of those who were nearest and dearest. Often was heard the sound of earnest intercession. Everywhere were souls in deep anguish pleading with God. Many wrestled all night in prayer for the assurance that their own sins were pardoned, or for the conversion of their relatives or neighbors.

All classes flocked to the Adventist meetings. Rich and poor, high and low, were, from various causes, anxious to hear for themselves the doctrine of the second advent. The Lord held the spirit of opposition in check while His servants explained the reasons of their faith. Sometimes the instrument was feeble; but the Spirit of God gave power to His truth. The presence of holy angels were felt in these assemblies, and many were daily added to the believers. As the evidences of Christ's soon coming were repeated, vast crowds listened in breathless silence to the solemn words. Heaven and earth seemed to approach each other. The power of God was felt upon old and young and middle-aged. Men sought their homes with praises upon their lips, and the glad sound rang out upon the still night air. None who attended those meetings can ever forget those scenes of deepest interest.

The proclamation of a definite time for Christ's coming called forth great opposition from many of all classes, from the minister in the pulpit down to the most reckless, Heaven-daring sinner. The words of prophecy were fulfilled: "There shall come in the last days scoffers, walking after their own lusts, and saying, Where is the promise of His coming? for since the fathers fell asleep, all things continue as they were from the beginning of the creation." 2 Peter 3:3, 4. Many who professed to love the Saviour, declared that they had no opposition to the doctrine of the second advent; they merely objected to the definite time. But God's all-seeing eye read their hearts. They did not wish to hear of Christ's coming to judge the world in righteousness. They had been unfaithful servants, their works would not bear the inspection of the heart-searching God, and they feared to meet their Lord. Like the Jews at the time of Christ's first advent they were not prepared to welcome Jesus. They not only refused to listen to the plain arguments from the Bible, but ridiculed those who were looking for the Lord. Satan and his angels exulted, and flung the taunt in the face of Christ and holy angels that His professed people had so little love for Him that they did not desire His appearing.

"No man knoweth the day nor the hour" was the argument most often brought forward by rejecters of the advent faith. The scripture is: "Of that day and hour knoweth no man, no not the angels of heaven, but My Father only." Matthew 24:36. A clear and harmonious explanation of this text was given by those who were looking for the Lord, and the wrong use made of it by their opponents was clearly shown. The words were spoken by Christ in that memorable conversation with His disciples upon Olivet after He had for the last time departed from the temple. The disciples had asked the question: "What shall be the sign of Thy coming, and of the end of the world?" Jesus gave them signs, and said: "When ye shall see all these things, know that it is near, even at the doors." Verses 3, 33. One saying of the Saviour must not be made to destroy another. Though no man knoweth the *day* nor the *hour* of His coming, we are instructed and required to know when it is near. We are further taught that to disregard His warning, and refuse or neglect to know when His advent is near, will be as fatal for us as it was for those who lived in the days of Noah not to know when the flood was coming. And the parable in the same chapter, contrasting the faithful and the unfaithful servant, and giving the doom of him who said in his heart, "My Lord delayeth His coming," shows in what light Christ will regard and reward those whom He finds watching, and teaching His coming, and those denying it. "Watch therefore," He says. "Blessed is that servant, whom his Lord when He cometh shall find so doing." Verses 42, 46. "If therefore thou shalt not watch, I will come on thee as a thief, and thou shalt not know what hour I will come upon thee." Revelation 3:3.

Paul speaks of a class to whom the Lord's appearing will come unawares. "The day of the Lord so cometh as a thief in the night. For when they shall say, Peace and safety; then sudden destruction cometh upon them, . . . and they shall not escape." But he adds, to those who have given heed to the Saviour's warning: "Ye, brethren, are not in darkness, that that day should overtake you as a thief. Ye are all the children of light, and the children of the day: we are not of the night, nor of darkness." 1 Thessalonians 5:2-5.

Thus it was shown that Scripture gives no warrant for men to remain in ignorance concerning the nearness of Christ's coming. But those who desired only an excuse to reject the truth closed their ears to this explanation, and the words "No man knoweth the day nor the hour" continued to be echoed by the bold scoffer and even by the professed minister of Christ. As the people were roused, and began to inquire the way of salvation, religious teachers stepped in between them and the truth, seeking to quiet their fears by falsely interpreting the word of God. Unfaithful watchmen united in the work of the great deceiver, crying, Peace, peace, when God had not spoken peace. Like the Pharisees in Christ's day, many refused to enter the kingdom of heaven themselves, and those who were entering in they hindered. The blood of these souls will be required at their hand.

The most humble and devoted in the churches were usually the first to receive the message. Those who studied the Bible for themselves could not but see the unscriptural character of the popular views of prophecy; and wherever the people were not controlled by the influence of the clergy, wherever they would search the word of God for themselves, the advent doctrine needed only to be compared with the Scriptures to establish its divine authority.

Many were persecuted by their unbelieving brethren. In order to retain their position in the church, some consented to be silent in regard to their hope; but others felt that loyalty to God forbade them thus to hide the truths which He had committed to their trust. Not a few were cut off from the fellowship of the church for no other reason than expressing their belief in the coming of Christ. Very precious to those who bore this trial of their faith were the words of the prophet: "Your brethren that hated you, that cast you out for My name's sake, said, Let the Lord be glorified: but He shall appear to your joy, and they shall be ashamed." Isaiah 66:5.

Angels of God were watching with the deepest interest the result of the warning. When there was a general rejection of the message by the churches, angels turned away in sadness. But there were many who had not yet been tested in regard to the advent truth. Many were misled by husbands, wives, parents, or children, and were made to believe it a sin even to listen to such heresies as were taught by the Adventists. Angels were bidden to keep faithful watch over these souls, for another light was yet to shine upon them from the throne of God.

With unspeakable desire those who had received the message watched for the coming of their Saviour. The time when they expected to meet Him was at hand. They approached this hour with a calm solemnity. They rested in sweet communion with God, an earnest of the peace that was to be theirs in the bright hereafter. None who experienced this hope and trust can forget those precious hours of waiting. For some weeks preceding the time, worldly business was for the most part laid aside. The sincere believers carefully examined every thought and emotion of their hearts as if upon their deathbeds and in a few hours to close their eyes upon earthly scenes. There was no making of "ascension robes" (see Appendix); but all felt the need of internal evidence that they were prepared to meet the Saviour; their white robes were purity of soul—characters cleansed from sin by the atoning blood of Christ. Would that there were still with the professed people of God the same spirit of heart searching, the same earnest, determined faith. Had they continued thus to humble themselves before the Lord and press their petitions at the mercy seat they would be in possession of a far richer experience than they now have. There is too little prayer, too little real conviction of sin, and the lack of living faith leaves many destitute of the grace so richly provided by our Redeemer.

God designed to prove His people. His hand covered a mistake in the reckoning of the prophetic periods. Adventists did not discover the error, nor was it discovered by the most learned of their opponents. The latter said: "Your reckoning of the prophetic periods is correct. Some great event is about to take place; but it is not what Mr. Miller predicts; it is the conversion of the world, and not the second advent of Christ." (See Appendix.)

The time of expectation passed, and Christ did not appear for the deliverance of His people. Those who with sincere faith and love had looked for their Saviour, experienced a bitter disappointment. Yet the purposes of God were being accomplished; He was testing the hearts of those who professed to be waiting for His appearing. There were among them many who had been actuated by no higher motive than fear. Their profession of faith had not affected their hearts or their lives. When the expected event failed to take place, these persons declared that they were not disappointed; they had never believed that Christ would come. They were among the first to ridicule the sorrow of the true believers.

But Jesus and all the heavenly host looked with love and sympathy upon the tried and faithful yet disappointed ones. Could the veil separating the visible from the invisible world have been swept back, angels would have been seen drawing near to these steadfast souls and shielding them from the shafts of Satan.

Reaping the Whirlwind

IN PREACHING the doctrine of the second advent, William Miller and his associates had labored with the sole purpose of arousing men to a preparation for the judgment. They had sought to awaken professors of religion to the true hope of the church and to their need of a deeper Christian experience; and they labored also to awaken the unconverted to the duty of immediate repentance and conversion to God. "They made no attempt to convert men to a sect or party in religion. Hence they labored among all parties and sects, without interfering with their organization or discipline."

"In all my labors," said Miller, "I never had the desire or thought to establish any separate interest from that of existing denominations, or to benefit one at the expense of another. I thought to benefit all. Supposing that all Christians would rejoice in the prospect of Christ's coming, and that those who could not see as I did would not love any the less those who should embrace this doctrine, I did not conceive there would ever be any necessity for separate meetings. My whole object was a desire to convert souls to God, to notify the world of a coming judgment, and to induce my fellow men to make that preparation of heart which will enable them to meet their God in peace. The great majority of those who were converted under my labors united with the various existing churches."—Bliss, page 328.

As his work tended to build up the churches, it was for a time regarded with favor. But as ministers and religious leaders decided against

The historic conflict between good and evil continues to be waged in human hearts, the outcome being decided by individual choice.

the advent doctrine and desired to suppress all agitation of the subject, they not only opposed it from the pulpit, but denied their members the privilege of attending preaching upon the second advent, or even of speaking of their hope in the social meetings of the church. Thus the believers found themselves in a position of great trial and perplexity. They loved their churches and were loath to separate from them; but as they saw the testimony of God's word suppressed and their right to investigate the prophecies denied they felt that loyalty to God forbade them to submit. Those who sought to shut out the testimony of God's word they could not regard as constituting the church of Christ, "the pillar and ground of the truth." Hence they felt themselves justified in separating from their former connection. In the summer of 1844 about fifty thousand withdrew from the churches.

About this time a marked change was apparent in most of the churches throughout the United States. There had been for many years a gradual but steadily increasing conformity to worldly practices and customs, and a corresponding decline in real spiritual life; but in that year there were evidences of a sudden and marked declension in nearly all the churches of the land. While none seemed able to suggest the cause, the fact itself was widely noted and commented upon by both the press and the pulpit.

At a meeting of the presbytery of Philadelphia, Mr. Barnes, author of a commentary widely used and pastor of one of the leading churches in that city, "stated that he had been in the ministry for twenty years, and never, till the last Communion, had he administered the ordinance without receiving more or less into the church. But now there are *no awakenings, no conversions,* not much apparent growth in grace in professors, and none come to his study to converse about the salvation of their souls. With the increase of business, and the brightening prospects of commerce and manufacture, there is an increase of worldly-mindedness. *Thus it is with all the denominations."—Congregational Journal,* May 23, 1844.

In the month of February of the same year, Professor Finney of Oberlin College said: "We have had the fact before our minds, that, in general, the Protestant churches of our country, as such, were either apathetic or hostile to nearly all the moral reforms of the age. There are partial exceptions, yet not enough to render the fact otherwise than general. We have also another corroborated fact: the almost universal absence of revival influence in the churches. The spiritual apathy is almost all-pervading, and is fearfully deep; so the religious press of the whole land testifies. . . . Very extensively, church members are becoming devotees of fashion,—join hands with the ungodly in parties of pleasure, in dancing, in festivities, etc. . . . But we need not expand this painful subject. Suffice it that the evidence thickens and rolls heavily upon us, to show that the *churches generally are becoming sadly degenerate.* They have gone very far from the Lord, and He has withdrawn Himself from them."

And a writer in the *Religious Telescope* testified: "We have never witnessed such a general declension of religion as at the present. Truly, the church should awake, and search into the cause of this affliction; for as an affliction everyone that loves Zion must view it. When we call to mind how 'few and far between' cases of true conversion are, and the almost unparalleled impertinence and hardness of sinners, we almost involuntarily exclaim, 'Has God forgotten to be gracious? or, Is the door of mercy closed?' "

Such a condition never exists without cause in the church itself. The spiritual darkness which falls upon nations, upon churches and individuals, is due, not to an arbitrary withdrawal of the succors of divine grace on the part of God, but to neglect or rejection of divine light on the part of men. A striking illustration of this truth is presented in the history of the Jewish people in the time of Christ. By their devotion to the world and forgetfulness of God and His word, their understanding had become darkened, their hearts earthly and sensual. Thus they were in ignorance concerning Messiah's advent, and in their pride and unbelief they rejected the Redeemer. God did not even then cut off the Jewish nation from a knowledge of, or a participation in, the blessings of salvation. But those who rejected the truth lost all desire for the gift of Heaven. They had "put darkness for light, and light for darkness," until the light which was in them became darkness; and how great was that darkness!

It suits the policy of Satan that men should retain the forms of religion if but the spirit of vital godliness is lacking. After their rejection of the gospel, the Jews continued zealously to maintain their ancient rites, they rigorously preserved their national exclusiveness, while they themselves could not but admit that the presence of God was no longer manifest among them. The prophecy of Daniel pointed so unmistakably to the time of Messiah's coming, and so directly foretold His death, that they discouraged its study, and finally the rabbis pronounced a curse on all who should attempt a computation of the time. In blindness and impenitence the people of Israel during succeeding centuries have stood, indifferent to the gracious offers of salvation, unmindful of the blessings of the gospel, a solemn and fearful warning of the danger of rejecting light from heaven.

Wherever the cause exists, the same results will follow. He who deliberately stifles his convictions of duty because it interferes with his inclinations will finally lose the power to distinguish between truth and error. The understanding becomes darkened, the conscience callous, the heart hardened, and the soul is separated from God. Where the message of divine truth is spurned or slighted, there the church will be enshrouded in darkness; faith and love grow cold, and estrangement and dissension enter. Church members center their interests and energies in worldly pursuits, and sinners become hardened in their impenitence.

The first angel's message of Revelation 14, announcing the hour of God's judgment and calling upon men to fear and worship Him, was designed to separate the professed people of God from the corrupting influences of the world and to arouse them to see their true condition of worldliness and backsliding. In this message, God had sent to the church a warning, which, had it been accepted, would have corrected the evils that were shutting them away from Him. Had they received the message from heaven, humbling their hearts before the Lord and seeking in sincerity a preparation to stand in His presence, the Spirit and power of God would have been manifested among them. The church would again have reached that blessed state of unity, faith, and love which existed in apostolic days, when the believers "were of one heart and of one soul," and "spake the word of God with boldness," when "the Lord added to the church daily such as should be saved." Acts 4:32, 31; 2:47.

If God's professed people would receive the light as it shines upon them from His word, they would reach that unity for which Christ prayed, that which the apostle describes, "the unity of the Spirit in the bond of peace." "There is," he says, "*one* body, and *one* Spirit, even as ye are called in *one* hope of your calling; one Lord, one faith, one baptism." Ephesians 4:3-5.

Such were the blessed results experienced by those who accepted the advent message. They came from different denominations, and their denominational barriers were hurled to the ground; conflicting creeds were shivered to atoms; the unscriptural hope of a temporal millennium was abandoned, false views of the second advent were corrected, pride and conformity to the world were swept away; wrongs were made right; hearts were united in the sweetest fellowship, and love and joy reigned supreme. If this doctrine did this for the few who did receive it, it would have done the same for all if all had received it.

But the churches generally did not accept the warning. Their ministers, who, as watchmen "unto the house of Israel," should have been the first to discern the tokens of Jesus' coming, had failed to learn the truth either from the testimony of the prophets or from the signs of the times. As worldly hopes and ambitions filled the heart, love for God and faith in His word had grown cold; and when the advent doctrine was presented, it only aroused their prejudice and unbelief. The fact that the message was, to a great extent, preached by laymen, was urged as an argument against it. As of old, the plain testimony of God's word was met with the inquiry: "Have any of the rulers or of the Pharisees believed?" And finding how difficult a task it was to refute the arguments drawn from the prophetic periods, many discouraged the study of the prophecies, teaching that the prophetic books were sealed and were not to be understood. Multitudes, trusting implicitly to their pastors, refused to listen to the warning; and others, though convinced of the truth, dared not confess it, lest they should be "put out of the synagogue." The message which God had sent for the testing and purification of the church revealed all too surely how great was the number who had set their affections on this world rather than upon Christ. The ties which bound them to earth were stronger than the attractions heavenward. They chose to listen to the voice of worldly wisdom and turned away from the heart-searching message of truth.

In refusing the warning of the first angel, they rejected the means which Heaven had provided for their restoration. They spurned the gracious messenger that would have corrected the evils which separated them from God, and with greater eagerness they turned to seek the friendship of the world. Here was the cause of that fearful condition of worldliness, backsliding, and spiritual death which existed in the churches in 1844.

In Revelation 14 the first angel is followed by a second proclaiming: "Babylon is fallen, is fallen, that great city, because she made all nations drink of the wine of the wrath of her fornication." Revelation 14:8. The term "Babylon" is derived from "Babel," and signifies confusion. It is employed in Scripture to designate the various forms of false or apostate religion. In Revelation 17 Babylon is represented as a woman—a figure which is used in the Bible as the symbol of a church, a virtuous woman representing a pure church, a vile woman an apostate church.

In the Bible the sacred and enduring character of the relation that exists between Christ and His church is represented by the union of marriage. The Lord has joined His people to Himself by a solemn covenant, He promising to be their God, and they pledging themselves to be His and His alone. He declares: "I will betroth thee unto Me forever; yea, I will betroth thee unto Me in righteousness, and in judgment, and in loving-kindness, and in mercies." Hosea 2:19. And, again: "I am married unto you." Jeremiah 3:14. And Paul employs the same figure in the New Testament when he says: "I have espoused you to one husband, that I may present you as a chaste virgin to Christ." 2 Corinthians 11:2.

The unfaithfulness of the church to Christ in permitting her confidence and affection to be turned from Him, and allowing the love of worldly things to occupy the soul, is likened to the violation of the marriage vow. The sin of Israel in departing from the Lord is presented under this figure; and the wonderful love of God which they thus despised is touchingly portrayed: "I sware unto thee, and entered into a covenant with thee, saith the Lord God, and thou becamest Mine." "And thou wast exceeding beautiful and thou didst prosper into a kingdom. And thy renown went forth among the heathen for thy beauty: for it was perfect through My comeliness, which I had put upon thee. . . . But thou didst trust in thine own beauty, and playedst the harlot because of thy renown." "As a wife treacherously departeth from her husband, so have ye dealt treacherously with Me, O house of Israel, saith the Lord;" "as a wife that committeth adultery, which taketh strangers instead of her husband!" Ezekiel 16:8, 13-15, 32; Jeremiah 3:20.

In the New Testament, language very similar is addressed to professed Christians who seek the friendship of the world above the favor of God. Says the apostle James: "Ye adulterers and adulteresses, know ye not that the friendship of the world is enmity with God? whosoever therefore will be a friend of the world is the enemy of God."

The woman (Babylon) of Revelation 17 is described as "arrayed in purple and scarlet color, and decked with gold and precious stones and pearls, having a golden cup in her hand full of abominations and filthiness: . . . and upon her forehead was a name written, *Mystery, Babylon the Great, the mother of harlots.*" Says the prophet: "I saw the woman drunk with the blood of the saints, and with the blood of the martyrs of Jesus." Babylon is further declared to be "that great city, which reigneth over the kings of the earth." Revelation 17:4-6, 18. The power that for so many centuries maintained despotic sway over the monarchs of Christendom is Rome. The purple and scarlet color, the gold and precious stones and pearls, vividly picture the magnificence and more than kingly pomp affected by the haughty see of Rome. And no other power could be so truly declared "drunken with the blood of the saints" as that church which has so cruelly persecuted the followers of Christ. Babylon is also charged with the sin of unlawful connection with "the kings of the earth." It was by departure from the Lord, and alliance with the heathen, that the Jewish church became a harlot; and Rome, corrupting herself in like manner by seeking the support of worldly powers, receives a like condemnation.

Babylon is said to be "the *mother* of harlots." By her *daughters* must be symbolized churchs that cling to her doctrines and traditions, and follow her example of sacrificing the truth and the approval of God, in order to form an unlawful alliance with the world. The message of Revelation 14, announcing the *fall* of Babylon must apply to religious bodies that were once pure and have become corrupt. Since this message follows the warning of the judgment, it must be given in the last days; therefore it cannot refer to the Roman Church alone, for that church has been in a fallen condition for many centuries. Furthermore, in the eighteenth chapter of the Revelation the people of God are called upon to come out of Babylon. According to this scripture, many of God's people must still be in Babylon. And in what religious bodies are the greater part of the followers of Christ now to be found? Without doubt, in the various churches professing the Protestant faith. At the time of their rise these churches took a noble stand for God and the truth, and His blessing was with them. Even the unbelieving world was constrained to acknowledge the beneficent results that followed an acceptance of the principles of the gospel. In the words of the prophet to Israel: "Thy renown went forth among the heathen for thy beauty: for it was perfect through My comeliness, which I had put upon thee, saith the Lord God." But they fell by the same desire which was the curse and ruin of Israel—the desire of imitating the practices and courting the friendship of the ungodly. "Thou didst trust in thine own beauty, and playedst the harlot because of thy renown." Ezekiel 16:14, 15.

Many of the Protestant churches are following Rome's example of iniquitous connection with "the kings of the earth"—the state churches, by their relation to secular governments; and other denominations, by seeking the favor of the world. And the term "Babylon"—confusion—may be appropriately applied to these bodies, all professing to derive their doctrines from the Bible, yet divided into almost innumerable sects, with widely conflicting creeds and theories.

Besides a sinful union with the world, the churches that separated from Rome present other of her characteristics.

A Roman Catholic work argues that "if the Church of Rome were ever guilty of idolatry in relation to the saints, her daughter, the Church of England, stands guilty of the same, which has ten churches dedicated to Mary for one dedicated to Christ."—Richard Challoner, *The Catholic Christian Instructed*, Preface, pages 21, 22.

And Dr. Hopkins, in "A Treatise on the Millennium," declares: "There is no reason to consider the antichristian spirit and practices to be confined to that which is now called the Church of Rome. The Protestant churches have much of antichrist in them, and are far from being wholly reformed from . . . corruptions and wickedness."—Samuel Hopkins, *Works*, vol, 2, p. 328.

Concerning the separation of the Presbyterian Church from Rome, Dr. Guthrie writes: "Three hundred years ago, our church, with an open Bible on her banner, and this motto, 'Search the Scriptures,' on her scroll, marched out from the gates of Rome." Then he asks the significant question: "Did they come *clean* out of Babylon?"—Thomas Guthrie, *The Gospel in Ezekiel*, page 237.

"The Church of England," says Spurgeon, "seems to be eaten through and through with sacramentarianism; but nonconformity appears to be almost as badly riddled with philosophical infidelity. Those of whom we thought better things are turning aside one by one from the fundamentals of the faith. Through and through, I believe, the very heart of England is honeycombed with a damnable infidelity which dares still go into the pulpit and call itself Christian."

What was the origin of the great apostasy? How did the church first depart from the simplicity of the gospel? By conforming to the practices of paganism, to facilitate the acceptance of Christianity by the heathen. The apostle Paul declared, even in his day, "The mystery of iniquity doth already work." 2 Thessalonians 2:7. During the lives of the apostles the church remained comparatively pure. But "toward the latter end of the second century most of the churches assumed a new form; the first simplicity disappeared, and insensibly, as the old disciples retired to their graves, their children, along with new converts, . . . came forward and new-modeled the cause."—Robert Robinson, *Ecclesiastical Researches*, ch. 6, par. 17, p. 51. To secure converts, the exalted standard of the Christian faith was lowered, and as the result "a pagan flood, flowing into the church, carried with it its customs, practices, and idols."—Gavazzi, *Lectures*, page 278. As the Christian religion secured the favor and support of secular rulers, it was nominally accepted by multitudes; but while in appearance Christians, many "remained in substance pagans, especially worshiping in secret their idols."—*Ibid.*, page 278.

Has not the same process been repeated in nearly every church calling itself Protestant? As the founders, those who possessed the true spirit of reform, pass away, their descendants come forward and "new-model the cause." While blindly clinging to the creed of their fathers and refusing to accept any truth in advance of what they saw, the children of the reformers depart widely from their example of humility, self-denial, and renunciation of the world. Thus "the first simplicity disappears." A worldly flood, flowing into the church, carries "with it its customs, practices, and idols."

Alas, to what a fearful extent is that friendship of the world which is "enmity with God," now cherished among the professed followers of Christ! How widely have the popular churches throughout Christendom departed from the Bible standard of humility, self-denial, simplicity, and godliness! Said John Wesley, in speaking of the right use of money: "Do not waste any part of so precious a talent, merely in gratifying the desire of the eye, by superfluous or expensive apparel, or by needless ornaments. Waste no part of it in curiously adorning your houses; in superfluous or expensive furniture; in costly pictures, painting, gilding. . . . Lay out nothing to gratify the pride of life, to gain the admiration or praise of men. . . . 'So long as thou doest well unto thyself, men will speak good of thee.' So long as thou art 'clothed in purple and fine linen,' and farest 'sumptuously every day,' no doubt many will applaud thy elegance of taste, thy generosity and hospitality. But do not buy their applause so dear. Rather be content with the honor that cometh from God."—Wesley, *Works*, Sermon 50, "The Use of Money." But in many churches of our time such teaching is disregarded.

A profession of religion has become popular with the world. Rulers, politicians, lawyers, doctors, merchants, join the church as a means of securing the respect and confidence of society, and advancing their own worldly interests. Thus they seek to cover all their unrighteous transactions under a profession of Christianity. The various religious bodies, reenforced by the wealth and influence of these baptized worldlings, make a still higher bid for popularity and patronage. Splendid churches, embellished in the most extravagant manner, are erected on popular avenues. The worshipers array themselves in costly and fashionable attire. A high salary is paid for a talented minister to entertain and attract the people. His sermons must not touch popular sins, but be made smooth and pleasing for fashionable ears. Thus fashionable sinners are enrolled on the church records, and fashionable sins are concealed under a pretense of godliness.

Commenting on the present attitude of professed Christians toward the world, a leading secular journal says: "Insensibly the church has yielded to the spirit of the age, and adapted its forms of worship to modern wants." "All things, indeed, that help to make religion attractive, the church now employs as its instruments." And a writer in the New York *Independent* speaks thus concerning Methodism as it is: "The line of separation between the godly and the irreligious fades out into a kind of penumbra, and zealous men on both sides are toiling to obliterate all difference between their modes of action and enjoyment." "The popularity of religion tends vastly to increase the number of those who would secure its benefits without squarely meeting its duties."

Says Howard Crosby: "It is a matter of deep concern that we find Christ's church so little fulfilling the designs of its Lord. Just as the ancient Jews let a familiar intercourse with the idolatrous nations steal away their hearts from God, . . . so the church of Jesus now is, by its false partnerships with an unbelieving world, giving up the divine methods of its true life, and yielding itself to the pernicious, though often plausible, habits of a Christless society, using the arguments and reaching the conclusions which are foreign to the revelation of God, and directly antagonistic to all growth in grace."—*The Healthy Christian: An Appeal to the Church,* pages 141, 142.

In this tide of worldliness and pleasure seeking, self-denial and self-sacrifice for Christ's sake are almost wholly lost. "Some of the men and women now in active life in our churches were educated, when children, to make sacrifices in order to be able to give or do something for Christ." But "if funds are wanted now, . . . nobody must be called on to give. Oh, no! have a fair, tableau, mock trial, antiquarian supper, or something to eat—anything to amuse the people."

Governor Washburn of Wisconsin in his annual message, January 9, 1873, declared: "Some law seems to be required to break up the schools where gamblers are made. These are everywhere. Even the church (unwittingly, no doubt) is sometimes found doing the work of the devil. Gift concerts, gift enterprises and raffles, sometimes in aid of religious or charitable objects, but often for less worthy purposes, lotteries, prize packages, etc., are all devices to obtain money without value received. Nothing is so demoralizing or intoxicating, particularly to the young, as the acquisition of money or property without labor. Respectable people engaging in these chance enterprises, and easing their consciences with the reflection that the money is to go to a good object, it is not strange that the youth of the state should so often fall into the habits which the excitement of games of hazard is almost certain to engender."

The spirit of worldly conformity is invading the churches throughout Christendom. Robert Atkins, in a sermon preached in London, draws a dark picture of the spiritual declension that prevails in England: "The truly righteous are diminished from the earth, and no man layeth it to heart. The professors of religion of the present day, in every church, are lovers of the world, conformers to the world, lovers of creature comfort, and aspirers after respectability. They are called to suffer with Christ, but they shrink from even reproach. . . . *Apostasy, apostasy, apostasy,* is engraven on the very front of every church; and did they know it, and did they feel it, there might be hope; but, alas! they cry, 'We are rich, and increased in goods, and stand in need of nothing.' "—Second Advent Library, tract No. 39.

The great sin charged against Babylon is that she "made all nations drink of the wine of the wrath of her fornication." This cup of intoxication which she presents to the world represents the false doctrines that she has accepted as the result of her unlawful connection with the great ones of the earth. Friendship with the world corrupts her faith, and in her turn she exerts a corrupting influence upon the world by teaching doctrines which are opposed to the plainest statements of Holy Writ.

Rome withheld the Bible from the people and required all men to accept her teachings in its place. It was the work of the Reformation to restore to men the word of God; but is it not too true that in the churches of our time men are taught to rest their faith upon their creed and the teachings of their church rather than on the Scriptures? Said Charles Beecher, speaking of the Protestant churches: "They shrink from any rude word against creeds with the same sensitiveness with which those holy fathers would have shrunk from a rude word against the rising veneration of saints and martyrs which they were fostering. . . . The Protestant evangelical denominations have so tied up one another's hands, and their own, that, between them all, a man cannot become a preacher at all, anywhere, without accepting some book besides the Bible. . . . There is nothing imaginary in the statement that the creed power is now beginning to prohibit the Bible as really as Rome did, though in a subtler way."—Sermon on "The Bible a Sufficient Creed," delivered at Fort Wayne, Indiana, Feb. 22, 1846.

When faithful teachers expound the word of God, there arise men of learning, ministers professing to understand the Scriptures, who denounce sound doctrine as heresy, and thus turn away inquirers after truth. Were it not that the world is hopelessly intoxicated with the wine of Babylon, multitudes would be convicted and converted by the plain, cutting truths of the word of God. But religious faith appears so confused and discordant that the people know not what to believe as truth. The sin of the world's impenitence lies at the door of the church.

The second angel's message of Revelation 14 was first preached in the summer of 1844, and it then had a more direct application to the churches of the United States, where the warning of the judgment had been most widely proclaimed and most generally rejected, and where the declension in the churches had been most rapid. But the message of the second angel did not reach its complete fulfillment in 1844. The churches then experienced a moral fall, in consequence of their refusal of the light of the advent message; but that fall was not complete. As they have continued to reject the special truths for this time they have fallen lower and lower. Not yet, however, can it be said that "Babylon is fallen, . . . because she made *all nations* drink of the wine of the wrath of her fornication." She has not yet made all nations do this. The spirit of world conforming and indifference to the testing truths for our time exists and has been gaining ground in churches of the Protestant faith in all the countries of Christendom; and these churches are included in the solemn and terrible denunciation of the second angel. But the work of apostasy has not yet reached its culmination.

The Bible declares that before the coming of the Lord, Satan will work "with *all* power and signs and lying wonders, and with all deceivableness of unrighteousness;" and they that "received not the love of the truth, that they might be saved," will be left to receive "strong delusion, that they should believe a lie." 2 Thessalonians 2:9-11. Not until this condition shall be reached, and the union of the church with the world shall be fully accomplished throughout Christendom, will the fall of Babylon be complete. The change is a progressive one, and the perfect fulfillment of Revelation 14:8 is yet future.

Notwithstanding the spiritual darkness and alienation from God that exist in the churches which constitute Babylon, the great body of Christ's true followers are still to be found in their communion. There are many of these who have never seen the special truths for this time. Not a few are dissatisfied with their present condition and are longing for clearer light. They look in vain for the image of Christ in the churches with which they are connected. As these bodies depart further and further from the truth, and ally themselves more closely with the world, the difference between the two classes will widen, and it will finally result in separation. The time will come when those who love God supremely can no longer remain in connection with such as are "lovers of pleasures more than lovers of God; having a form of godliness, but denying the power thereof."

Revelation 18 points to the time when, as the result of rejecting the threefold warning of Revelation 14:6-12, the church will have fully reached the condition foretold by the second angel, and the people of God still in Babylon will be called upon to separate from her communion. This message is the last that will ever be given to the world; and it will accomplish its work. When those that "believed not the truth, but had pleasure in unrighteousness" (2 Thessalonians 2:12), shall be left to receive strong delusion and to believe a lie, then the light of truth will shine upon all whose hearts are open to receive it, and all the children of the Lord that remain in Babylon will heed the call: "Come out of her, My people" (Revelation 18:4).